Kate
Richards
O'Hare

Kate Richards O'Hare

Selected Writings and Speeches

Edited, with Introduction and Notes, by
PHILIP S. FONER AND SALLY M. MILLER

Louisiana State University Press
Baton Rouge and London

Copyright © 1982 by Louisiana State University Press
All rights reserved
Manufactured in the United States of America

Designer: Patricia Douglas Crowder
Typeface: L/202 Caledonia
Typesetter: Graphic Composition, Inc.
Printer: Thomson-Shore, Inc.
Binder: John Dekker & Sons, Inc.

LIBRARY OF CONGRESS CATALOGING IN PUBLICATION DATA

O'Hare, Kate Richards, 1877–1948.
  Kate Richards O'Hare, selected writings and speeches.

  Includes index.
  1. O'Hare, Kate Richards, 1877–1948.
2. Prisoners—Missouri—Biography. 3. Socialists—
United States—Biography. 4. Pacifists—United
States—Biography. I. Foner, Philip Sheldon,
1910–   II. Miller, Sally M., 1937–
HV9468.O35A25   1982   365'.924 [B]   81–15667
ISBN 0–8071–0988–6   AACR2

To Kim with love
and
To Nikki

Contents

Acknowledgments   ix
Introduction   1

Part I   Socialist Writings

How I Became a Socialist Agitator   35
The Girl Who Would   41
"Nigger" Equality   44
A Crack in the "Solid South"   49
As a Bud Unfolds   52
The Leaven Doing Its Work   56
The Wages of Women   63
War in the Copper Country   70
Drink, Its Cause and Cure   78
The Story of an Irish Agitator   85
Over the Sea and Back Again   91
Three Weeks   93
Shall Women Vote?   97
Priscilla at Her Loom   106
Blame It on God   108
Margaret Sanger   110
The Tale of a Rib   114

Part II   Antiwar Writings

Socialism and the World War   121
Our Martyred Comrade   143

Shall Red Hell Rage?   146
World Peace   151
My Country   163
Good Morning! Mr. American Citizen   165
Hold the Fort!   168
Speech Delivered in Court by Kate Richards O'Hare
    Before Being Sentenced by Judge Wade   170
Waiting!   181
Guilty!   183
The End of Act One   188
Farewell Address of Kate Richards O'Hare   194

Part III   Letters from Prison   203

Part IV   In Prison   305

Part V   Postprison Writings

Smoldering Fires of Unrest   327
The Children's Crusade   333
The Cleveland Conference   340
What Commonwealth College Means to the Workers   344
Are We Headed Straight for Perdition?   351
We Protest Stop or "Congressman's Nightmare"   355

Index   359

Illustrations   *following* 118

Acknowledgments

We wish to thank the staffs of the Tamiment Institute, Elmer Bobst Library, New York University; Duke University Library; the State Historical Society of Wisconsin; Peace Archives, Swarthmore College Library; and the Missouri Historical Society for their assistance. We owe debts of gratitude also to the staffs of the Library of Congress; the National Archives; New York Public Library; Columbia University Library; Nebraska State Historical Society; Boston Public Library; University of Pennsylvania Library; University of Wisconsin Library; and Yale University Library. We also wish to thank the members of the staff of the Langston Hughes Memorial Library, Lincoln University, and of the Irving Martin Library, University of the Pacific, for their continuous assistance in obtaining materials through interlibrary loan from libraries, historical societies, and other institutions. Most important, we sincerely thank Eugene R. O'Hare, a son of Kate Richards O'Hare, for granting permission to reprint some of his mother's letters from prison, and we wish to acknowledge the University of Washington Press for permission to reprint material from *In Prison*, edited by Jack Holl. In addition, we wish to express thanks to Neil K. Basen, of the University of Wisconsin's School for Workers, an authority on the life of O'Hare, for kindly directing us to sources containing her writings and speeches and for making available some of his own materials. Finally, hearty thanks are due Louise Sasenbery for her enthusiasm for the project over the years of typing drafts of manuscripts on Kate Richards O'Hare; also thanks to Janet Bleyl for typing the final manuscript; and warm appreciation to the University of the Pacific and its Faculty Research Committee for generously providing funds to cover the costs of preparing the manuscript for publication.

Kate
Richards
O'Hare

Introduction

From the plains of Kansas emerged the most renowned socialist woman of the "golden age" of the Socialist party of America, Kate Richards O'Hare. The tall, gangling speaker and writer was perhaps the only woman, among the many women activists in the party, who managed to play a role in the first rank of party leadership. A close comrade of Eugene V. Debs, to the public the embodiment of American socialism early in the twentieth century, Kate O'Hare was a popular agitator on the Great Plains and in mining locales in the West. The party's rank and file knew her through her columns in the widely circulated periodical, the *National Rip-Saw*, and through her writings for the most popular radical sheet of the period, the *Appeal to Reason* of Girard, Kansas. She was a familiar personality to the party faithful throughout the country because of her constant speaking tours and her participation in various party campaigns in all regions of the country. A frequent candidate for party and public office, she became unique among American socialist women as a recognized leader in the international socialist movement and a comrade of the giants of the Second International. Late in her socialist career, she became known as Red Kate and, in that guise, she gained the distinction, shared with a few other women of the Left, such as the IWW and communist leader Elizabeth Gurley Flynn and the anarchist Emma Goldman, of serving time in a penitentiary as a political prisoner.

O'Hare, the party propagandist of the first two decades of this century, was also a social critic who touched on virtually every major issue with which the twentieth century would grapple. No aspect of American society or politics escaped her scrutiny. She applied her radical perspective to an impressive variety of topics, some of which were of concern to her contemporaries and others of which she highlighted for later generations. She was an educator in society and in the classroom who sought to enlighten the public and to demand meaningful and relevant liberal and vocational education. As a woman, she recognized keenly the many ways in which pervasive and unlimited exploitation characterized the lives of the masses of women. A former church worker, she badgered clergy who eschewed social responsibilities. As a onetime prison inmate, she applied the pioneering works of psychology to promote and eventually to implement penal reforms. She took the South to task for its inability to understand how its racial policies prevented regional progress. She was an internationalist and war dissident in an era of exaggerated patriotism who recognized modern war's inhumanity along with its economic logic and was an early commentator on how war preparations starve the civilian sector of a country. In sum, O'Hare represented the best in an indigenous radicalism that, whatever its own limitations, set high standards for American society. Her ambitious range of concerns was undercut by degrees of narrowness, especially evident in matters of race and of gender, where some of the timelessness that characterized her other views was markedly lacking. Yet Kate Richards O'Hare was a significant figure whose fame of long ago merits renewal. O'Hare is important in the history of the American Left, the Plains states, and the Southwest, in women's history, and in the development of modern penology.

Little of Kate Richards O'Hare's correspondence survives, but her voluminous writings during her twenty years of party activism delineate her life and, more important, the contribution she made to the social history of her times.[1] Born in 1876 on a farm in Ottawa County, Kansas, she had as her earliest memories romanticized romps and outdoor adventures in post–Civil War Kansas, where homesteading had only in that

1. See "Kate Richards O'Hare—Candidate for Congress," *Socialist Woman*, IV (August, 1910), 2; David A. Shannon, "Kate Richards O'Hare Cunningham," *Notable American Women*, I, 417–19; Melvyn Dubofsky, "Kate Richards O'Hare Cunningham," *Dictionary of American Biography*, supp. 4, p. 635. There is yet no biography of O'Hare, but see Neil K. Basen, "Kate Richards O'Hare: The 'First Lady' of American Socialism, 1901–1917," *Labor History*, XXI (Spring, 1980), 165–99; David A. Shannon, *The Socialist Party of America* (Chicago: Quadrangle, 1967), 25–27; James Green, *Grass-Roots Socialism: Radical Movements in the Southwest, 1895–1943* (Baton Rouge: Louisiana State University Press, 1978), 48–52. O'Hare's correspondence was destroyed during her marital breakup in the 1920s. Without these primary sources, it is unlikely that a full-length biography will ever be attempted. Hitherto, Kate Richards' date of birth has been listed as 1877, but recent research indicates that she was born in 1876. See Basen, 169.

generation succeeded frontier strife and bitter territorial politics. The
security of those years as one of five children in a well-to-do farming
family was abruptly terminated by the drought of 1887 and the subsequent financial panic. Her father, Andrew Richards, became a machinist
in Kansas City, Kansas, where Kate, who had attended elementary
school in Ottawa County, continued her education, and she later attended briefly a normal school in Nebraska. Her memories of her family's
decline from the middle class to the precariousness of a wageworker's
income led her, years later, to write of the experience as scarring her
permanently, so that her "whole soul" forever after revolted when she
witnessed strong men needing to beg for work.

After a season of schoolteaching, which she discovered paid less than
a living wage, she worked as a bookkeeper in the machinist shop where
her father was by then a partner. But as she "hated ledgers and daybooks
and loved mechanics" she became a machinist's apprentice and a member of the International Association of Machinists despite its males-only
membership practice. By then, she was seventeen years old and, as so
many young women of the last decades of the nineteenth century, she
was deeply religious and became involved in temperance work in her
community. Active also at a local mission for "fallen women," she was
acutely sensitive to the problems of alcoholism and prostitution she observed in the slums and among workers' families. She believed that such
social ills created the endemic poverty of the community, and her prayers
and her energy were devoted to undermining vice and spreading Christian belief. Gradually, however, through her machine-shop union exposure, she began to learn that poverty was an effect rather than a cause.
She read some of the popular social critiques of the time, *Progress and
Poverty* by Henry George, *Wealth Against Commonwealth* by Henry
Demarest Lloyd, and *Caesar's Column* by Ignatius Donnelly. In addition, the young woman attended union meetings and, unlike many of her
comrades, groped toward the perception that even established and
healthy unionism, if confined within the capitalist system, meant political
and economic impotence. Though patronized by her male shop mates for
"daring to talk politics," she found such issues irresistible. After listening
to two socialist speakers, one of whom was the already legendary Mary
Harris "Mother" Jones, she found her road to a socialist commitment.
Hearing Mother Jones, a "mile-post" in her life, as she later termed it,
led to the maturation of her social philosophy.

Kate Richards became an earnest student of socialist classics and tracts as a member of a Kansas City socialist group. She met J. A. Wayland, the somewhat eccentric socialist publisher, and in 1901 under his sponsorship she enrolled in the training school for Socialist party workers recently established by Walter Thomas Mills at Girard, Kansas. She became acquainted with a fellow student and party member, Frank P. O'Hare of St. Louis, and they were married on January 1, 1902. Their honeymoon, characteristic of activist partnerships in various social movements, was spent lecturing and organizing in the vicinity for the year-old Socialist party of America.[2] Thus commenced two decades of mutual ideological and matrimonial commitment that began simultaneously and in effect fragmented the same way. This, too, is a not uncommon phenomenon in activists' relationships. Perhaps the shared ideology served as the cement of the marriage.

Kate Richards O'Hare's socialism was of the reformist variety despite her radical reputation. Upon examination her views resemble those of Victor Berger, whose bossism and bombast she despised, and those of Morris Hillquit, whose suave and legalistic elitism she deplored. Like them, she neither eschewed political action nor dismissed gradualist reforms. She was in fact quite comfortable with the dominant reformist direction of the party and its revisionist ideology, despite her affection for the more Marxist-oriented Debs. On no issue did she challenge the revisionist thrust of party policy. Her militant image stemmed from her grass-roots familiarity with the lives of miners, millworkers, machinists, farmers, and housewives, her humane empathy for them, and her rhetorical re-creation of their struggles. She surely believed, as did the party leadership, that the continued exploitation by industrial capitalism of the masses, marginal farmers as well as dependent urban wage earners, working women as well as children, would inevitably lead the workers to embrace the message of socialism. The ongoing class struggle would result in the proletariat's assuming its historically determined role on the revolutionary stage; only more time and propaganda were necessary. When some socialists sensed a moment of revolution at hand and the party experienced its cataclysmic schism after World War I, she stayed

2. Bits of Frank P. O'Hare's early life can be traced in "Frank P. O'Hare to Mrs. Margretta Scott Lawler and Miss Mary Porter Scott, April 26, 1960," *Missouri Historical Society Bulletin*, XX (October, 1963), 56–58. The O'Hares had four children between 1903 and 1908.

with the reformists and the remnants of the party rather than join the revolutionary wing and its newly created Communist party.[3]

O'Hare's published writings demonstrate that there were three cornerstones to her thought. The combination of mass education, political action, and a stronger unionism would lead to the cooperative commonwealth, gradually and inevitably. No force or violence was required to promote the millennium, and even compensation to expropriated capitalists to ensure a peaceful transition (as Victor Berger also acknowledged) was conceivable. Such a moderate and evolutionary approach seemed feasible in the United States because the workers, unlike others elsewhere, were armed with universal manhood suffrage. Thus, through indigenous conditions and strategies, including cooperation with Progressives, the collective ownership of the means of production and distribution would be attained one step at a time. O'Hare's confidence was firm.

Kate O'Hare's commitment to the struggle of working people to achieve the cooperative commonwealth saw her emphasize specific reforms. She supported various types of social reforms, whether a shorter workday, better working conditions, protective legislation for women workers, or prohibition of child labor. Further, she supported the craft union movement as represented by the American Federation of Labor despite her belief in its shortsightedness and narrowness. From her days as a member of a machinists' local throughout her years as a socialist propagandist, she refrained from attacking the AFL directly. While she was capable of biting references to "Sammy" Gompers, its perennial president, she generally preferred the approach of the party's right wing—keeping lines open to the craft unionists. When the Industrial Workers of the World (IWW) emerged in 1905, she did not embrace the new industrial unionism. Although throughout her career she spoke fondly of individual Wobblies and applauded their efforts to fend off sporadic right-wing attacks, her personal warmth toward specific Wobblies seemed to be only that. Hers was an occasional spontaneous reaction toward a genuine rank-and-file effort, but institutionally she lined up against the IWW. Indeed, she used her position as international secretary of the Socialist party in 1913 to implement party policy directed against the Wobblies in the international arena. She supported the inser-

3. This thesis is convincingly argued in Basen, "O'Hare: The 'First Lady,'" 177–86; Green, *Grass-Roots Socialism*, 50.

tion of a clause in the party constitution which decreed expulsion for alleged saboteurs, and she unsuccessfully promoted a discussion of this issue at a meeting of the International Socialist Bureau in London.[4]

Racism, which was an issue in a variety of ways in this period and perhaps a party characteristic, did not touch O'Hare in one way but in another marked her very clearly. Party policy toward immigration restriction was hammered out painfully over a several-year period. The dilemma of those who controlled party machinery seemed to be how to align themselves with the increasingly racist and restrictionist anti-immigrant attitude of organized labor while simultaneously respecting the Second International's condemnation of racial or nationality exclusion. Convention proceedings reveal an antipathy among party members toward non-Anglo-Saxon immigrants: since workers from eastern or central Europe and the Orient were unorganizable, a view shared by organized labor, they would not be welcomed by a party that hoped to represent the workers of the country. Kate O'Hare revealed no such exclusionist and bigoted sentiments. At most, in her writings here and there a patronizing attitude was shown toward immigrants from eastern Europe.[5]

In contrast, O'Hare's views of American blacks were sharply etched in bigotry and racism. O'Hare felt an affinity toward the South, despite being the daughter of a Union army veteran. While she vigorously condemned the antebellum slavocracy as a feudal economic system, she nonetheless empathized with white southerners. Their heritage, she wrote, denied them an inherent respect for work and prevented them from politically and economically organizing themselves against the bonds of capitalism. Toward black Americans, whom she perceived to be still economically enslaved, she felt little sympathy. Her greatest concern was that they delayed economic progress in the South. She believed blacks to be inferior, unable to profit from higher education, and incapable of competing with whites. However, O'Hare bore them no ill will and, in fact, wished that they might achieve whatever progress they could without arbitrary interference. Thus, she argued for equality of opportunity for black Americans in a segregated society. In any future

4. *Party Builder*, February 7, 1914; see Sally M. Miller, "Americans and the Second International," *Proceedings of the American Philosophical Society*, CXX (1976), 376–77.

5. See, for example, party discussions of immigration restriction in *Proceedings of the 1908 National Convention* (Chicago: Socialist Party, 1908), 105–122, and *Proceedings of the 1910 National Congress* (Chicago: Socialist Party, 1910), 75–101. O'Hare was not involved in the anti-immigration movement within the party.

socialist commonwealth, she proposed setting aside a section of the nation for blacks.[6]

A great many of her writings dealt with social problems that she believed were inherent to capitalism. She devoted particular attention to the role of the church as an institution that misled people about the social problems of the day and was often controlled by "bought preachers." She was especially venomous in her writings against the Protestant clergy. Indeed, her general passion in this vein is probably reflective of her status as a convert. Although she had aspired to enter the ministry of the Disciples of Christ, in her mature years as a socialist agitator she wrote bitterly against clergymen who would neither recognize human exploitation nor act to oppose it. Her articles addressed to Archbishop John J. Glennon of the St. Louis Archdiocese were given major coverage in the *National Rip-Saw*, demonstrating the importance she attached to this subject. While in prison she was particularly bitter about organized religion's neglect of society's despised. She quoted Jesus: "I was sick and in prison and ye visited me not." Further, she wrote, she realized that she had sought Jesus most of her life in the various movements she had followed, and that she found him when she entered prison on Easter.[7]

O'Hare wrote voluminously on the plight of women workers and child laborers. If any one theme could be cited as suggestive of her social concerns, it would be the helplessness of such economically exploited individuals. In every few issues of the prewar *National Rip-Saw*, she addressed herself to the vulnerability of these most insecure of workers. While women had always worked in clothing and food processing, their inability to own the tools of production under industrial capitalism destroyed any semblance of independence. Further, she emphasized the constant danger of sexual exploitation that proletarian women and girls faced. Consequently, O'Hare pushed through a party declaration on

6. For an overview of racism and the socialists, see Philip S. Foner, *American Socialism and Black Americans: From the Age of Jackson to World War II* (Westport, Conn.: Greenwood Press, 1977), 94–311; Sally M. Miller, "The Socialist Party and the Negro, 1901–1920," *Journal of Negro History*, LVI (July, 1971), 220–29; Laurence Moore, "Flawed Fraternity: American Socialist Response to the Negro, 1901–1912," *Historian*, XXXII (November, 1969), 1–18.

7. O'Hare, "He Beats Around the Bush," *National Rip-Saw* (May, 1913), 3, 10–12. While in prison, she noted the number of priests and rabbis who had written to her, but the lack of interest by Protestant clergymen probably affected her more. O'Hare to her family, July 13, 1919, in Kate Richards O'Hare Collection, Missouri Historical Society, St. Louis. All her prison letters cited hereafter are in that collection.

white slavery's economic base, and her major leaflet published by the party's Woman's National Committee dealt with prostitution. In *'Wimmin' Ain't Got No Kick* and in the *Rip-Saw* pamphlet *Law and the White Slaver*, O'Hare focused on the likelihood of prostitution trapping any underpaid or unemployed woman. She wrote with melodramatic emphasis of the phenomenon of vice rings, the involvement of politicians, and the insanity that so many prostitutes eventually experienced. She believed that not until socialism succeeded capitalism would prostitution, as well as divorce (given that marriages were often for economic security), disappear. She saw some signs of improvement in the new minimum wage law for women workers, passed in California and Illinois, but only the appearance of the cooperative commonwealth would eliminate prostitution—the supreme exploitation—and all other social problems. Indeed, while ameliorative reforms might soften some of the system's worst abuses, the final solution to capitalist-inspired exploitation awaited the triumph of socialism.[8]

O'Hare believed, as did most other party members, that the ballot was simply a tactical weapon to be used wisely by the proletariat. She chided American men for having voted for old parties and old programs rather than voting in the interest of the masses. She also scolded them for not committing themselves to women's suffrage. Although as a socialist she never saw the winning of the ballot as an end in itself, she certainly believed that American women needed the same tactical weapons men had. Thus, she immersed herself in many campaigns for women's suffrage. In St. Louis she was prominent in suffrage groups, collaborating with bourgeois women. Like other socialist women, such as Theresa S. Malkiel, who spearheaded New York's socialist suffrage drive, O'Hare believed that it was permissible to cooperate with middle-class nonsocialist women in suffrage campaigns. While the Second International as well as the Socialist party cautioned against indiscriminate collaboration, many socialist women argued that such cooperation with suffragists was defensible as long as the socialist distinction of the vote as a means but not an end was emphasized. In spring of 1913, O'Hare served as marshal of the socialist section of the massive suffrage parade in Washington, D.C., and she was pleased to point out that the party's bloc of five hundred marchers was the largest in the parade. Later that year, while

8. O'Hare, *'Wimmin' Ain't Got No Kick* (Chicago: Socialist Party, Woman's National Committee, n.d.); O'Hare, *Law and the White Slaver* (St. Louis: *National Rip-Saw*, 1911).

on a national tour, she specifically went to New York City to support the
Socialist Suffrage Campaign Committee. She attended a mass rally at
Carnegie Hall and spoke as a supporter from the West.[9]

In discussing the basic value of the ballot to women, O'Hare viewed
women in two specific ways: as subservient creatures without means of
self-defense and as individuals who naturally bore central responsibility
for the home. She argued that any group without suffrage lived in servitude, and that for women the ballot had to be seen as "a sex right [and]
a class right." Enfranchised women would have the opportunity to advance the workers' cause, protect the American home, and solve health
and consumer problems by immediate political reforms. In an approach
not too different from that of Jane Addams and other Progressives, that
is, bourgeois, women reformers, O'Hare argued in a manner which
placed women in a domestic framework.

O'Hare should not be considered an overt socialist feminist and did
not, in fact, think of herself in those terms. Only years later, as a conse-
quence of her imprisonment, did she begin to confront feminism directly. Not only the experience of shared helplessness with other women
inmates but a bitter sense of her neglect by the Socialist party[10] and the
national media, both of which publicized the plight of male political prisoners, led her to write (June 8, 1919) to her husband: "You know I have
never been a particularly rampant feminist; I have always felt that the
'woman question' was only a part of the great 'social problem' but my two
months here have changed my views materially, and I know now, as
never before, that 'women bear the heaviest burdens and walk the
roughest road' and that this is true in all walks of life, and becomes more
damnably true as you descend the social scale, until it reaches the very
extreme here in prison." But O'Hare never resolved this issue. During
the height of her party activity, with her deep concern for the exploitation of women and belief in the need for protective legislation, she remained convinced that only the cooperative commonwealth would settle
the Woman Question. Thus that question was subsumed in the class
question. Her behavior more than demonstrated her distance from the
issue. Her participation in the activities of the Woman's National Committee can be termed no more than peripheral. Her failure to contact

9. O'Hare, "The Power of Your Ballot," *National Rip-Saw* (October, 1912), 10–11;
O'Hare, "Suffragists and Slavers," *National Rip-Saw* (April, 1913), 24, 26.

10. See O'Hare to her family, May 31, 1919.

the leaders of the International Conference of Socialist Women when she was abroad is noteworthy. She, unlike most prominent women, voiced few criticisms of party discrimination against women. Also indicative of her lukewarm feminism, O'Hare had few women friends and, indeed, showed a clear preference for the company of male comrades. Two women party members with whom she shared a sense of closeness were Theresa S. Malkiel of New York City and Grace D. Brewer of Girard, neither of whom had unambiguously embraced feminism. Malkiel, perhaps O'Hare's most frequent party correspondent while she was in the Missouri State Penitentiary, was the most vociferous critic of the lack of true equality within the party. But she also believed that the Woman Question must be treated within the class question. Brewer, who accompanied O'Hare when she surrendered to the federal marshal, argued that women's mode of reasoning differed from men's and that they had to be prodded along toward socialism by arguments that reflected the female experience and viewpoint. Neither woman apparently had challenged culturally accepted views any more than had O'Hare.[11]

Kate Richards O'Hare epitomized the dilemma that the Woman Question represented for her generation of socialist women and, indeed, for all women. Despite her awareness of varieties of exploitation that women experienced, she, like most of her socialist women comrades, did not fully confront the issue of women's liberation, which was obscured by both Marxist ideology and societal mores. Socialist women as different as midwestern, middle-class types such as May Wood Simons, who headed the Woman's National Committee and who like O'Hare and many others came to socialism from temperance or evangelical campaigns, and Theresa Malkiel, an immigrant who came to socialism from sweatshop work and labor organizing, shared this dilemma. O'Hare's personality may have made it even more difficult for her than for some of her socialist sisters to commit much of her energy to the Woman Question.

Kate O'Hare understood through socialist classics, such as Engels'

11. "Theresa Malkiel," *Socialist Woman*, II (May, 1909), 2; "Grace D. Brewer," *Socialist Woman*, I (January, 1908), 2; O'Hare to her family, March 17, 1920. The prison letters refer to Grace Brewer's escorting O'Hare to the place of surrender; they also mention that party organizer Florence Wattles accompanied her. Frank O'Hare left early because there were rumors that the O'Hares would "pull something," and he wanted to ensure a calm atmosphere. See Sally M. Miller, "From Sweatshop to Labor Leader: Theresa Malkiel, a Case Study," *American Jewish History*, LXVIII (December, 1978), 189–205; Basen, "O'Hare: The 'First Lady,'" 166.

Origin of the Family, Private Property and the State and August Bebel's *Woman Under Socialism*, that women were the proletariat of the family. She expanded on those insights with her firsthand knowledge, for example, of the wives of farmers and their special burdens. But shaped as she was by society's norms, she never resolved her ambivalence about the Woman Question or transcended her limited view of it, and she wandered between socialist feminism and pure-and-simple socialism. An overt struggle for women's liberation would dilute and weaken the class struggle, she believed. While she acknowledged that women bore the double exploitation of class and sex, she failed to envision shared and equal parental, household, occupational, and community responsibilities and freedoms. Social institutions under a socialism that freed women as it did men were not suggested in her writings, and she refrained from endorsing the day care centers espoused by sometime socialist Charlotte Perkins Gilman. The women's liberation with which O'Hare felt comfortable was predicated on economic security in the cooperative commonwealth that enabled a woman to remain home in her natural sphere, safe from the exploitation of industrial capitalism. O'Hare's was a traditional view of the structure of the family and of historical role assignments, held by many socialist women and men, but O'Hare was farther away than some from a synthesis of socialism and feminism.[12]

O'Hare's socialist career exactly paralleled the rise and fall of the Socialist party of America. The Socialist party was founded in 1901, when fragments of nineteenth-century socialist groups coalesced into a national party. Except for the Socialist Labor party of Daniel De Leon, the new party reflected a unity hitherto unknown to the American Left. Also differentiating the party from its forerunners was the native-born composition of its membership. A dozen years later a survey demonstrated that 70 percent of the members were born in the United States, but it was

12. Marilyn J. Boxer and Jean H. Quataert (eds.), *Socialist Women: European Socialist Feminism in the Nineteenth and Early Twentieth Centuries* (New York: Elsevier, 1978), 6, 16, define a socialist feminist as one "who saw the root of sexual oppression in the existence of private property and who envisioned a radically transformed society in which man would exploit neither man nor woman," but they note that family reconstruction was an issue dodged by most socialist feminists. O'Hare fully represents an American reflection of that phenomenon. On the socialism-feminism nexus in the American context, see Sally M. Miller, *Flawed Liberation: Socialism and Feminism* (Westport, Conn.: Greenwood Press, 1981); Mari J. Buhle, *Women and American Socialism, 1870–1920* (Urbana: University of Illinois Press, 1981).

clear from the beginning that the Socialist party was an indigenous expression of militance and social criticism.[13]

The socialists organized locals in every region of the country—the Plains states and the Southwest, where the party showed impressive vitality in formerly Populist Kansas and the newest state in the Union, Oklahoma; midwestern and eastern cities where immigrant communities were the root of party strength; and small towns everywhere (with least success in the South). By the end of its first decade, the Socialist party maintained a membership of 118,000 and elected mayors and city council members in such scattered locales as Milwaukee, Wisconsin; Schenectady, New York; Butte, Montana; Berkeley, California; Lima, Ohio; Coeur d'Alene, Idaho; New Castle, Pennsylvania; Star City, West Virginia; Kalamazoo, Michigan; Winslow, Arkansas; and Granite City, Illinois. Pockets of strength across the country were mirrored also in a flourishing socialist press, so that three fourths of the forty-eight states enjoyed at least one socialist periodical.

A party profile suggests that the typical member was a middle-class or professional man, often a journalist, with workers making up a minority. Women, approximately one tenth of the membership during the party's first decade, were active in the party, possibly because of its ideological commitment to equal rights, but no official effort to attract women members was made in the early years. The same was true regarding minorities. The party pledged racial equality, and it was one of the few American organizations in that era which did not bar racial minorities from membership. On the other hand, racially discriminatory attitudes, or, at best, indifference to racial injustice, seem clear. Accordingly, the party's black contingent was quite small.

The Socialist party, dominated by its reformist or revisionist faction, supported immediate demands and favored various step-at-a-time social reforms, many of which were not unlike the goals of Progressive reformers. While a Marxist or more doctrinaire faction always vied for influence, the reformist or right wing of the party, led by Morris Hillquit of New York and Victor Berger of Milwaukee, directed party policy and emphasized election to political office as the wellspring of the party's program. The years 1910 and 1912 were spectacular for the party's electoral hopes, as local offices across the land were won, the first socialist

13. *Campaign Book* (Chicago: Socialist Party, 1912) provides these data.

entered Congress when Berger was elected to the House of Representatives, and Eugene V. Debs, its perennial candidate for the presidency, won nearly 6 percent of the vote. In the remaining years of the pre–World War I golden age, membership and level of activity fluctuated, but essentially the party sustained itself at a time when the country was ending its flirtation with reform movements.[14]

Kate O'Hare, from 1902 until the time of her trial and imprisonment in 1918–1919, toured the country ceaselessly for her party. As an example of her schedule, in April, 1914, she spoke throughout Illinois and in the St. Louis vicinity, in May and June, she toured in Iowa, Nebraska, the Dakotas, Colorado, Utah, and Idaho, then went to Arkansas, Louisiana, Texas, and Oklahoma, and thereafter paused for ten days. From the third week in July through August, she and Frank devoted their energies to the encampments in Arkansas, Texas, and Oklahoma. In the fall she traveled alone once again, spending the last three months of the year in the Midwest, the Great Plains, the Southwest, and California.[15] Kate O'Hare's impact was undoubtedly greatest in the Southwest at the summer encampments, where she was thoroughly at home, building on the evangelistic techniques she had long used in rural environments. As described by party organizer Oscar Ameringer, these "summer camps" for rural families were "lineal descendants of the religious and Populist camp meetings of former days." Farm folk, believers and others, came to break the monotony and isolation of their routines, and merchants and even chamber of commerce representatives joined them as participants or as promoters of good customer relations. Throngs of five thousand and more would gather for a week or two under the broiling southwestern sun to hear O'Hare, Gene Debs, Mother Jones, and others, to sing socialist songs set to gospel and other familiar melodies, and to attend economic and historical "educationals." This setting enabled "the party's or-

14. See Sally M. Miller, *Victor Berger and the Promise of Constructive Socialism, 1910–1920* (Westport, Conn.: Greenwood Press, 1973), 17–116; James Weinstein, *The Decline of Socialism in America, 1912–1925* (New York: Monthly Review Press, 1967), 1–118, esp. the tables, 93–102, 116–18. James Green, "The 'Salesmen-Soldiers' of the *Appeal* 'Army': A Profile of Rank-and-File Socialist Agitators," in Bruce M. Stave (ed.), *Socialism and the Cities* (Port Washington, N.Y.: Kennikat Press, 1975), 13–40, argues that in certain regions, especially the Plains states, the party rested on a working-class base, but most secondary writings agree that the party nationally was middle class in composition.

15. *National Rip-Saw* (April, June, 1914), 12, 14, lists O'Hare's various speaking engagements. There are some contradictions, suggesting that her schedule was revised as she traveled.

ators, agitators, and educators to reach rural poor people the traveling organizers never touched" and it proved so successful that European socialists considered adopting this inherently American practice. And Kate O'Hare, second only to Debs as a crowd pleaser with these audiences, even in the last years of her life relished her memories of the encampments.[16]

This draining schedule was maintained year after year, requiring frequent separations from her four young children. O'Hare was clearly one of the most formidable among socialist organizers, with perhaps only Lena Morrow Lewis, another indefatigable organizer and propagandist, and Gene Debs himself surpassing her in speaking commitments. But O'Hare seemed oblivious to the toll such a schedule might take and did not seek to lighten her load.

Her touring was the essence of her socialist commitment. Like Debs, she was not a Socialist party functionary. She did not wheel and deal with the party bosses and manipulators like Hillquit and Berger. While she did assume, unlike Debs, some responsibilities as a party officeholder, she never developed a coterie of party bureaucrats or a vested interest in policy making, either because of her temperament or because of the party leadership's distaste for granting power to women members. Her socialist fame lay in her hold on the rank and file.

In 1910, Kate Richards O'Hare ran for the House of Representatives in the Second Congressional District of Kansas, two years before women won the right to vote in that state. In 1916, she became the first woman to run for the United States Senate, as a candidate in Missouri. That same year, she was also a serious candidate for the Socialist party's nomination for the vice-presidency. She lost to George R. Kirkpatrick, a lesser-known figure, by two to one, but her try for the nomination was the first such effort by a woman.[17] In 1920, genuine sentiment emerged for her nomination to that position, but since both she and Debs were serving prison terms, it was deemed unwise to name candidates neither of whom could campaign.

O'Hare attended party conventions, even "carrying my babies with

16. Oscar Ameringer, *If You Don't Weaken: The Autobiography of Oscar Ameringer* (New York: Henry Holt and Co., 1940), 263–67; Green, *Grass-Roots Socialism*, 40–41, 154.

17. The vote was 20,597 to 11,118. See *American Labor Year Book*, 1916, p. 129. She lost despite her greater fame than the winner's, which may mean that the party was simply not ready to nominate a woman for that high office.

me sometimes," as she later nostalgically recalled, where she actively participated in the proceedings. At the National Congress of 1910 she served on the Farmers' Committee and at the 1917 Emergency Convention, called at a time when American intervention in the European war seemed imminent, she chaired the Committee on War and Militarism, which drafted the party's policy on the war. In that role, she presided over the most significant policy-making committee ever established by the Socialist party.

In 1912 and 1913, she sat on the National Executive Committee, the policy-making body of the party. She was only the second woman elected to the NEC and she served merely that one term. She had come to the NEC directly from a year of service on the Woman's National Committee, where she played a muted role, especially for such a prominent party leader. She missed a number of WNC meetings because of the press of her other responsibilities, and she failed to submit several votes to the woman's general correspondent, even on subjects in which she was much interested, such as a proposed campaign against white slavery. She also inexplicably failed to vote on a resolution to publicize women's suffrage as the party's May Day theme. The committee invited her to prepare an antiwar statement in May, 1911, to circulate to party locals during the military occupation at the Mexican border during that country's revolution, but the WNC ended up tabling its invitation. Thus, except for O'Hare's contributing the proceeds of ten of her speaking engagements in 1912 to the WNC, she had little impact on the woman's sector of the party. Her NEC service also seems to have been unimpressive, which may explain why her candidacy for another term, after a year's absence from that body, was not successful. While on the National Executive Committee she was promoted for membership on an *ad hoc* committee to investigate an imbroglio in West Virginia, where miners and local socialists faced martial law and violence. But those appointed by her NEC comrades to what became a controversial fact-finding mission were Gene Debs, Victor Berger, and Adolph Germer.[18] Her own term ended without any such excitement.

In 1913 and again in 1919, O'Hare was elected the party's international secretary, its representative to the Second International headquar-

18. David A. Corbin, "Betrayal in the West Virginia Coal Fields: Eugene V. Debs and the Socialist Party of America, 1912–1914," *Journal of American History*, LXIV (1978), 987–1009.

tered in Brussels. She thoroughly enjoyed her trip to the 1913 bureau
meeting held in London. She toured the British Isles and apparently
made an impact through her speeches in Dublin during the general
strike then in progress. She also impressed some of the leaders of the
international socialist movement, especially the French socialist Jean
Jaurès, who invited her to come to France to advise the movement there
how best to attract the peasantry.[19] At the business meetings of the International Socialist Bureau, she tried in vain to have the issue of direct
action placed on the agenda for the meeting of the International Socialist
Congress scheduled for 1914 in Vienna. Six years later, during her confinement in the Missouri State Penitentiary, she was elected international secretary once again. However, not only was she unable to represent her party, the party schism as well as the upheaval in international
socialism precluded a return trip.[20]

During these years, Kate Richards O'Hare lived with her husband
Frank and their growing family in Oklahoma and in Girard, Kansas, and,
after 1912, in St. Louis. In Girard the O'Hares were based at the *Appeal
to Reason*. At the end of 1912, Kate O'Hare became associated with
Gene Debs on the staff of the *Appeal* following the suicide of J. A. Wayland, her mentor. Soon thereafter, both O'Hares were invited to work
with the *National Rip-Saw*, a St. Louis socialist monthly. They moved to
St. Louis, where Frank assumed editorial duties and Kate continued to
write and lecture, now in association with the publisher of the *Rip-Saw*,
Phil Wagner.

The war in Europe, which erupted in the summer of 1914, modified
the emphases in Kate O'Hare's writings and speeches and served eventually to alter the pattern of her life. As early as that fall she focused her
readers' attention on the bloodletting in Europe. She mourned the waste
in human lives and, that first year of the war, wrote of American businessmen discovering the "value" of preparedness. Those already killed
in the war, she insisted, were murdered by capitalism. In an article entitled "To the Mothers and Maids of America," she wondered whether
women could make a difference. She stressed the particular cost of war
to women and urged them to write to President Wilson demanding that

19. Shannon, *The Socialist Party of America*, 26.
20. For O'Hare's party activities, see the Socialist party convention proceedings, various party newspapers, such as the *Party Builder* (1912–14) and the *American Socialist*
(1914–17), and the independent magazine, *Socialist Woman* (1907–1913).

the United States remain out of the war. But she predicted pessimistically that the stage was set for the country to be "gobbled up" by the zealous efforts of the warmongers. As other governments promoted war babies while they sent their sons to their deaths, so, too, might the United States.[21]

The National Executive Committee of the Socialist party scheduled an Emergency Convention for April 7, 1917, following the resumption of unlimited submarine warfare by the German navy that February and the subsequent break in diplomatic relations between Germany and the United States. In the frenzied days of February and March, the Socialist party cooperated with various antiwar groups to flood Congress with demands for continued neutrality. Simultaneously, fissures appeared within the party as American intervention inexorably approached. Some prominent party personalities, such as A. M. Simons and May Wood Simons, William English Walling, and J. G. Phelps Stokes, chose nationalism over socialism, a dichotomy O'Hare dismissed as cant. Her argument that socialism involved the highest form of nationalism, i.e., internationalism, was unpersuasive to a number of erstwhile party leaders.[22]

The Emergency Convention met in St. Louis for eight days. There, it hammered out an antiwar statement that adhered to its noninterventionist position, despite the American declaration of war a few days earlier. Thus, the party's proclamation, reaffirming the principle of internationalism and its own unalterable opposition to the war, reflected O'Hare's early antiwar writings and invited conflict with the federal government and any jingoistic spirit which war might engender in the public. The party had demonstrated more consistency with its prewar principles of international solidarity than had many of its European comrades who supported their nations' war efforts. But the cost of such principles included a membership drain and government prosecution.

The committee of fifteen, including most of the leadership of the party,[23] met in secret session and returned two minority reports as well

21. For representative selections of her early antiwar writings, see her articles in *National Rip-Saw* (October, 1914–August, 1915); "To the Mothers and Maids of America," *National Rip-Saw* (August, 1915), 5–6. The *Rip-Saw*, with which the O'Hares worked for a dozen years, was later called *Social Revolution* and then *American Vanguard*.

22. On the party splits of that spring, see Miller, *Victor Berger and the Promise of Constructive Socialism*, 145–63.

23. Committee members, besides Kate O'Hare, were Victor Berger, Morris Hillquit, John Spargo, Algernon Lee, Job Harriman, Kate Sadler, Louis B. Boudin, Charles E. Ruthenberg, Dan Hogan, Maynard Shipley, and four less well known individuals. Some

as the majority report. Kate O'Hare, who presided over the Committee on War and Militarism, supported the majority report and suggested the insertion of a clause specifically warning against the "delusion of so-called defensive warfare." A referendum endorsed the majority antiwar statement, by a wide margin. Those socialists still loyal to their party were thereby committed to opposing military or industrial conscription, encroachments on civil liberties, and massive food exports and to supporting propaganda against militarism, expansion of worker education, and a program of socialization of major industries and national resources.[24]

Kate Richards O'Hare seemed to have no second thoughts following the most tumultuous party convention up to that time. She returned to the antiwar activity in which she had pioneered, and her militant stand on the war remained firm. Unlike so many members of the Anglo-Saxon Protestant wing of the Socialist party who claimed party anti-Germanism, Kate O'Hare did not abandon her commitment to international brotherhood. In contrast to the majority of European socialists, she held to Marxist internationalism before and during the war. The war was an economic struggle among capitalist nations, she continued to insist, and the masses were being led to the slaughter. Her antiwar leadership, so clear at the party's Emergency Convention, was the American equivalent of that of the major European socialist wartime dissenters, Karl Liebknecht and Rosa Luxemburg. And while O'Hare would be imprisoned for her ideological position, their fate would be imprisonment and then murder.

O'Hare crisscrossed the country, speaking out against an embryonic ultranationalism which the federal government's new Committee on Public Information promoted with the help of unofficial loyalty leagues. Sharply she condemned the conscription of the nation's sons. In "Good Morning! Mr. American Citizen," she informed him that Uncle Sam demanded his son and also indirect taxes on food and other necessities, as evident in the wartime inflation. She railed against the suppression of the socialist press and, thereby, the threatened loss of the Bill of Rights. She witnessed her own magazine, now called the *Social Revolution*, and all other dissenting magazines and newspapers, including the New York

party leaders had already dropped their membership and were not present to support a policy on behalf of the American war effort.

24. Alexander Trachtenberg (ed.), *The American Socialists and the War* (New York: Rand School of Social Science, 1917), 39–45.

Call, the *Appeal to Reason*, the Milwaukee *Leader*, the *Masses*, the *American Socialist*, and the *International Socialist Review*, virtually excluded from the U.S. mails. The denial of second-class-mailing privileges was decreed by the postmaster general, who held them to be in violation of the Espionage Act stricture against reporting inexact news.[25] Despite the assistance of the National Civil Liberties Bureau and influential attorneys Clarence Darrow and Frank P. Walsh, the government attack on domestic critics continued. That fall and into 1918, much of the left-wing leadership in the United States was indicted for violations of the Espionage Act. The Dakota-based Non-Partisan League, the Industrial Workers of the World, and the Socialist party all found themselves in constant litigation for the duration, their ranks thinning. The American show trials of the first Red Scare inexorably proceeded.

Kate O'Hare gave one basic speech in the spring of 1917 and honed it to perfection in the seventy-five times she delivered it.[26] She presented the standard socialist argument on the economic causes of war. Capitalist competition had brought on the war, and the prewar socialist movement had not been effective enough to prevent it. However, she advised her listeners, the peoples of the world would be purified by the war experience, and an international community would emerge. She was convinced, she said, that war would bring socialism. For the duration, nations were adopting state socialism, and therefore socialism itself was being promoted by the capitalist governments now turning toward it. And, thus, the dead would not have died in vain.

Nowhere in her speech did she advise young men not to register for the draft or to violate the law in any way. But when she spoke before a small audience in Bowman, North Dakota, on July 17, 1917, she was quoted later as having departed from her text to say "that the women of the United States were nothing more nor less than brood sows, to raise children to get into the army and be made into fertilizer." In her text, she described the special loss that war always represented for women, a point she had made in her writings since the beginning of the European war. In an article published in 1915 entitled "Breed, Mother, Breed," she had written of women figuratively placed in "breeding pens."[27] She had

25. Miller, *Victor Berger and the Promise of Constructive Socialism*, 191–94.
26. Some secondary accounts state that she gave this address almost 150 times, but she refers to delivering it 75 times.
27. O'Hare, "Breed, Mother, Breed," *National Rip-Saw* (September, 1915), 5.

long been convinced of and written about the cheapness with which capitalist governments viewed the lives of the masses of the people: men
could be killed in battle while women could produce future generations
in an endless cycle. Later, in her testimony during the trial, she reported
that in her Bowman speech she had said: "When the governments of
Europe, and the clergy of Europe demanded of the women that they
give themselves in marriage, or out, in order that men might 'breed
before they die,' that was not the crime of maddened passion, it was the
cold-blooded crime of brutal selfishness, and by that crime the women
of Europe were reduced to the status of breeding animals on a stock
farm." But O'Hare denied that she had made the irreverently phrased
remark attributed to her in Bowman. For that alleged remark, Kate
O'Hare was indicted under the Espionage Act for intending to interfere
with the national war effort, specifically, conscription. The indictment,
evidence implies, actually arose from local politics, a squabble over a
post-office appointment, having no relation to O'Hare or to war issues.
The Bowman postmistress Lillian Totten was reported, by two anonymous letter writers, to have heard O'Hare's remarks and to have approved of them. Totten, whose husband led the local Non-Partisan
League and whose brother-in-law had edited a local league newspaper,
was apparently the target of a powerful Bowman Democrat who had earlier held the position of postmaster. Kate O'Hare happened to be handy
and useful for the local antileague faction.[28]

Kate O'Hare was tried that fall, the first important figure indicted
under the Espionage Act. Her trial was highly publicized because of her
stature and also because a mother of young children might be sentenced
to prison. Her trial, like those of the other socialists, was held in an
atmosphere not in the least conducive to justice. The jury was unsym-
pathetic to her politics and the judge, Martin J. Wade, actively hostile.
He was described as having "developed a sort of mania for denouncing
'traitors' on all possible occasions." In his statement late in the proceedings, the judge himself said: "Well, I tell you, if that is the sort of stuff
the socialist party stands for, if its gospel is the gospel of hate, and contempt of religion and charity, it has not any place on the American soil
either in times of war or times of peace."[29] Later, in a letter from prison,

28. Bernard J. Brommel, "Kate Richards O'Hare: A Midwestern Pacifist's Fight for
Free Speech," *North Dakota Quarterly*, XLIV (Winter, 1976), 5–19.
29. Lawrence Todd to Roger Baldwin, December 28, 1917, quoted in H. C. Peterson

O'Hare reported amusement at encountering in her readings the traditional Catholic concept of the just war and realizing she had supported
that principle against the Roman Catholic, Martin J. Wade. But at the
trial, faced with the judge's intransigence, she found little to amuse her.
The judge disallowed one third of her witnesses, despite the efforts of
her able attorney V. R. Lovell of Fargo, North Dakota, and the verdict
of guilty was a foregone conclusion. She was convicted on December 14,
1917, and sentenced to five years in the state penitentiary at Jefferson
City, Missouri. Frank O'Hare immediately organized the "Liberty Defense Union" to raise funds for her appeals and to publicize her plight.
Her old comrade Gene Debs, soon himself to be in the dock, was in-
credulous that she could be convicted for expressing an honest belief,
and he wrote to her that if she actually did serve time in prison, "I shall
feel guilty to be at large."[30]

During the year and a half of legal proceedings following her conviction, Kate O'Hare was free on bail supplied by millionaire socialist William Bross Lloyd, who also provided bail for Victor Berger, Big Bill Haywood, and others. But one legal maneuver after another failed: the
Circuit Court of Appeals affirmed her conviction in October, 1918, and
the Supreme Court denied a petition the next March. In early April,
1919, she traveled to Bowman to surrender to the federal marshal there,
delivering a farewell address to sympathizers along the way. On April
15, 1919, during Easter week, the doors of the Missouri State Penitentiary, the largest state prison in the country, closed behind her.

O'Hare was absent from party activity during the most volatile period
in its history. Because of the exigencies of the war situation, the composition of its membership altered and, at the same time, the party's showing at the polls improved. People joined or supported the party to demonstrate solidarity with its wartime dissent, to show allegiance to the
worldwide revolutionary situation symbolized by the Russian Revolution, or to underline support for civil liberties. As a result, the Socialist
party's foreign-language federations by 1919 had grown to 51 percent of
the membership, compared with 30 percent prior to the war. In addition,

and Gilbert C. Fite, *Opponents of War, 1917–1918* (Madison: University of Wisconsin
Press, 1957), 36; Zechariah Chafee, Jr., *Free Speech in the United States* (Cambridge:
Harvard University Press, 1942), 76.

30. Eugene V. Debs, "Conviction of Kate O'Hare," *Social Revolution* (January, 1918),
5; Peterson and Fite, *Opponents of War*, 248; Ray Ginger, *Eugene V. Debs: A Biography*
(New York: Collier Books, 1962), 369.

a number of those who had abandoned the party in the spring of 1917 returned, sporting a new militancy. Under the impetus of such evolution, in early 1919 an organized left-wing bloc began to emerge in Chicago, New York, Boston, and in the Ohio and Michigan state organizations. It demanded a firmer allegiance to the Bolshevik regime in Russia, an end to cooperation with nonsocialists in the amnesty campaign and other programs, the minimizing of political action and immediate demands, and the maximizing of the class struggle by aggressive unionization efforts. Competition between the new left wing and the old leadership led to the existence of two National Executive Committees, each claiming legitimacy. At the end of August, a climactic convention was held in Chicago, the party's first regularly scheduled meeting since the convention of 1912, which, under far different circumstances, had succeeded in terminating the IWW presence in the party. The 1919 gathering, rather than simply muting the impact of a party bloc by inserting some new clause in the constitution, witnessed a major schism in the American Left. A number of erstwhile party leftists met nearby and organized the Communist party of America, ignoring the official party proceedings. The remaining members of the left-wing section, unable to capture the convention after contested delegations were seated at the only party convention that ever required the police to restore order, bolted and organized the Communist Labor party. This fragmentation marked the end of the Socialist party as the nucleus of the American Left as O'Hare had known it.[31]

Kate O'Hare's impatient and helpless observations of the proceedings from four hundred miles and a lifetime away in the penitentiary contrasted with her fascination with the signs she saw of upheaval and social change. The year 1919 was marked by more expansive strike activity than perhaps any year since 1877. When O'Hare entered prison in April, the Seattle general strike, which had tied up that metropolitan area, had recently occurred. In May, she read of the Winnipeg general strike. Together, the strikes seemed harbingers of a new mood of militancy in the North American labor movement. The May Day letter bombs that ap-

---

31. Miller, *Victor Berger and the Promise of Constructive Socialism*, 227–39. Years later, O'Hare wrote that it was only a half-truth to say that the world war wrecked the Socialist party. She alluded to "the Hillquit-European-minded wing," *i.e.*, also Berger's Milwaukee contingent, working to remove her, Debs, the *Rip-Saw*, and the *Appeal to Reason* from the scene. See O'Hare to Samuel Castleman, September 9, 1945, in Debs Collection, Tamiment Institute, Elmer Bobst Library, New York University, New York City.

peared everywhere in the country only underlined the desperation marking demands for change. The next six months witnessed industry-wide strikes in steel and coal and a police strike in Boston. While the strikes were not successful—indeed, for the police and for the steelworkers, they ended in disaster—still, from O'Hare's perspective American workers clearly had joined the social revolution.[32]

When the prison doors closed on Kate Richards O'Hare, she could have had no inkling that in a strange way her fourteen months there would be the highlight of her life. The intensity of the experience can only be compared with the wartime service of soldiers who, ever after, look back on that trauma as a time of the most intimate human connectedness, of great significance found in normally mundane incidents, and of indignities that held much meaning in being shared. Nor could she have known that a line was irrevocably dividing her adult life into halves, the socialist era and the reform decades.

Kate O'Hare entered prison a forty-three-year-old woman, in good health yet menopausal, to settle into a regimented existence in an antiquated penal system. The American prison system in the first decades of this century still clung to discredited nineteenth-century precepts of punishment and rehabilitation. Innovations in other areas of criminology, such as the creation of juvenile courts, the suspended sentence, and probation and parole, were reflected in penology by a halting movement toward specialized institutions, such as first-offender reformatories, prisons for the criminally insane, and minimum, medium, and maximum security prisons. Pioneering penologists, such as Dean G. W. Kirchwey of Columbia University and Thomas Mott Osborne, both onetime wardens of Sing Sing, sought to undermine archaic practices of solitary confinement, darkened cells, bread-and-water diets, the silence system, striped clothing, and underpaid contract labor. Rejecting these practices as inhumane and unsuccessful in reshaping prisoners in socially useful directions, the so-called New Penologists, often looking toward the developing field of psychiatry, flailed about, seeking a workable program in a transitional era. The fundamental approach of these reformers, as in other fields, was to gather data, analyze problems, and establish appropriate institutional responses, and the result would be the rehabilitation of deviants by a state that could adjust offenders to society. The prison,

32. See Robert K. Murray, *Red Scare: A Study in National Hysteria, 1919–1920* (New York: McGraw-Hill, 1964).

often likened to a school or a hospital, would thus better serve society
and its individual inmates.[33]

Kate O'Hare occupied a small cell in which she was permitted to keep
books and other reading matter, plants, food, and knickknacks. While
silence was imposed except for one hour of the day, she communicated
regularly with the women in the surrounding cells. Recreation periods,
the only time the inmates were permitted to speak, involved one hour
in an open courtyard on certain days or a class in chorale singing. On
Saturday afternoons in summer, there were park outings; on weekend
afternoons in other seasons, films. Male prisoners, incarcerated on the
opposite side of the prison, had these activities and also more varied
types of recreation available to them. For the most part, a rigid system
of sexual segregation applied.

The women prisoners spent nine hours a day at sewing machines in
the industrial shop, making denim jumpers and jackets for the Oberman
Manufacturing Company, despite Missouri law prohibiting prison contract labor. As a recent study has demonstrated, the prison industries
system of the nineteenth century, including convict leasing, piecework
arrangements, and contract labor, was being dismantled in these years,
but southern and rural-dominated states discarded such practices slowly.
Contract labor did not disappear entirely until the Great Depression,
under the impetus of the opposition of manufacturers and labor unions
and the passage of federal legislation. Abominable working conditions,
characteristic of prison shops, existed at Jefferson City: poor ventilation,
inadequate lighting, and stifling temperatures for most of the year. The
task system still prevailed, a method utilizing piecework that required
that the "task be made" or punishment be incurred. The quantity and
quality of the work were judged by an abusive young shop foreman or
overseer. An incompleted daily task usually meant that a woman finished
her work at night in her cell. To O'Hare, a socialist and a staunch supporter of union labor, prison contract labor was the most contemptible
aspect of her confinement. To be forced to scab meant the prison system
was the ultimate capitalist exploitation. The elimination of such contract

33. Gerhard O. W. Mueller, *Crime, Law and the Scholars: A History of Scholarship
in American Criminal Law* (Seattle: University of Washington Press, 1969), 67–68; David
J. Rothman, *Conscience and Convenience: The Asylum and Its Alternatives in Progressive
America* (Boston: Little, Brown, 1980), 117–58.

labor became for her, as Jack Holl has written, the moral equivalent of the abolitionist crusade.[34]

The prison meal system was intolerable. The imposed silence lent a surrealistic quality to mealtimes. Warden Osborne, writing about his experimental week posing as an inmate, remarked: "Fourteen hundred men sitting at dinner—and no sound of the human voice;—it is a ghastly thing. I had no appetite; and so spent the few minutes allotted for dinner in studying the backs of the men in front."[35] Kate O'Hare acknowledged that some of the food was decently prepared, but hot food was cooked hours in advance on the men's side of the prison and sent over to the women's section. The cold stews and soups were impossible for the prisoners to eat and so, for some, the actual mealtime became the snacks shared in their cells. O'Hare constantly received food packages from party comrades, friends, and strangers, and the food would be handed down the line from cell to cell. Emma Goldman, who was in the adjacent cell for O'Hare's first few months, spoke of feeding the monkeys, an endearing term for all of them, as they shared tidbits and even full meals in their cages.

Kate O'Hare was one of four federal prisoners confined at Jefferson City. Less than a half-dozen years later, the first federal prison for women would be opened at Alderson, West Virginia, but at this time such "federals" formed a kind of elite among the prostitutes, dope addicts, thieves, the deranged, and other victims held in the state prisons. Two of the politicals, Gabriella Antolina and Molly Steimer, were young immigrant girls, novices in leftist activities, for whom O'Hare felt great affection, especially for Ella, whose struggle against deportation was later handled by Frank O'Hare. But the political stars were O'Hare and the charismatic Emma Goldman, La Pasionaria to her generation of international anarchists. To radicals outside Jefferson City, the possibility loomed large of great conflict between these representatives of competing movements. But incarceration enabled the human elements to prevail over the ideological. O'Hare described Goldman as "the tender, cosmic mother, the wise, understanding woman, the faithful sister, the loyal comrade" who played an enormously important role in sustaining the

34. Rothman, *Conscience and Convenience*, 139–42; O'Hare, *In Prison*, ed. Jack Holl (Reprint; Seattle: University of Washington Press, 1977), xviii.

35. Thomas Mott Osborne, *Society and Prisons: Some Suggestions for a New Penology* (New Haven: Yale University Press, 1916), 125.

prisoners' morale and whom O'Hare herself missed in a childlike way after Goldman's departure. In return, Goldman wrote of her erstwhile socialist antagonists with whom she now shared the bonds of incarceration: "What terrible commentary on our so-called democracy . . . men like sweet Gene Debs, women like Louise [Oviereau], and Mrs. O'Hare must serve." Their mutual ordeal created a respect that lasted beyond their imprisonment and Goldman's deportation from the United States.[36]

The essence of O'Hare's prison experience was twofold: relationships with her sister inmates and her development of a penal critique. O'Hare's very presence symbolized the intrusion of political ideas and attitudes into the prison and, to one degree or another, into the psyches of the inmates with whom she lived. This not uncommon phenomenon in American history, as H. Bruce Franklin has noted recently, was marked by informal instruction.[37] O'Hare sought unsuccessfully to teach classes for the other inmates but she did win for them access to the library in the men's section, hitherto closed to women inmates. She read aloud to them during recreational periods, either fiction or mild political literature, and she lent books and magazines to those she deemed self-educable. O'Hare developed a tremendous fondness for these women, including the most unfortunate, those with contagious diseases, and she tried to exploit her fame to improve their conditions in every way possible. She had friends correspond with individual women, she distributed little gifts that she received, especially to those completely neglected by the outside world, and she had her own children contact the most forlorn. She brought to the warden's attention unique problems of particular women. With Frank O'Hare's support outside the prison walls, she used her influence to have the dining room and the women's wing of the cellblock painted, warm meals served, showers installed, and, in general, to achieve some semblance of civilization. Her greatest campaign was for segregation of the contagious. Hers was, nevertheless, a markedly hierarchical approach to the prisoners. Unlike Emma Gold-

36. O'Hare to her family, May 31, 1919; Emma Goldman to Agnes Inglis, April 17, 1919, in Emma Goldman Papers, Joseph A. Labadie Collection, University of Michigan, Ann Arbor; Emma Goldman, *Living My Life* (New York: Knopf, 1931), II, 677–79, wrote: "Had we met on the outside, we should have probably argued furiously and have remained strangers. . . . In prison we soon found common ground and human interest in our daily association."

37. H. Bruce Franklin, "The Literature of the American Prison," *Massachusetts Review*, XVIII (Spring, 1977), 55.

man, whose emotional relationship with them was deeper, Kate O'Hare was the observer, the scientist in prison. She was distant, though working side by side with them. She was their evaluator, a patronizing almsgiver. She judged the clean and the unclean, the educable and the ignorant, the white and the black. The black prisoners, two thirds of the inmates, were those for whom she seemed to have the most pity but as society's matron to society's deprived rather than as social equals.

Kate O'Hare was more the reader than the writer while in prison. Her nine-hour, or more, daily stint at the sewing machine to "make her task" precluded concentration on writing, unlike political prisoners in other societies who were not required to work. In addition, the prison administration foiled her plans to conduct a scientific investigation of the other prisoners and to write a casebook on criminology. She did manage to develop a number of case studies in her free time, but these materials were eventually confiscated and lost. Her extant prison writings, thus, are her letters to her family. She was allowed to write one five-page letter per week, eventually three letters, which included an occasional letter to a friend or comrade, about 10 percent of which were confiscated by the prison censor. While she was still incarcerated, Frank O'Hare issued sixteen of her letters in the booklet *Kate O'Hare's Prison Letters*, which was circulated widely. But these were not substitutes for what could have been a valuable firsthand clinical addition to the emergent New Penology by an amateur social scientist. Kate O'Hare's report immediately after her release, called "In Prison," and her prison memoirs of the same name published three years later, served as her assessment and critique of the American penal system. Her environmentalist approach to the "criminal" represented one of the major tenets of contemporary criminology. She placed far less emphasis on heredity, and much more on the influence of external surroundings, in shaping an individual toward lawbreaking. As a socialist, she believed that many of the nonpolitical inmates were in fact imprisoned because of the exploitation and injustice inherent in the system of capitalism. But at the same time, as a well-informed person in the Progressive era, familiar with Freud's work and other psychological studies, she believed that society required criminal law and courts and even penal institutions. Society must protect itself from the socially irresponsible and offer a healthy environment and a program through which the state might shape positive personality development. Her program was vague and undeveloped, especially as compared with her fully delineated critique of the penal system, but clearly she was willing to promote immediate ameliorative reforms within the existing system. Nevertheless, with the eventual coming of the cooperative commonwealth, the prevalence of social justice would so alter the environment that socialist society might well lack such problems.

Kate O'Hare's prison letters, subject as they were to censorship, contained few substantive political discussions. Through the variety of labor and radical periodicals she was allowed to read, as well as the voluminous correspondence from comrades, she was able to follow the outline of the earthshaking events affecting the Left during her fourteen months in prison. Moreover, her usual weekly visit with her husband provided the opportunity to obtain fuller information, although their time was limited. She mourned only slightly the passing of the Socialist party as she had known it. She remained basically future-oriented and optimistic. Again and again she wrote of a possible wide coalition on the Left and speculated that perhaps the old Socialist party was a stepping-stone to a grander and less bureaucratized leftist movement.

The successes of the Non-Partisan League in the upper Midwest, the emergent Farmer-Labor party, the militancy among railroad brotherhoods, and the appearance of the broad-based Committee of Forty-Eight inspired her. The Socialist party schism and the resultant three-way division, with the socialists and the newly formed Communist party and Communist Labor party competing for the same followers, seemed to her worthy of little attention. These signified the moribund past, while the newer groups, especially those which represented agrarian-based militants cooperating with urban workers, pointed toward a more promising future.

Following three bouts with illness, including influenza during the great epidemic, and after becoming thoroughly exhausted from the wearying months at the archaic sewing machine, Kate Richards O'Hare had her prison sentence commuted by President Wilson on May 29, 1920. While she had chosen not to ask for a pardon, with its implication of guilt, she and her husband had promoted as best they could the national amnesty campaign of the Socialist party. Almost two years after the Armistice, she walked away from the Missouri State Penitentiary, leaving behind in the prisons of the United States at least one hundred political prisoners, some of whom would remain incarcerated another half-dozen years. But her devotion to the cause of the modernization of the nation's prisons was now her driving commitment.[38]

Upon taking up her life, O'Hare seemed to move in several directions at once: the amnesty and prison reform campaigns held priority, but she also tried to resume party work. She launched into her speaking schedule almost immediately, traveling across the country as in the old days, although now sometimes accompanied by her daughter, Kathleen. She and Frank began publication of their magazine, but apparently the fragmentation of the socialist and communist Left precluded the type of full-time educational effort that had marked Kate O'Hare's earlier career. Within two years of her prison release, the institutional Left was no longer her focus.

Both O'Hares spearheaded the ongoing campaign for amnesty for World War I political prisoners. They sought the release of Gene Debs from the federal prison in Atlanta, tried to raise funds for Kate Debs, and went to Terre Haute as part of the welcome home party when Debs returned during Christmas week, 1921. For the less famous political prisoners, Kate O'Hare organized the so-called Children's Crusade, leading a group of prisoners' children to Washington, D.C., to draw attention to their plight. At the same time, she challenged the contract labor system, becoming perhaps the most prominent journalist to publicize its evils since George W. Cable's attacks on its prolongation of black chattel slavery in the 1890s. She conducted a nationwide survey of prison contract labor, under the auspices of the Garment Manufacturers' Association and the United Garment Workers. For this investigation, as well as for her other publications on prisons, she was recognized by the Missouri Welfare League, and her writings were utilized by congressional committees and women's groups dealing with prison conditions and the need for separate facilities for women "federals."[39]

Labor education became the natural focus of her work during most of the 1920s. The O'Hares moved to Louisiana and, along with their monthly, now called the *American Vanguard*, became part of the Llano Co-operative Colony. This socialist colony, in the image of nineteenth-

38. *Frank P. O'Hare's Bulletin* (June 12, July 17, 1920). President Coolidge restored her citizenship in recognition of her prison reform work.
39. Ginger, *Eugene V. Debs*, 431–33; Shannon, "K. R. O. Cunningham," I, 419; O'Hare, *In Prison*, xxii.

century utopian experiments, had been formed by Job Harriman, a one-time Socialist party vice-presidential candidate and a lawyer, who had founded Llano in California in 1914. In 1917 the colony, forced out by drought, moved to Louisiana and then, shortly after the O'Hares joined the enterprise, relocated in rural Arkansas. Kate O'Hare, whose experience several years before with labor education at Ruskin, a colony in southwestern Florida, had led to friendship with socialist professor William E. Zeuch, became a member of the faculty at Llano's Commonwealth College under the directorship of Zeuch. From 1922 to 1928, during and after Commonwealth's affiliation with the colony, she served not only as sociology professor but also, at various times, as curriculum coordinator, trustee, and field director. In these several capacities, she encouraged the small student body to analyze American society, world problems, and proletarian literature.[40]

Another sharp demarcation in her life followed. In 1928 the O'Hares were divorced and Kate Richards O'Hare married Charles C. Cunningham, a California engineer, and moved to the West Coast. By then, she had clearly distanced herself from left-wing politics, having become a staunch foe of communism, and approached the liberal center. In the 1930s she supported Upton Sinclair's "End Poverty in California" gubernatorial campaign and she served on the staff of a Progressive congressman, all the while critical of the inadequacies of the New Deal. Her path to pure-and-simple reformism was completed in 1938, when Governor Culbert L. Olson of California appointed her assistant director of the Department of Penology. More important perhaps, it was a high point in her prison reform years and provided a framework for the period after 1920. Working with the department's director John G. Clark, she helped modernize and streamline the California prison system, which became one of the more progressive in American penology. While O'Hare, then in her sixties, occupied the position for only one year, during that time civil service status for prison administrators was initiated, young offenders segregated from mature and hardened inmates, and the first American minimum-security prison established at Chino, California. A full-scale investigation of conditions at notorious San Quentin and the

40. On Ruskin, see *Socialist Woman*, V (April, 1912), 6; on Commonwealth College, see Harold Bronco, "Kate Richards O'Hare," *World Tomorrow*, IX (February, 1926), 56–57; William H. Cobb, "Commonwealth College Comes to Arkansas, 1923–1925," *Arkansas Historical Quarterly*, XXIII (Summer, 1964), 99–122.

appointment as warden of Clinton T. Duffy led to the elimination of a number of O'Hare's most concrete complaints when she was an inmate: inedible food, unsanitary conditions, and prisoner abuse. O'Hare's sense of achievement won official recognition a few years later when Governor Earl Warren invited her to attend sessions of the State Crime Commission.[41]

Kate Richards O'Hare Cunningham died in January, 1948, in California at the age of seventy-one, of a coronary thrombosis. The wire-service obituary, announcing the death of Red Kate of World War I fame, noted her retirement from the left wing of the American political spectrum while saluting her continued fight for "causes" until the end of her life.[42] While she had not seen emerge the social democratic revolutionary order she had once endorsed, her lifelong activism had helped promote and realize a great number of reforms for the benefit of the masses of Americans. Her historical record is that of a militant reformer who had hoped for even more, a social transformation.

The significance of Kate Richards O'Hare's career and writings is clear. She was a woman of vision who in many ways voiced twentieth-century concerns. She was an outspoken critic of political and religious oppression, an ideologue with solutions to economic and social problems, and a defender of the most vulnerable of her era: working women and children, tenant farmers and textile workers, prison inmates and prostitutes. Finally, her antiwar record in itself decisively speaks to later generations. Although O'Hare was sometimes narrow in her approach, as her inability to see the full dimensions of the so-called Woman Question, or blinded by some of the teachings of her era, as on racial issues, she remains an important figure of the first decades of this century. Thus, the following selections from O'Hare's writings should be welcome to readers interested in any of the topical issues underlined therein.

41. O'Hare, *American Guardian*, July 23, 1937, wrote that the New Deal "failed to mend the old wreck"; on her record as a penologist, see Robert E. Burke, *Olson's New Deal for California* (Berkeley and Los Angeles: University of California Press, 1953), 181–86; Shannon, "K. R. O. Cunningham," I, 419.

42. Stockton (Ca.) *Record*, January 12, 1948, p. 10.

PART I
Socialist Writings

How I Became a Socialist Agitator

My earliest memory is of a Kansas ranch, of the wide stretches of prairie, free herds roaming over the hills and coulees, of cowpunchers with rattling spurs and wide hats, free and easy of speech and manner, but brave and faithful to their friends, four-footed or human; of the freedom and security and plenty of a well-to-do rancher's home.

Those were wonderful days and I shall never cease to be thankful that I knew them. Days that laid the foundation of my whole life, gave me health and strength and love of freedom, taught me to depend on myself, to love nature, to honor rugged strength of mind and body and to know no shams in life. Everything is very real, very much alive and in close touch with nature on the broad sweep of the prairie amid the longhorns.

Then comes the memory of a Kansas drouth, followed by one of the periodical panics which sweep over our country. Days and weeks of hazy nightmare when father's face was gray and set, when mother smiled bravely when he or we children were near, but when we sometimes found tears upon her cheeks if we came upon her unexpectedly. Of course, it was all beyond our comprehension. A horrible something that we could not fathom had settled down over our lives, but the day when the realness of it was forced home came all too soon. The stock was sold, the home dismantled and one day father kissed us good-bye and started away to the city to find work. He who had always been master of his own

"How I Became a Socialist Agitator" was first published in *Socialist Woman*, II (October, 1908), 4–5.

domain, who had hewn his destiny bare-handed from the virgin soil, forced to go out and beg some other man for a chance to labor, an opportunity to use his hands. Though I could not comprehend it then the bitterness of it all was seared upon my memory and I never see a strong man vainly seeking and begging for work that my whole soul does not revolt.

Then came the day when we left the ranch and went to the city to take up the life of a wage-worker's family in the poverty-cursed section of the town. For, of course, no other was possible for us for father's wages were only nine dollars a week and nine dollars is not much to support a family of five. Of that long, wretched winter following the panic of 1887 the memory can never be erased, never grow less bitter. The poverty, the misery, the want, the wan-faced women and hunger pinched children, men trampling the streets by day and begging for a place in the police stations or turning footpads by night, the sordid, grinding, pinching poverty of the workless workers and the frightful, stinging, piercing cold of that winter in Kansas City will always stay with me as a picture of inferno such as Dante never painted.

Of the years that followed when father had regained to some extent his economic foothold and poverty no longer pinched us though it encompassed us all about like a frightful dream that could not be shaken off, it is hard to write intelligently.

I, child-woman that I was, seeing so much poverty and want and suffering, threw my whole soul into church and religious work. I felt somehow that the great, good God who had made us could not have wantonly abandoned his children to such hopeless misery and sordid suffering. There was nothing uplifting in it, nothing to draw the heart nearer to him, only forces that clutched and dragged men and women down into the abyss of drunkenness and vice. Perhaps he had only overlooked those miserable children of the poor in the slums of Kansas City, and if we prayed long and earnestly and had enough of religious zeal he might hear and heed and pity. For several years I lived through that Gethsemane we all endure who walk the path from religious fanaticism to cold, dead, material cynicism with no ray of sane life-philosophy to light it.

I saw drunkenness and the liquor traffic in all the bestial, sordid aspects it wears in the slums, and with it the ever-close companion of prostitution in its most disgusting and degraded forms. I believed, for the good preachers and temperance workers who led me said, that drunkenness and vice caused poverty and I struggled and worked, with only the heart-breaking zeal that an intense young girl can work, to destroy them. But in spite of all we could do the corner saloon still flourished, the saloon-keeper still controlled the government of the city and new inmates came to fill the brothel as fast as the old ones were carried out to the Potter's field, and the grim grist of human misery and suffering still ground on in defiance to church and temperance society and rescue mission.

Gradually I began to realize that the great Creator of the universe had placed us here to live under fixed natural laws that were not changed at the whim of God or man and that prayers would never fill an empty stomach or avoid a panic. I also learned that intemperance and vice did not cause poverty, but that poverty was the mother of the whole hateful brood we had been trying to exterminate and that the increase of her offspring was endless. Dimly I began to realize that if we would win we must fight the cause and not the effects, and since poverty was the fundamental cause of the things I abhorred, I began to study poverty, its whys and wherefores, and to try to understand why there should be so much want in such a world of plenty.

About this time father embarked in the machine shop business and I added to my various experiences that of a woman forced into the business world there to have every schoolday illusion rudely shattered, and forced to see business life in its sordid nakedness. Possibly because I hated ledgers and daybooks and loved mechanics, and possibly because I really wanted to study the wage-worker in his own life, I made life so miserable for the foreman and all concerned that they finally consented to let me go into the shop as an apprentice to learn the trade of machinist. For more than four years I worked at the forge and lathe and bench side by side with some of the best mechanics of the city and some of the noblest men I have ever known. The work was most congenial and I learned for the first time what absorbing joy there can be in labor, if it be a labor that one loves.

Even before my advent into the shop I had begun to have some conception of economics. I had read "Progress and Poverty," "Wealth vs. Commonwealth," "Caesar's Column,"[1] and many such books. Our shop

1. These three books, *Progress and Poverty* by Henry George, *Wealth Against Com-*

being a union one I naturally came in contact with the labor union world and was soon as deeply imbued with the hope trade unionism held out, as I had been with religious zeal. After a while it dawned upon me in a dim and hazy way that trade unionism was something like the frog who climbed up to the well side two feet each day and slipped back three each night. Every victory we gained seemed to give the capitalist class a little greater advantage.

One night while returning from a union meeting, where I had been severely squelched for daring to remonstrate with the boys for voting for a man for mayor whom they had bitterly fought four months before in a long, hard strike, I heard a man talking on the street corner of the necessity of workingmen having a political party of their own. The man's words were balm to my ruffled spirits, for I had been unmercifully ridiculed for daring to talk politics to a lot of American Voting Kings; "a woman, the very idea!" I asked a bystander who the speaker was and he replied, "a Socialist." Of course, if he had called him anything else it would have meant just as much to me, but somehow I remembered the word. A few weeks later I attended a ball given by the Cigar Maker's union, and Mother Jones[2] spoke. Dear old Mother! That is one of the mile-posts in my life that I can easily locate. Like a mother talking to her errant boys she taught and admonished that night in words that went home to every heart. At last she told them that a scab at the ballot-box was more to be despised than one at the factory door, that a scab ballot could do more harm than a scab bullet; that workingmen must support the political party of their class and that the only place for a sincere union man was in the Socialist party.

Here was that strange new word again coupled with the things I had vainly tried to show my fellow unionists. I hastily sought out "Mother" and asked her to tell what Socialism was, and how I could find the Socialist party. With a smile she said, "Why, little girl, I can't tell you all about it now, but here are some Socialists, come over and get acquainted." In a moment I was in the center of an excited group of men all talking at once, and hurling unknown phrases at me until my brain

monwealth by Henry Demarest Lloyd, and *Caesar's Column* by Ignatius Donnelly, were late-nineteenth-century best sellers on the social ills of contemporary society.

2. Mary Harris "Mother" Jones (1830–1930) was a legendary labor organizer, agitator, and quasi socialist. From the 1880s to the end of her long life, she traveled to every area of labor strife, especially the coal mines, and sought to represent the workers.

was whirling. I escaped by promising to "come down to the office tomorrow and get some books." The next day I hunted up the office and was
assailed by more perplexing phrases and finally escaped loaded down
with Socialist classics enough to give a college professor mental indiges-
tion. For weeks I struggled with that mass of books only to grow more
hopelessly lost each day. At last down at the very bottom of the pile I
found a well worn, dog-eared, little book that I could not only read, but
understand, but to my heart-breaking disappointment it did not even
mention Socialism. It was the Communist Manifesto, and I could not
understand what relation it could have to what I was looking for.

I carried the books back and humbly admitted my inability to understand them or grasp the philosophy they presented. As the men who had
given me the books explained and expostulated in vain, a long, lean,
hungry looking individual unfolded from behind a battered desk in the
corner and joined the group. With an expression more forceful than ele-
gant he dumped the classics in the corner, ridiculed the men for expect-
ing me to read or understand them, and after asking some questions as
to what I had read gave me a few small booklets. Merrie England and
Ten Men of Money Island, Looking Backward,[3] and Between Jesus and
Caesar, and possibly half a dozen more of the same type. The hungry
looking individual was Comrade Wayland,[4] and the dingy office the birth-
place of the Appeal to Reason.

For a time I lived in a dazed dream while my mental structure was
being ruthlessly torn asunder and rebuilt on a new foundation. That the
process was a painful one I need not tell one who has undergone it, and
most of us have. At last I awoke in a new world, with new viewpoints,
and a new outlook. Recreated, I lived again with new aims, new hopes,
new aspirations and the dazzling view of the new and wonderful work to
do. All the universe pulsated with new life that swept away the last vestige of the mists of creed and dogma and old ideas and beliefs.

For some time I worked with our group in Kansas City, and seven

3. Of these several titles dealing critically with capitalism, Looking Backward by Edward Bellamy was the most renowned. One of the most widely read books of the era, it
was a utopian socialist tract in novel form which contrasted a future socialist society with
the social problems of contemporary capitalist America. A middle-class movement favoring nationalization of industry flourished briefly, stimulated by the impact of Bellamy's
fiction.

4. Julius A. Wayland (1854–1912) was the publisher of the Appeal to Reason, probably the most influential of all socialist periodicals. It was published in Girard, Kansas, as
a weekly from 1895 until World War I.

years ago when Walter Thomas Mills[5] opened his training school for Socialist workers in Girard, Kansas, I was one of its students. There I found
not only a congenial group of comrades, the best and most forceful
teacher I have ever known, but that crowning, finishing touch of human
life, love. In the school as a fellow-student I met my husband. Of our
marriage at the home of Comrade Wayland at the close of the school and
our life since that time little need be said. All who are at all acquainted
with the Socialist movement know more or less of it for our story has
been the story of the Socialist movement, it has been our life.

Taking up the work of traveling speakers and organizers the next day
after our wedding we have followed the stony, rough hewn path from
that day to this. From the coal fields of Pennsylvania and West Virginia
and Indian Territory, to the farms of Kansas and Iowa and Missouri,
through the plains of Texas and into the cotton fields of Oklahoma and
Arkansas and Tennessee, from the Ghetto of New York to the Rocky
Mountains we have gone wherever and whenever the economic pressure
has made men and women receptive to the philosophy of Socialism. We
have stood on the street corner and in the pulpit, at the shop door and in
the college assembly room, in the country school houses and trades
union hall, in the legislative chambers and temples of justice, in all manner of places and appealing to all manner of men. We have worked and
have seen the Socialist movement grow from a handful of men and
women sneered at, derided and ridiculed, into the mighty force it
now is.

Twice in the seven years my work in the field has been interrupted
by the cares of maternity and now a curly-haired boy of five and a brown-
eyed girl of two share our hearts and make the fight seem all the more
worth while.

Seven years, yes, seven long, weary, toilworn, travel-tired years.
Years when the path was often dark and the road rough; when the heart
grew sick and the soul faint because the world is deaf and dumb and
blind, has eyes that see not and ears that do not hear, hearts that do not
feel either their own needless suffering or that of their fellow-men. Yet
they have been glorious years, years of battle with the forces of ignorance, years that have tried men's souls, that have left many a noble
comrade lying by the wayside, dead upon the field of battle for economic

5. Walter Thomas Mills (1856–1942), socialist teacher and writer, was a sometime
minister who was especially successful as a propagandist in the Great Plains area.

justice, yet years of such achievement as the world has never known, years filled with success still unmeasured, of revolutionary forces we cannot even guess. Our thought in so short a time has dominated the thought of the world, our literature setting the standards, our philosophy shaping the political forces of the nations and round the world glows the spark of human brotherhood, ready to spring at our call into living flame.

The Girl Who Would

Times without number I have been asked why I, a woman, happened to become a machinist, and why I chose to trade so far from woman's prescribed sphere of action. When I attempt to answer the question, I find there are a number of reasons, all good and valid, and yet I cannot point to any one of them that quite answers the question fully.

Perhaps it was because Nature, that sly, wise old mother, placed in my brain an unusually strong desire to create.

At any rate I remember that as a little child no pastime sufficed, unless it was the making of something. . . .

At eighteen I found myself an overgrown, slender girl, my physique wrecked by over-study, in miserable health, and the problem of self support confronting me. I had tried successively school teaching at $30 a month, vest making at $1 a day, and stenography at $9 a week, and realized, that with my poor health I could never make a living at any of them. I looked over all the field of women's work and saw no hope; all were over-crowded and under-paid, and I was beginning to wonder if marriage was the only way left for a girl to make a living, when I made the acquaintance of one of those wonderful mechanical geniuses that our present system so effectually crushes.

In his company all my old love for mechanics came back to me, and he, delighted to find so apt and interested a pupil, taught me all he could of the theory of mechanics. Soon my father became interested, and finally we three combined our small capital, and started a little machine shop. I was supposed to do office work, but as our establishment was a very modest one, I could attend to all my duties and still find much time to spend in the shop. I teased, coaxed and cajoled the men into letting

"The Girl Who Would" was first published in *Wilshire's Magazine* (January, 1903), 27–29.

me try my hand on their work, until the discipline of the shop was ruined, and in desperation, one day the foreman said that I must either keep out of the shop altogether or come in and work under his orders. I immediately replied that I would report for duty the next morning, and I did.

At first the men laughed at me and teased me, but that had no effect. Then they tried giving me the dirtiest, greasiest work in the shop thinking I would get discouraged and quit, but all of my Irish will was up, and I would not yield. Finally when the men realized that I meant to stick, they grumbled long and loud, and finally threatened to revolt, not because they disliked me personally, but because they feared I was establishing a precedent. If one girl learned the machinist trade, others would, and soon the shops would be overrun by women, and wages would go down as they have in every trade that women have entered.

Teddy [Roosevelt] had not turned the lime light on the path to the strenuous life at this time, but nevertheless I lived it, the first two years in the shop. Between learning the trade, conciliating the men, and pulling wires for admittance to the Union I was not troubled with *ennui*.

Naturally the dirt and grime was distasteful to me, and I decided it unnecessary. Since I had broken one unwritten law by entering the shop, I decided to break another, and have the floors cleaned, and the windows washed. So by judicious distribution of gumdrops and smiles, I gained the co-operation of the apprentice boys, and soon we had the shop as clean as a Dutch frau's front steps.

I realized that if I kept pace with the boys I could not be hampered with superfluous clothing. I discarded corsets and long skirts, and wore a short neat suit of blue duck, with the regulation machinists cap. Of all the costumes I have worn since I left the shop, none have ever seemed so comfortable or becoming as my shop uniform. Manual labor in congenial surroundings had given me back my health, and wielding a hammer and pushing a file had developed a pair of shoulders and arms that would have been the envy of many a society belle.

Was not the work hard, heavy and disagreeable?

It was hard; sometimes so heavy that I must needs call some of the boys to assist me; but it was never disagreeable, for I loved it.

There is nothing else that brings the exultation, the consciousness of power, like taking hard, unyielding steel, and conquering it, shaping and forming it to your will. Then the joy of taking an ugly, sodden piece of iron and watching it grow under your hand to a beautiful polished thing of use and beauty. Think what it means to a true mechanic, when with a touch as tender and as gentle as a mother's, he carefully fits together the parts of a delicate mechanism he has created. Weeks, months, aye perhaps for years, he has been forming it piece by piece, and at last all is done, carefully each part is fitted to the whole. Each tap and screw is tightened, each bearing oiled, and with eager heart and bated breath the power is applied. For an instant the belts slip on the polished pulleys, then look! It's off! It runs! It works! Eureka! We have won! Our hands and brain have given something useful to humanity, added to the comfort of mankind, and lightened the load of the toiler.

No brush can ever paint the glowing tints of the forge, and no artist ever watches his colors with the intensity of the mechanic in tempering his tools.

You wonder, no doubt, why I changed the hammer for the pen, the shop for the platform, if I loved my trade, my art, so much? I'll tell you why I did it. Because my work brought me the contact with the great wage-earning class, and there I saw the wage system in all its accursedness. There I saw men dumb and paralyzed with an unsatisfied longing for the brush, the pen, the soil, or for the whispering forests, bound to a lathe or forge, in the roar of machinery that is music to him who loves it, and hell to him who hates it.

On the other hand I saw men who were born mechanics chained to a desk, or pulpit, miserable misfit failures, because they were denied the opportunity to do the thing Nature intended them for. I saw women denied the right to use their strong creative instinct in healthful work, and forced into the factory, the sweat-shop, the brothel, to earn their bread.

Here I saw manhood and womanhood wither and crumble away beneath the crushing weight of economic servitude. I saw men created in the image and likeness of God fall to miserable, servile, cringing slaves, afraid to hold up their heads and say they were men, because some man had it in his power to take their means of life away—not only theirs but that of their wives and babies. I saw fathers robbed of two-thirds of the products of their labor, and little children's lives coined into profits.

At last my soul revolted at the crime and injustice of it all. I could stand it no longer, so I hung up my cap, laid aside my calipers and rule, and went out in the fight for Socialism. And here I stay until the Co-operative Commonwealth is ours.

"Nigger" Equality

There is a reason why the cry of "Negro Domination" strikes terror to the hearts of the Southerner and is such an effective weapon in the hands of the capitalist class and their tools, the politicians. My father was a Federal soldier and I was born and reared in Kansas, the abolition state of all states, but my heart was bled and my blood boiled as I have listened to the frightful stories of those accursed days when the "Carpet Bagger"[6] ruled the southland and added his damnable wrongs to a country already cursed by war's devastation. To the man or woman who lived through those miserable days when the vile politicians from the north by their arrogant power forced the defeated southerners not only to face the bitterness of war's reverses, but the stinging disgrace of having ignorant blacks placed in positions of power and authority over them, "Negro Domination" means something more than words. Naturally they revolt at any political movement which they can be induced to believe sanctions such a thing.

In the South the great bug-bear used by the Democratic politicians to keep the voters in line behind the Democratic party is the cry that Socialism would mean "Nigger Equality." At every Socialist meeting some earnest seeker after the light gently whispers the question or some politician sneeringly hurls it at me, "Don't you Socialists believe in nigger equality?"

Now listen, you white voters of the South; let us settle this question fairly and definitely and forever. It is absolutely true that the very basic principle of Socialism is EQUALITY and the very goal of the whole Socialist movement of the world is EQUALITY.

"'Nigger' Equality" was first published as a pamphlet, by the *National Rip-Saw* (St. Louis, 1912).

6. Carpetbagger was a derogatory term applied to northerners who participated in Reconstruction. They were held to be transients exploiting the already defeated white South. In actuality, such individuals more often simply hoped to find postwar opportunities in the New South.

"There, I told you so, I knew you wanted nigger equality," every Democratic politician in the South shouts.

Sure! but just wait a moment until we decide what kind of equality we want.

There are several kinds of Equality:

Social Equality.

Physical Equality.

Mental Equality.

Equality of opportunity, or economic equality.

"Do we want Social Equality?"

Certainly not; there will never be such a thing. Men and women always form social groups according to their various tastes and differences in social tastes and preferences will always remain and Social Equality is impossible and would be undesirable.

"Do we want Physical Equality?"

No. Socialists would like to see a condition that would enable every human being to be the best physical specimen possible, but there will always be tall men and short men, fat men and lean men, plain women and beautiful women and such a thing as physical equality can never exist.

"Do we want Mental Equality?"

No. We want every man and woman to have the opportunity to develop their mentality to the highest point compatible with their personal wishes in the matter, but inequalities will always remain. Law can never make a bright man dull or a dull man brainy.

"Well, what kind of Equality do you Socialists want?" you ask.

"Why, just one kind, EQUALITY OF OPPORTUNITY."

SOCIALISTS WANT TO PUT THE NEGRO WHERE HE CAN'T COMPETE WITH THE WHITE MAN.

The whole aim of Socialism is that every human being, white, black, red or yellow, shall have equal opportunity to have access to the natural resources which nature has supplied and to the machinery which man has created and then to have the full social product of his labor.

"And do you want the 'nigger' to have equal opportunity to use natural resources, and machinery of production and to let him have all the wealth he creates by his labor?" you ask.

Certainly—not because we love the "nigger," but because we know that every chain of economic servitude that is shackled on the ankle of the "nigger" is riveted on the wrists of the white workers. Just as long as a "nigger" can be robbed of the product of his labor by the capitalist class by being shut out from access to the means of life, just that long he can be made the club and chain that will drag and beat the white workers down into the mire of poverty. As long as the "nigger" can be forced to be a wage slave, so can the white man; as long as the "nigger" is a tenant farmer, so long will the white man be; as long as an idle capitalist can live off a "nigger's" labor, so can he live off a white man's labor.

No, we Socialists don't love the "nigger" any better than he loves us; we don't admire the shape of his nose or the color of his skin any more than he likes our insolence and intolerant attitude, but we have sense enough to know that capitalism chains us to the negro with iron chains of economic servitude and we would rather have the negro free from the chains. Because if the black man is chained it spells slavery for the white man and woman and girl—we must share it.

Wake up, you southern voters. You have let the scare-crow of "Nigger Equality" keep you ignorant of the Socialist movement and what it means to you without understanding that you endure the very thing you dread. You have Jim Crow laws[7] that keep the negroes out of your railroad coaches, but where is the Jim Crow law for the factory, workshop, mines or cotton field? A negro can't ride in a white street car in Memphis, but I saw a hundred men digging in a sewer ditch. Half of them were blacks and half white Democrats; there was no Jim Crow law there; it was a "nigger" and a white man, a "nigger" and a white man, as nicely placed as the stripes on a calico apron. When the water boy came along with the water pail and one dipper a "nigger" took a drink and then a white man, another "nigger" and another white man, and not a politician shouted "nigger equality." In the laundries of that aristocratic southern city the daughters of white Democrats work side by side with big, black negro men; in the cotton mills, the white children compete with negro children. In the cotton fields the white daughters of white voters drag the cotton sacks down the cotton row next to "nigger bucks" and the Democratic politician of the chivalrous South where womanhood is placed on

7. The name Jim Crow was adopted from a nineteenth-century minstrel-show character introduced by T. D. Rice in about 1828. Jim Crow laws were passed following the end in 1875 of Radical Republican legislation, which dealt with black equality. A pattern of segregation, both by law and by custom, came to dominate the South.

a pedestal and worshipped, where it would degrade women to have a vote, raise no voice in protest.

No, we Socialists don't want that kind of "Nigger Equality" in the north or south. God knows we have had enough of it. Negro and white alike have the equality of wage slavery, tenant servitude, capitalist exploitation, illiteracy and bitter poverty. Socialism would replace that "equality" with equality of opportunity for black and white to have access to the means of life and the opportunity to develop the best there is in both races instead of the worst.

"Nigger Equality!" Good Heavens; If the tenant farmers of the south had equality with the niggers they would be lots better off than they are. All over the south wherever I have traveled I find the good land, down in the bottoms where cotton grows shoulder high and the soil is rich and fertile, is rented to the blacks. Every landlord in the south rents every acre of land he can to negroes and the poor land up in the hills, the worn out land, the land that produces least, he allows the Great American Sovereign Voting King, the white Democrat of the south, to till; and then the same white Democrats shy at Socialism like a frisky colt because Socialism would mean "Nigger equality." Well, nigger equality would be better than the Democratic "equality" which you have now, with the nigger getting the best of it all around, which best, God knows is bad enough.

The "Negro Equality" which Capitalism forces on us to-day is not peculiar to the south alone; we have it in the north as well. In Kansas City black men have replaced white men in the packing-houses wherever possible, and the white daughters of both Republican and Democratic voters are forced to associate with them in terms of shocking intimacy. In the coal mines of the whole United States black men have been used to replace white miners until there is not a shred of race distinction left.

Remember there is a vast distinction between the economic equality of opportunity for the black man along with his white neighbor to have access to the means of production and the product of his labor and the revolting equality of degradation which capitalism forces on us. We Socialists simply want the negro to have this opportunity to have access to the means of life, so he can quit competing with the white man, not because we love or hate him, but in order that he may not be used to keep down our wages. I neither love nor hate a negro. I am no more anxious to associate with him than he is to associate with me. I don't want to associate on terms of social equality with him and I know he is just as willing to dispense with my society as I am with his, but capitalism forces us into a social, economic and physical relation which is just as revolting to the negro as it is to me, and as both the negro and I want to escape, the only way we can do so is by Socialism giving us both an equal opportunity to have access to the means of life and the product of our labor; then we can dump the capitalists off our back and work out our own problems, freed from the curse of race antagonism.

But you ask what is the solution of the race question?

There can be but one. Segregation. If you ask me what I am going to work and speak and write and vote for on the race question when it is to be settled under a Socialist form of government, I can tell you very quickly. Let us give the blacks one section in the country where every condition is best fitted for them. Free them from capitalist exploitation; give them access to the soil, the ownership of their machines and let them work out their own salvation. If the negro rises to such an opportunity, and develops his own civilization, well and good; if not, and he prefers to hunt and fish and live idly, no one will be injured but him and that will be his business.

Be sensible men, you white voters of the south, and refuse to be frightened by an empty scarecrow. "Nigger Equality" has served the politicians and the capitalist class for a long time to keep you in blind servitude; demolish it and think for yourself.

You are yoked up as tenant farmer or wage slaves with the negro today. Vote for Socialism and be free.

Be wise, you black men of the South. While Abe Lincoln and the boys in blue were smashing your shackles of chattel slavery the capitalist class of the North was forging the shackles of economic slavery on both you and the men who fought to free you. Now you are both slaves of the same master, you are bound together by the same chains of economic servitude. Socialism is the only force on earth that can free you both, free us all, black and white, man, woman and child. White men of the United States, black men of our country, use your ballots to sever the chain that binds you together and binds you to slavery. Black men, vote to free your wives and daughters from the despoilation of your white masters; white men, vote to free your womenkind from the debasement of wage slavery yoked to Negro Equality.

A Crack in the "Solid South"

For years the South has been looked upon by all as the strong-hold of capitalism. The masters have felt that the Southern working people were so completely blinded by prejudice and enslaved by poverty that they were perfectly "safe" and would always remain blind devotees to the moss-grown Democratic party.

No land on earth has ever been so shamefully wronged. Dixie bore the crushing weight of one of the most hellish wars the world has ever seen. That the northern manufacturers and traders might reap richer profits from the south its homes were ruined, its fields despoiled and its people forced to bear the brunt of war and suffer the bitter humiliation of defeat. That venal politicians might be rewarded for not spoiling the capitalists' game the South was cursed with the "carpetbagger." The propertied class were reduced to penury, the working class to abject poverty. The negro slaves over whom the whole cursed war was ostensibly fought are learning that they were not freed from slavery by the Republican party, for while the shackles of chattel slavery were struck off the master class were busy riveting the shackles of wage-slavery on them. The only thing the Republican party has ever given the black voters has been the opportunity to stop bullets in strikes and to do the "dirty work."

Naturally all Southerners since the war are Democrats. Because of the livid scars the South bears, its hatred of all things "Republican" and "Yankee" is understandable and quite excusable.

For forty years the Punch-and-Judy show has been played. The scars have been rasped in the South and the "bloody shirt"[8] has waved in the North. The workers of each section, north and south, have distrusted

---

"A Crack in the 'Solid South'" was first published in *National Rip-Saw* (August, 1916), 5, 9.

8. The bloody shirt was a vote-getting device used by northern Republicans for a generation after the Civil War. Relying on sectional hostility and rivalry, they waved the bloody shirt in countless campaigns.

each other, and voted against each other, while the masters gathered in the wealth the workers of both sections produced.

Firmly entrenched in power in the South the Democratic party has become more and more corrupt, as corrupt as the Republican party in the North. Each year the politicians show themselves more and more completely the tools of the great outside corporations that are stripping Dixie of her natural resources and reducing Dixie's workers to plundered wage slaves. Without a shadow of legal right or moral reason corrupt officials of the South have given the great forests, coal lands, phosphate mines, water power, and other natural resources bodily to the capitalist class. The world has never known such an orgy of ruthless robbery and despoilation of natural resources as has taken place in the South in the last twenty years.

The testimony before the Industrial Relations Committee proves beyond doubt that the condition of the tenant farmer of the South, whose cotton clothes the world, is more insecure and cursed than that of the black slave before the war; that the workers of the Southern mills, mines and lumber camps are robbed ruthlessly and dominated as completely as was the negro. Black and White, the workers of the South are enduring a condition that every day becomes more unbearable.

In camps where whites can not be secured vile enough to do the bidding of and stoop to crime for the Lumber Trust, black men have been made deputies, armed with guns and clubs and given the power of life and death over the white men, women and children. Fifty years ago white men cracked the whip over the backs of black women, but in Dixie today white men wield the economic whip over thousands of white women and children and compel obedience. In cotton field, mine and factory, economic and social equality with negroes is forced upon the whites, and in bitter rebellion the workers of the South are realizing that the "social equality" and "negro domination" about which the Democratic politicians have shouted are Democratic facts, and the unbearable conditions of "reconstruction" days are being re-enacted.

In places all the horrors of chattel slavery have been revived and for the workers, white and black, a whole new list of sorrows have been added, that black slavery never knew. In no nation on earth, not even in Russia, are large sections of the workers more completely in the power of the capitalist class and nowhere is wage-slavery more bitter and de-

grading. When the blood-stained pages of Dixie's history since '66 is written for the world the Democratic party will be eternally damned for having permitted and assisted in the exploitation of the masses of the
Southern people.

A few years ago all over the Southland Socialist literature began to
pass from hand to hand and be quietly discussed. Ranting politicians who
tried to fill the minds of men with age-old lies were called upon to prove
their assertions and were often routed in derision. The RIP-SAW, the AP-
PEAL TO REASON, the REBEL,[9] and other Socialist papers found their way
into coal mine, lumber camp and plantation house. Like outlaws skulking
about at night, lumber jacks and coal miners carried their little bundle of
precious literature and sometimes read it aloud by a smoking lamp or
flaring pine torch to their fellow workers who could not read. Gathered
about the cotton gin or the country store the farmers read, discussed and
finally understood what Socialism offered the farmers as a class.

Whenever a matter affecting the welfare of the working class came up
the Socialist agitators were always ready to do their part and more. If the
Farmer's Union needed a speaker the Socialist was there loaded to the
guards with good, big chunks of fact and logic. If a strike was on he was
on hand again and ready for business; if an empty pulpit needed someone
to resurrect it and give the hungry sheep some real spiritual food, the
Socialist preacher was on the job. The Renter's Union and Brotherhood
of Timber Workers[10] fighting for life, know now that they have an ally
worth while, and a means to tell their story to the world through the
Socialist press, a press that cannot be muzzled. Dimly the workers in the
cotton mills know that the men and women who wear the red button are
working and fighting for them. The tenant farmers in the cotton field
have found that the man who carried [sic] a red card and tells them [that]
to vote the master's ticket is a crime, knows their condition and holds out
the only hope that has ever illuminated their darkened lives. The men
and women of culture in the South find in the comradeship of the So-

9. The *National Rip-Saw* was a socialist monthly published in St. Louis from 1904 to
World War I, for which both Frank P. O'Hare and Kate Richards O'Hare worked. The
Rebel was a socialist weekly published in Texas from 1911 to 1917.

10. These unions represent fleeting grass-roots efforts to find strength in unity. The
Brotherhood of Timber Workers existed in Louisiana and Texas from 1911 to 1913. It
enrolled several thousand lumber workers in an unsuccessful unionizing effort against the
open-shop policy of the enormous Kirby Lumber Company.

cialist writers and speakers the only real companionship they have
known in forty long, dark, bitter years.

As a Bud Unfolds

Of all the civic ills that beset us there is none that has been so widely
discussed as Child Labor. So many crocodile tears have been shed, so
many hypocritical sighs heaved, so much bemoaning and bewailing of it,
and so little intelligence displayed in the superficial and silly attempts to
meet the problem that the very mention of the subject irritates me, and
as far as possible, it is the one that I taboo. Not because I do not realize
its horrors, but because I detest the maudlin twaddle that press, pulpit
and platform are always sending forth.

There are perhaps few women who have seen more of the horrors of
child labor than I. I have stood beside the breaker boys, gnomelike in
the murky darkness, bending to their endless task. I have watched ragged children weave youth and health into shining silks, and human life
and quivering heart throbs into soft velvet. I have followed the children
into mine and mill and sweatshop; into the cotton fields and over the
sunny, fruitland slopes; oh, I know where the icy blasts chill blood and
marrow, and where the fires of Hades scar body and mind and soul! I
have seen the slaughter of innocents in all manner of hideous and needless forms, and having seen, hate as only a mother can. But what avail?
If tears could wash away the crimson stain of murdered childhood, our
civic robes would be white as snow (God knows enough have been shed),
or if heartache could atone for wasted life, we might call ourselves "A
Christian nation." But tears and heartaches are of no value unless they
arouse the heart and mind of mankind, not to weep and wail, but to seek
and find the underlying causes, and knowing, dare to act.

One of the clearest statements of the Child Labor problem and its
fundamental causes that I ever heard came from a capitalist, a very large
employer of children. I was working in a machine shop then. One day
the owner of one of the largest soap factories in the West sent for me,
and taking me out into the wrapping room where the soap was wrapped
and packed for shipment, he pointed to where long rows of children,

"As a Bud Unfolds" was first published in *National Rip-Saw* (November, 1912), 2, 3.

stoop shouldered, narrow chested, chalky faced, and with hands eaten by the alkali, were working with the racking swiftness of piece-workers.

"In all your shop," he said, "is there not mechanical skill and inventive genius enough to make us a machine that will wrap soap as quickly and as cheaply as those children? The cost is of little moment; all I ask is that you build the machine. We will pay the price. I am so sick of it all, so tired of watching that crowd of children glide into the gates at morning like felons and out at night like ghosts; so heartsick with hearing sad-faced mothers lie their children's childhood away; so disgusted with lob-bying legislatures, bribing inspectors and juggling laws, that I want to escape it if I can."

Seeing the look of surprise on my face, he added: "O, I suppose you are like all the rest. You think because I am a factory owner and work children that I am a monster of greed. You forget that I, too, am a man, a human being with eyes that see, ears that hear, a man with a heart and mind and soul, yes, and a conscience too. Do you think that I cannot see that disease and death stalk through these foul-smelling rooms, that con-sumption lurks in each dark corner and epidemic holds high level here! Do you think that we enjoy taking the urchins from their play in the street, bubbling over with animal spirits and latent mischief, and con-verting them into mere machines like these?"

"Then why do you do it? Why don't you pay living wages and employ men?" I asked.

"Why don't I, indeed," he replied, "when my competitor across the river pays starvation wages and uses children? I would last just about sixty days in this business, then the bankruptcy court. I must make soap just as cheaply as any one else, and compete in the market for trade, or I perish. As long as that exists" (and with a comprehensive wave of his hand, he pointed to the Patch, the slum of Packingtown), "as long as poverty and want exists there, there will be parents forced to lie that the children may work. And as long as my competitors employ children, I must give them work, revolting as it may be to me."

"Then why don't you work for better Child Labor Laws?" I asked. "Why not help to secure better legislation instead of fighting it?"

"Labor laws! Labor legislation!" he cried. "O, you Laborites, you Trade Unionists, you are so tiresomely verdant, so disgustingly gullible! You prate about laws and legislation, overlooking the fact that the Em-ploying class have always made the laws and are still doing so. Can you hope for a law that will protect life at the expense of profit when those who lose life have no voice, and those who control profits have power in the making of laws? If the very best Child Labor law were placed upon our statute books, would it protect the children and free me from the distasteful position of child labor employer? Not at all. Somewhere there will be a soap manufacturer, whose conscience is not troublesome. In order to reduce the cost of production and gain the market, he will wink at law, bribe officials and employ children, thus forcing me to do it too, or go to the wall.

"Granted that we might secure the best Child Labor laws, who would be elected or appointed to enforce them? The fathers of the children working in the factories? Well, I guess not. It would be the same old crowd of political grafters, who have fattened off the public purse and private bribes since the political game began. Child Labor laws cannot solve the problem. They only mean more laws that we must break, more lies legal and illegal, and a whole gang of political harpies that we must bribe. Legislation, laws and penalties! Why is it you good people cannot understand that since the day when the Draconian code was framed, laws have been piled mountain high, but crime has not abated. The motives that impel men to right living must be made stronger than those which impel him to crime. Law and penalty never uplifted the human race.

"Don't you know that for ages theology has held the human race by the nape of the neck, dangling over a pit of fire and brimstone? It has transgressed in spite of eternal fire sizzling at its feet, and sulphur fumes filling its nostrils. If everlasting, infinite punishment cannot coerce mankind into paths of rectitude, what hope of finite human penalties? Mark my words, machinery, the inventive genius of mankind alone can free the child slave from his task and the employer of children from his enforced moral and civic transgressions. Give your inventive genius full play, test your mechanical skill, use the brains God gave you and make us machines. MACHINES, that shall shoulder the burden of toil and make the children free."

Since then, I have listened to the babble of countless tongues and floundered through seas of written words, all prating of the problem of "Child Labor," but I have never heard more common sense and less sophistry than in that hard headed old businessman's statement. I can say that there is but one solution: - Machinery, to do the work, and the collective ownership of the machine, in order that all may share in their production and be freed from the curse of slavish toil.

Sometimes we hear ardent Socialists declare that under Socialism there will be no more child labor. I hope quite sincerely that these people are mistaken. In fact, I am sure they are. For while we all admit that "all work and no play makes Jack a dull boy," we are learning that all play and no work makes Jack a mental, moral and physical degenerate. The sons and daughters of our millionaires today are living proof of this trite saying, quite as much as are the child toilers of the preceding.

In discussing the question of child labor, we must remember that there are two kinds: child labor in which the best that is in life, in which life itself is transformed into wealth for the owner of the factory, mill or mine, and child labor for the best development of the child, mentally, morally and physically. Child labor for profits, or child labor for learning by doing. Under a sane social order the former will not exist and the latter will be the basis of our school system.

We never see children of the rich at the loom, lathe or spindle. For them the whistle never shrieks its warning call; for them there are no long hours of nerve and body racking toil; they never creep home at night dull, dazed and toil broken. When all the mills, mines and factories of the world belong to all fathers and mothers, yes, even to the children, there shall be no more murder of childhood. When they are owned by just a few fathers and mothers, the mass of fathers and mothers cannot keep the wolf from the door without offering up their children as a living sacrifice on the altar of private ownership.

Under capitalism, the child whose father owns a factory is taught that it is degrading to have to work; that ownership means the right and power to despoil childhood, debase womanhood and enslave manhood. Under Socialism, the child will be taught that it is degrading to eat the fruits of another's toil without a just return; that labor is honorable, and that ownership means a sacred responsibility that can only be met by faithfully developing the highest qualities and capabilities.

With the ideal of service to mankind replacing the ideal of using mankind for service, living off the fruits of another's labor will become as repulsive to the child of the future as dining off the flesh of another is to the child of the present. When Love, Labor and Brotherhood are crowned the Graces of human life, children will be born in love, reared as brothers and educated in the art of useful joyous labor. The workshop will be a school, and the school a workshop. The field shall be a university, and leaves of grass and ears of corn, textbooks. From weaving bits of colored paper into mats in the kindergarten to designing a dynamo in the draughting room or making a home run on a ball ground, none will draw the line between work, play and education.

There will be child labor under Socialism, but it will be the labor that trains the head, heart and hand; that develops men and women fit to inherit, to dress and keep this beautiful, bountiful old earth of ours. The child labor that can not exist is that which snatches the child away from its mother's breast and thrusts it into the factory to toil and moil for the gain of the idle owners of the marts.

The Leaven Doing Its Work

There is a vast difference between the Socialist movement and the Socialist Party. The Socialist movement is in one sense the awakening social consciousness of the race, the Socialist Party is the organized expression of the interest of the world's workers; the visible recognizable portion that can be definitely counted by means of dues and votes, but the general movement toward Socialism is immeasurably greater.

At the last election there were a million American citizens who expressed their allegiance to organized Socialism by their votes and there are possibly another million men and women who would have done so except for the fact that they were disenfranchised. How many millions more semi-Socialists there are we can not know but we do know that Socialist thought has permeated every institution today and is shaping the thought and action of the race. Socialist thought has leavened the church until the church must be revolutionized, must forswear its allegiance to Mammon and stand forth with the propertyless Nazarene in its teachings or it will crumble into dust.

The public schools have been socialized to an extent almost astonishing to the average mind. In St. Louis our children are furnished all their books, pens, paper, pencils and other supplies by the city and in many of the schools lunches are served at cost or very near it for the school

"The Leaven Doing Its Work" was first published in *National Rip-Saw* (March, 1913), 3, 12.

children. No one ever questions the fact now that books and school supplies are now as much a social right of a child as a teacher, school room or heating appliance. Yet only a few years ago when the Populist Party of Kansas[11] put in their platform a plank favoring free school books, a perfect howl of derision went up all over the state. I remember that the children of Democratic and Republican fathers turned up their noses at me and said that my father wanted to pauperize them by having the state furnish free school books. The drouth in Kansas was broken that year by the rivers of very wet tears shed by the people who did not want their children pauperized by having the state furnish the books as well as the teacher, school house and coal to heat it. To-day every one including Democrats and Republicans turn up their noses at the state or city so behind the times and antiquated as not to furnish free school supplies, and no politician in the most benighted state would dare oppose free school books. The lobbies maintained at seats of government by the school book trust are forced to work under cover and would immediately bring the wrath of the most ignorant voter down upon themselves by an open opposition of free school books.

This Socialistic idea has permeated the minds of the people, yet they do not know it is Socialistic and it is accepted by the adherents of all parties as a fundamental need of society.

During the last year the Nurses Association of Missouri at their own expense and by their own initiative made a social survey of the conditions of jails and almshouses of the state. From their own funds they printed splendid booklets setting forth their findings in the most startling manner, and they are maintaining a traveling lecturer to hold public lectures and awaken the citizens to the frightful social conditions of these state and county institutions.

Here is a group of young working women, possibly the most highly paid as a class of any working women in the state; women who have nothing in common with jails and almshouses, neither are they concious [sic] Socialists to any extent. They are simply women who by contact with the world and a broad culture have had their social consciousness

11. The Populist party, organized in 1892, was the culmination of decades of farmer agitation over falling agricultural prices. The Populists, whose strength lay in the Plains states, promoted a variety of socioeconomic and political reform measures, many of which became law in the Progressive era after the party's demise.

developed, have unconsciously become a part of the Socialist movement and fighting for the downmost dog, the most helpless and hopeless part of mankind, the jailbird and the pauper.

The revolting conditions they found in the Missouri Jail are told in the graphic and yet matter of fact manner and make a booklet well worth reading. It not only tells the sordid story of Fifteenth Century methods still used in Twentieth Century Missouri but tells the inspiring story of awakened womanhood fighting for social justice and struggling to bring the light of science into the darkest, most sordid and hopeless places on earth. . . .

It is not that the Nurses Association has brought out any new facts, told us anything we did not know that is valuable. Every resident of the state of Missouri and all other states for that matter knows everything that is told in the little book. We know what dreary, miserable, sordid damnable places almshouses are and we know that "over the hills to the poorhouse" is the most bitter tragedy that can come into an old man or woman's life. Long before Will Carlton wrote the tender poem that has endeared him to every heart, and since he told us of the ride that mother took,[12] the "poorhouse" has been the black tragedy that has furnished the background for many a writer's verse and story. It has been the spectre that has haunted the lives of millions of American citizens, the fear of it has urged men to crime and women to sell their virtue; the saddest end that could come to a human life was to die in the Poorhouse and be buried in Potter's field.

The Nurses Association has told us nothing new concerning jails. We knew it all long ago. None of us can plead guiltless of the knowledge of their filth, mental, moral and physical condition.

We know jails are placed in dark cellars, their windows are but slits in stone walls, that ventilation, sanitation and sunlight are considered by jail builders as fatal to reformation and only filth, darkness and fetid air conducive to moral uprightness. We all know that jails are breeding places for crime, incubators where all that is beastly inhuman and vicious are nursed into life.

Great God! We all know the grim tragedy of the Poorhouse and we

12. Will Carleton (1845–1912) was the author of *Farm Ballads* (1873), which contained his best-known poem, "Over the Hill to the Poor House," *Farm Legends* (1875), and *City Ballads* (1885).

know the social crime of jails, these things are old and hoary, the new
note, the inspiration, the hope, is that the Nurses should have developed
a social consciousness sufficient to induce them to spend their hard
earned wages and needed strength to make a fight on these hoary wrongs
and best of all that the mass has developed social consciousness to assist
them in their efforts. I don't care whether there is a single Red Card in
the whole Nurses Association or not (of course I wish there were as many
as there are members), those women are my Comrades, they are lifting
the burdens of the helpless, fighting the battles of the hopeless, helping
to lift the burden of oppression from the most downtrodden until they
can climb out of the mire and stand erect; and best of all they know why
they are doing it. They may not have read a single word of Socialism;
these girls possibly would not recognize Karl Marx if they met him on
the street; they might not know whether Economic Determinism is a
new fangled bandage or a baby food, but they understand the basic law
of life—the law of "cause and effect," and when that filters through your
cranium you are on the road to Socialism whether you know it or not.

We know that "God moves in a mysterious way his wonders to perform," and we can somehow comprehend Socialist thought squeezing
through the frozen respectability that guards the church portals, dodging
the Mammon worshippers and digging down deep into the debris of the
past and finding poor, buried Jesus there; we can understand how Socialist thought found ready access into public schools for the school itself
is Socialistic; we can readily understand how the women who give their
lives to healing the sick should find the keynote of human brotherhood,
but we must have faith in miracles before we can accept the statement
that it can reach a Democratic politician. But the fact is here, the impossible has happened and a Democratic Governor, an Arkansas Democratic
governor at that has made a step so radical and revolutionary that I doubt
if any man in the Socialist Party of Arkansas were in Donaghey's[13] place
could have had the courage to do the same.

If there is any human being on earth that I am suspicious of, and just
naturally don't like on general principles, next to a Republican politician,
it's a Democratic politician, and the Southern Democratic politician is

13. George W. Donaghey of Arkansas, governor from 1909 to 1913, was a Democrat.
Originally a carpenter, he later served on the State Board of Education. As governor, he
built the new state capitol in Little Rock.

about the worst of the breed of bipeds without feathers. I have sworn eternal vengeance on them. It was said "that the only good Indian was a dead Indian," and I have claimed that the only good Democratic politician is one laid safely away 'neath the magnolia's shade. But I hereby almost retract, almost apologize. I have a new hope and a new inspiration. I know now that some good can come out of "Nazareth" and even an Arkansas Democratic politician can be reached and forced into action (noble, brave, fearless action) by the great wave of social consciousness that is rolling over the world.

In all American history, perhaps no braver act has ever been performed by any Capitalistic public official than the pardoning of practically every prisoner in Arkansas jails and penitentiaries by Governor Donaghey. Unaided and alone, fighting the party that elected him to office, standing against the most powerful, corrupt and vicious interests not only of Arkansas, but of the whole plundered South, Governor Donaghey struck the death blow at the most brutal, beastly, hellish survival of savagery in our country—the convict leasing system.

To the people of the South no explanation of the "convict leasing system" need be offered. They know enough to make their blood run cold, to sicken them with horror and chill their heart with despair. Words are superfluous there. To the people of the North who know nothing of the accursed thing no words are adequate to give even an inkling as to just how damnable the system of convict leasing is.

The law of the state of Arkansas and of many other Southern states is, as nearly as I can give it without legal jargon, that any citizen of the state of Arkansas fourteen years of age or over, male or female who is convicted of a crime or misdemeanor may be fined at the discretion of the presiding judge any sum the judge sees fit. The convict shall then be sold or leased to the highest bidder. The convict is forced to work out his time at the rate of a few cents per day for the contractor. The contractor feeds and guards the prisoners in the case of county contracts but I think the state guards the state prisoners. The state or county receives the sum paid by the contractor, which is usually very small.

This bald statement of the purport of the law is disgusting enough, but if you could know the South as we who have lived or traveled extensively there know, it becomes positively loathsome.

Remember that the convict lumber camps, cotton farms and turpentine camps and tie camps are all owned by a gang of the most greedy, soulless capitalists on earth. They are managed by hired foremen and overseers, the most brutal, inhuman animals that wear trousers; and the governments, both county and state, are in the hands of the most corrupt aggregation of politicians on the face of God's creation. Great railroad corporations are building their lines through the swamps and into the lumber and coal fields. The pious and godly Lumber Trust fathered by R. A. Long, Kirby and their associates,[14] are slashing out the timber. The U.S. Naval Stores Co. is denuding the South of turpentine bearing trees; there are levees to be built, land to be cleared, swamps to be drained and the great need of the greedy capitalists and blood sucking overseers is plenty of cheap, docile labor. It is the task of the officials and officers of township, county and state to see that this need is met, and the convict leasing system has furnished them with a slave system which for the purposes is a vast improvement over the chattel slavery of the old days.

"Befo de war" if a plantation owner or levee contractor needed a slave he had to buy him, pay out good cold cash for the lazy scoundrel, and if he ran away or died he lost his investment; to-day if the plantation owner or levee contractor needs a slave he just sends word down to the local county officers, they arrest the first poor white man or black man they see, an accommodating judge finds him guilty, he is sentenced to a year or more in jail. Everything is nice and smooth, fine and dandy for all concerned except the white man or the black, and they don't count. The county gets ten cents a day, which goes to the officials and the contractor who is always a political boss and who gets a good slave; a slave that did not cost him anything except a little political favor, a slave over which he holds the power of life and death, that he can starve, flog, outrage, and murder quite within the law. Remember that this law applies to male and female alike, and that when overseers or contractors wish women for their lust it is only necessary to convict a fourteen year old girl of a misdemeanor and the girl of a black woman or a mother of the working class can always be convicted when the boss needs her body. Under this hellish system the workers of Dixie have endured conditions too loathsome to talk of, too beastly to think of. If the English language had words and

14. R. A. Long, a well-known manufacturer, originally of railroad passenger-car interiors, was a leader of the open-shop movement. John J. Kirby was head of the largest lumbering operation at the time.

I had the power to write what I have seen and heard myself in my travels, no issue of the Rip-Saw could pass through the mails that carried it and I would land behind the bars at Leavenworth. If I could tell my story, the story for which Warren[15] and Wayland were indicted would sound like the chatter of a tea party made up of old maids from Boston, so prudish would it be in comparison.

But I can't tell it; no human being on earth can tell one thousandth of its horrors. Not until the greasy waters of the bayou give up their dead, not until they who sleep in the graves in the cypress swamp come forth, not until the scroll of life unfolds can the story of the convict slaves of Dixie be told.

Seven years ago when I first came in contact with the "convict leasing system" in Arkansas I was assured by all that it was an institution too deeply rooted to be destroyed. Business men told me the economic development of the state depended on it, politicians sneered at me and asked, "What are you going to do about it?" Preachers gravely assured me that it was a God given institution to protect the womanhood of the country from the attacks of black men. Even Socialist Comrades begged me with tears in their eyes not to mention it in my speeches as I could do no good and would only be endangering my life. Seven years ago in Arkansas to raise your voice against the convict leasing system was to court the assassin's bullet and many a Socialist agitator had hairbreadth escapes for mentioning it in his speeches.

Seven years of agitation and education, seven years during which time the Socialist thought had leavened the whole Southland and a social consciousness had been born, and today a Democratic Governor defies the party that elected him, defies the strongest, most corrupt political ring in the United States, and throws the gauntlet in the face of the whole capitalist class of the south by pardoning every convict slave in his state.

What the outcome will be we do not know at this time, but we do know that the convict leasing system has had its death blow and that the capitalists of the south will have to devise some more up-to-date method of robbing the workers.

15. Fred D. Warren (1872–1959), who edited Wayland's *Appeal to Reason*, was often embroiled in libel suits, many of which were evidence of government interest in undermining the publication.

The Wages of Women

Have you ever had the experience of standing on some lofty skyscraper and watching the glaring light of a modern searchlight flash over a city, throwing into a startling relief here, a mighty office building there, a sordid slum? Or did you ever turn over a stone and watch the denizens of darkness scuttle away before the blinding sunlight? If so then possibly your imagination can picture the scenes that have been staged at the sessions of the Senatorial Minimum Wage Commission that have been held at the Planters' Hotel here in St. Louis.

Within the last few decades factories, department stores and office buildings, towering mountain high, have become a part of our industrial life. Each morning the modern Pied Piper sounds the searching notes of the call of want and thousands of girls scurry forth with the dawn to answer the call of his pipe and are swallowed up by the doors of the mountain of modern industry. Of the interior of that mountain the world has been ignorant, what went on within we did not know and cared less. That the girls must creep forth at night and find a place to rest and food to eat that she might have the strength to answer the call again when morning came has not concerned us. We have left that matter entirely to Providence.

But of late years disquieting things have happened. Now and then there came a muffled cry of agony and protest from behind the walls: sometimes we found that a girl had fallen by the wayside, too weak from lack of food to answer the call, too broken by her labor to sustain herself, and society was compelled to assume the unpleasant task of caring for a broken woman until she died and then furnishing her a hole in the potter's field as a resting place. Shocking to our sense of decency and morality has been the fact that an ever increasing number of girls turned from the door of the mountain of toil and entered the scarlet door of sin. We are very resentful also of the fact that these scarlet sisters have not decency enough to stay hidden behind the closed blinds of the Red Light, but openly flaunt their shame under our noses on the public streets and lie in wait for our sons at the alley's corner. So one after another things most unpleasant and disquieting have happened; and at last the world has conceived the idea that possibly it might be well to

"The Wages of Women" was first published in *National Rip-Saw* (July, 1913), 2, 6–9.

look behind the closed doors of the mountain of toil and see just what is happening there. Possibly also it might be well for society in self protection to state a minimum wage at which girls might be employed in order that there should be no shocking of public decency by women falling by the wayside on account of hunger and want, or taking the wide road to sin to escape their terrific and sordid struggle with poverty.

So, all over the country, legislative commissions have begun the investigation of women's wages and cost of living. Illinois, California, and other states lead off. And the state Senate of Missouri bestirred itself and appointed a commission to investigate the wages and working conditions for women and girls.

Like boys with a new and wonderful toy, but with no knowledge of its scientific working, this commission proceeded to turn the searchlight on industrial St. Louis.

Down through the walls of the mountain of Toil the glaring beams of the searchlight plowed showing up with shocking distinctness the sordid, damnable, hellish things that had been hidden from our view. All the world was given a view of the woman who works, the reason she works and the pay she gets.

With entire earnestness, but with astonishing ignorance of the whole question of woman's industrial problems, the Missouri Commission settled down to work.

Through the doors of the palatial Planters' Hotel were herded hundreds of girls who never before entered a first-class hotel, and up the marble steps hurried the women, who were more used to filthy factory stairs. Trembling with nervousness and shivering with fright these women and girls, some of them old grandmothers and some so small their heads would hardly reach above the table, laid bare the pitiful details of their lives. All felt the fear of losing their jobs, all knew how the wrath of the boss would be visited on them if they told the whole truth, and yet they all felt the majesty of the power of the state. Haltingly and badly scared many of them lied. A trembling child of twelve went white and red and shook with fright until one of the committeemen asked her if she was cold while she swore she was sixteen. Girls from the paper box factories hastily assured the committee that they were perfectly happy and entirely satisfied, while the fat, gross, brutal factory boss watched them out of his pig-like eyes.

Each girl's testimony was a vivid bit of drama that fitted perfectly into every other girl's until they blended into a complete picture of toil and poverty, hopeless struggle and crushing sordidness. Each sordid bit of human drama held certain facts common to all, and out of these facts an accurate summary of existing labor conditions is formed.

Industrial evolution has brought us to a state where an ever increasing percentage of the female population works at wage labor. These women and girls work at all kinds of useless and useful labor; they do every conceivable kind of useful service, from acting as trained nurses when we are born, to making the casket and shroud in which we make our exit from the earth. In this investigation the fact was made strikingly prominent that the very foundation of twentieth century civilization rests upon the slender toil-bowed shoulders of working women and children.

In return for this labor the women are paid a certain sum of money in wages and turned out to shift for themselves, voteless, voiceless, unorganized and absolutely unprotected by our man-made governments.

Working girls in St. Louis start to work at fourteen, usually, because their fathers are either physically disabled and unable to longer feed them or because the father's job is so fleeting and unstable that he can not support his family; others are widows, women with sick or worthless husbands and women whose husbands are not able to support them from their scanty wage and insecure employment.

These young girls start to work at from $2.50 to $4.50 per week. By twenty-five and fifty cent raises at infrequent and long-drawn out intervals they finally reach a wage of $5.00 in factories where weekly wages are paid and from $5.00 to $8.00 on piece work. The general wage of working women in several large factories was shown to be about $5.50 per week. . . .

They all worked because they were compelled to work. No feminine unrest there; no struggle for a "wider life," no suffragette tendencies, no revolt against home, husbands and babies. The whole question resolved itself into the problem of bread. If the girls expected to eat they must go out and earn their bread; not only earn their own bread but earn bread for the mother who must stay at home and act as a breeding machine to provide children like themselves for the factory. The girl must sometimes earn bread for the father, who had been worn out or broken at his job and tossed on the human scrap pile, a human wreck, whose only value now is to act as a fertilizing machine for a human breeding machine, who are breeding more children for the factory boss.

Many of these women were mothers who were not only breeding wage slaves for the factory owners, but were working as wage slaves themselves to support their offspring until they were old enough to be profitable to the boss. The most soul-sickening stories of all were the simple, halting tales of these mothers working with Spartan courage to feed their children until they are old enough to work. There are thousands of women in St. Louis working for $6.00 a week or less and supporting one or two children. Simply these women told of how they arose at 4:30 or 5 o'clock in their little furnished rooms, cooked their scanty breakfasts, dressed one or more children, hurried them away to some kind-hearted neighbor or a charity, day nursery, then rushed away to the factory or laundry, worked all day and hurried home again, fetched the baby, cooked supper and tumbled into the knobby bed in the sordid room; just to arise in the morning and do it all over again the next day. On Sunday they varied the programme by doing their washing, ironing, sewing and housecleaning, all this for $6.00 a week and the privilege of breeding a wage slave or two. Verily our Christian civilization, our man-made governments are chivalrous and tender of woman and motherhood!

The Senatorial Commission seemed to feel that its real task was to strive at an accurate estimate of just how much real money it takes to keep a working girl in working order. Farmers, by long experience have arrived at the accurate knowledge of just how many ears of corn a day it takes to keep a mule in working condition. If you give the mule too much corn he gets too frisky to be manageable, and if you feed him too little, he either gets too weak to do your work or dies on your hands. Girl-power is now taking the place of mule-power, and it behooves our users of female labor to get some expert knowledge of the cost of keeping a girl in good mule condition. Sufficient food is, of course, the first essential of good mule condition and the cost of food was carefully inquired into.

The commission got real peeved because they could get few girls to admit that they lived away from home. The commission wanted to know what the absolute cost of decent board was in St. Louis, and no witness seemed able to give it. I offered to go out and investigate more than a score of boarding houses, rooming houses, and furnished rooms for light house-keeping. These ranged from good and safe to filthy and indecent. Table board in St. Louis ranges from $3.00 a week for impossibly bad and incredibly dirty to $5.00 for good, clean meals in a respectable neighborhood. Room and board ranges from $4.50 for a very bad to $6.00 for reasonably good, two people in a room. Furnished rooms range from $2.00 in the slums, dirty, unsanitary, and surrounded by frightful influences, to $5.00 a week in respectable neighborhoods and clean, sanitary houses.

One of the most striking facts that came to my notice was that only two furnished room houses I visited had parlors where company could be entertained, and that the landladies expected the girls to take gentlemen friends to their bedrooms. Another was that out of the score of houses I visited I found only one boarding house and one furnished room house that was even approximately safe and decent where girls were desired as boarders or roomers. If a house bore the earmarks of decency the landladies would tell me flatly and emphatically that they would not take a girl. The reason they all gave was that the prevailing wages for girls adrift were not sufficient for the usual girl to live on, and they could take no chances. With few exceptions the only houses open to working girls I found were such places as no girl could endure its environments and long remain self-respecting and decent. . . .

What is the minimum or lowest wage on which a girl dependent upon herself and not living at home can get along on in St. Louis?

The summary of the testimony offered by hundreds of working girls finally reduces itself down to this simple proposition. If a girl worker living alone in St. Louis (or any other city for that matter) does not receive as much as $11 a week, she cannot maintain herself in good mule condition. . . .

Mrs. Raymond Robbins,[16] of Chicago, who has spent many years studying this very problem, testified before the commission that the minimum living wage for a girl living alone in Chicago was twelve dollars per week. . . .

The stories of the girls and women who testified before the commission were largely the same, except as to the details as to how they squandered their magnificent wages. But in spite of the rash extravagance possible on six dollars a week, the lives of the girls by their own stories were drab, dreary and sordid in the least extreme. Music, literature and art are closed books to them. St. Louis has no parks in the working-class districts; they are all out in the South Side and West End, where the "better class" live. In order to reach them ten cents carfare must be do-

16. Margaret Dreier Robins (1868–1945) was president of the National Women's Trade Union League.

nated to the St. Louis Street Railway Trust, and there are no loose dimes
in a $6.00 wage. Few of the girls seemed to know that there was such a
thing as our beautiful new Carnegie Library; all, when questioned, said
they had no time to read since their sewing, washing and ironing had to
be done nights and Sundays. St. Louis has a most beautiful art gallery,
but it is in Forest Park, and out of the reach of the working class. Shaw's
Garden is one of the noted botanical gardens of the world, but one must
pay streetcar fare to get there. Most of the girls had no place to entertain
company, and if they had beaux they must meet them on the street corner, at the dance hall and at the nickel shows. The few rooms of a tene-
ment home are too fully occupied in the prosaic business of providing
the family a place to eat and sleep to give any room to a parlor where
beaux may be entertained. The landladies of rooming houses must rent
every available inch of space, and poor Cupid gets a hard deal. The only
places of amusement open and in reach of the working girl and her working young man friend are the dance halls and the cheap shows, and neither of these are safe places for young people to find social life. . . .

It was quite evident from the beginning that the commission did not
intend to let the investigation stumble into the question of vice conditions.

However, in spite of the precautions of the commission, now and then
some testimony would reveal the grisly form of vice. One girl told the
commission that she got $4.50 per week in wages; that she had to pay car
fare, and that she paid $3.00 per week board. When asked what it cost
her to dress she looked the chairman of the committee square in the eye
and replied, "Three dollars per week, and no girl can do it on less and
hold her job." Another clerk from a department store told the commission that she earned $7.00 a week, that it cost her every cent of it to stay
alive, that she had just returned from the hospital where she had been
ill three weeks. The hospital bill was $27.00 for three weeks, her doctor's
bill was additional, and no man on the commission had the courage to
ask her how she met the cost of her illness.

A beautiful girl of seventeen told of working for $4.00 a week, paying
her mother $3.00 for board, and being compelled to dress herself, pay
carfare and find recreation on $1.00 a week. She was rather fashionably
dressed, and when the chairman of the committee pressed her to tell
how she managed she stammered and said, "Well, you see, I buy my
clothes on the installment plan," and since the suit and hat she wore must

have cost as much as her whole surplus for one year, the commission could not ask her to tell what form of installment payments she meant.

In the space at my command in this issue of the Rip-Saw I will not have time to dwell on the question of what girls really earn in industry.

I have in the last year seen men who were averaging $25.00 per week, replaced by four girls, who each draw $8.00 per week. This is due to the invention of a new machine. The employer makes an extra profit of $13.00 per week on each girl. But it took four years to learn the trade followed by the men. It takes four weeks to learn the work done by the girls, and in four months they are as rapid at the work as they will ever be. . . .

I tell you that with our modern machinery the little sixteen year-old chit, frivolous, ribbon-loving, giggling and careless though she may be— this little child is producing two or three times as much wealth as the skilled mechanic could produce in the last generation.

But the wealth she produces—who gets it?

Not her father—he is "on the dump."

The trust gets it. Here is where the swollen fortunes of the Big Biz comes from—from the use of six million women and girls at starvation wages while they are producing watches, and clothing and silks and velvets and screws and bolts and sewing machines and telephones and cash registers and all sorts of wealth—turning it out in piles mountain high, to be appropriated by the trust owners. . . .

There is no doubt but this wage hearing is the most important thing that has ever happened in St. Louis for years. No picture ever painted could be more realistic, no novel of real life so absorbing, no drama ever staged so gripping in human interest, at no time have facts vital to our national life, our civilization itself been so wonderfully staged. Yet in spite of this not one single priest, preacher or representative of a church organization attended. Not a club woman or organized charity expert put in an appearance or offered help. The only social "uplifter" who appeared at all was the manager of the City Club, who was compelled to appear and who admitted that he paid dishwashers and scrub women five dollars a week, and did not concern himself with their physical, mental or spiritual welfare, considering them only pieces of machinery to be bought at the lowest possible price.

The only people who attended the sessions, followed the inquiry, and gave assistance to the commission were Nellie Quick from the Women's

Trade Union League,[17] Mary Bulkly, from the Consumers' League,[18] and myself, representing the National Rip-Saw.

There is no doubt but the commission will recommend in their report to the State Senate that a law shall be enacted placing and establishing a minimum wage that shall be paid female labor. I rather think the commission will set that minimum at about $7.50 to $9.00 per week. Naturally the big employers of labor will fight the bill, money will flow like water, lobbyists will get busy and everything possible will be done to fight the bill. If the recommendation ever becomes a law we must fight for it. I am going to turn prophet and wager my bonnet that when the crisis comes the same people who were absent from the hearing will be silent and only the working-class forces that assisted in the investigation will be on hand to fight for the law. . . .

I know the law will not be Socialism, it will not bring the co-operative commonwealth, it will not abolish the infernal wage system, but it is an important skirmish in the class war. It is one outpost to be taken from Big Biz, and every victory makes the great victory that much nearer. A minimum wage is not the goal of Socialism; we want all we produce, but a minimum wage is another hardtack in our knapsack to fight on and we know that a soldier with two hardtacks will do twice as much fighting as a soldier with one.

War in the Copper Country

The copper miners' strike at Calumet[19] is merely one great battle in the world's class war and can be viewed in no other light. It is to be regret-

17. Nellie Quick, of the Women's Trade Union League, is a rather anonymous figure. We find no evidence of her except an article by a writer of that name, "How I Earned My College Degree," *Delineator*, XCI (November, 1917).

18. Mary Bulkley represented the National Consumers' League, one of the variety of middle-class organizations that together formed the Progressive movement. She also chaired the St. Louis Commission on Industrial Conditions, of the Central Council of Social Agencies.

"War in the Copper Country" was first published in *National Rip-Saw* (December, 1913), 2–3, 16.

19. On July 23, 1913, twenty copper mines, located on the Keweenaw Peninsula of Upper Michigan, were struck by the Western Federation of Miners. Almost fifteen thousand miners walked off the job, demanding union recognition by the mineowners. This was one of the era's most highly publicized strikes and received wide coverage in the labor

ted, of course, that the race has not progressed beyond the point of set-
tling issues with clubs and guns and writing history in human blood, but
the brutal, naked truth remains that we have not. Just as long as there is
one master who can exploit the labor of a wage slave, and one wage slave
who can be exploited, war will live. Real war is always a grisly, hellish
thing and can not be written of in perfumed, gentle language.

I was sent to Calumet to get the story of the strike, and naturally
expected to see real war, and it is needless to state that I was not disappointed. It is hard for the average citizen who quietly goes about his
humdrum life to realize that here in the United States, in a Christian
country with a church on every corner, in a land overburdened with laws
and courts, that the mere decision of a group of working men to lay down
their tools could plunge a cultured city into savagery and fill the souls of
men and women with blood lust, yet those things have happened in the
copper country.

I had not reached the mining districts on my way north until I began
to feel the suppressed excitement and quick surge of blood, the latent
hate and intense desire for action that will sway the best balanced man
or woman when once they smell the smoke of battle. The passengers in
the Pullman had been a well-bred, amiable, polite group of friends at
night, but when morning came and we entered the strike zone, we felt
the tingle of class war and each responded according to his class interests.
The wall paper manufacturer across the aisle glared at me and said I was
a crazy anarchist, though the night before he had called me a brilliant
and charming woman. I retorted that he was an ignorant, heartless ex-
ploiter of child labor, though I had found him most agreeable the previous evening and had been pleased to dine with him.

The Calumet Copper strike is a fitting climax to the marvelous story
of wealth, creation and human evolution. For forty years the copper barons have owned the mines and operated them with European peasant
labor. These capitalists piled up untold wealth and bred a race of physical
and mental giants. Through it all unusual industrial peace has existed
there. The killing cold, the black-list and the time check have kept the
workers fairly well controlled. The absorbing occupation of building a
working-class culture and social life has kept the workers so intent with

---

and socialist press. After almost nine months, the miners admitted defeat and voted to
return to work in April, 1914, having failed to achieve recognition of the union.

their own concerns that they have given the employers little trouble. Now and then there would a sudden flare of protest break out among a little group of men in some isolated mine, but no general organization or systematic revolt had taken place.

Five years ago the Western Federation of Miners[20] sent organizers into the copper country and they found the field ripe for their work. Soon the whole district was solidly organized. At first the copper barons paid no attention to the organizers, thinking their work merely some new expression of the miners' boundless energy. In the past the miners' activities had not touched the barons' dividends and they had been very tolerant.

When the miners were solidly organized and well drilled in discipline, they formulated a list of very mild demands, looking to the abolition of some minor wrongs in their work. They asked for an eight-hour day, two men on a machine and a minimum wage of three dollars per day. Most important of all, they asked recognition of the union and the right to collective action.

The copper barons flatly refused the demands, refused to allow the matter to be arbitrated and notified the miners that they would only deal with them as individuals and declared that no "handful of common miners could dominate the copper industry."

The strike was called and fifteen thousand men walked out of the mines and commerce was paralyzed in the copper country. It was as if the electric current had been switched off of a mighty machine, and it stood there silent and impotent. The barons blinked a little in uncomprehending wonder and sat down to wait until the "vulgar cattle" should go back to work. These employers could not comprehend that they were facing a new epoch in the history of copper mining. They did not know enough of science to realize that the cold and killing conditions of labor had killed off the weaklings and bred a race of men so strong that they would not be satisfied with an added crust of bread, but would demand the whole product of their labor.

---

20. The Western Federation of Miners was organized in the West in 1893 among metal miners. For the next twenty years it was involved in a series of major and dramatic events, eventually becoming the International Union of Mine, Mill and Smelter Workers within the American Federation of Labor.

The amusing thing I found in the copper country was the genuine surprise and hottest indignation of the copper mine owners, towards the revolt of the miners. They felt exactly as the average housewife would feel if she went down to her kitchen some morning to build a fire in the good, old family cookstove, that had warmed and fed the family for years, and found it rearing up on its hind legs breathing smoke and spitting fire brands, gone on a strike against the job of cooking food. For forty years the miners had dug out of the mines mountains of wealth; uncomplainingly they had given it to the barons without a murmur. Why should they rebel at this late day? The copper operators could not realize that in breeding up this magnificent breed of superior working men they had also bred men of superior brains and unusual efficiency. They could not understand that when you breed a race of workingmen who can run one of the greatest industries on earth under frightful climatic conditions and produce millions every year for the weakened, bald-headed, sickly stockholders down in New York or Boston, that you are quite likely to breed a race of men who will demand more than a slave's wage.

I found Calumet and Hancock beautiful and cultured towns, but there was no mistaking that they were battlefields. The streets swarmed with deputies, the hotels were full of thugs and gunmen and soldiers clattered by on horses. The streets were filled with automobiles that went honking up and down loaded with thugs, armed to the teeth and bent on murder. Now and then I would meet a man with a bandaged head or an arm in a sling and at the hotel I found quite a hospital of disabled scabs and gunmen who had come in contact with a rock or club. Out at Kearsarge I saw a 15-year-old girl with a bullet from a deputy's gun through her head and looked on the fair white breasts of girls beaten black and blue with soldiers' sabers. I found rosy-cheeked children with the marks of horses' hoofs on their tender bodies, and watched a schoolboy throw a red pepper in a schoolmate's eyes because the latter was the son of a striker.

Though Michigan is a civilized, Christian state, with a constitution and statutes and a full corps of law officers and officials, I found that there was no law in the copper country except the will of the copper barons, and that human life had no protection except that of a good strong arm and a handy club. Men could be beaten down, women assaulted and young girls forced to listen to the most degenerate and revolting language, and the law of Michigan was dead, and its enforcers were too busy protecting profits to take notice.

Drunken thugs and gunmen upset a stove in their boarding house and caused a fire and all the newspapers of the copper country shouted that the strikers had committed arson. A fuse was planted along a railroad track and a locomotive engineer who knew just where to look for it discovered the rising smoke, and all over the country the capitalist press bewailed the fact that the strikers had attempted to wreck a train.

Every brutal, hellish thing that is a part of war has taken place up in the copper country. There is no more freedom there than in Mexico, no more enforcement of written law, according to statutes, than in West Virginia[21] or Russia, no more security for womanhood and virtue than in the Balkans, and this is the United States of America in the year of our Lord, nineteen hundred and thirteen. This fact can teach the thoughtful but one lesson, and that is that the capitalist system itself breeds war, and peace can never exist as long as there is a master to exploit or a slave to be exploited.

I do not suppose the scenes that were enacted when the militia invaded the peaceful homes of the miners were materially different than those that take place whenever an armed force is called by the capitalist class to shoot the working-class into subjection.

Men were shot down, women and children trampled by the soldiers' horses, girls were outraged and lewd women imported to satisfy the lust of the invaders, and all of the soul-sickening things that are a part of every strike where the militia is used took place.

Strange to say, the armed invasion of state militiamen was not a success from the copper barons' standpoint. You may dress a callow snip of a boy in khaki, arm him with a gun, fill his brain with the drunkenness of power and for a time evil passions will sway him; but the blood lust of the modern youth is soon glutted and he sickens of it all. Ten days in the copper country changed nearly every militiaman from a tool of the copper barons, whose sole object in life was to outrage, maim and kill vulgar working men and women, into a disgusted youth whose soul was sick with the sight of blood, whose mind responded to the plea of the working

21. In West Virginia, labor-management strife resulted in martial law and suspension of civil liberties when the United Mine Workers sought to win union recognition in the coalfields.

men that they were brothers and whose uniform became a thing of shame. I talked to many of the boys of the state militia and without a single exception they voiced just what I have said.

When the militia proved worse than useless to the copper barons, they tried another plan. The slums of adjoining cities were scraped of their lowest dregs. Thugs, thieves, murderers, gunmen and criminals of all sorts were rushed into the Upper Peninsular by the Waddell and Ascher Agencies, armed and deputized as special policemen. They, too, were proving a nuissance, and when I was in Calumet the copper operators were having vastly more trouble caring for their gunmen than in fighting strikers. They would not stay in that clean, decent little city without the prostitutes they were accustomed to consort with, and provision of fallen women to satisfy their demands was a sore trial to the godly, pious copper barons.

The thugs insisted on getting drunk, as usual, and a drunken gunman is not at all particular which way he points his gun. They had to be fed and cared for and no hotel keeper wanted the disgusting job. These vicious criminals proved to be so untrustworthy, that the copper barons found it necessary to compel the small businessmen to allow their high school boys to be deputized and work with the gunmen, that some sort of check might be provided. Nearly all the small traders in the copper country hired their automobiles to the barons to be used in hauling thugs and gunmen about, and usually a son acted as driver.

I saw real war up there; I heard heads crack and bones snap. I walked over bloodstained snow. I heard bullets whistle and watched a passenger train riddled with stones and clubs, but the most sickening sight of all was that of fresh-faced high school boys consorting with vicious criminals. These boys, just in the first warm flush of youth, marched side by side with the lowest dregs of the city slums. They walked with men whose faces bore the marks of every vice, crime and evil passion known to man, and their plastic boyish minds received a deluge of such filth and loathsome horror as no words can express.

Each morning I spent in Calumet a group of several hundred strikers, including men and women, went out on the picket lines and I accompanied them. These were the finest, cleanest girls I have ever seen, and they walked between rows of thugs and gunmen who hurled language at them so vile that the girls could not understand its loathsome lewdness, while the high school boys listened to it all. Militia and gunmen both proved worthless to the copper barons, and while I was in Calumet they were trying the plan of wholesale arrest and imprisonment.

I stood in front of the court house and saw strikers, including men and women, driven into jail like droves of sheep into the shambles. Men were clubbed and beaten like wild beasts, and beautiful young girls dragged through the ranks of deputies, subjected to vile insults and jammed into jail, trailing their American flags behind them. As I watched them I thought of old Betsy Ross, and wondered if from that other side of life one may look back upon this one, what she thought of the depths to which her stars and stripes had fallen.

When I left it seemed as if jailing the strikers would prove a failure also, for when the miners saw their comrades being thrown into prison they went down by hundreds, admitted taking part in the riots and filled the jails to their limit. It's an expensive job feeding several hundred miners and saving the union funds. A county judge who rode down on the train with me cursed like a pirate as he talked of the debt that would be piled up on the county. There is little to be gained by throwing a man in jail if he is willing to be there, no balm to the soul of an operator in feeding a striker so that the union funds may keep the strike going.

From what I can gather now, the whole situation has settled down to a game of waiting. The miners are waiting until the frost and snow will so injure the operators' mines and machinery that a settlement will have to be made. When the temperature drops down to forty degrees below zero and the snow piles five feet deep, the men must fight frost like demons to save the master's property. A railroad unused for a single day is so clogged with snow and locked in ice as to become useless until the spring sun releases it. Pumps and steam pipes left without a full head of steam freeze as hard as steel, and are totally ruined.

Gunman and thug will swing a club and swagger with a pistol, but he will not dig copper, shovel snow, fight frost or feed the engines. The scabs gathered up from the slums of nearby cities will run the risk of cracked heads in order to fill their stomachs with the good hotel meals the operators pay for; they will accept the five dollars a day and loaf, but they never will dig a ton of ore, and when the winter comes and grips the Peninsular in its iron grasp their poverty and dissipation-warped bodies will crumble like dry leaves in a gale. There is only one group of men on earth that can run the copper industry, and that is the members of the Western Federation of Miners now out on strike. Either they must go back into the mines or one of the most marvelous industries of our country will crumble into decay; ships will rot in the harbor, railroads turn to rust, towns be given over to timber wolves, and the wonderful land of copper be no more. I interviewed lawyers, doctors, businessmen, priests, preachers and operators, and all agreed that this was true.

The issue at stake is how shall they go back? Shall they return like curs whipped to their kennels, or like free men? This and this alone is the issue at Calumet. I interviewed many mine officials and each declared that the issue at stake was not hours, wages or conditions, but the solidarity and organization of the workers. More than one copper company official said that the copper companies could afford to give the men an eight-hour day, two men on a machine and five dollar minimum wage. If the miners would just be sensible, go back to work and drop their organization, the operators would profit by their bitter lesson and give the men more than they asked for. But the operators must crush the Federation into dust, or the miners would sooner or later demand that the whole people own and control the copper mines and entirely eliminate the private owners. As one mine owner expressed it to me, "The whole strike is not one of wages, hours or working conditions; it's just plain socialism. Either the operators must rule the copper country with an iron hand or the damned Finnish socialists[22] will, and you know what that means to us."

This, comrades of the working-class, is the whole story. The miners have conducted one of the most remarkable strikes in history. Fifteen thousand men walked out on the strike order. Of that number but six have proven traitors to the union and scabbed upon their brothers. It has been the most orderly strike ever known, involving so large a body of men. Its management has been systematic and scientific in the extreme. Though the membership of the Federation is made up of several language groups who speak no common tongue, there has not been a ripple of discontent and word of censure or criticism of organizers or leaders.

22. While the miners were of many different nationalities, Finnish miners and lumberjacks throughout the United States were known for their strong support of the socialist movement. The Finns formed the backbone of the Socialist party in Michigan's Upper Peninsula.

Men and women have stood solidly together, race and creed lines have
been obliterated, and those thousands of workers have acted together
like one great body. . . .

Drink, Its Cause and Cure

I remember very distinctly as one of the vivid things of my childhood
the mental picture of a dear old preacher, tall and spare, with patriarchal
beard and snowy hair. Every Sunday he stood in the pulpit of that tiny
country church and thundered forth in awesome words his denunciation
of "Rum." How I thrilled in terror of his forceful speech and resonant
tones, and how that demon rum did stalk through my dreams; in a thousand frightful forms he haunted me day and night. I had never seen a
saloon, never known a saloonkeeper, never looked upon a drunken man,
yet my childhood was haunted by wild unreasoning hate, and shadowed
by frightful pictures that I did not understand.

Perhaps the most bitter sorrow I ever knew up to ten years of age was
when I accidentally heard my father say he had gone into a saloon to find
Bob, my favorite cow-puncher, my dearest friend and childhood play-
mate. The horror of it haunted me by day and night. To know that Bob—
dear old Bob, whom I loved so much, Bob who let me wear his spurs
and ride his pony and taught me to shoot without shutting my eyes—was
in the clutches of Rum. Many nights I cried myself to sleep, only to
dream of leaning over the jasper walls of heaven and watching Bob sizzle
in the flames of hell below.

How I longed to be a woman that I might go out and fight and slay
and kill. The peace of my childhood was shadowed, the sweetness of
girlhood turned to consuming hate, and the early years of my womanhood spent in a fruitless battle with forces I did not understand. My soul
responded to that wild, incoherent battle cry of the temperance crusade,
but my mind was chaotic, my knowledge nil, and my forces all undi-
rected and therefore wasted.

I was not alone in having my life shadowed and my days filled with
unreasoning fear; thousands have felt the same influence. The church
has insisted on giving the whole problem a religious trend and trying to

"Drink, Its Cause and Cure" was first published in *National Rip-Saw* (September, 1913),
3, 6.

deal with it as if it were a question of morals and religion or a lack of
them. One half of the world cowers in fear of the spectre of drunkenness,
and the other half illogically dismisses the whole matter as unimportant;
accepts it as inevitable, or rants a lot of foolish nonsense about the "right"
of a man to drink if he feels like it, and the "right" of men to engage in
any kind of business. Both positions are untenable and unscientific. The
"Demon Rum" is no more frightful than the demons of poverty, unemployment or overwork. Neither can we rightly use the word "freedom"
in connection with drunkenness. No man is free to do a thing that harms
another. That is license. There can be no human right to engage in a
business that wrecks bodies, ruins brains and murders souls.

There is a problem of drunkenness, just as there is a problem of poverty, overwork, child labor and prostitution. It is a part of the great master problem of human life, and if it is ever to be solved it must be by a
rational, scientific study of cause and effect, and not by canting "freedom"
or fighting windmills like Quixote.

The Socialists, being primarily interested in human welfare rather
than in mere material prosperity, are vitally interested in the solution of
the question of intemperance. All over the world the Socialist organizations are holding up to the working class the ideal of a clear-brained,
clean-bodied, conquering proletariat. We believe we have the right answer to the problem. We have found intemperance to be a disease, the
fruit of capitalism.

Drunkenness is a disease, and like all diseases, largely vocational.
Certain diseases are common to certain trades. Miners have rheuma-
tism, railroad men kidney disease, printers consumption, hair workers
anthrax and matchmakers phossy jaw. Each trade and vocation develops
a disease peculiar to its surroundings and the disease of drunkenness
finds proper culture medium in excesses—of idleness or work, excessive
cold or heat, excessive speed or deadly monotony, unnatural nerve ten-
sion or exhausting muscular strain. The physical causes for inebriety are
as easily traced as the physical causes for consumption. The cure must
be physical also.

Miners in both coal and metal mines develop the disease of drunkenness to a considerable extent. Their work is excessively hard, carried on
underground, in constant danger, and always in darkness, slime and
damp air. They live and labor knowing that every moment of their life
hangs by the slenderest thread. A misplaced blast, the flicker of a lamp,

the careless lighting of a match, and coal dust may flash into an explosion that will leave them only a seared lump of human flesh. The slightest miscalculation of the strength of rock or coal, the snapping of a timber may crush them into pulp. The deadly black damp is always lurking in readiness to grip their throats and throttle them. The life of a miner drags on in endless grappling with powerful unseen forces, and the disease of drunkenness finds fertile soil for culture.

Telegraph operators who sit with their fingers on the pulse of commerce, the click of whose keys sends trains thundering down countless tracks with their burden of wealth and human life; these tense-nerved men know that the slightest twitching of their weary fingers, the least dullness of their sense of hearing, a single dot or dash misplaced or misunderstood means death and destruction. They live and labor keyed to concert pitch, and naturally many brace their shattered nerves with drink and seek relaxation in drunkenness.

In the glass factories the heat and nervous strain is so great that men are worn out in a few years. The glass furnace demands strong, lusty young men, with more than the usual degree of health, brain, muscle and nerves as delicate and responsive as a violin string. With strength, mastery, and delicacy expressed in each graceful movement, he swings the iron blowpipes and molds the molten glass into perfect form. For just a few short years the glass furnace uses these magnificent men. Then, suddenly their lives snap out, just as their great rollers smash if only a fraction too much force is used. These men look death in the face in the white-hot furnace, blow their lives into the brittle glass, and die as their handiwork is shattered by the slightest overstrain on tense wrought nerve and muscle. It is not strange that they should drink. Why not? They know their fate is sealed; they have seen their brothers die. They know their day of reckoning with outraged nature is near at hand. Drink cools their heated blood, eases the nervous strain and helps them to laugh in the face of the grim reaper. That is why they drink.

For wherever men are driven to labor beyond their strength under unnatural conditions and live abnormal lives, they will demand stimulants to spur the jaded brains and bodies on to renewed effort, and to provide a substitute for the thrill of life of which they are robbed. Many men seek this spur in drink, some in sex debauchery, and some in religious frenzy. The drunken man reeling to his lonely boarding house after a day of abnormal labor and a night of wild carousal is not an example of natural depravity—he is but a product of the abnormal state of society in which we live. He is not a bad man—he is just a robbed man, robbed of all that makes life worthwhile. He has sought the only substitute within his reach and understanding. The drunken orgy of the brothel is not a demonstration of the vileness of men and lewdness of women—it is but one phase of the blind, but world-wide search for happiness in an abnormal system in which happiness for the many must be impossible. The insane religious frenzy of a Gypsy Smith revival or a holiness camp meeting is merely the howling drunk or sex revel given a religious trend. It has the same cause and the same effect on its victims. No matter whether men seek spur and relaxation in drink, religious or sex expression, the effect is just the same in either case, a wrecked body, a warped brain and a murdered soul. . . .

Man must have companionship and social intercourse, or become a raving maniac or mumbling imbecile. Capitalism has largely robbed the workingman of the opportunity for social life. Family life is broken up, the boys and girls are herded into the cities, crowded into boarding houses, jammed into factories, become a part of the mighty crowd that can never assimilate, and become social companions. The young working man or woman has no opportunity for social intercourse, for becoming part of a social circle or enjoying life. It is a law of nature that men and women denied social expression either sour into misanthropes, dry up into moving mummies, or degenerate into vice.

There are great theaters and concert halls, there are balls and receptions and social life in the city, but they are not for the workers. Their earning capacity is not great enough to give them access to intellectual or social life.

There are big, beautiful churches in the cities, filled with artistic beauty, music, and the things men and women crave, but they are built for the glory of God and not for the use of man. They are only used three hours a week and shut up to moulder and get musty all the rest of the time. The church complains that the working class is drifting away from its influence, becoming irreligious, and that the saloon is gaining the ascendancy with men. This is no doubt true, but there must be a reason for this deplorable condition. Possibly if the church looked at the question with both eyes, it would find the reason in this fact, deplorable also. . . .

Just as long as we try to deal with the problem of drunkenness as THE problem and not a part of the whole problem of social life, we must fall short of our ideal. I know the frightful effects of drunkenness, realize the menace of the saloon, comprehend its demoralizing grip on mankind, yet insist that it is only one of the minor problems of capitalism. I dread it no more than I dread many other problems and know that the solution can only come with a better organized system of life.

We have preached and prayed, legislated and labored for prohibition and local option. We have allowed this one phase of the problem of life to obscure our view of the other and larger questions demanding solution. We have wept and wailed over the terrible effects of drink, and overlooked the fact that private ownership of the means of life has caused more misery, suffering, poverty and prostitution, wrecked more homes, ruined more lives, murdered more men, women and children than the drink traffic a hundredfold.

The private ownership of railroads has taken more lives, robbed more homes of their breadwinners, despoiled and levied tribute on the whole people to a vastly greater extent than has the liquor traffic. The private ownership of packing houses and flour mills have made more bare cupboards and hungry human beings than the saloon. The private ownership of the textile mills and shoe factories have caused more people to be cold, ragged and ill-clad than drink. The private ownership of homes by landlords have caused more men, women and children to be homeless, wandering vagabonds than drunkenness. The private owner of the machinery of production is a more despotic tyrant, has power to kill, maim and crush a thousand times more than the "Demon Rum." The slave to the private owned machine is a more pitiful sight than the slave to drink. The waste of private ownership is a hundred times more useless and appalling.

The mortality reports published by the United States government for the year 1906 gives the number of deaths from alcoholism at about 2,707 for the whole United States. During the same year the railroads killed 3,929 employees and injured 80,630 more. There are no statistics available giving the number of passengers killed and crippled, for the private owners of the railroads have the power to muzzle the press, still the moans of the dying and hush the cry of the bereft.

During the time alcoholism killed three thousand, industry claimed a toll of 616,295, and each of this vast army, almost as many as lost their life in the Civil War, died or were maimed for life as a direct result of the private ownership of the machinery of production and distribution. Drink is deadly, but the private ownership of the machinery of life is a thousandfold more so.

The waste of wealth in drunkenness is frightful, almost beyond belief, but the waste of wealth by private ownership is so vastly greater that our minds find it hard to grasp the figures. In the year of 1909 our nation expended in war appropriations $1,044,014,398, and war is but the plaything and the servant of the owners of the means of life. Drunkenness damns, war kills, industries crush and maim, poverty debases, and unearned wealth debauches, and the private ownership of the means of life is the fundamental cause of all!

Socialism and Socialism alone can offer a sensible solution to the liquor problem, and until it is solved by Socialists under a Socialist form of government, it will remain the problem it is to-day.

Drunkenness now exists as a direct result of certain causes inherent in capitalism. When Socialism succeeds capitalism, the cause will be abolished and, naturally, drunkenness also.

If there were no intoxicants manufactured, the inveterate toper would find it impossible to acquire a "jag" of even moderate proportions. There can be but one incentive to induce men to manufacture intoxicating drinks, and that is the opportunity for private gain.

All over the world there are great breweries, distilleries and wineries. The sole excuse they have for existing is that men make profits from them and are enabled to add to their private bank accounts by the manufacture and sale of their products. Why, even the good monks of Chartreuse are not wholly unworldly wise; they own great wineries and convert the profits into cold cash for the glory of God! Aside from the owners of liquor-producing machinery, there is a great army of salesmen, saloonkeepers, bartenders, porters and scrub women, as well as those actually employed in its manufacture, who are dependent upon the profits of the liquor traffic for their lives. Nor is that all. Church and state would be in a bad way but for ungodly liquor makers and dispensers. Our nation's finance is built on a whiskey barrel, for the revenues to keep its wheels moving come largely from the tax upon liquors and dispensers' licenses. Why, if all the brewers, distillers and saloonkeepers were to be suddenly converted and give up their evil ways, the whole nation would be bankrupt in no time in the panic that would ensue. A large percentage of that ornamental and more or less aggregation of officials who manage or mismanage our nation would remain unpaid. Then again, if all the saloons, distilleries and breweries should suddenly cease paying taxes, in all possibility the church would be compelled to pay its taxes (they are exempt now) and that would make frightful inroads on the Anti-Saloon League and Anti-Vice Crusades[23] funds. Of course, there would be a great saving in the cost of maintaining courts and penal institutions, but think what an army of judges, lawyers court ataches, policemen and inmates of jails and prisons there would be looking for jobs, and jobs at a premium already! As long as we support our present system we dare not look too closely to the source of our revenues. We might be forced to consider them "tainted," and this would make it inconvenient for us to accept them and still more so not to do it.

Under Socialism things would be quite different. Private profit would be forever abolished. No man or group of men could have it to their advantage to make or sell liquor. If liquor were needed and the majority of the people voted that it should be made, the nation would manufacture the purest, and best, would supply it entirely without profit to anyone; and by abolishing gain, the very cause of the existence of liquor would be done away with.

The army of men and women who now live upon the profits of the sale of liquor, would, under Socialism have free access to the means of production, continued employment, and the full product of their labor, and would busy themselves in making and distributing food, clothing, and the comforts and luxuries of life, adding to the sum total a human happiness instead of its misery and degradation.

Socialism would abolish the classes of the idle rich and idle poor and put both the parasite who lives in a palace and the parasite who exists on charity work at honest labor and insure him the full product of his toil. The strain of overwork for intervals and no work at all for long periods would be abolished. All would work long enough to produce the things necessary for the best life for all, and all would share according to the measure of their labor.

Unsanitary and dangerous conditions of labor would be remedied. Mill, mine and factory would no longer be human slaughter pens, but

23. The Anti-Saloon League was one of the major groups to promote national prohibition. From its founding in 1893 through the next twenty-five years, it was instrumental in establishing dry laws in various areas. The Anti-Vice Crusade was an allied group that triumphed in 1919 with the passage of the Eighteenth Amendment and the Volstead Act. The activities of these groups represent the start of organized special-interest politics.

palaces of industry, owned, operated and managed by free workers. Labor would cease to be a brutalizing drudgery and become the highest form of human activity, and the happy, active, live human being would loathe brutalizing liquor.

When the fullest, freest social intercourse is made possible for men and women, one of the compelling causes for drunkenness will be abolished. When the lecture hall, the conservatory of music, the theater, the ballroom, the art gallery and the recreation parks are opened up to all, made possible for all, we will be too busy with the better things of life to seek the lower.

When the slum, the shack and the hovel shall be razed; comfortable, sanitary homes be built for all; when men can earn enough to maintain homes and support their families, life will be clean, sane, secure and happy, and few will care to lose a single moment of it in drunken stupor.

The Story of an Irish Agitator

Quite the most thrilling and wonderful experience of my trip to Great Britain was a visit to Dublin on the invitation of the Strike Committee.[24] I arrived on the scene at the most dramatic moment of the great struggle, when the Strike Committee carried back the message from the British Trades Unions that they repudiated the general strike, but would sustain the Dublin workers financially. That visit to Dublin will always be a vivid memory of a great life tragedy staged by a master hand.

No written words can ever carry to another mind the haunting beauty of Ireland and that strange blending of brains and stupidity, beauty and sordidness, doltish acceptance of wrongs and passionate revolt that only the religious fanaticism between Orangemen and Catholics could have made possible.

Ireland is perhaps the most poverty stricken land on earth; her slums are hellish, her housing conditions notoriously frightful, her working class exploited and tyrannized over to the last degree, and yet the physi-

"The Story of an Irish Agitator" was first published in *National Rip-Saw* (April, 1914), 6–7, 9.

24. The strike (1913–14) of the Irish Transport and General Workers' Union was also a lockout by employers. The workers, who sought the right of union recognition, tried to involve British-based trade unionists. The Dublin strike failed.

cal and mental degeneration that is produced by abject poverty the world over is lacking. I saw tens of thousands of the poorest of the poor massed in solid bodies at strike meetings, and I have never seen finer physical specimens, more handsome men, or crowds that grasped the point of a speech so quickly and could turn such shrewd wit upon the speaker who was not master of the situation.

I visited the most appalling slums in Ireland and found there men, women and children fit for artists' models. The schools of Ireland are a disgrace to the British Empire, and yet the street gamins and beggar girls speak the most perfect English. I suppose there must be vice in Ireland, but the evidence of virtue is most striking. Among hundreds of thousands of men, women and children, all abjectly poor, I did not notice a single obvious case of physical degeneration. The dirtiest little ragamuffins seemed physically clean.

The Irish working class will submit like oxen to the most frightful wrongs for years, then suddenly burst into a flame of passionate revolt over some trivial thing. The whole history of Ireland is that of long periods of doltish submission to terrible wrongs and sudden wild orgies of revolt. The story of Irish uprisings and Fenian rebellions would fill a whole volume of the Rip-Saw, and the Dublin Strike was but an Irish rebellion, a Fenian uprising expressed in a strike. . . .

About five years ago there appeared on the horizon of the labor world of Ireland one of the most spectacular men, assisted by one of the most remarkable women the labor world has ever known—Jim Larkin[25] and his sister, Margaret. Margaret Larkin is an Irish woman of the highest type, beautiful, sweet, cultured, perfectly poised, sympathetic, efficient to a marvelous degree and very modest. Though she was quite the most interesting character I met while in Dublin, no picture of her could be secured.

No word picture can ever make you know Jim Larkin, for no two people ever see him in the same way. He seems to be a mirror which reflects the hearts and souls of those with whom he comes in contact. Larkin is very slender and loose jointed, with the lean, homely face of Lincoln. Sometimes his eyes are like blue steel, again like pansies; sometimes they are red and bloodshot with the glare of a wild beast in them.

25. James Larkin (1876–1947), a leader of the Dublin strike, was a labor agitator, Irish nationalist, and, earlier in the United States, an organizer for the Industrial Workers of the World.

At times Larkin walks with the cringing slouch of a criminal, and again with the swinging stride of a born leader of men. Sometimes his voice has the raging snarl of a wild beast at bay, and again it is as soft and caressing as the low notes of a violin. At times his language is coarse, vulgar and repellant, and at other times it is wonderfully sweet, cultured and attractive. Larkin is a man of wonderful magnetism. I have known many men in my life, but never one into whose soul the iron had sunk so deeply, never one with such an overmastering passion to serve his fellow-men. Never have I known a man who apparently loved and served so passionately and unselfishly and hated so deeply and vindictively.

No one knows from whence Jim and Margaret Larkin came or how. Their past is hidden in the mists of Irish revolutionary history, and it is neither wise or kind to press an Irishman as to his antecedants; some of the noblest men Ireland ever produced were crushed by the iron heel of England and sleep in felon's graves. It is not well for children to speak of the past, lest the long arm and the mailed fist fall upon them also.

The story is told in Ireland (and there seems to be much to substantiate it) that Jim Larkin is the son of James Carey, the informer and traitor of the troubled days of the last Fenian uprising. I studied the pictures of Carey in the magazines and newspapers that I found in the libraries, and they are certainly strikingly like the Jim Larkin of today. If this strange tale be true (and stranger tales are true in Ireland), it adds a wonderful element of romance and tragedy to the activities of Larkin and explains much that is hard to understand about the man. If the tale is true, then Larkin must have been a boy of seven or eight at the time his father played the traitor's part and paid the traitor's penalty. He no doubt lived through the horror of the arrest of his father and his associates, the tragedy of the confession and the subsequent execution of the five Fenians and the frightful experience of seeing his father shot. The sorrow, the shame and horror of it all would explain also Larkin's insane hatred of England, of law, of policemen, of prisons and soldiers, for Larkin becomes a maniac when he speaks of these. This story would also explain Larkin's fanatically passionate devotion to the Irish working class, and the religious fervor with which he throws himself into his work and makes of it a penance for his father's sins.

But whether the story be true or not, the Larkins appeared on the scene just at the time when Ireland was emerging from thirty years of the inertia of despair and making ready for another outbreak. The old

Fenianism was dead, the newer Shin-fane movement existed only among the students and younger members of the upper class, and upon the shoulders of the working class fell the burden of a new revolutionary movement. The trades unions were compelled to fight the battles of Ireland and of labor, and Jim Larkin became their prophet. But Larkin was not a trades union agitator, he was an evangelist, a John the Baptist, crying in the wilderness; he was not an organizer, he was a religious fanatic, and his religion was the freedom of Ireland and the emancipation of the working class. Larkin is not as was Jesus of Nazareth. Like all religious fanatics, Larkin is an intolerant bigot, suffering from an aggravated case of exaggerated egoism. He has no common sense of every day efficiency, and he flatly refuses to be guided or helped by anyone who has these humdrum qualities. But he is a marvelous evangelist, a man who can arouse masses of human beings to their very depths; but he can never organize the sentiment he arouses, and he is too egotistical to allow others to do it without interference. Men follow him with blind adoration, and he with his head in the clouds leads them into a ditch.

Larkin spoke to the people of Ireland not only in the language of the labor agitator, but in the sweet, passionate tongue of the Fenian and Irish patriot. He appealed to the young men of his day with the battle cry of labor, and to the old men of his father's generation with the demand for Ireland's freedom. . . .

Like a spark to tow the message of Larkin and Larkinism spread until it flamed into an outbreak in the Tram Car Driver's Union strike in Dublin. Sympathetic strikes broke out everywhere among all classes and soon the whole island was in the throes of the most spectacular struggle of the age. It was more than a labor strike, it was an uprising of the Irish people who for six hundred years have been uprising periodically and fighting the tyrannical rule of England. Into it was injected not only the bitterness and rancor of labor against capital, but of Ireland against her oppressors.

I cannot think calmly yet of the great strike meeting I addressed where ten thousand human beings were packed into one solid mass in a dingy square in the most sordid slum of Dublin. By the flickering glare of the torches I could read in the eyes of the people the concentrated hate, bred by six hundred years of tyranny and oppression. In the hoarse shouts of my audience I could hear the war cries and the death songs of the uncounted thousands who have died for Irish freedom. Never to me again perhaps will there come so great a moment as when the crowd recognized in my speech the voice of brotherhood from across the sea and accepted me as one of the clan. Never again will I be so deeply moved as when two hundred Irish policemen stood with lifted helmets to make a path through the seething mass of people through which two stalwart Irishmen carried me on their shoulders to the jaunting car in which I rode to my hotel while the thousands marched beside as a guard of honor such as perhaps no woman ever had before and which I will never know again. . . .

In every other uprising of the Irish people hunger has been the ally of the master class, and starvation has forced the rebels back into slavery. But in the last thirty years a new spirit has quickened the minds of men, a new religion had birth—the spirit of working class solidarity—the religion of the brotherhood of man. When the master class of Ireland would have starved the workers into subjection, the working class of England, Scotland and Wales rallied to the call of their brother workers in Ireland, and great food ships loaded with the necessities of life steamed across the Irish sea and were landed to the idle quays in Dublin. Striking dockers quickly unloaded them and soon the stomachs and backs of the Irish workers were better supplied than they had been for many a day.

In the meanwhile Jim Larkin annoyed Great Britain, and I doubt if ever any one man ever set a whole nation in such an uproar. He tweaked the noses of the conservative, reactionary trades union leaders, and set the rank and file against them; he flouted the respectables and loomed larger on the political horizon than King George or Lloyd George. When I was in Great Britain Larkin and Larkinism was the bogey-man before which the whole nation quaked, while Jim Larkin set all Great Britain sneezing with the mold he kicked up. Margaret Larkin and James Connolly[26] (former editor of the *Harp* and author of *Socialism Made Easy*) stayed in Dublin to manage the strike and distribute the relief funds, and each accomplished their tasks with marvelous ability. This quiet little woman was commissary chief of a hungry army of two hundred thousand

26. James Connolly (1870–1916), also a strike leader, was a theorist as well as an organizer. He, too, had been active as an agitator for the IWW in the United States, where he was editor of the *Harp* from January, 1908, to December, 1909. The *Harp* was moved to Ireland in 1910 and the editorship was transferred from Connolly. (The *Harp* ceased publication later that year.) Connolly, after his return to Ireland, became involved in labor and nationalist causes. He was executed by the British for his part in the Easter Rebellion of 1916.

men, women and children, and never did a chief feed his army with greater skill. Under her orders were the food ships unloaded, food depots established, food distribution organized and carried on; under her watchful eyes were the hungry fed, the naked clothed and the sick cared for. You can well realize that it is no small task to feed, clothe and care for two hundred thousand poverty-cursed, hunger-pinched human beings and do it without uproar and friction, yet the food distribution of the Dublin strike was as quiet and orderly as a prayer meeting.

Jim Connolly's task was to keep the men in line and direct the activities of the strike, to act as commander-in-chief of the labor army. A right doughty little general was Connolly, and very efficient; but Larkin's continual interference made it impossible for him to handle the strike with any system or order. If Larkin had only possessed common sense enough to have stayed on the job of evangelizing and let Margaret and Connolly run the strike, the end of the story might have been far different. I devoutly prayed every day that Larkin would break his leg or have some other interesting accident happen [to] him that would have put him in the hospital for a month and allow Margaret and Connolly to bring the strike to successful termination. I am absolutely sure that if they could have had a free hand in the management of the strike without doing anything to shake the confidence of the strikers in Larkin, the victory would have been with the workers to a far greater degree.

However, the strike ran its spectacular course for several months and was finally settled with some slight advantages to the workers from a material standpoint. The gain in dollars and cents for the workers was not worth the outlay of life and energy, but the mental and moral gain cannot be estimated.

The Dublin strike taught the workers of Great Britain many valuable lessons; first, that evangelists are very useful as evangelists, but we must keep them evangelizing while organizers run our strikes; second, syndicalism and direct action are all right to talk about, but that an organized, disciplined, trained working class is necessary to fight the battles of the working class; third, that the man who is not educated to vote right is rarely educated to strike right, and that political education and political organization must keep pace with industrial development.

The trades union leaders of Great Britain learned that they can only lead in the direction the rank and file want to go. The rank and file of the British trades unionists had a most illuminating example of the difference

between a soapbox oration on the beauties of direct action and syndicalism and the conduct of a great strike according to their principles.

Naturally, the most valuable thing accomplished by the Dublin strike
was the victory of class solidarity over national prejudices, and the
freeing of the working-class from priest domination.

The most valuable lesson learned by the Irishmen themselves was
that the tyranny of England is only the tyranny of the owning class; that
the oppressor that they must fight in the years to come was not England
but capitalism, be the capitalist class English, Irish or what not. The Irish
workingman found that Mr. Murphy, good Irishman and Catholic that he
is, used the scarlet coated soldiers to shoot down Irish workingmen as
quickly as England would. They found also that an Irishman killed by an
Irish policeman at the behest of an Irish employer was just as dead as if
he had been killed by an English soldier under orders from an English
king. This was a bitter lesson for Irishmen to learn, but it will have a
splendid effect. From this time on, much of the heroism, patriotism and
splendid energy that has been expended in the various movements to
free Ireland from England, will be thrown into the Socialist movement
to free the workers of the world from the hell of capitalism. Irish nationalism has been merged into world-wide Socialism, and that means much
to the workers of the world in every nation; for Irish brains and Irish
brawn have fought the battles of every nation; now they will fight their
own battles, the battles of workers of the world.

Over the Sea and Back Again

The men who made up the membership of the International Socialist
Bureau[27] were wonderfully interesting. Some of them, like Jaurès of
France, and Molkenbuhr of Germany,[28] belong to the old guard, the men
who have spent their lives fighting for Socialism, and the never ending

"Over the Sea and Back Again" was first published in *National Rip-Saw* (March, 1914),
26–27.

27. The International Socialist Bureau served as the central clearinghouse for the
Second International. The headquarters were in Belgium.

28. Jean Jaurès (1859–1914) was the unifying force in the French socialist world and
one of the most influential leaders of the Second International. He was perhaps equally
known for his pacifism and, ironically, was assassinated as World War I began. Hermann
Molkenbuhr (1851–1927), of the German Social Democratic party, was a specialist on labor
legislation.

marvel is that they are just as full of fire and enthusiasm as the newest convert. Vandervelde of Belgium, and Huysmans, the International Secretary,[29] belong to a little later school, but they are no more keen and alert than the older men. The Russian Comrades, whose names no American could pronounce if I could spell them (and I can't), were an interesting group. One man had been in every Douma, and I bitterly regretted my inability to speak his language when I thought of the wonderful stories he could tell.

Comrade Longuet,[30] the editor of the French daily Socialist paper, L'Humanité, was one of the most brilliant and kindly men I met. He speaks French, German, English, and I don't know how many more languages, and was always ready to act as interpreter when I found myself in the frightful predicament of having plenty to say but only one language to say it in.

Dan Cameron, a Scotch Highlander, with his delightful Scotch brogue, was one of the most charming Britishers I came in contact with. If we could only induce him and George Dallas to come to America in kilts and with their bagpipes to talk Socialism, they would back Grape Juice Billy[31] clean off the boards as a Chautauqua attraction.

Comrade Keir Hardie[32] was the same gentle, sweet, comradely Hardie that all American Comrades know him to be. He is one of the best loved men of the Socialist movement, and certainly deserves to be.

Every man on the International Bureau was a wonderful character study but I wondered if it would not be good for the Socialist movement of the world if instead of always sending the old men to such meetings it would be well to add a few younger comrades now and then. A few of the younger generation could not possibly do any harm, and it would be such a wonderful education for them, and add so much to their usefulness. . . .

29. Émile Vandervelde (1866–1938) was the dominant figure of the ISB executive body through this period. Camille Huysmans (1871–1968) was the secretary of the bureau from 1905 until the demise of the Second International during World War I.

30. Jean Longuet (1876–1938), a grandson of Karl Marx, was especially marked by his sense of French nationalism. L'Humanité, founded by Jaurès and Aristide Briand in 1904, was the most influential leftist newspaper in France.

31. William Ashley Sunday (1863–1935), the famous Billy Sunday, was a leading revivalist and temperance advocate.

32. Keir Hardie (1856–1915), the founder of the Scottish Labour party, a forerunner to the Independent Labour party of England, and a member of Parliament, had been a coal miner and was one of the few leaders of the Second International with a working-class background.

I was the only woman delegate on the Bureau. In fact, the first woman who ever was a member,[33] and naturally this fact caused considerable comment. Every courtesy was extended and everything that could add to my pleasure and make me feel at ease was done, but it was easy to see that the idea of accepting a woman as an absolute equal, even in a Socialist Bureau meeting, was quite startling to the European male mind, particularly the English.

One of the most impressive and interesting happenings of the Bureau meeting was the public demonstration against militarism. The British comrades took advantage of the presence of Socialists from abroad to hold a huge anti-militarist demonstration in Kingsway Hall, London, on Saturday, December 14, over which Keir Hardie presided. The speakers were Vandervelde (Belgium), Molkenbuhr (Germany), Jaurès (France), O'Hare (America), A. C. Cameron (Labor Party), and Dan Irving (British Socialist Party). Anatole France, the great French writer and Socialist, came to the platform and made a wonderful plea for world peace. . . .

The European comrades never tired of hearing me tell of our southwestern Socialist encampments. They felt that they were the most wonderful and ingenious propaganda machines they had ever heard of, and every man I talked to expressed a great desire to visit a string of encampments. One of the happiest moments I remember was to see the glow of joy on Comrade Kautsky's face as I told him of how Oscar Ameringer[34] and I had sold thousands of his "Road to Power" in Oklahoma. . . .

Three Weeks

Don't be shocked, this is not the sultry love story of a young English nob, but the simple tale of the easy and leisurely life of a socialist agitator.

I left St. Louis on October 12 with two things on my mind; first, I wanted to visit as many of the Eastern municipalities as I could reach and see what was being done or had been done in dealing with the prob-

33. O'Hare is mistaken. Rosa Luxemburg (1871–1919) was a member of the International Socialist Bureau as a Polish representative in 1904.

34. Karl Kautsky (1854–1938), of the German Social Democrats, was the leading theorist of the so-called center. Oscar Ameringer (1870–1943), born in Swabia, was a socialist speaker and writer popular in the Great Plains area and the Middle West.

"Three Weeks" was first published in *National Rip-Saw* (August, 1914).

lem of unemployment, and second, share in the work of the Socialist
Suffrage Campaign Committee of New York City. I visited a number of
municipalities and will visit a great many more during the winter, and
hope that my investigation will be useful when finished.

I reached New York Saturday evening, and Theresa Malkiel, the
greatest human dynamo extant, met me at the Ferry and sent me back
to the wilds of Jersey to talk Suffrage to the Jersey Cityites which I did
while the great crowd waited for Debs to arrive. Sunday I spoke with
Congressman Meyer London and Gene Debs[35] in the great Carnegie
Hall meeting in New York. Right here I want to remark that this meeting
was one of the biggest, best managed affairs I have ever attended, and I
have seen some meetings in my life. The Socialist Suffrage Campaign
Committee (a group of New York Socialist women led by Theresa Malkiel
as organizer) had charge and the meeting was arranged for, handled and
officered entirely by the women. Every seat was sold and the "Standing-
Room Only" sign put out twenty minutes before the opening time. One
hundred young girls dressed in white and wearing great red "Votes for
Women" sashes acted as ushers and I have never seen a great crowd
handled as efficiently. Meta Stern[36] made an ideal chairman, Meyer London was at his best, Gene charmed his hearers as he always does, and I
attempted to sustain the reputation of the West in general and my sex in
particular to the best of my ability. When the Carnegie Hall meeting was
glorious history, then the fun began, and I had a chance to find out what
real, downright hard work meant. I spoke from three to five times every
day in every manner of place where human beings gather in masses.

New York city was the vortex of the great Suffrage cyclone[37] that was
sweeping over the conservative, mossbacked, rock-ribbed East; and the
Socialist Suffrage Campaign Committee seemed to be the dynamic center of the storm. For the first time in the life of New York, the women
were IT and the male was only a background for female activities. New

35. Theresa Malkiel (1874–1949) was an immigrant garment worker who became a
Socialist party leader and organizer in New York. Meyer London (1871–1926), born in
Poland, was a lawyer, a socialist activist, and, representing the Lower East Side, was a
member of the House from 1914 to 1918 and from 1920 to 1922. Eugene V. Debs (1855–
1926) was of course the much-loved perennial presidential candidate of the Socialist party
from 1900 to 1920. Debs never held a party office, preferring to write and speak for the
cause rather than involve himself in policy making or in internal squabbles.

36. Meta Stern Lilienthal was a Socialist party activist and a journalist for the New
York *Call.*

37. Woman suffrage did not carry in New York State until 1917.

York was OURS, and every man and woman wanted to hear what we had to say on Suffrage, and we said it—indeed we did. From soapboxes and cart-tails, autos and trucks, piles of lumber and stacks of brick, we hammered home the economic need of Equal Suffrage and always there were just as many people to listen as our voices could reach. I am sure the work done by the Socialist Suffrage Campaign Committee breaks all records, and there is no doubt but Theresa Malkiel and her loyal helpers have set a pace that will be hard to equal.

In one day we distributed sixty thousand English leaflets, fifty thousand Jewish; sold twenty-five hundred one-cent books, fifteen hundred five-cent books, put up forty thousand stickers, held one hundred meetings, and collected money enough on the street corners to pay the cost of the day's work. The Campaign Committee started without a cent in the treasury, carried on seven months' work, using some of the best known speakers in the country and finished without one cent of debt. Can any bunch of men anywhere on earth equal that record?

Suffrage did not carry in New York, but no one ever dreamed that it would. Great revolutionary changes are not made in one campaign, but are won by long years of constant work and education. The vote was far greater than the most hopeful anticipated and the new campaign is now on and will be continued until the male Henry Dubb is really educated. The Campaign of the Socialist Party of New York was just as wonderful and inspiring as the Suffrage campaign, in fact they were one. I never knew whether it was the Socialist Party or the Suffrage Campaign Committee I was speaking for, and which ever it was I talked the same kind of Socialism I talk in Oklahoma, and the people ate it up in just the same way. On the lower East Side I was speaking at a nice, dignified suffrage meeting in a schoolhouse, and a bunch of young comrades rushed in and kidnapped me and demanded that I go out on the street and take a Democratic politician's crowd away from him—which I did in just three minutes, and we held five thousand people for two hours in a nasty drizzling rain. At the McKinley Square Casino in the Bronx, Debs was the principal speaker. At eight o'clock the great hall, seating about four thousand was filled, and the smaller hall seating fifteen hundred packed. The police closed the doors and four thousand people were in the streets. U. Solomon,[38] with only three speakers - Debs, London and myself - man-

38. U. Solomon was a New York Socialist party functionary.

aged to keep all the meetings going and get a collection of $100 over and above ticket sales.

In the Brownsville District in Brooklyn I spoke to two monster meetings in one evening, and thereby helped share the joy of helping to send [Abraham] Shiplicoff [sic], the first Socialist Assemblyman, to Albany.

From New York I went to Philadelphia to speak for the Socialist Literary Society in the Broad Street Theatre. Here I found just the type of work that is so sorely needed in every city, and it is quite possible if we would use good common, horse sense in the management of our propaganda meetings. The Socialist Literary Society is furnishing the working class just what they are hungry for: music, culture, social life, artistic expression, and all founded on the bedrock of Socialism. To speak in the Broad Street Theatre is a joy, and to see the work being done there is an inspiration. How I wish other cities would do the same splendid work.

From Philadelphia I made the long jump over to Dubuque, Iowa, where two college boys from a Catholic college felt equal to the task of "smashing Socialism." The Dubuque Comrades brought me over to champion the cause against the onslaughts of the sophomores. The largest hall in town was packed to the doors, and every one had their money's worth in uproarious fun. Incidentally, two very nice young men know now that they can't "smash Socialism" with the weapons furnished by their college textbooks, while the local has taken on new life and added sundry bits of filthy lucre to the treasurey.

The next day I spoke in Des Moines, Iowa, where a splendid meeting was held on Sunday afternoon in the West Side High School Building. It was an ideal meeting in every way. On the same evening with a group of comrades I attended Peter Collins'[39] meeting and heard him annihilate Socialism in his usual manner. From the floor of this meeting I challenged him to meet me in debate and he agreed to do so, but up to the present time no definite arrangements have been possible. If any gentle reader happens to see Peter Collins rampaging about his vicinity, will he please rope Collins and tie him down until that debate can be arranged? I am just aching to get at the doughty Peter.

My last meeting was at Centerville, Iowa, a typical county seat town, in a rich Iowa county. It was a splendid example of what one good live Socialist can do if he has the right stuff in him. There is no local at Cen-

39. Peter Collins, an antisocialist lecturer, specialized in responding to socialist public speakers.

terville, but Comrade Willes, a coal miner, handled a Debs meeting there last summer which packed the largest hall. Encouraged by this, Comrade Willes tackled another meeting for me, filled the largest meeting place, was forced to turn people away who could not squeeze in. Don't this make some of you comrades who sit down and wail, "We can't do nothin," feel a bit ashamed?

And here endeth the tale of three weeks' adventures of a Socialist agitator.

Shall Women Vote?

Home is the logical location of womanly activity; biology and the natural division of labor have placed her there, and all the ologies and isms can never remove her from the home as long as the human family arrives in this vale of tears in the manner now in vogue. Some time in the future science may produce an incubator that will relieve woman of her primary occupation, but not until then need we fear the danger of the disappearance of home.

In the home of past days everything used in the home was produced in the home under the watchful eyes of the mother, and hers was the direct responsibility for conditions existing there. On the mother's loom and spinning wheel was the fabric made, and by the mother's needle was it fashioned into garments. All the food for the family was prepared under the eyes of the mother, and if it was lacking in flavor or cleanliness she was directly responsible.

Today everything used in the home is produced outside the home in a factory, and the mother has absolutely no control of the conditions existing there; neither has the mother any control over the location, sanitation or healthfulness of the house that must be the family home. If a textile mill is unsanitary, operated by sickly women and children and a veritable breeding place of disease, the mother who buys the fabric made there is helpless. If a food factory is reeking with filth and germs and sends poisoned food to the family table the mother is powerless to protect her own. The sources of food supply are often at the ends of the earth; an Asiatic with bubonic plague may send us death-dealing tea; a

"Shall Women Vote?" was first published in *National Rip-Saw* (July, 1914), 5–6; (August, 1914), 5–7; (October, 1914), 10–13.

filthy packinghouse in Argentina may send diseased meats to our table. A girl with tuberculosis or worse in a London sweatshop may send her curse to our baby in a silken garment. The loathsome horrors bred down in the slums where the workers who make the commodities used in our homes dwell, are no respectors of persons; they creep up the avenue and travel by routes of trade until they invade our homes, and we mothers are helpless before their invasion.

We can not expect men to usurp woman's natural place in the scheme of things and do the work of women in caring for and protecting the family. Man's concerns are the masculine ones in the direction of harnessing the elements, conquering nature and creating and directing the machinery of production and distribution. Our prehistoric ancestors settled the question of man's and woman's place in life back in the far past when instinctively the men went out to hunt the game and left the women and children to tend the fires, prepare the food and dress the skins.

It is idiotic to presume that we wish to or can upset the natural order of life and compel men to forsake their own vocations to assume the duties of women, simply because the industries of home have left the four walls of a cabin and gone to a factory and workshop.

Cooking, cleaning and clothing, sewage and smoke, dirt, disease and death always have been and are still woman's problems and must be dealt with by women. Men have problems of their own to solve. But these problems have ceased to be individual problems of individual women and become the civic problems of motherhood collectively, just as the loom, smokehouse and preserving kettle have ceased to be the individual property of individual women and become the collectively operated means of production.

Our responsibilities as mothers are just the same, but the methods of meeting them have changed. Women cannot cope individually with their responsibilities; only collectively can women solve the problems of the wider home. This collective action is political. Not the politics of the old school—but something different and finer. An enlightened democracy gives representation to every distinct interest. This is the meaning of Equal Suffrage. . . .

No Equal Suffragist says that "Men are too bad to be trusted." We simply say that no man can do our thinking for us or represent us in controlling the conditions under which our children shall live and labor. . . .

I, as a Socialist, most emphatically state that I demand Equal Suffrage not merely as a sex right, but also as a class right. I demand not only better laws and better enforcement of laws for my sex, but more particularly for my class.

Mrs. Ruler[40] says, "There always seem to exist in the mind of the suffragist some obscure connection between the right to vote and the expediency of wearing 'pants.'" I confess that I know nothing of the "expediency of wearing pants," but I do know that any sex, class or race that has been denied the right to vote has always worn the chains of servitude. The negro wearing the chains of chattel slavery in the South before the War was no more a slave than the disfranchised black man wearing the chains of wage slavery today. The white woman slave in the cotton mill is no more a slave than the white man slave in the lumber camp; both are disfranchised, and both are slaves. I, as a Socialist and a Suffragist, want to give each of them a ballot and protect them in the use of it, that working together, standing shoulder to shoulder, they can by the intelligent use of that ballot wipe the curse of wage slavery out of our social system.

It is the working class in which I am interested; it is the working class to which I belong. The working class is ninety-three percent of the whole people; and as half of that ninety-three percent of the people are women, I want the women of my class enfranchised, not alone that they may help me fight the battles of my sex, but also of my class. I know that "all legislation in the interest of man must necessarily be in the interest of woman"; hence, I want the power to help make better legislation in the interests of man that as a woman I may be helped. Don't worry, Mrs. Ruler, about us Socialist women "not understanding what we are doing, why we are doing it, or how it can be done." We know why we are demanding the ballot; we are doing that because we want to use our ballot to peacefully bring about the social revolution which shall eliminate wage slavery and establish the collective ownership and democratic control of the collectively used means of life. We know this can be done only by the

40. O'Hare held a debate on this issue. Her opponent was Bessie Ruler, a St. Louis attorney opposed to suffrage for women.

intelligent use of the ballot, and we can't use it until we get it—and there is the whole question in a nutshell.

Mrs. Ruler is much mistaken when she states that "on a plea of sex equality, we desire to seize upon the 'soft snaps,' the learned professions and politics." We demand our franchise that we may peacefully take over the earth and the machinery of production and distribution out of the hands of the greed-crazed spoilers who are making of it a charnel house of poverty, misery, disease, degradation and death. We demand the right to use the earth God made and the machinery man made to feed, clothe, shelter, educate and bless mankind and we further demand the right to use our brains and our ballots to harness the forces of nature and the power of machinery to lift from the shoulders of the human race the brutalizing load of needless drudgery. Certainly we are not "hastening to enlist our services as a miner, a puddler, a sewer-cleaner or a stoker." We are intelligent enough to know that puddling and stoking are far better done by machinery today than by hand, and that mining and sewer-cleaning can be much better done by machinery also, and will be so done when poverty forces no man to brutalize himself by loathsome labor better done by iron and steel.

We women are also well aware of the fact that it is not necessary for us to "enlist" for the loathsome, filthy jobs under our present system. The woman who cleans sausage casing in a packing house, who scrubs office and restaurant floors, or who works in a rope factory, does work infinitely more hard and repulsive than that of a miner, puddler, sewer-cleaner or stoker, and does it for a one-third the wage men receive. Machinery can do the work far better, and we want to use our ballots to gain control of the machinery and do away with loathsome labor for both men and women. . . .

Mrs. Ruler assures us that "women in America are fortunate in having under the law equal privileges without equal responsibilities." This is just as true and wise a statement as the altruistic attitude of anti-suffragists and the solution of domestic service for labor problems. Most emphatically, women have not equal privileges without equal responsibilities. The most sacred right, the fundamental privilege of life, is the privilege and right of self protection; and that, no voteless human being, man or woman, can have. Even if Mrs. Ruler's statement were true (which it is not), no right-minded woman wants privilege without responsibility; that is the position of the slave, the child, and the mentally incompetent, and

we deny that we are any of these. Grant again that Mrs. Ruler's statement is true (which it is not), that the laws of all states relating to all
women are exceedingly fair, and give a distinct advantage to women over
men, the position would still be abhorrent to all intelligent, right-think-
ing women. I am not asking for better laws for women; I am asking for
no special privilege; I am whining for no privilege without responsibility.
I demand better laws for the working class and the power to convert the
whole human race into useful workers and to eliminate the parasitical
idlers. I want no special privilege for myself, for my sex, or for my class.
I merely demand equal opportunity for all. I want to shoulder my own
responsibility and I ask for the ballot to strengthen my arm for its task.

Mrs. Ruler challenges me to point to some specific law that places
women at a disadvantage and I will name but three out of the many that
exist. But remember, these are laws aimed not directly against women
as a sex, but against women as a part of the working class. The women of
the property owning class are fairly well protected, for laws are made for
the protection of property and not human life.

In Missouri, law places the whole burden of responsibility on the
shoulders of the unmarried mother. By law the father of an illegitimate
child must be protected and a birth certificate bearing his name will not
be accepted by the Board of Health. By the laws of Missouri no illegitimate child may bear the name of its father, nor may it inherit any of his
property or make any claim upon him for support.

The age of consent in many states is placed at from ten to fifteen years
and no punishment can be laid upon the man who seduces a girl of that
age and no responsibility can be placed upon him for the care of the fruit
of his lust.

In Georgia and South Carolina the age of consent is ten years and a
man may make a girl the victim of his lust three years before she has
reached the age of puberty.

Even these unjust laws work little hardship upon the daughters of the
owning class, for they have always money enough to shield themselves
from shame; it is only upon the daughters of the working class the heavy
burden falls. The sons of the idle rich may prey with impunity upon the
daughters of toil and the laws of our states will protect them.

Mrs. Ruler closes with the statement that certain altruistic gentlemen
would deny us the vote, "not because we are not good enough to vote,
but because we are too good." How charming! How perfectly delightful

these altruistic gentlemen are. We are not "too good" to be the prey of
their lust; not "too good" to toil in their factories; not "too good" to do
their dirty work; not "too good" to be the producers of their wealth, but
"we are too good to vote."

We women of the working class thank you altruistic gentlemen very
kindly but we have some ideas on that subject ourselves. IF WE ARE
GOOD ENOUGH TO BEAR THE CHILDREN WE ARE NOT "TOO GOOD" TO
USE OUR BALLOTS FOR THEIR PROTECTION. IF WE ARE GOOD ENOUGH
TO PRODUCE THE WEALTH OF THE WORLD WE ARE NOT "TOO GOOD"
TO USE OUR BALLOTS TO GET POSSESSION AND ENJOYMENT OF WHAT
WE HAVE CREATED. IF WE ARE GOOD ENOUGH TO BEAR THE BURDENS
OF CIVILIZATION UPON OUR SHOULDERS WE ARE NOT "TOO GOOD" TO
DEMAND THE RIGHT TO SHARE IN THE BLESSINGS OF THE CIVILIZATION
WE HAVE MADE POSSIBLE. . . .

Mrs. Ruler states that there are two kinds of taxes, "money tax," the
money tax being levied on the property of men and women alike, while
the service tax is levied on men only and calls for jury service, police
service and military service. She argues that "Representation," or the
franchise, rightly goes with the service tax, but not with money tax.

Very well, Mrs. Ruler, let us carry your argument to its logical conclusion. Men, you say, should vote because they serve the nation in time
of war, but so do women serve the nation in time of war. Not only do the
women remaining at home till the fields and produce the rations the men
consume in the battlefield, but they also tend the loom, run the spindles
and sew the fabric that they have made into the clothing that the soldiers
wear, the tents they sleep under and the flags they carry. A modern army
without its corps of female Red Cross nurses would be routed in short
order, and women nurses armed with medicine kits and antiseptic ban-
dages are just as much a part of modern army equipment as men-armed
guns.

Men do police duty—so do women. There is scarcely a city in this
country so benighted and barbaric that it does not have its corps of
women police matrons, juvenile officers, truant officers, and special
women officers who do the work that men cannot do.

Men serve on juries; so do women. They serve too possibly as well if
not better than the average jury rounded up in the saloon and barrel-
house. Not only do women serve on juries in suffrage states, but in states
where women are still denied the ballot, that dearly beloved "Public

Opinion" with which Mrs. Ruler would replace the franchise, has already forced the appointment of women judges in Morals Courts and Courts of Domestic Relations.

Not all women serve as jurors or judges, go to war or act as police officers, but neither do all men—, and yet the exempt men vote. It is worse than silly to measure a woman's service to her nation by military service. It smacks of the Middle Ages when the bloody trappings of War were considered badges of honor. Mrs. Ruler, being a lawyer, naturally draws all her inspiration from the same place she acquired her legal lore—the Dark Ages of the past, and it is quite natural that she should not have progressed beyond the point where the man who could spill the most blood would stand highest in her estimation.

If service to city, state or nation, and not sex, should determine the right to the franchise, then women have proven themselves ready and willing to serve at all times and under all conditions when called upon, from the days of Molly Pitcher, Florence Nightingale and Mother Bicherdike, down to Mother Jones and Big Annie of Calumet. Yet Mrs. Ruler would deny the ballot to Jane Addams, Rose Schneiderman, Ella Flagg Young and Kate Bernard[41] and give it to thugs, gunmen and Pinkerton spies because they can carry a gun. In St. Louis we have a little woman not much larger than a pint of soap—Charlotte Rumbold. She possibly doesn't know one end of a gun from the other and could not lift a bayonet, yet she worked in season and out for years and compelled the establishment of public playgrounds, swimming pools and vacation schools. This little woman has handled single handed and alone thousands of the toughest, most troublesome boys from the worst slums of the city and never had to call for a policeman's club or a soldier's bayonet to manage them. Who has served the city of St. Louis best, Charlotte Rumbold or the white slaver living on the price of some girl's shame? Yet Mrs. Ruler would deny Charlotte Rumbold the ballot and give it to the procurer because he can carry a gun.

41. Molly Pitcher (1754?–1832) was a legendary heroine of the American Revolution; Florence Nightingale (1820–1910) was the Englishwoman considered the founder of modern nursing; Mother Bickerdyke, born Mary Ann Ball (1817–1910), was a Union nurse during the Civil War; Jane Addams (1860–1935) was the leading woman Progressive reformer, renowned for her work at Chicago's Hull House; Rose Schneiderman (1884–1972) was an immigrant garment worker who became an organizer for the International Ladies Garment Workers Union and president of the Women's Trade Union League; Ella Flagg Young (1845–1918) was superintendent of the Chicago public schools, the first woman to hold such a position in a large school system; Kate Bernard, or Barnard (1875–1930), the

I have worked in many strikes and faced a few mobs and I have always found one cool, level-headed woman equal to about ten average men in such crisis. Who stood forth in the best light in the shirt waist makers strike, Inez Milholland[42] or the policemen who clubbed the girls?

It was the women in Lawrence[43] who led the peaceful picketing; it was sweet-faced, home-loving women led by Big Annie, who was always at the head of the parades in Calumet and carried the American flag; it was the women in Colorado and West Virginia who served so loyally the working class, and it was the men sworn in as special constables in each instance who committed the fiendish murders. It was a "special constable" who shouted, "Fire," and blocked the stairway at the Christmas festival in Calumet and caused eighty children to be crushed to death; it was a "special constable" who fired into the crowd in Lawrence and killed the men and women; it was "special constables" who fired the tent colony at Ludlow, Colorado and roasted men, women and children alive.[44] Always on Labor's battlefields it has been the women who have struggled so bravely and nobly for better conditions that make for peace and harmony, and always it has been the "special constables" as thugs, gunmen, mine guards, Pinkerton cutthroats, militiamen and other Hessians that have spilled the blood and committed murder. If "service is the rightful price of the ballot, then women have paid that price and should have what is rightfully her own."

Every Socialist is well aware of the fact that "property is protected by government." Certainly we know that by bitter experience. I am not weeping over the woman whose "property" is not protected. I am not concerned with the woes of the women who pay taxes on property with-

first commissioner of corrections and charities in Oklahoma, established a record of reform which included the construction of a new prison.

42. Inez Milholland Boissevain (1886–1916) was a lawyer and a journalist, active in the suffrage movement and also in support of the labor movement, especially in the 1909–1910 garment workers' strikes in Chicago and New York. She rode horseback as the "American Joan of Arc" in the March, 1913, huge suffrage parade in Washington, D.C.

43. Lawrence, Massachusetts, a city dominated by its textile mills, was the scene of a massive strike in 1912 that was led by immigrant workers, with women and children playing prominent roles. The strikers evacuated their children from the city to ensure their safety. The publicity led to a congressional hearing, and for a time at least, the workers' wages were raised.

44. The so-called Ludlow massacre of 1914 occurred at the Rockefeller-owned Colorado Fuel and Iron Works. Striking workers were shot at by machine-gun-wielding troops, and tents, inhabited by miners' families, caught fire and the occupants died. Nearly one hundred people died during over a week of violence. A congressional investigation followed.

out votes to decide what rate they shall pay or what the taxes shall be used for; I know that her property is going to be well protected, not because she is a woman, but because it is property and property is sacredly protected by the capitalist system.

The woman for whom I demand the ballot has no property; she owns nothing, not even her life; she is the woman who is not able to sell her labor power for enough to possess enough property to be taxed—the woman of the working class. If service be the price of the ballot then in God's name these women have paid it a thousand times. They have mothered all the soldiers, policemen and jurymen; they have clothed us and fed us; they have trained our children in the schools; they have fought our battles on Labor's battlefield; they have washed our linen and scrubbed our floors; they have served us at the table and waited behind the counters; they have toiled and moiled for our well-being; they have nursed us when we were sick and stitched the shrouds for us when we die. From the cradle to the grave the women of the working class have served mankind and Mrs. Ruler and her ilk would deny them the one weapon with which they in some measure might protect their lives because they don't carry guns and spill blood. . . .

I am demanding the ballot, not because I am a woman, but because I belong to the working class and I want the workers to be represented on the board of directors of every industry on earth. By the use of the ballot I want my class to have the power to take back from the Land Trust the land God made, and from the other Trusts the machinery man made. By the use of the ballot I want the working class to vest the ownership of the sources of the means of life in the commonwealth, and by the ballot to have representation in the control of these things. By the use of the ballot I want to eliminate the indirect taxation of the capitalist class and give the workers the full social product of their labor.

I know that in the last analysis the question of votes for women will be settled on exactly the same basis as the American Revolution was settled. The colonists were strong enough to win their demands for independence; when the women who want the ballot are numerous enough and determined enough the voting males and the antiquated females will cheerfully and gracefully surrender as they have already done in ten states, regardless of the doctrines and vaporings of the legal fossils who have filled the musty tombs with their hair splitting contentions as to the why's and wherefore's thereof. Law follows the will of the people and when equal suffrage prevails, curiously enough it will appear to be the only logical and reasonable plan for democracy. . . .

Priscilla at Her Loom

No one doubts that one of the causes for decreasing marriage, increasing divorce and race suicide, is woman labor; yet women have always labored and we have never looked upon it as a problem or a curse until in the immediate past. Strange, too, but women are doing to a great extent the same kind of labor they have always done, and with vastly improved tools; and, notwithstanding this fact, woman labor has grown to a problem which is demanding the attention of the legislators, publicists, philanthropists and reformers.

Women have always been the weavers of the world's clothing, and the maid or matron at her loom or distaff has long been the theme for painter's brush and poet's lay. Today she is still the weaver of the world's raiment but she no longer inspires song or picture unless it be the song of misery and the picture of human suffering.

Priscilla, strong and rosy, sat at her wheel while John Alden pleaded the cause of love. She was a pioneer in a new land, surrounded by wilderness and savages, but history shows her well fed, well clad and happy. Science and invention have come to the aid of the modern Priscilla. Her distaff and loom, touched by a magic wand have grown wondrously, and the latter now whirrs and roars from morning until night, and a touch now and then of her fingers is all that is needed to keep it spinning and weaving countless yards of finest fabric. Her loom and spinning wheel have been harnessed to steam, and with almost human intelligence the wheels revolve and the shuttle flies back and forth so fast that the eye cannot follow, and at night there is more cloth than Priscilla could have woven in a long year.

The housewife of old rendered her lard and cured her hams and bacon by hand process, but today the packing-house takes the pigs and with the aid of just a few men and women transforms numberless pigs into lard, hams and bacon, and does it with incredible swiftness. The old dairy house and churn have been replaced by the cream separator, and

"Priscilla at Her Loom" was first published in *Socialist Woman*, II (July, 1908), 8.

the great creameries and the butter making of the world has had its labor reduced ninety per cent. And so we might go on through all the avocations of womankind. Women are doing the work they have always done and with the assistance of machinery and modern equipment, while science has added a whole list of new activities which modern civilization has made possible, yet woman labor has grown to be a curse to mankind. Since it cannot be the labor itself which is harmful, we must look for the harm in the way in which the labor is done.

When the Priscillas of old spun and wove with their clumsy hand-tools they were rosy, well-fed, well-housed and happy. They could only weave a little cloth in a day, but by being industrious they easily kept the whole family comfortably arrayed. Priscilla today weaves many, many yards of cloth each day, and is poorly fed, poorly housed, and she and her loved ones lack decent clothing, the harder she works the less she receives, and is denied the happiness which is the natural right of mankind; possibly we may find the reason here:

Priscilla of old owned her loom and spinning wheel, and though she wove but little it was all hers. Priscilla's loom to-day is owned by a capitalist and though she weaves much it is not hers, but belongs to the man who owns her loom, who gives her only a very little in return and calls it wages. The modern Priscilla bends not alone under the burden of providing all manner of luxuries for an idle class of men and women who do no useful labor, but suck like vampires the life blood of the women and children who feed and clothe them in purple and fine linen and enble [sic] them to fare sumptuously every day.

When butter was made by hand there was butter for the bread of all who were willing to work for it, and now the workers eat unwholesome, unclean oleomargarine because the creameries belong to the Creamery Trust, and those who eat butter and those who make it must pay the tribute which builds up the colossal fortunes of the owners.

When the women cured the meat in the kitchen and the smokehouse there was meat for all, and now when it is cured in packing houses they who cure it and who eat each contribute so large a share to the Armour's and Swift's holdings that their own must go without meat, or pay an unwarranted share of their income for it.

It is an indisputable fact that woman labor is not bad, but the way she labors. Labor is a joy when we perform it for those we love and reap the fruits of our industry, but is a curse when we labor for a master and the wealth we create means added misery for us and our loved ones and added power to despoil for our masters.

Since the workers have lost the ownership of their tools, and the world has ceased making things for use, and everything is produced for profit, when a woman works for wages she works for a master, and that master sets the price of her labor, fixes the hours, says how much shall be done and what conditions must be, and always with the idea of making the largest profits for himself. As a result we see an army of five million women working in all manner of industries and under the conditions and at the wages the master, who has no eye but for profit, decrees. There could be but one result where a few men have such control of many women's lives—low wages, long hours, unsanitary conditions, dangerous work, poor food, poor lodging, insufficient clothing, poverty, misery, want, degradation, crime and vice.

Blame It on God

Cardinal O'Connel delivered a eulogy in St. John's Church, Peabody, Mass., after the frightful fire in the Parochial School there, in which he says: "The accident seems to have happened through the fault of no one.

"What can one say in the face of such things? You fathers and mothers know that what words fail to express, faith and hope make strong and clear. Search your Christian hearts, bring out today from that storehouse of confidence in God, in his all-seeing wisdom, which in a moment like this must be your greatest strength, as they must also be the only answer to all your questions." Again: "Your little ones are with God. A moment and God has enfolded them in His loving arms, taken them home to Himself. . . . God's happiness claimed them for an eternity of bliss. Their sweet souls were unsullied; their innocence still angelic. In a moment of trial all the suffering of mortal life was over, and they were in the loving arms of their God, their Father; and not for all that earth contains would they now leave the heaven which they possess forever."

It seems to be one of the strangest kinks in human nature for people (particularly clergymen) to lay the blame for every catastrophe from war to syphillis on God.

"Blame It on God" was first published in *National Rip-Saw* (February, 1916), 18–19.

The losses of Europe in the war up to May 31, as compiled by the French ministry of war, are as follows:

	Killed	Wounded	Prisoners
France	460,000	660,000	180,000
England	181,000	200,000	90,000
Belgium	49,000	49,000	15,000
Russia	1,250,000	1,680,000	850,000
Germany	1,630,000	1,880,000	490,000
Austria	1,610,000	1,865,000	910,000
Turkey	110,000	144,000	95,000
Totals	5,290,000	6,478,000	2,630,000
Grand Total	14,398,000		

No human mind can grasp the horrors represented by these figures. Five and a quarter million slaughtered men means practically the same thing as if we sent out an army and killed every man, woman and child in the state of Illinois. Six and a half million more wounded, mutilated, crippled men almost equal the total population of the state of Pennsylvania. The killed and crippled of this war number more than the combined population of all New England, Maine, New Hampshire, Vermont, Massachusetts, Rhode Island and Connecticut, with the population of Delaware, New Jersey, Maryland and West Virginia thrown in. If you can imagine these ten populous states with everything in blood-soaked wreck and ruin and with every human being wounded, crippled or dead, you can have some conception of the horrors of the European war. And every king, statesman, diplomat and practically every priest and preacher emphatically declare that "God did it."

When we Socialists suggest that decent fire escapes, doors that swing outward, or better still, fireproof school buildings would have saved the lives of the children roasted in the school building at Peabody, Mass., we immediately become impious, irreligious and atheistic; when we insist that all the ghastly horrors of war are caused by the stupid, insensate greed and inefficiency of the capitalist system, the properly pious declare us to be blasphemers and heretics; when we seek to teach the world that the economic slavery of women is responsible for prostitution and venereal disease, with one accord the "men of God" shout that we are obscene, vile and licentious.

"God wills it so!"

Sure! Blame it on poor God; He can't help Himself, and it's so much easier to sit down and twiddle our thumbs and mumble, "God's will be done," than it is to stand up like men and women, give God a square deal and rebuild society in a decent, sane, humane manner.

Margaret Sanger

Margaret Sanger is a trained nurse; for ten years she did nursing for a charity organization in the lower East Side of New York City. Her work took her among the poorest of the poor, where the birth rate is the highest of any place in the world and where the baby death rate is higher still. She not only nursed poor mothers through the agony of unwanted motherhood of surplus babies for the potter's field, but she was often called upon to watch the death agony of a woman who had braved the dangers of abortion in preference to bringing into the world a child for whom there was no place.

When Mrs. Sanger changed her work and went into private practice, and was employed not by the poor but by the well-to-do and rich, she found little call for maternity nursing; for babies are few and far between on the Upper West Side; most of her patients required her services for other ailments besides babies. Down on the East Side Mrs. Sanger found that women bore the many babies that could not possibly survive because they knew no way of avoiding forced motherhood; on the West Side the women who were physically and financially able to give a baby a fair chance in life had few babies because they were able to buy from their physicians the knowledge of how to prevent undesired maternity. This seemed bitterly unfair to the little trained nurse and she decided that if it was right for the rich woman to limit her family to the desired number of children, then it was right for the carpenter's or hod-carrier's wife. What was good for the "Captain's lady" was also good enough for "Judy O'Grady." So Margaret Sanger began giving free to the women of the working class that information that the rich have always purchased at high prices from their fashionable doctors.

Then the storm broke over her head!

The church, the state, and the press piled on her. No woman would

"Margaret Sanger" was first published in *National Rip-Saw* (July, 1916), 5.

take a stand by her side, no man would openly espouse her cause. Her little magazine was suppressed by the postal authorities and she was indicted for the crime of circulating "obscene" matter (the word obscene matter being material that has long been circulated through the mails in medical books). The story of Mrs. Sanger's departure to England, the arrest of her husband by trickery for passing out her literature, his conviction, her return to this country and the farce of her trial has all been told in the RIP-SAW as well as in hundreds of other newspapers and magazines. In one year Margaret Sanger has risen to national and international prominence; and no woman in the United States today has more friends and sincere admirers.

So when Margaret Sanger invaded the city of St. Louis on May the twentieth, for three whole days the city trembled in abject fear.

A stranger arriving in our fair city and observing the fear and consternation of certain bankers, clergymen and lawyers would no doubt have concluded that Margaret Sanger was a cohort of the Kaiser, armed with Lyddite shells, carrying a supply of poison gas, charging about the country in airships laden with gun-cotton and machine guns!

It would have been hard indeed to convince such a stranger that Margaret Sanger is just a tiny scrap of a woman, the typical trained nurse, dainty, sweet and soft-spoken, with soft brown eyes, alluring curves, and the most kissable mouth imaginable, and that her only weapons were her voice and an array of terrific facts; for she jarred sleepy, reactionary old St. Louis as it has not been jarred since the cyclone twenty years ago.

Margaret Sanger ruffled the serenity of the most hidebound, conservative city in the country simply because she was a woman who dared, and she came loaded with an idea. Every human being worthy of the name admires a woman who is willing to fight the whole world barehanded and alone for her opinions and every right-minded man or woman must agree with Mrs. Sanger that the most sacred thing in life is the creation of life and that the creator should have the right and power to say when a life shall be called into being.

In the most astounding manner the people of St. Louis responded to the message of this brave little woman. The largest crowd of businessmen that ever attempted to enter the City Club diningroom listened to her address with rapt attention and cheered her words. At the Town Club the business women of St. Louis overran the facilities of the American Hotel, and the doors were closed while many clamored for admittance.

The Victoria Theatre had been rented for her public lecture. At the last minute the manager refused to open the doors to the thousands of people who had purchased tickets and who thronged the street. When Mrs. Sanger attempted to address the immense crowd from an automobile she was unceremoniously prohibited from saying a word by a police sergeant at the head of his squad. The people cheered Mrs. Sanger and jeered the police when she was refused the right to speak in the theatre that had been hired for the occasion, or on the public street. The St. Louis folk were sent home to bed for fear that they might be contaminated by such dangerous doctrines.

The people of St. Louis welcomed Margaret Sanger; they wished to hear her message whether they agreed with it or not and they had every desire that the right of free speech should be maintained in this city, yet a few powerful men were able to insult this woman whose shoes they are not fit to touch; these men were able to put the Constitution of the United States to naught and deny a whole city the right to pay for and to hear a lecture on a vital topic.

Who were these men and wherein did their power lie? Mr. Festus Wade, one of the most powerful bankers in the middle west and a capitalist unrivalled in the art of attracting other people's earnings to his own pockets. Archbishop Glennon, head of the Catholic Church of this city, and a lawyer named Schneiderhahn who did the dirty work for these gentlemen.

The manager of the Victoria Theatre was approached and was given to understand that if he dared to carry out his contract with Mrs. Sanger he would be boycotted and ruined in business by the societies controlled by the above-named gentlemen. As Robert Minor[45] remarked, "These gentlemen and the Black Hand societies use the same weapon, the threat."

The newspapers, which at first gave Mrs. Sanger fairly favorable notices were likewise bludgeoned into a silence so thick that it would have served for armor plate!

In this way were the "common people" of St. Louis denied the right to see and hear Mrs. Sanger discuss the question of Family Limitation.

One can understand that the Festus Wade class of society is able to

---

45. Robert Minor (1884–1952), a socialist journalist, wrote for the New York *Call*, the *Liberator*, the *Daily Worker*, and other papers and periodicals. He later became a member of the Communist party and served as an official.

buy and is buying all the "birth control" information it needs, and that his Grace is not supposed to need it, but what of the rights of the thousands of women of St. Louis who honestly feel that motherhood is too sacred to be abused, that the power to give life is a sacred responsibility and that its control should be in the hands of the woman who gives life rather than at the caprice of the man whose only responsibility is the gratification of physical passion.

If the Archbishop and the Catholic church are sincere in their teaching that women should accept motherhood without question or revolt as often as the stork decides to come, whether once or twenty times in twenty years, then let the Catholic church use its mighty power for the protection of motherhood and childhood by uniting in an effort to secure:

Maternity compensation laws;

Widows' pensions;

Certain jobs and adequate wages for the bread winner;

The abolition of child labor;

The abolition of the tenant system of farming;

The abolition of Mr. Wade's control of the cotton market.

When the church has used its power to make society as a whole responsible for the welfare of all children, provide every prospective mother with funds enough to care for herself and her unborn child in such a manner that the highest state of mental and physical fitness shall be insured; when there is care during confinement, freedom from harmful labor following childbirth and security of life and opportunity for the offspring; when such conditions prevail then and not until then has any male biped without feathers the right to forbid to any woman the scientific knowledge that will enable her to decide when and under what conditions she shall call a new life into being.

I know that the great mass of men and women who read the RIP-SAW feel with me that neither Archbishop Glennon nor Festus Wade have any right to demand that the women of the working class shall continue as breeders of child slaves to perish in capitalism's shambles for the glory and profits of the American plunderbund.

Margaret Sanger is fighting a brave battle on behalf of the working class. Write to her and tell her so. She needs the hand of comradeship and appreciation to give her courage to walk the danger-beset path that lies before her. Every word of cheer from a comrade now will be worth tons of flowers on her grave. Let us see that she gets it now. Margaret

Sanger's address is 163 Lexington Ave., New York City, and every right-
minded man and woman will send her a word of comradely greeting.

The Tale of a Rib

Ancient theological authorities disagree as to whether the eternal question mark was made from a tail-bone or a rib-bone, but with one accord
they all called it woman. There is one thing of which I am absolutely sure
however, and that is judging from the subservient position woman has
held in historic times it was not a back-bone. . . .

In spite of the variety and lucidity of the theories furnished by the
various theologies of the world concerning woman's advent, there have
been men who were not quite willing to accept these explanations of the
whichness or the wherefore of our being here on earth and they insisted
on digging deeply into the debris of the past that more scientific explanations may be forthcoming, so they say.

Charles Darwin is, of course, the most famous of those men and his
work is too well known for it to be necessary for me to comment on it. Of
course, Darwin has always been very unpopular with the clergy, possibly
because he insisted on introducing woman into the world on exactly as
respectable a basis as man.

Following in the wake of Darwin came men like Morgan, McLennan,
Bachofen, Westermark, Cunow, Mason[46] and many others. These men
did not depend on Holy Writ for their information concerning the in-
fancy of and early childhood of the race. They went out to the uncivilized
places of earth and hunted out the scattered remnants of savage tribes,
who, being the backward children of the race, still live in the same stages
of development through which our ancestors passed untold ages ago.
Morgan traces the crooked windings of the path of progress through six
periods of pre-civilized life. . . .

"The Tale of a Rib" was first published in *National Rip-Saw* (October, 1916), 5–6, 8;
(December, 1916), 5–6; (February, 1917), 5.

46. Of the anthropologists cited here, the key name is Lewis Henry Morgan (1818–
1881), who was a pioneer in American anthropology. He was trained for the law, but in
the 1840s he studied the social organization and culture of the Iroquois Indians, following
which he made the study of culture his lifework. In 1871 his monumental *Systems of
Consanguinity and Affinity of the Human Family* was published, the founding study in
the field of kinship. His work influenced Marxists, especially Engels' *Origin of the Family,
Private Property and the State.*

The sixth and last period of barbarism began with the smelting of metals, when iron tools were made to till the soil and iron weapons to wage war. The groups federated into nations; strong men fought for the possession of favorite women, and the possession of a large number of women became the mark of a chieftain's success, and a necessary adjunct to a man's comfort and happiness. Of course, not all men could have a lot of women, only the military leaders who were very powerful in war were so fortunate.

The sacred Hebrew writings, the Homeric legends and the songs of the Northern Sages tell the story of this period of human progress, when the gentle art of warfare on the one hand and of annexing women on the other became the favorite pastime of the masculine part of the human race. And such it has remained down to this day with addition of the modern art of money grabbing.

As long as the race lived in savagery, possessed little information, few tools and crude methods of production, men could only supply their own needs, and these in the most sparing manner and private property was unknown. Slavery could not exist side by side with the collectively-used property, for a master must own property and a slave must be propertyless.

Gradually primitive women invented new methods and established new industries. They tamed the animals and founded the herds, they tilled the fields and raised the crops, they made the pots and built the homes, until at last the men found that the women working about the fires could produce enough food to feed the men while they waged wars and enjoyed themselves at such manly sports. It was during this period that the adage, "let the women do the work" was coined, and we have been doing it ever since.

War had long been the favorite pastime of the men, but they had to stop now and then to do a little hunting and fishing to help the women out in providing the food. Captives had long been taken in war, but not until the women established the industries did captives have any but a culinary value. Previously after each battle the captives were killed and roasted and eaten for dinner. One man made one dinner which was very extravagant. When women demonstrated that they could with tools and better methods of production produce enough to feed the warriors, then some old John D. of that day conceived a brilliant idea. He no doubt reasoned thus: "If we kill these captives they furnish one dinner, but if we keep them alive and leave them at home to work with the women we can eat off of them all the rest of our lives." And thus slavery was established, a working class set apart to do the work of the world and the downfall of woman came about. And from the day when slavery first became a part of human development, the waging of wars, the capture of slaves and the subjugation of women became the principal business of the menfolk.

Until the establishment of slavery there had been no private property and no degradation in woman's position in society; on the other hand they had really been the dominant portion of the race. Morgan in his *Ancient Society*, and Mason in his *Woman's Share in Primitive Culture*, both declare that all during these ages such governments as existed were matriarchal. The members of a group claimed one common ancestress to whom the females traced their descent and the children belonged to the mother's group and not that of the father. Women were the leaders and rulers of the simple social organizations of that day, their opinions ruling in the households as well as in the affairs of the tribe. The woman was the peacemaker, judge and priestess as well as the mother of the group. . . .

With the invention of writing and the establishment of slavery the race passed from the period of development called barbarism into what we have dignified by the name of civilization. War ceased to be a pastime and became a business, captives in war became slaves, captured lands and herds became the private property of the captors. The collective ownership of property passed away, collective production ceased and society was divided into two classes—those who had forcibly taken the earth, and their slaves, and to the latter class women belonged.

So in the days of the Old Testament, the slave system was in full force. The military class was the ruling class and they were firmly established on the basis of the RIGHT of any man who had the MIGHT to own his working class as private property. The productive work of that time was done by bondmen and bondwomen—in other words, slaves. Whenever and wherever men have been allowed to own their working-class as private property, they have steadfastly held that they had a sacred right to own anything else they needed in their business in the same way. And if we read secular history and religious history rightly, men since the beginning of the slave system have needed plenty of women in their business. They were quite justified in getting the women by any method they found convenient. Purchase, capture or abduction, in fact any method that supplied plenty of women was satisfactory as well as moral and pious.

If the subjugation of women had only existed among the Hebrews and Christians we might with justice attribute it to the "rib story," but since we find it among all nations and a part of the life all the people of all religions and realize that it came along with the private ownership of property we must in justice decide that the "rib story" did not create the slavery of women, it just sanctioned and defended it as did all other religions.

Walter Thomas Mills in his *Struggle for Existence*, says: "It is seen from a study of primitive industry that when man came to use the resources of the earth, it never occurred to him for a thousand centuries that it could belong to only a portion of the race. When he did come to that conclusion, slavery and the subjugation of women came along with the private appropriation of the natural resources." August Bebel in his *Woman* says: "The matriarchate or mother rule, implied communism and equality for all. The rise of the patriarchate or father rule, implied the rule of private property and the subjugation and enslavement of women."

With the institution of private property came the vital question of inheritance. The father who by his trusty sword had acquired broad acres and numberless slaves did not care to run the risk of having his hard-earned wealth pass at his death into the hands of the child of some other man, who might have poached on his preserves while he was away at war. The enslavement of women and the enforcement of the most drastic laws concerning her chastity was the only solution for the problem. Religion and law, both being the servants of the men of the ruling class, joined hands in enforcing the subjugation of women and the mastery of men; and naturally before such a combination, women were helpless. . . .

When we pass from the story the Bible tells of woman's status, there is little in ordinary history that is worth while. Painfully and with infinite patience, one must thresh mountains of "historical" chaff to gather here and there a grain of wheat. With painstaking care one may plod through a thousand years of the history of the Turkish race as given by Sir Edward Creasy in his *History of the Ottoman Empire* only to find that there were neither women nor workingmen in all these years of history; only warriors. In all of the two fat volumes of Hallman's *History of the Middle Ages* there is not one single line dealing with the life and conditions of the women of the times of which he writes, and these instances may be multiplied a thousand times.

A study of the laws of the nations is the most fertile field for one who cares to delve into the story of woman's past. For in laws we find woman's position accurately defined, and law, like religion, tells the story with no intention of doing so. If we wish to construct anything like a true picture of woman's march across the ages, we must depend upon the evidence found in laws and religions; for conventional history is almost worthless for the purpose.

Women wrote no history, and men could not if they wished to tell the story, and certainly they had no wish to tell it. No book has ever yet been written that lays bare the woman heart and soul, and no voice has ever spoken the secrets of her mind. No man can know what women feel and no woman dare tell it. If, for but a single day, every woman spoke the exact truth and expressed her thoughts without disguise, chaos would reign and society would be turned up-side-down. This book will not tell the story of womankind as I see it, because if it did tell it so, the book would never be printed. We live in a man's world, and in it women speak not by right, but by permission. Men own the publishing houses and the avenues of publicity; men buy and pay for the books published and it is men's tastes and pocketbooks that must be consulted; so naturally this book will be well shaped to masculine thought before it sees the light of day. A few generations hence perhaps, when women own and manage publishing houses and are economically free enough to buy such literature as they choose, our great-great-grand-daughters may write exactly what they feel to be true, but it is not for the women of my generation. If, even in our own time, the true story of women may not be told, how much less possible it was two thousand years ago.

Kate Richards O'Hare with her newborn twins, Eugene and Victor, and her older children, Dick and Kathleen. 1908
Courtesy of Mrs. Theresa Taft

Frank P. and Kate Richards O'Hare and children about 1910. Her caption says, "A rad. example of what Socialism does to the home and family."
Courtesy of Tamiment Institute Library, New York University

Kate Richards O'Hare as journalist, about 1913
Courtesy of Perkins Library, Duke University

On the lecture circuit, about 1913
Courtesy of Perkins Library, Duke University

PART II

Antiwar Writings

Socialism and the World War

Foreword

During 1917 I made a transcontinental lecture trip and at each appointment I delivered this lecture, and always in the presence of a representative of the U.S. Department of Justice. My seventy-sixth appointment
was at Bowman, N. D., on July 17, 1917.

On July 23, 1917, Senator McCumber[1] of North Dakota read into the
Congressional Record a letter from Bowman, N. D., whose author was
not willing to have his identity known. This letter dealt with a postoffice
feud at Bowman and connected me with the sordid affair because the
postmistress, whom the writer wished to have removed from office, had
attended my lecture. . . .

A few days later Jas. E. Phelan, a banker-politician of Bowman, appeared before the Grand Jury at Fargo, N. D., accompanied by one man
who had attended my lecture and four who had not even been in the
vicinity of the meeting place. On the testimony of these men, an indictment was returned charging me with an "intent to interfere with the
enlistment and recruiting service of the United States["] by the use of
language first made use of in the letter read by Senator McCumber.

I was tried in Bismarck, N. D., during the December term of court,

"Socialism and the World War" was first published as a pamphlet, by Frank P. O'Hare (St.
Louis, 1919).

1. Porter James McCumber (1858–1933), a Republican in the Senate from 1899 to
1923, specialized in banking and finance.

Judge Martin J. Wade of Iowa City, presiding. The prosecution produced two witnesses who had attended my lecture and three who had not entered the opera house. Eight witnesses for my defense were allowed to testify, and four were denied that right by the judge. The eight witnesses who were permitted to testify, swore that I had not used the language imputed to me, but had used the language printed in black face type. I was found guilty and sentenced by Judge Wade to five years at hard labor. The Circuit Court of Appeals and the Supreme Court of the United States have affirmed the findings of the trial court, and I must begin serving my sentence in a few days.

Since all legal efforts to secure justice have been exhausted, I feel that it is time to carry the case to the great court of the American people. I feel that the time is opportune. President Wilson is now making heroic efforts to establish the League of Nations, and his efforts to that end coincide perfectly with the prophecy that I made two years ago.

I am presenting now for the judgment of the American people the absolute and exact reproduction of my lecture at Bowman. I wish to say in fairness to the jury that the lecture was not submitted in evidence because of my ignorance of the fact that I had the right to present it in its entirety.

If the American people decide that these words of mine are "seditious" or "disloyal," I am ready to pay the penalty for my crime. If you decide that they are not, then make your voice heard in Washington.

Fraternally,
KATE RICHARDS O'HARE

St. Louis, Mo., March 20, 1919

Socialism and the World War

In this, the most trying hour of the life of not only this nation but of the human race, I am glad that I am to have the privilege of speaking to this audience of sober, thinking men and women. These are days that try men's souls; and, if ever in all the history of the world the need for deep, clear and heart-seeking thought has been necessary, it is necessary today. I shall discuss with you the effect that I think that this world-war is having and will have on the great world movement to which I have given my life—the International Socialist Party [sic].

It is a comfort to me to know that in the last few months, for the first time in all my life, I have been able to give my whole time and energy to a rational discussion of Socialism, its principles, its aims and its ultimate goal. I have been in the Socialist movement for a long time, more years than I like to contemplate or to admit. I am not going to tell you just how many years, for you know that when women get along to my age they are just a bit sensitive about having you men begin to figure on how old they are. Suffice it to say that, for many years I have traveled up and down this earth preaching the gospel of Socialism. Until within the last few months I have always been required to give at least three-fourths of my time and energy, not to teaching Socialism or expounding its theories and ideals, but to discussing and answering certain prejudices carefully planted in the minds of the people by the capitalist-controlled means of public expression.

Cultivated Prejudices

I have found, in my long years of work, that it did not matter where I spoke, or to what manner of audience, this condition existed. Before I could begin to explain what Socialism really means and what goal we Socialists really have in mind, I had to deal with these carefully planted and cultivated prejudices. If I started on a discussion of the fact that all experiments so far tried seem to prove that the collective ownership and public control of public utilities are more efficient and economical, more just and righteous than the private ownership and irresponsible control of men actuated only by hunger for profits, and that we Socialists feel that all the things used by the people collectively would be better owned by the people and controlled by them, then some good, staunch Democrat or Republican would at once interrupt—

"Say, do you mean that the Government should confiscate and run all of the great public utilities?"

I would reply that we Socialists are not saying how the Government should get the public utilities, but that we want it to get them in the most fair and just way, then to own and operate them to serve the people and not to make profits for a few bondholders.

Then my good Democratic or Republican friends would shout:

"Sure! We know that the public ownership of public utilities has proven best; but you must remember that these great profit paying industries are owned by the capitalists; they bought and paid for them; they are private property, protected by the laws of the country, and if you Socialists try to take that property away from them, you will plunge this country into a bloody war."

This charge that the Socialists would plunge the world into war has been a stock argument against Socialism. It has been hurled at us from every quarter in all manner of forms. We have been called violent and blood-thirsty breeders of war and disorder so often that we have become quite hardened to the cry. . . .

Socialism Would Destroy Religion

Nor was that all. We were not only very bad people, but marvelously powerful, as well. There was another nightmare which haunted the dreams of clergymen and nervous old ladies of both sexes. That was that we Socialists were atheists, agnostics, irreligious, impious and un-Christian. In every campaign in which I have taken part, this cry has been raised in all its variations. We asked the voters to vote for social righteousness, for industrial and political democracy. We asked them to choose their public servants from among their own class instead of the class that preyed upon them. When we made this appeal the cry was always raised that Socialism would destroy Christianity. About a week before election the clergymen would preach impassioned sermons in which they would call upon the voters to save Christianity from the menace of Socialism. With anguish shaking their voices, and with tears in their eyes, they would declare that, if a Socialist mayor and governor should be elected, the next day after that ungodly man took his seat, the blood-thirsty Socialists would go out and burn all the churches and hang all the preachers, and utterly destroy Christianity.

I could never quite grasp the logic of these timid Christians. According to their faith, Christianity is the divinely ordained institution of an all wise and all powerful God. God is absolute; He speaks to the winds and they are still; He speaks to the tossing storm waves and they are at peace; He holds the destiny of mankind in His grasp; yet, according to the wail of these timid Christians, a handful of wild-eyed, wicked Socialists can destroy God's divinely ordained institution and eliminate God from the universe. I could never quite decide where they thought God would be and what they thought He would be doing while we worked such havoc with His institutions. Perhaps they think He has lost interest in this footstool of His.

Nor was this all the danger that lurked in Socialism, according to the capitalist mouthpiece. There was a danger so frightful and loathsome that it would only be discussed in whispers. It was said that we Socialists were immoral; we did not believe in marriage; we would replace the Christian home with illicit sex relations; we would debase womanhood, degrade motherhood, debauch childhood; we would usher in an orgy of lust and passion, rapine and free love, and people the earth with illegitimate children.

And there were yet other dire dangers lurking in Socialism. I presume that Bowman has not suffered a visitation of Peter Collins or Davy Goldstein.[2] They rarely visit a town of this size. However, you are all quite familiar, through the press, with the particular scarecrow which these gentlemen were wont to dangle from the string of their oratory. These self-appointed protectors of public morals insist that we Socialists teach that the child is the property of the State, and not of its parents. They shudder over the fact that we hold the State superior to the individual, and that the State has a right to demand of the individual any service needed by the State—even to the bearing of children to serve the State on demand. There is no doubt that many a poor mother's heart has been torn as she realized what it means to her to have the State demand her child for its service, and enforce that demand by law and court and military power.

There was one more crime that we were alleged to seek to commit, which makes our black record complete in essentials. That was that Socialists believe in confiscation; that we hold that the property needed by the whole people should belong to the nation. These gentlemen declared that we Socialists maintain that if the private owners of public property will not sell their property at a fair price, and relinquish it willingly, that it should be taken from them by force if necessary.

So, for years, we Socialists went about our work, always having to meet these ignorant prejudices and explain why the capitalistic interests of the country were so eager that these prejudices should be insistently planted and so tenderly cultivated. Over and over again we had to meet

2. Peter Collins and Davy Goldstein were antisocialists who followed socialist speakers in order to offer rebuttal lectures.

the charge that the Socialists would plunge the world into war, destroy civilization, tear down Christianity, degrade womanhood, debase motherhood, people the world with illegitimate children, take the child from the parent and give it to the State, and confiscate the property of the industrious and frugal. I am sure that I have answered every one of these charges at least a thousand times. . . .

The World War Comes

When the first shock and horror [of the war] had passed, men began to reason clearly, and it suddenly dawned on us that, though the Socialists had been charged with seeking to provoke war, they could not be held guilty of causing this war. The only thing that could be said against them was that they had not done their utmost to keep the world out of the war.

I remember that just a few days after the war came I met the clergyman who had been most insistent that I was a dangerous person who would sooner or later bring about a war by preaching Socialism. He was white and quivering with excitement, and he stopped me with an imperative wave of his hand. He said:

"I thought you said there would never be another war. I thought you declared that the Socialists of Germany would not slaughter the Socialists of France. I have heard you insist that Socialists were opposed to war. Why in the name of God did not the Socialists stop this war? . . ."

Not Caused by Socialists

I shall not at this time discuss the real cause of the war; but if we take the newspaper statements that it was forced on the world by the lust for power and greed for territory of certain kings, then there are two kings that must be held responsible. One of them is the deposed Czar Nicholas, and the other Kaiser Wilhelm. And, friends, I want to impress upon your minds this fact—that neither Czar Nicholas nor Kaiser Wilhelm ever carried a red card in the Socialist party. These gentlemen were no friends of ours, I assure you. In the realm of Nicholas, for persons to have a scrap of Socialist literature meant arrest, prison, dungeon, Siberia and death. Why, that long, bitter, ice-bound, blood-stained path to Siberia was paved with the bones of Socialists. In the kingdom of Wilhelm there was nothing feared and hated so much. Long ago, in the lifetime of Wilhelm's father, the iron hand of Bismarck had been used with brutal and tyrannical power to crush out the growing power of Socialism. For more than forty years all the power of autocratic Germany was used to destroy the Socialist party. Its teachers were jailed and thrown into dungeons, its editors were imprisoned and exiled; its publications were barred; but Socialism grew and grew, until it was the only thing on earth that the Kaiser feared with a deadly fear. He said just before the war came that the greatest danger to his empire was the ungodly, unpatriotic Socialist party which was seeking to overthrow the emperor, destroy the empire and build a co-operative republic on the ruins of Imperial Germany. He said that, if nothing else would stop the growth of Socialism a war would be necessary, and he knew that if he could employ the people in waging a defensive warfare they would have no time to study Socialism.

The one big, outstanding, undeniable fact brought home to men's minds is that this war was not caused by Socialists or Socialism. It did not come because of us; it came in spite of us; it did not come because we had taught the gospel of industrial and political democracy, it came because there were so many blind, ignorant fools in the world who would not try to understand these things, or help to make them possible.

Not only did we discover in the first few days of the war that the Socialists were not responsible for it; but, when the black cloud settled down over Europe, there was just one group, one organization, one voice that dared to cry out for peace and sanity and civilization in the midst of madness and slaughter.

In that hour of world tragedy, who was it that took their stand with Moses who said: "Thou shalt not kill!" Was it the Rabbi? Not if he numbered capitalists among his synagogue. Who was it lifted up the cry of the prophets: "Beat your swords into plowshares and your spears into pruning-hooks?" Was it the priests? It was not. Who was it that raised the cry of Jesus: "Love thy neighbor as thyself and do unto others as ye would that they should do unto you?" Was it the preachers? Not so you could notice it! When the war god sounded his brutal blast; when a mad Kaiser and greed-crazed capitalists were willing to plunge the world into war to sate their insane lust for power and hunger for profits, so far as we have any record, priest, rabbi, and preacher forgot their gospels, turned their back upon the teachings of Moses and Jesus and the prophets, and they seem to have with one accord espoused the cause of the god of war. When a mentally diseased and power-mad king sought to make a shambles of the earth, we must admit that church and clergy aided and abetted him. There is no record, so far as we have been able to find, where in any nation at any time the Christian church and the Christian clergy made the slightest protest against the world being blasted by war. So far as we know, almost without an exception, the church became a recruiting office, the clergy became recruiting officers; and, dressed in the vestments of the Church of God, they took their places before the altars and called to the men of Europe: "Shoulder your guns, unlimber your cannons and go forth to wage this holy war. God and the king is calling you, it is your Christian duty to obey." According to the clergy of every nation it was a holy war of defense, and in no country could they discover that it was an unholy war of robbery and plunder. In that dark hour, the only men who dared to proclaim the commands of God, to uphold the message of the prophets and take their stand by the side of Jesus were the ungodly, irreligious, warlike, brutal, un-Christian Socialists.

Socialists Stand True to the Ideals of Jesus

The brutal hand of tyrannical power fell with crushing force upon those men who remained true to the ideals of Jesus and the prophets. In Germany hundreds of Socialists were stood up against the wall and shot for opposing the war. Karl Liebknecht[3] and Rosa Luxemburg were too powerful to shoot, so they were thrown in prison. In France, Jean Jaurès, the greatest orator and the greatest statesman of this generation, was murdered by a hired assassin because the forces that hoped to fatten on war in France dared not let Jean Jaurès live and speak for peace. In every nation in Europe the Socialists were cursed and reviled; they were called seditious, traitorous enemies of their country because they dared to oppose human slaughter as a method of solving the problems of the race.

In the few weeks that marked the beginning of the war, we saw the non-Socialists perform some wonderful mental gymnastics. A week before the war came we were damned for wanting to start a war; a week after it came we were damned for not stopping it; then a week later we were damned just as bitterly for wanting to stop it. It seems that we can't possibly please you non-Socialists, no matter what we do or don't do.

3. Karl Liebknecht (1871–1919) led the antimilitarist proponents of the German Social Democrats and proposed direct appeals to servicemen, for which he served a prison sentence. He was the first Social Democratic member of the Reichstag to vote against war credits in 1914.

Possibly because your mental processes are such that you never quite know just what you do want.

This is a bloody, brutal war. We had no part in bringing it, but it has performed a mighty service for us. Never again will any human being be so stupid or so ignorant as to say that we are the provokers and defenders of war. Why, even Postmaster General Burleson[4] admits that much. We are branded now. Like Cain, we wear a brand upon our brow: the brand of being the followers of the Prince of Peace. We could not lose that brand if we would, and would not if we could. The cry that we would plunge the world into war is stilled forever. Now we can turn our attention to the work of building a world democracy.

Thankful as we are, that we are forever freed from the false charge of seeking to create war, we must count the price that the world has paid for our vindication. No doubt the contemplation of that price is more vivid to me than to many others here. I had the wonderful privilege of visiting Europe just a few months before the war and of learning to know and love many of the men who have died on the battlefield, and many of the women whose lives have been utterly shattered. . . .

Sweet and Sacred Memories

. . . Memories sweep over me, and then—I try to imagine what Europe must be like now. I know that beautiful cities, with their busy marts of trade, are either blackened ruins, or given over wholly to the grim and wasteful trade of making war. I know that the wonderful roads are scarred by cannon and exploding shell, and deeply rutted by the traffic of war. I know that the tenderly tilled fields are ruined wastes that never can be brought back to fertility. I know that the quaint cottages of the workers are shattered; that the castles have been turned into hospitals; that the churches are battered down and the priceless works of art destroyed. I know that the Europe that I loved is but a howling wilderness now, a blackened, war-scarred ruin, an inferno such as Dante never painted.

I know that, in this blood-stained hell which war has made, death has come in most frightful forms to men whom I knew and loved, and worse than death to the women they loved. I know that on the bloody fields of France and Belgium, Serbia and Poland, there is festering in the July heat the bodies of millions of men. I know that, scattered there, are the

4. Albert A. Burleson (1863–1937) was postmaster general from 1913 to 1921. During the war he decided whether a periodical could be circulated through the mails.

bodies of the boys with whom I worked in Dublin; there are the miners who sang for me in Wales; there are the Scottish Highlanders and the London newspaper men. I know also that it is not only the workers who have died, but the men of brains and learning and culture as well. I know that, side by side with the humblest peasant, or the most illiterate serf, there lies the artist and the musician; the doctor and the scientist; the college professor and the inventor. Dead and decaying on these battle-fields are the pick and flower of modern civilization. In the masses of corrupting human flesh there lies all that ten thousand years of civiliza-tion, of science, of knowledge, of culture, and all that two thousand years of Christianity could do for the human race.

I know also that it is not alone the achievements of the past that decay there, but the hopes of the future as well. When I picture the bearded face of a man, swollen and bloated in the July heat, it is not only the man I see, but the women he left behind. Oh! I see his wife the victim of invading soldiers, his children starved and maimed and mutilated; and I wonder what hope the future holds for that man's wife and chil-dren? . . .

I can sense the agony and hopelessness and despair of the mother whose boy lies dead on the battlefield, for I am a mother and I have sons. True, none of my sons are old enough to be drawn into this war, and I pray God that, long before they are old enough to be sent to the battle-field, the workers of the world shall have learned their bitter lesson. I hope that they will have thrown territory-mad kings and profit-mad capi-talists into the scrapheap of discarded things, and established a social and economic system to which wars will never come. . . .

The Price of Our Vindication

Heavy as are our hearts, sick as we are with the appalling price that mankind has paid and will pay for the vindication of the Socialist position, we do find some comfort in the fact that the lies and the vilifications of the capitalist-controlled means of public expression are being thrown back into their teeth with the vengeance of outraged justice. And we do know that the price of this war will not be paid in vain, that the world purified by the flames of war must be a cleaner world than existed before the test of fire.

Our traducers have declared that we would destroy civilization, tear down constitutions, abolish courts and laws, prostitute ethics and morals, and bring anarchy and chaos to the world. Socialism never came, but the world-war did come, and remember—we did not bring it. Strange to say, when that war came all of these things happened. Civilization was destroyed wherever battles raged. The first thing to go down under the shock of war was international law. It was declared a "scrap of paper" by the Kaiser who shouts so loudly that he and God are running this war and whose position is so ably supported by the church and clergy of his empire. The sacredness of treaties was found to be only as sacred as the corrupt heart of a king and the greed for profits of the capitalists of his kingdom.

It has long been known that democracies are poor war makers, and that just as soon as war comes to any nation, democracy must be laid on the shelf and autocracy takes its place. Constitutions, civil laws, individual rights, justice and humanity are also clogs of war-making powers, and must be placed in cold storage until the war is done, in order that the war makers may have the power to wage a successful war.

War can have but one aim and that is victory. Victory can be achieved under the operation of but one law and that is the law of military necessity. Military necessity does not concern itself with constitutional or civil laws, individual rights or individual wishes. All things must of necessity become secondary to the laws of military necessity when for any reason a war for victory becomes imperative.

We find that grim necessity turns our standards of ethics and morals all topsy-turvy also. In Europe one month before the war came, if a man had plunged a bit of steel into the heart of another man (citizen of another nation or not), that man would have been a murderer. He would have been convicted of a capital crime; he would have been antisocial, unethical, immoral and un-Christian. The state would have sentenced him to the hangman's noose, and public opinion would have consigned his soul to hell. One week after an insane Kaiser had loosed the dogs of war on Europe and had been supported in the act by the clergy and the capitalists of his nation, if then thousands of men took pieces of steel and thrust them into as many hearts as they could reach, why the men who did the thrusting were noble heroes, the government decorated them with the iron cross if they lived, and the priest was quite sure that if they died they went to Heaven on a through ticket and with a pass that St. Peter must honor, no matter what their lives had been.

Just as strangely do our concepts of morality as related to our sex relations change overnight when war comes. In Europe before the war if a woman loved a man so completely that she was willing to give herself without marriage, the woman was a harlot, she was a scarlet woman, and a thing to be spat upon and spurned. If perchance a child should result, it was an ill-begotten, illegitimate child. The mother was an outcast, and the child was cursed by God and man because of the mother's sin. Then war came, and millions of men were dying. The birthrate was falling far behind the deathrate; there was great need of babies to replace the waste of war. Then, if a woman gave herself to a man that he might "breed before he died," she was not a harlot or a scarlet woman, she was a perfectly honorable heroine and her child was a patriotic "war baby."

We know now that when war came civilization was beaten down into the blood-stained mire. We know now beyond any doubt that war and civilization cannot both occupy the same battlefield at the same time, that when battles rage civilization flees away to await the dawn of peace. . . .

Outrage Ran Riot

I wonder how many of you men in my audience ever went about saying that Socialism would degrade womanhood, debase motherhood, debauch childhood and people the world with illegitimate children? If any of you did say these things your words have come home to you with brutal, chilling force. For our souls sicken when we think of how these things have come to pass. Never in all the history of the human race, not even among our cave dwelling ancestors or the Indians who lived on these plains, has womanhood been so degraded, and motherhood so debased as in the most civilized and cultured countries of Europe. No language can tell the tale; no brain can grasp the horrors and no soul can sense the degradation that has come to the women of war scarred Europe. Lust and rapine and outrage ran riot. The women have not only been forced to endure the horrors of unleashed passion; of blood drunken lust; of the unholy embrace of enemies; they have not only been forced to pay the price of millions of men being forced to live unnatural lives; but they have had a greater degradation forced upon them by state and clergy.

When the governments of Europe, and the clergy of Europe demanded of the women that they give themselves in marriage, or out, in

order that men might "breed before they die," that was not the crime of maddened passion, it was the cold-blooded crime of brutal selfishness, and by that crime the women of Europe were reduced to the status of breeding animals on a stock farm.

You sneered at us and said that Socialism would people the world with illegitimate children. Socialism never came, but the war did, and our faces scorch with shame when we think of the illegitimate children of the war zone. In Europe there are thousands of babies, and thousands more will be. These are illegitimate children; they are ill-begotten children; they are children whose fathers they will never know; whose fathers' language they will never speak. These children are not the fruits of marriage; they are not the flowers of love; they were not begotten in wedlock and decency. These are the children of invasion and rapine and outrage. They were conceived in lust, nurtured in hate, born to poverty and pestilence and famine. All of you know something of the laws governing the coming of a human life, and you know that children so conceived and so nurtured and so born cannot be normal human beings. I have talked with physicians who have been in the war zone, and they tell me that the very sight of these children is enough to turn the soul sick with horror. They are deaf, dumb, blind, idiot, imbecile and deformed monstrosities that can be nothing but a burden to themselves and a curse to the race. And remember, you dear old, rock-ribbed, hide-bound, moss-backed democrats, these are not Socialist babies—they are war babies.

The State Has a Right to Your Service

Again, do remember, you perfectly respectable, smug, self-righteous gentlemen, you men who sit about on dry-goods boxes and grocery store counters, do you remember the dire threats you used to make of what an awful fate would befall "them durned Socialists." You were wont to get a stick and a jack-knife and a generous chew of tobacco and expound thusly:

"Ya, them durned Socialists, they think that our children ort to belong to the government, by Jimminey! They say that the government has got a right to take our children away from us and make 'em serve the state, if the state needs 'em and we ain't got a right to say a word. But, by cracky! if any low-down Socialist official ever tries to come inside my door and take one of my boys away from me, I'll fill his dirty hide so full of buckshot that it won't hold corn shucks."

Well, my dearly beloved, Socialism never arrived. We never elected a President and only achieved one lone, lorn congressman, but strange to say, on the fifth day of June,[5] your Democrats who voted for Wilson because "he kept us out of war,"[6] suddenly awakened to the fact that your sons did not belong to you. You also discovered that they did not belong to themselves; they were the actual, physical property of the United States, and its Government had a perfect right, and exercised that right, to come into your home and take your sons and demand their service, even to the giving of their lives. Not only did the Government exercise that right, but enacted stringent laws, punishing with the utmost severity any one who made the slightest protest against it.

If your wife, the woman who gave life to that boy, so much as suggested that before the state should have the right to demand the life of her son, she at least should be given a vote in the government, if your wife should make this statement and a Federal officer should overhear her, legal authorities tell us that she can be arrested, convicted of a crime, sent to prison, dressed in stripes, forced to do the most menial and degrading labor for a long term of years.

This is not the time or place to argue the question of whether the conscription law is right or wrong, moral or immoral, constitutional or unconstitutional. I am not making any argument whatever, I am just telling you what happened to you, that is all. Of course, I want to impress upon your mind at this time the fact that this principle was not enunciated and this law was not enacted or enforced by a Socialist administration, but a Democratic administration.

When we have reached this point in the survey of the world war and its effects on mankind, we are forced to realize that it has ceased to be a European war and has become an American war as well.

It is but natural, in a great world convulsion which shattered the very

5. June 5, 1917, was declared national Conscription Day. The Selective Service Act (May 18, 1917) applied to all male citizens between the ages of twenty-one and thirty-one, with exemptions for those with dependents, essential occupations, or certain religious beliefs. Later, the age limits were eighteen to forty-five.

6. This slogan was utilized in Wilson's campaign for reelection in 1916. The original statement, "we didn't go to war," was made by Martin H. Glynn of New York, the Democratic convention's keynote speaker. The change in wording, and the implied promise for the future, appeared in the platform.

foundation of our lives, that there should be grave differences of opinion and that prejudices and passion should run rampant. In a time like this it is very hard, indeed, for any one to keep a firm hold upon sanity and retain the ability to think clearly and to a purpose, without bitterness or bias.

I don't think for a moment that I am superhuman, but I do earnestly try to keep my poise and balance. We have been told that the time for reason and consideration is past, and that we must perforce shut our eyes, stop the processes of our brains, and let our divinely chosen politicians and editors do all our thinking and reasoning for us. The time may come in this country when we will be forced to turn the wheels of progress backward, and enthrone again the old, discarded theory of the "divine right" of rulers to act and think for us, but at this time I cannot feel that it is either wise or necessary. I think if ever there was a time that demanded that we all think for ourselves, it is now.

I feel that it is the very highest and most intelligent sort of patriotism for the people of this country and of all countries to seek with intense earnestness the cause of this war. It is only in knowing the cause, in analyzing and scrutinizing the hidden forces that direct nations in time of war, that we can hope to make this the last of wars.

There is no man or woman, with an atom of reason or logic or common sense, who believes that this war was brought about merely by the inflated ego of a half-insane Kaiser, or the maudlin weakness of a neurotic Czar. Not that Kaiser and Czar are not mad enough to provoke a war, but we all know that no Kaiser or Czar has the power in modern society to cause or to wage a war. War in these modern times is not the mere waving of plumes, brandishing of swords and sounding of trumpets. War is a highly organized, and very businesslike bit of business that can be carried on only by the business forces of a country. Before a war can be waged, the bankers must provide the money for war bonds; the manufacturers must provide the munitions of war, and the business men must provide the business management for this highly organized business venture. Bankers and manufacturers and business men are hard-headed, far-sighted, keen-minded men, and, before they give the necessary sanction to a war, it is evident that they must see very clearly just what profits they can hope to secure.

It seems quite evident to me that, in consideration of this war, we can look upon the Kaiser and the Czar principally as the spectacular figureheads who furnish the theatricals while the business men furnish the money and the brains with which to wage the war. A family squabble between Cousin Nickie and Cousin Willie is hardly sufficient to explain the world tragedy.

The Time to Discuss Causes

There must be some mighty fundamental, economic, financial cause behind the quarrel of Kaiser and Czar to induce the business men to take the mighty risks that a war entails. This economic cause is not hard to discover. The capitalist and trading interests of the European nations have been rapidly expanding for several decades. The traders of each nation have exhausted the trade possibilities of their own land, and have been forced to reach out for the trade of weaker and less developed nations. They have also developed a ravenous hunger for colonies in out-of-the-way places of the earth. This hunger was no doubt whetted by the gratifying profits made by King Leopold of Belgium in the Congo. It is but the natural result of trade expansion, that the traders of the different nations should have encroached upon each other's trade territory. It is perfectly natural that they should battle for each other's trade, and fight tooth and nail to grasp each other's profits. In the battle for trade and profits, wars and armies have always played an important part. The musket has always followed the drummer's grip, and the warship the trader's sloop. When that titanic struggle of the European trades for world commerce had reached its apex, it was but natural that a war of guns and cannons should follow the war of trade. "Cannons are the last argument of kings," you know—political kings or industrial kings. So, in the fullness of time, the ego-mad kings and the profit-hungry traders joined in an unholy league and the world war was the result.

When it comes to a discussion of our part in the war, human nature is just the same on one side of the ocean as on the other; and it seems logical that the same conditions must exist. We have been fortunate enough to stay out of the war for almost three years; we elected our president on the slogan—"he kept us out of war." It is evident by this that the hearts of the people are against war and for peace, yet we are at war.

Our politicians and editors tell us that we must not reason, or think, or discuss, but this is not possible. No human being can stop the processes of mind and live; and we must think, and must reason, and must grope through the darkness that encompasses us, for that is the law of life.

Thrice armed is that man or nation whose cause is just, and if this war is a just war there is no surer method of securing the solid, self-sacrificing, loyal support of every man and woman than by an intelligent discussion which will satisfy our reason. We are asked to reverse every one of our well loved principles of Americanism, and that cannot be done without thought and study and a sure sense of the necessity for such reversal.

We women feel that, particularly, we have the right to weigh and consider, discuss and understand, for we are called upon to make the supreme sacrifice. It is not enough for us to be told by a lot of politicians that they will do our thinking for us. We know to our sorrow that the politicians have told us many things that were not true. They have told us that we did not need the vote, because they, out of the greatness of their hearts and the ponderosity of their wisdom, would care for our interests, and we know that they have often betrayed us.

They tell us that the war in which we are engaged is a war for humanity and democracy. God knows, we hope this is true. Humanity has suffered long and bitterly enough that some great power should become her knight. Democracy is a principle big enough and noble enough to live for; to fight for; to die for. Real democracy is all that we women have ever desired when we demanded the vote. But we cannot deny that we women could give more loyal and more whole-hearted support to a war for democracy in Germany, if we had a little of it at home.

We have been told that this war has been entered into with no consideration for the profits of the capitalist class. If this is true then the capitalist class must be made up of a choice lot of doddering idiots. The whole war itself is the supreme struggle of the capitalist class to decide which group of capitalists shall rule the world markets. When the German U-boats began to sink the ocean liners laden with food and munitions of war, they struck a death blow at the very heart and soul of the capitalist system—the right to trade whenever profits can be made. If that right of free and unrestricted trade can be denied, the whole fabric of capitalism crumbles like a house of sand. The man who believes that capitalism is right and just, and the only system under which the race can exist, would be a fool if he did not demand that war at any cost of life and blood should be invoked to protect the fabric of civilization.

Of course, I don't believe that capitalism is either right or just, or that it is the only system under which the race can survive; so the only quarrel between the capitalists of this country and your humble servant is not whether this war shall protect the capitalist system but whether the capitalist system should be protected. If the capitalist system is right, then the war is right; and on that basis I am sure we can find agreement. We have been told that nothing but service to humanity is involved in this war. Once again I say that, if by humanity you mean the humanity of the capitalist system, again we agree that war is the only possibility. If you mean by humanity, the lives and happiness and welfare of the whole human race, then we feel that there is room for discussion. You know we women have long, long memories—you men have not. You never remember longer than the day before yesterday. That is the reason why the corrupt politicians fool you so easily. When we think of humanity, we don't think of barter and trade, ocean lines, and traffic in munitions. We think of living, breathing, suffering human beings.

Women Have Long Memories

We women can't forget the invasion of Belgium; the sinking of the Lusitania;[7] the desolation of France and Serbia and Poland; or the crushing of the Irish republic; and we do feel that if justice and right had a sacred right to demand our service, that they called long and hopelessly for three bitter years.

I remember that we Socialists protested against these horrors, and that we were sharply rebuked. I was billed to speak at a meeting to protest against the invasion of Belgium and memorial meetings for Jim Connolly who was so wantonly murdered. I was requested by Government Officials not to speak at these meetings because they said to do so would be unneutral. I remember that, as I traveled, I found over every postoffice window and on every bank tellers' counter a placard that said: "We must be neutral in word and thought," and it was signed—Woodrow Wilson.

You say: "Oh, yes! We know; but President Wilson is a patient man—patient and long suffering."

I answer: "Yes, I know he is patient. But sometimes I have wondered

7. The *Lusitania*, a large Cunard liner, was sunk without warning by a German submarine off the coast of Ireland on May 7, 1915; 1,959 persons were on board, of whom 1,198 died, including 128 Americans. The ship carried thousands of cases of small-arms ammunition and shrapnel. Intense indignation in the American press followed the sinking.

if a little less patience would not have better protected the working class. I remember that when women were brutally murdered at Ludlow; I remember that when more than fifty children were murdered by hired thugs of the copper trust in Calumet; I remember that when the coal miners were shot down in West Virginia and Arkansas; I remember that when the employees of the Standard Oil Co. were killed in cold blood at Bayonne, that we workers of the country appealed to President Wilson for protection for the lives of these American citizens, and we found that he was patient and long suffering with the outrages of the capitalist class. I cannot help but wonder if a righteous anger in these cases would not have been more noble than patience."

We know from the study of all past history that the flag, and the army, and the navy have always followed bonds and investments; and we know that it is an inevitable part of the capitalist system that the army and the navy should follow the investment of more than four billion by the house of Morgan in British war bonds. That is why we felt a throb of fear when that investment was made.

And now, friends, since we must face the tragedy and the misery and the soul-searching questions that must come to us, I am glad that I can close with a great message of hope and cheer. Under all the horror of this war there is a divine comedy. It is this—the world has been plunged into this bloody abyss, not by Socialism, but for a lack of it. We Socialists have always opposed war and wanted to settle the problems of the race by ballots instead of bullets; but, nevertheless, this war is bringing Socialism a hundred times more quickly and decisively than we ever hoped to bring it by education. This war has proven that individualism, run amuck, can plunge a world into war, but only intelligently applied Socialism can save the race from suicide.

The Nations Turn to Socialism

Every nation that has entered this war has been compelled to junk the capitalist system and make use of at least a modified form of Socialism. This has been true in Germany and France and England, and it is rapidly coming to pass in the United States.

Germany had more State Socialism[8] than any other country in the

8. State socialism is the ownership or operation of important industries by a government that is not controlled by the masses of its people. This was, in effect, the wartime policy of the U.S. government and its allies, for the sake of efficiency.

world, and it was in this that her efficient preparedness lay. So Germany
got into the war in about fifteen minutes after war was declared. France
had less State Socialism than Germany, but vastly more than Great Britain; and France got into the war in about fifteen days. Great Britain was
the last stronghold of individualism. She has eyes in the back of her head,
drew her inspirations from graveyards, and took her political economy
from John Stuart Mill. Britannia did not bother with such new-fangled
notions as State Socialism; so, when the war came, she was frightfully
handicapped. It was really about fifteen months before she got into the
war with any degree of efficiency. This was not because her sons were
not brave or her statesmen loyal, but because she had not machinery
with which to make war.

The first thing that broke down in Great Britain was the railroad system; and she was compelled to take over the railroads and put them
under government control before she could mobilize her troops.

The next thing that broke down under the strain of war was the coal
production. It was a strike of the Welsh miners, led by Bob Smilie,[9] that
forced Great Britain to take over the coal supply and make it possible for
the war to be carried on. This strike, and the government control of the
coal supply, teach a very necessary lesson which this country will be
forced to learn before we can meet the demands of a successfully managed war. When the war came the private owners of the coal mines (who
were, of course, all good patriots) raised the price of coal to the government from about two dollars and fifty cents a ton, to five dollars. And at
this price it was impossible for the operators to supply sufficient coal and
keep the men at work. Finally, labor unrest became so acute that the
miners went on a strike, and their demand was not for more pay or
shorter hours, but for government control of the coal industry. This was
finally agreed upon by the government; and, when the private coal operator was displaced by the government co-operator, the hours of labor
for the men were reduced, wages were substantially increased, production almost doubled, and the price of coal was reduced.

The food situation was the same. Just as soon as war was declared,
the profiteers hoarded the food, raised the prices, and starved the
people. In those first dark days of the war, when the British army was

9. Robert Smillie (1857–1940) led the Miners' Federation and was one of the Scottish
founders of Britain's Independent Labour party.

suffering such heart-breaking reverses, we know now that they failed not because they were bad soldiers, but because they had no ammunition with which to wage the battle. While the soldiers died in the trenches for lack of ammunition, the ammunition makers dropped in front of their benches in the exhaustion of starvation. Their wages could not reach the extortionate prices of food. While the soldiers died and the ammunition makers starved, the warehouses of Great Britain were crammed to bursting with the food that the profiteers had hoarded and were holding for blood-wet profits. When the condition became unbearable, Great Britain was forced to turn to the Socialists for a remedy. The government took over the food supply, eliminated the profiteers, and set just prices for food as well as searched the earth for food supplies.

The results were amusing to us Americans, if we have any sense of humor. For instance, last winter in St. Louis potatoes reached the amazing price of four dollars a bushel. I suppose it is unnecessary to tell you that the little O'Hares did not have potatoes in their Irish stew—not at four dollars a bushel. When I was at my wits ends to know what to give the children to eat, our divinely inspired editors told us to eat rice. Now, just imagine telling any one by the name of O'Hare to eat rice instead of potatoes! But we have to have something to eat, and I went shopping for rice. I found that it was twelve cents a pound. At the very time that we were paying four dollars a bushel for potatoes in St. Louis, the British food commission came over here, bought potatoes by the train load, shipped them to London, and sold them for one dollar and seventy-five cents a bushel. While we paid twelve cents for rice grown in Texas, the British food commission bought that rice, shipped it across five thousand miles of submarine-infested sea, and sold it for four cents a pound. We paid ten cents a pound for sugar; and sugar grown in the same beetfield was shipped to London and sold for five.

War Brings Socialism

We are in the war now, and every single step we take towards winning the war is a mighty step towards Socialism. We did not want Socialism to come by war, but "God moves in a mysterious way His wonders to perform" and it may be that "He doeth all things well." Does it not seem strange that you men would not listen to us; that you would not reason or think or educate yourselves; that you rejected Socialism when we offered it to you in peace, by means of the ballot; and that now you are having it thrust into you on the end of a bayonet? Well, if it suits you better that way, we are not to blame.

They have told you that we Socialists are unpatriotic, seditious and treasonable. I will simply leave you to judge from what I have said whether you think this true or not.

They have told you that we were hindering the President in waging a successful war. That is not true. We hoped that Socialism would come without war. It did not, but it is coming just the same. A successfully waged war will mean a war waged by Socialist methods, and certainly that means success for us. If you are willing to pay the price of a world war for Socialism, we must submit.

They tell you that we are attempting to hinder the draft. That is not true. Once again I say that it would not have been our method, but the draft is forcing on every human being, in the most striking manner, the fact that the State is superior to the individual. Of course, since the conscription of life had been demanded, we are going to demand the conscription of wealth. I am free to confess that we don't relish the idea of having a small group of men pass on the matter of life and death for millions of other men, particularly when the men who do the passing also pass up the fighting, because they are either too old, or too fat, or too busy to go to war.

They tell you that we are opposing enlistment. This is not true. Please understand me now and do not misquote what I say. If any young man feels that it is his duty to enlist, then with all my heart I say—"Go and God bless you. Your blood may enrich the battlefields of France, but that may be for the best."

There is just one other point that I want to touch upon, then [I] shall have finished this long lecture. They told you that Socialists would bring confiscation. Socialism never came, but confiscation is here in full force. The mighty mountain of war debts that have been and will be piled up by this war, can be paid only by confiscation. It will mean the confiscation of the workers' very bread and butter, but it will also mean the confiscation of the profiteers' unholy war profits. They may escape for a time, but it must come eventually.

When we used to suggest that the Government should buy the railroads, you would shout: "Ya, but where are you going to get the money?"

Gentlemen, the price of this war would buy the railroads and almost everything else in sight; and the Government will get the money by frying it out of your dear old Democratic skins. Certainly we Socialists can smile as the aroma of the frying is wafted to our noses.

The United States of the World

I shall close now, Comrades, and I wish to leave this thought with you. Dark as are the days, heavy as are our hearts, sick as are our souls, we are not hopeless. We know that out of this war must come peace; let us hope it will be an everlasting peace. We know that out of this struggle will come strength; let us hope it will be righteous strength. We know that out of this clash of the capitalist struggle will come co-operation; let us hope it will reach around the earth until every land is welded into the great United States of the World.

I have finished now, Comrades, and the last message that I want to leave with you, the last prayer of my heart, is that you will think and reason and seek diligently for light that you may know that only through intelligence, and co-operation, and brotherhood, and faith, and loyalty to God, and country, and fellowman, can salvation come for this war-sick world.

Our Martyred Comrade

Perhaps in all the world there is not a man whose heart ached so bitterly because of war, race prejudice and inharmony as Jean Léon Jaurès. Peace between nations was his passion and harmony in the world wide Socialist movement his religion. This man was the first martyr of peace to fall in the hell of war that rages in Europe today.

Jean Jaurès was all that power maddened monarchs and gold lusting capitalists hate. He was first of all a man, who stood upright in the might of his manhood and feared nothing in the universe but the ignorance of his fellow workers. He was a student, a thinker, a philosopher, a master of oratory and the ablest parliamentarian of his day. He hated war, he

"Our Martyred Comrade" was first published in *National Rip-Saw* (September, 1914), 10–11.

loved his fellowmen and he used all his powers of brain and soul to educate and organize the workers of the world against war. How natural then
that king, priest and capitalist should hate and fear him, and that when
ready to let loose Hell in Europe, that first an assassin should strike down
the one man who was bigger and more powerful than all the kings,
priests, and emperors of earth.

I had one week of close association with Jean Jaurès at the International Socialist Bureau meeting in London in 1913, and to me it will
always be one of the big events of my life. To me the memory will always
come of the bigness, the sweetness and the power of the man.

Always for peace and concentration of the power of the workers,
Jaurès had been active in the work of harmonizing the factions of the
British Socialist movement, and the first meeting of the International
Bureau was given to that problem. I entered Clifford's Inn Hall, London,
just as the roll call of nations was taking place, and when I rose to answer
for the United States, a burst of applause startled me until I forgot everything I wanted to say and stood there blushing like a schoolgirl. It was
the first time in the history of the International Socialist Bureau that a
woman had ever come to represent a nation and the Comrades seemed
to feel that it marked an epoch in the solidarity of sexes as well as class.
Painfully embarrassed and desperately trying to gather my scattered wits
I stood there waiting until the noise subsided. Suddenly I saw a little old
man with shaggy white hair and beetling brows step towards me. His
eyes were tender and smiling and grasping both my hands he whispered,
"Bravo, Comrade, take courage; with all our hearts we welcome you
here. America is a great nation and it is a splendid token of her greatness
that she should send one of her daughters to council with us." Straightway my embarrassment was gone and I responded to the words of welcome extended me. The old man was Jean Jaurès, tender and gentle
enough to rescue a woman from stage fright, strong enough to shake
every throne in Europe. . . .

In accordance with the instructions from the National Committee of
the American section I presented the question of "sabotage and direct
action" for the agenda of the next International Congress. With a look
that I can never forget Comrade Jaurès turned to me and cried, "My
God! Comrade, don't we have enough of war and hate thrust on us by
the capitalist class without hunting an opportunity to fight in our own

ranks? If we would successfully fight the enemy we must have peace at home."

Jaurès loathed race prejudice as he did anything that made artificial divisions among the working class. At a luncheon given to the members of the International Bureau he gazed about the table and turning to me said: "Look, Comrade, here we sit, men and women of many tongues and countries, we are all born in the same way, we live and labor, love and die just alike; for what should we make war and kill each other."

Of never failing interest to Jaurès was the American Socialist movement and the great Socialist encampments of our farmers. This method of propaganda was a theme on which he never tired of talking. His love for peace extended to peace among the different economic groups and he gloried in the fact that in America we could make the farmer and the wage worker both understand that they were members of the same exploited class.

Whenever there was a little leisure time Comrade Jaurès would seek me out and, with Paul Longuet to interpret when we became mired in a language bog, he would say, "Now, Comrade O'Hare, tell us more of your farmer encampments." As I talked of the work we are doing his eyes would glow with animation, the shaggy gray head would nod and now and then he would pound the table until the dishes rattled and cry, "Bravo! You have reached the soul of things." His joy was so infectious that the stolid English waiters hovered about our table and smiled in sympathy.

The last words Comrade Jaurès spoke to me expressed the wish that he might come to America in 1916 and visit our farmer encampments, and he looked forward to it as the most wonderful holiday of his life. It was his dream that he could secure some of the speakers and managers who had made the encampments so successful to return to France with him and help to arrange encampments among the farmers in Southern France. As he stated it, "We will teach the French farmer also to sing and dance and laugh while he gets his economic education. The joy of life and economic education shall go hand in hand; what a glorious dream! . . ."

Jean Jaurès sleeps that sleep that no cannon's roar can disturb; the earth he loved is soaked with human blood; the working class for whom he gave his life writhes in the cursed hell of war, but Jaurès lived and taught not in vain. For a little time power-mad monarchs and gold-crazed capitalists may make Europe a shambles, but sooner or later the soul of the working class will revolt at the stench of blood and they shall beat their swords into pruning hooks and their lances into plow shares and forever overthrow the powers that wage war. Out of the soil, wet with human blood, will spring the corn for man's bread and the grapes for their vintage. King and monarch shall disappear, kingdoms will fall and the United States of Europe will take their place—a Democracy owned, controlled and administered by a united working class. The soul of Jaurès will dominate that Risen Europe even though the body sleeps. Monarchs and exploiters will find the Jaurès, dead by an assassin's hand, a million times more alive and powerful than the Jaurès in the flesh.

LONG LIVE THE SPIRIT OF JEAN LÉON JAURÈS, THE INCARNATION OF PEACE AND BROTHERHOOD, AND THE INTERNATIONAL RACE OF WORK-ERS!

FAREWELL BELOVED COMRADE OF THE SOCIAL REVOLUTION!

Shall Red Hell Rage?

Shall the Red Hell of War rage in the United States; shall murder become the business of our nation; shall our sons become cannon meat?

At last the American nation stands face to face with these grim, grisly, ghastly questions. They have ceased to be academic problems for scholarly discussion and have become living, throbbing, personal questions to each human heart. For almost a year we Americans from our smug position of fancied security have discussed the European war in the most approved academic manner. Hysterical women have frantically stitched botched nightshirts and knitted lumpy socks while professional philanthropists gathered up our loose change and old clothes and shipped them to Europe, for War Relief. We have prayed, philosophized, moralized and shed crocodile tears over the European War, but it was still the European War, three thousand miles away, and not a vital life-and-death problem to us American citizens.

But every day that passes brings the Red Hell just a wee bit nearer

"Shall Red Hell Rage?" was first published in *National Rip-Saw* (June, 1915), 6–7.

us; nearer our firesides, our sons, our daughters and our means of life. Already we can see the lurid flames of War lighting our horizon, our souls are beginning to writhe under its scorching menace and in imagination our nostrils can detect the smell of fresh blood and rotting corpses.

War is striding in seven-league boots across the Atlantic and none of us know just how near it may be. By day and by night our nerves are strained to the snapping point listening for the strident cry of the newsboys shouting, "Extra! War Declared on Germany!" That cry may not come today, it may not come next week, but so sure as the capitalist class rules and the working class slumbers in ignorance and stupidity, it will come and we shall face not the European War, but the World War, including America.

How do I know that the Red Hell is drawing closer and that the strident voice of the War god shall wake us from our dreams of fancied security? I know because for months I have been watching the great human drama unfold upon the world stage and history has taught me that with a given cause there must always be a given result.

War rages in Europe today because the bankers, armament makers and powerful group of capitalists know that when the world is glutted with unsold goods and the highways are filled with unemployed men, war and destruction becomes a far more profitable game than peace and production. But modern warfare is so destructive that it makes short work of gutting a nation or continent. In nine short months the capitalist butchers have drunk the blood and picked the bones of Europe and in the blood soaked charnel house of that continent there is little left for their unglutted appetites.

The best men of all the European nations have been killed and those left are scarcely worth wasting bullets on and will be needed as seed by which to sow in the wombs of the European women the crop of workers needed in the future. The bankers of Europe are loaded up to capacity with war loans; the food supplies are so nearly exhausted that there are but small profits possible for the speculators; the armament manufacturers must have access to a new supply of raw material and the war game in Europe has reached a point where it offers no worthwhile inducements to capitalists of the front rank. It is a land now fit only for vultures and scavengers. Europe has been gutted, skinned and picked to the last bone, but America is fat and juicy for the slaughter.

Here in the United States there are billions of dollars waiting for profitable investment, three million jobless men just ripe for cannon meat. We have endless food supplies for profitable manipulation by speculators and a world of raw material for making arms and ammunition and, most important of all, a completely cowed, stupid, unorganized working class waiting like patient sheep to be led to the slaughter. It is unthinkable that the great captains of finance will overlook this golden opportunity to ravish America as they have ravished Europe and our dance with the Red Hell is just about due.

The stage has long been set; the hysterical frothings of loud mouthed jingoes and the rabid howlings of the harlot press was the overture, the sinking of the Lusitania the curtain call. Kaiser Wilhelm the villain is called to account by Woodrow Wilson the hero, and hurrah! The greatest tragedy-drama of the ages is off with a swing and roar! Let cannons roar; swing wide the gates of hell, kill and destroy; murder and ravish; it's all for the glory of God, the defense of humanity, the honor of our nation, the reverence we owe our flag and the expression of our love for human kind.

"But," you cry, "Kaiser Wilhelm did sink a passenger ship and murder in cold blood innocent men, women and children. One hundred and thirty-seven were American citizens; honor demands that we retaliate and we have a moral right to punish him for his brutality."

O certainly! I know all that. The capitalist interests that pulls the strings that makes the puppets Wilhelm and Woodrow dance, did build, equip and send forth on its mission of death the submarine that sent the Lusitania to the bottom of the sea, but what of that? They have been building submarines, battleships, aeroplanes and a thousand other machines of death, and their only mission has ever been the mission of slaughter. Why get finicky now over the faithfully executed work of one machine of death when we have gloated over the efficiency of the thousands we have made? If machines of slaughter are not to be used to kill human beings, why expend millions of dollars making them?

"But a thousand innocent men, women and children were killed and that was a damnable crime," you say.

Certainly! We know it was a damnable crime, but is not the killing by wholesale of human beings always a damnable crime? The same capitalist interests that built the submarine and sent it forth to kill have slain or wounded ten thousand times a thousand human beings in the European war up to date; these same capitalist interests murder in times of peace, here in the United States every year in our industries and slums a hundred times a thousand human beings and you never turn a hair. If any ungodly socialist calls attention to this fact the world piously exclaims, "God wills it so. The Lord hath given, the Lord hath taken away, blessed be the name of the Lord."

"But the murder of the passengers on the Lusitania was so brutal, so uncalled for and contrary to the laws of nature and of nations," you insist.

Sure! I know it. But Rockefeller, Morgan and Long have instigated the murder of hundreds of helpless human beings right here in the United States in times of peace, not only on the bleak hillside at Ludlow but in the valleys of West Virginia, the tamarack swamps of North Michigan and in the pine woods of Dixie. These American citizens were murdered more brutally and with far more cold blooded cruelty, yet Woodrow-the-Wise never burned any midnight oil inditing any notes to these transgressors of human and national laws insisting that they must cease murdering American citizens.

If I am not misinformed it is only a little more than a year ago when Woodrow-the-Wise took a hand in the killing game (not on his own account but on orders from Rockefeller, Morgan, Hearst and Pearson[10]), President Huerta of Mexico objected to turning his nation over body and soul to these eminent gentlemen as Woodrow-the-Wise had so thoughtfully turned over the United States. President Huerta's method of expressing his unwillingness to meet the modest request of these gentlemen was by declaring that he would only shoot six times at our flag. Woodrow-the-Wise insisted on twenty-one shots and Huerta stood pat. Then Woodrow-the-Wise sent a few gunboats and a lot of young boys down to Vera Cruz[11] to demand the twenty-one shots and likewise the Mexican nation for his masters. Huerta didn't shoot, neither did he give possession of his nation, but nineteen American marines were killed and something more than two hundred Mexicans (a number reported to have been school children on their way home from school) suffered the same fate. The American marines, the school children and Mexican citizens

10. *Pearson's* was the last major muckraking magazine, adopting that policy only in 1912 under the guidance of Arthur West Little. Among the contributors were such socialist journalists as Charles Edward Russell and Allan L. Benson.

11. Victoriano Huerta (1854–1916), insurgent president of Mexico, arrested several U.S. Marines in April, 1914, for trespassing. President Wilson dispatched a fleet to Veracruz and a brief U.S. occupation ensued, apparently in an effort to eliminate Huerta.

are just as dead as are the dead millionaires now feeding the fishes off the coast of Ireland.

But why continue? Great God! The story of innocent men, women and children murdered by the insane greed of the capitalist interests that would open the gates of hell and toss us into the pit, is so long, so brutal, so cursed that I can not bring myself to write of it. And now fools, knaves, cowards and mental prostitutes are clamoring that we mothers of America shall sing, "Praise God From Whom All Blessings Flow," while our nation is ravished and our sons are murdered in the interests of the blood-soaked money changers of New York, Berlin, Paris and London.

To me a human life is a human life, one as sacred as another, and the taking of a human life is murder whether done on the battlefield, on the high seas or in a labor strike. When Rockefeller has been indicted for the murder of the victims of Ludlow; when Woodrow Wilson and his advisors have been brought to the bar of Justice for the deaths of the American marines, the Mexican school children and the Mexican citizens who were murdered in Vera Cruz; when the hundreds of industrial masters have been brought to trial for the murder of the hundreds of thousands of the victims of industry, then and not until then have we a moral right to demand a reckoning from poor puppet Wilhelm.

I know that when the blood-drunken, greed-crazed capitalist masters are ready they will turn the hell of War loose on us. If only the workers would have listened to the voice of reason and intelligence instead of ever harking back to prejudice and ignorance, we Americans might have been strong enough to have stopped the Red Hell on its way to our firesides, but I fear that is now too late. But when our nation is ravished, our sons slain, our daughters defiled, our industries in ruins, perhaps the mass of mankind will awaken. It seems a cursed price to pay for stupidity, prejudice and ignorance, but Nature always takes her toll in the most relentless manner and all humanity must pay for willful, wanton blindness of mankind.

IN THAT DAY WHEN THE CANNONS ROAR AND THE HELL OF WAR CRASHES ABOUT YOUR HOMES, REMEMBER THAT WE SOCIALISTS CRIED OUT OUR WARNINGS FOR YEARS BUT YOU HAD EARS THAT HEARD NOT: WE POINTED OUT THE DANGERS THAT ENCOMPASSED US, BUT YOU HAD EYES THAT SAW NOT: SO WHEN THE BLOODY DAY OF WAR'S HELL COMES HOME TO YOU, JUST REMEMBER THAT YOU ARE PAYING THE PRICE OF WILLFUL IGNORANCE.

World Peace

Act II

> [LEFT STAGE] *The peasant women of the warring nations are grouped in a semi-circle, each national group huddled together and seated on low stools. Their children are crouching at their feet and hiding behind their skirts. The neutrals are grouped together at the extreme left and slightly behind the warring nations. The women of the warring nations are anguish-stricken and weeping, and the people of the neutral nations seem frightened and anxious. The noise and turmoil of war is heard in the distance and with each fresh outbreak the people of the neutral nations grow more agitated.*
>
> [RIGHT STAGE] *America and Columbia are seated on a flag-draped dais. The American business man, American banker, American speculator and the "drummer" are grouped near. They listen to the thunder of war and gaze on the terror-stricken women and children with pity.*

COLUMBIA.   Great God! How frightful. It makes my senses reel and my soul sick to think of such horrors. How can such things be in a world of culture and civilization? Has the world gone stark, raving mad with the lust for blood?

AMERICA.   Not at all. This war is but the outcome of civilized industrial life. It is distressing, it is true, but you should not allow sentiment to overshadow your practical common sense. Just think what a wonderful opportunity for business. [*Columbia shudders and hides her eyes from the appalling scene.*]

COLUMBIA.   How terrible to think of business, when millions of human lives are lost, culture and art trampled into the dust, and civilization dragged back into savagery.

AMERICA.   Quite true, but it is business that rules the world to-day and not sentiment.

A continuous stream of porters, carrying shoes, harness, saddles, clothing, bags of wheat, guns and boxes of ammunition, enter [right],

"World Peace" was first published by the *National Rip-Saw* (St. Louis, 1915), 27–44.

The play, by Frank P. and Kate Richards O'Hare, was popular in 1915–16 on the socialist lecture circuit and was performed throughout the country before U.S. intervention in the war.

cross in front of the weeping women and pass on their way to the battlefield.

AMERICA.   There! Observe how foolish your objections. A stream of wealth is pouring from our shores to the warring nations and a stream of good European gold will come back to us.

COLUMBIA.   But the gold is all stained with human blood, and our own working people are starving for the food we send to feed this war.

AMERICA.   Mere Socialistic cant! The priests, bishops and church dignitaries have all expressed their opinion that it is a holy war. I have questioned my statesmen and they declare that it is being conducted according to the rules of world diplomacy; I have received advice from our great captains of finance and they declare the war good for business. God ordained these wise men to guide our destinies. Be content woman, be content!

Peasant women rise one by one and cluster in center of stage for conference. They appeal to a Hungarian woman to carry a message to America pleading for intercession.

GERMAN WOMAN.   Go, sister, to the great land across the sea and beg mighty America to stop this slaughter.

FRENCH WOMAN.   Hurry, sister, ere it is too late. The great Napoleon once said that armies travel on their stomachs, and the granaries of Europe are bare of food. If America will sell our war lords no more food, the war must cease. We may starve, but better far to die of hunger than to be maimed with shot and torn with shell.

AUSTRIAN WOMAN.   America is tender of heart and mighty in power; go tell how bitter are our sufferings, that her mighty strength may bring us peace.

RUSSIAN WOMAN.   Go, tell the generous America that the arms she sends across the sea but prolong this hell of war. Every bullet may make a widow, every shrapnel a dozen orphans, and the dum-dum kills not alone the body of the man on the firing line but the heart and soul of the woman left behind.

ENGLISH WOMAN.   Go, sister, and voice the cry of the harried, war-stricken women of Europe, and surely the great, tender heart of America will heed our cry and send us help.

SERVIAN WOMAN.   America is called "The Home of the Brave and the

Land of the Free." God grant that the "free" may hear the cry of the slaves of the war gods and make of our bravery our salvation.

MESSENGER.   I will be your messenger.

ALL WOMEN.   [*In unison*] God speed you on your way. God send us peace.

The Messenger crosses stage and kneels before America to make her plea.

MESSENGER.   Oh! Great and powerful nation, I come as the living voice of all the war-cursed women of Europe. I kneel at your feet and supplicate for the strength of your might and the humanity of your heart that alone can save the continent of Europe from utter ruin and despair. Europe to-day is one vast charnel house, her highways are shambles, her farms are graveyards, her fields are quagmires soaked in human blood and polluted with rotting human flesh. Our factories, mills, mines and workshops are idle while the workingmen fight, die and rot in the trenches. Already the pick and flower of European young manhood have been transformed into bloated corpses whose stench pollutes the air, while famine and pestilence hover like vultures over every nation.

AMERICA.   True, my dear madam! You have my heartfelt sympathy. I will call my people to gather in the churches and hold a day of prayer.

MESSENGER.   A most pious thing to do, no doubt, but long and bitter experience has taught us that God is always on the side of the army with the best guns, and since there are guns enough in Europe and being manufactured in your armament factories to shoot the happiness of the women of Europe into fragments we are loath to wait until the guns decide whom God shall help. If agonized prayers could have brought us peace we would not have appealed to you. From a million agonized souls in Europe prayers are ascending at this moment.

AMERICA.   My heart is with you, but, of course, I can take no official notice of your plea. Home is the place for women; men must settle the quarrels of nations in the manly way. Go home to your children and in God's good time the war will end.

MESSENGER.   But listen, O! great nation, we have no homes. Millions of our men have been taken from us. How many are slain we do not know, but we do know that every time the sun passes from east to west thousands die. Our homes have been destroyed and more crumble every time a cannon roars or a shrapnel falls. Our protectors are gone and thousands of women in Europe bear beneath their anguished hearts the little lives that have been conceived in force, that will be nurtured in blazing hate and that will be born to deeds of violence and insanity. In a few weeks the Belgian women will give life to the hated offspring of the German invaders; the outraged Polish women will bear the fruit of the hellish lust of the Russian soldiers, and so the cruel, brutal story runs, involving every warring nation and bearing in its train horrors too frightful for human mind to grasp.

AMERICA.   Madam, what would you have me do?

MESSENGER.   I would have you order back into the harbor every ship loaded with food, either for sale or to be given in charity. Every pound of food you send the warring nations but helps the war lords to continue the slaughter. I would have you forbid the exportation of arms and ammunition. But for the armament you make and sell the warring nations, the murder must cease. In the name of womanhood, childhood and humanity, I demand that you stop the sale of war supplies and proffer mediation to the warring nations.

AMERICA.   But, Madam, why do you come to me? I am only one nation and have problems enough at home without interfering in your European war.

MESSENGER.   True you are only one nation, but you are the dominant nation of the Western world. You set the precedent of dictation of European politics when by your Monroe Doctrine you said no king or emperor should come to the Western world and extend his dominions. You have enforced that edict, not with battleship and cannon, but with moral power, and because of it two great continents are made up of sister republics who live in peace and harmony. Two score of republics stretch from pole to pole and their thousands of miles of boundary lines are unprotected by forts or soldiers, and these two-score governments are free from the curse of militarism. America is the mother of republics, and when you speak it will not be for one nation, but for the twenty that occupy the Western continent. Every ruler of the Western world will join in the proffer of mediation, but you must lead the way in this, as in the building of republics.

The neutral nations of Europe are only waiting for your leadership. They hate this war, but are powerless to act lest they be crushed.

The common people of the warring nations have no quarrel with each other and loathe the part they play in the orgy of murder, but they, too, are helpless victims. The power to stop not only this war, but cast the War-God chained into the pit, and to rescue all mankind from his domination, is yours. Have you the courage to act?

AMERICA.   Great God! How I long to take the step, but I am bound by unseen bonds—the domination of business interests—and Europe will not listen.

MESSENGER.   Warfare is to business what drunkenness is to a weary man; false strength, false power that must be paid for in deadly reaction. And Europe will be glad to listen.

The porters continue to carry their wares across the stage.

America calls the American banker, speculator and business man for consultation.

AMERICA.   [*Pointing to messenger*] You have heard the woman's plea. What is your answer?

AMERICAN BANKER.   Preposterous! What insolence and presumption. Pray tell me what do women know of war or finance!

SPECULATOR.   Impracticable! We have no call to interfere.

DRUMMER.   [*Elbowing his way to the front*] Say, Sam, take it from me, if you let women butt in on this proposition hell will be popping. They don't give a damn for business; they are sentimentalists. Duck the petticoats, old man, or we are in for trouble.

AMERICAN BANKER.   My friend is a little crude in his manner of expression, but quite sound as to logic. Allow me to donate half a million dollars to a fund to send doctors and nurses to Europe. It has always been the duty of womankind to bind up the wounds of the fallen, and if we can fix the minds of women on the noble work of nursing, they will not trouble us about an embargo or mediation.

DRUMMER.   Good. I'll help in that. [*Hastily draws a roll of bills from his pocket and tosses it to banker.*]

America turns and pats the Messenger on the head with a fatherly air.

AMERICA.   Madam, my heart bleeds for you and the women of your unhappy continent. I shall send Medical Science, one of God's best gifts to man, and Red Cross, the concrete expression of tender womanhood, to aid you in your day of sorrow.

*America beckons and Medical Science, a young man physician, and
Red Cross, a young woman nurse, enter [right]. America gives each
an emergency case and they pass over to the weeping women, who
view them without interest, and the pair pass on to the battlefield.
[Leave stage left.]*

MESSENGER.   [*To America*] Believe me, I am grateful for your tender-
ness of heart and for your desire to succor us in our day of need, but
I am not satisfied. Of what value to us will it be to have Medical
Science and Red Cross bind up the wounds and heal the hurts of our
loved ones, if, when they are healed, they must again go back to
murder and be murdered?

Red Cross or Medical Science can bring no happiness to the hearts
or ease to the souls of the women and children of war-cursed Europe.

AMERICA.   Ah! Quite true, Madam, I understand. We must care for the
women and children also. I will call my faithful aids, who have always
been able to comfort my working people when strikes and lockouts,
gunmen and Cossacks have brought death and suffering to their humble homes. I shall call Charity and Religion to you. [*America beckons,
and Charity, a young woman dressed in black, and Religion, a young
clergyman, enter right. They stand before America, who hands to
Charity a basket of bread and to Religion a Bible. Charity and Religion start to go.*]

[*The drummer, suitcase in hand, is starting for Europe. He bumps
into Religion accidentally and almost topples him over.*]

DRUMMER.   Beg your pardon, parson! I have to hustle to keep up with
my job these days; business is simply humming.

RELIGION.   I am happy to hear you say so, brother, for I am on my way
to carry the consolation of religion to the unhappy continent of Europe and I trust you will contribute liberally.

DRUMMER.   Sure! Just hold this stuff while I write a check. [*Thrusts his
sample case, order book and grip on Religion, who stands and holds
them awkwardly. The drummer writes a check, speaking as he
writes.*] Well, take it from me, parson, the poor ginks need all the
consolation they can get over there. That country is sure messed up
something fierce.

RELIGION.   I am happy to perceive that you have a tender heart and a
realization of your Christian duty.

DRUMMER.   Sure, Mike!

RELIGION.   I am happy to have been chosen to carry the message of Christ to our unhappy brothers and sisters.

DRUMMER.   What! Carry the message of Christ? Say, do you think I am going to put up my good money to have you spilling that "Peace on earth, good will to men" bunk around over Europe now? I should say not! Peace on earth! Nix! Not when our factories are running twenty-four hours a day, not when we are getting a hundred per cent advance on our shoes, not when unemployment here in the United States makes it possible for us to work our employes twelve hours a day and cut wages to the bone. Say, we can get a full grown man for nine dollars a week, a peach of a girl for four and kids! Pshaw! They are so cheap we buy them by the carload.

RELIGION.   Brother, I rejoice in your prosperity, but is there not serious danger of undermining the morals of your females by compelling them to work for so inadequate a wage as four dollars per week?

DRUMMER.   Morals! What in hell has morals got to do with making shoes? I don't suppose it is particularly moral for us to send our shoes over there so the poor boobs can wade through the snow to shoot each others' head off, but it's darn good business. See, here, parson, if you haven't a better line on morals and business than that, I don't think I can trust you to spend my money. [*Starts to put the check back in his pocket.*]

RELIGION.   [*In agitation*] You misunderstood me quite, brother! I see your viewpoint clearly. It is the message of Paul I wish to carry.

DRUMMER.   Sure! Paul was all right! He was a good old scout. You just throw that stuff of Paul's about "servants, obey your masters," and "women, if you want to know anything, ask the old man at home" around in good big chunks and send me a bill for the chunks. So long! I got to keep moving. [*Drummer thrusts check in Religion's hand, snatches his sample case and rushes away.*] [*Exit left.*]

Religion and Charity pass over to the weeping women, who dumbly accept their offerings, impatiently reject them, or sadly turn away.

RELIGION.   [*Stoops and speaks to a Belgian child*] Here, my dear little child, is a tract and a nice bun this good, sweet lady and I have brought you. You must pray God every night to bless the kind gentleman in America who sent us.

BELGIAN CHILD.   I don't want no bun. I don't want no tract. I want my
father. I want to go home. My grandpa is shot and my auntie is lying
in the ditch all bloody. I don't like tracts and buns and war. I want to
go home.

RELIGION.   What shocking manners.

BELGIAN MOTHER.   Leave the child alone. He had better starve than to
grow up to be cannon meat.

*Religion and Charity pass down the lines of women and children,
meeting with indifference or rebuffs. They pause near left exit.*

RELIGION.   [*Speaks with deep sadness*] Sister, it is very evident that this
is no place for us. These people are stiff of neck, hard of heart and
adamant to the gentle voice of piety. Let us retire to some quiet spot
and meditate and pray for their conversion. [*Both leave left.*]

MESSENGER.   [*To America*] Bear with me, O! mighty nation, if I still
plead. My sisters in yonder unhappy land are in desperate plight and
you are our only hope. Do not think us ungrateful for all your charity.
We know the heart of America is tender and the sympathy of America
is universal, but every loaf of bread you send across the water but
leaves another penny in the war lord's chest with which to wage the
war.

AMERICA.   Oh! Begone, woman. Begone! You drive me mad with your
insistence. Governments do not take into account womankind. There
is no place in our world diplomacy for the voice of woman. Leave me
in peace that I may consult with those to whom I must account for my
every official act for the furtherance of the business interests and the
material prosperity of my nation. [*America turns from the woman
and consults with bankers and business men who stand grouped near
the dais.*]

*The messenger rises and passes over to Columbia and starts to kneel.
Columbia hastily raises her to her feet and places an arm about her
shoulder.*

COLUMBIA.   Do not kneel to me, sister. To-day it is your sons who fall
in battle, to-morrow it may be mine. In the travail of giving life to
sons we have been initiated into the holy sisterhood of mothers. The
blood seal of giving life has sealed us unto a sisterhood that shall withstand the assault of creed and race, hate and war, death and the grave.

Like you, I now have no voice in political government. The time has come for united womankind to declare that if we bear the sons, we, too, shall have a voice in the parliaments that send them forth to murder and be murdered. [*Addressing herself to America*] I array myself beside this woman. I am in accord with her demands that the exportation of foodstuffs and munitions of war shall stop and that America shall demand and secure mediation.

AMERICA.   For God's sake, be quiet. Do not interfere with mighty problems that you do not understand. I have consulted with my advisers and they refuse the woman's plea. What can I do?

The drummer re-enters [right] and stands near America, looking on.

AMERICAN BANKER.   It would be contrary to all the rules of world diplomacy.

AMERICAN BUSINESS MAN.   It would interfere with business.

COLUMBIA.   Diplomacy! Business! I care as little for these as you care for the millions of human lives that have been sacrificed upon the altar of greed. Such gods may satisfy men who never gave life to a child, but to us women who have paid the price for a human life they are but trash.

AMERICA.   Be reasonable, woman! Be reasonable! We must be content with watchful waiting.

COLUMBIA.   Watchful waiting! Yes, no doubt, that is sufficient for you men, but we women want quick and decisive action.

AMERICA.   [*In desperation*] Ye gods! These women!

DRUMMER.   Sam, I told you that if ever you let the petticoats get a look-in they would play the devil with things!

COLUMBIA.   Are our children to blush for us in everlasting shame because of your inaction now? In all the history of the world no nation ever faced so sublime an opportunity to serve mankind as we; no ruler ever grasped so god-like a power; but once in the lifetime of the race does such an opportunity come, and all the future ages will loathe and despise us if we fail humanity in this crisis. From the crash and roar of war that grips the world to-day we are free; while the nations of Europe writhe in a death struggle like wild beasts in a jungle fight, we are at peace. The only powerful nation not hopelessly embroiled, we hold the confidence of all nations and the power to arrest carnage, to still the roar of war, to dam the rivers of blood and to bring peace to nations unable to secure peace for themselves. Like Jesus, who stood by the wind-tossed waves of Galilee, we have the power to say to the war-tossed nations of Europe, "Peace, be still," and no matter how strong the surge of hate, no matter how blind the passion, no matter how deep the hold of the war demon—if we but speak, war will cease.

AMERICA.   In God's name! Will you never cease your importunities? This is not our war. Militarism is to blame; Kaiser, King, Emperor and Czar are responsible; we must maintain our neutrality.

COLUMBIA.   How Christlike! Militarism—that word seems to have a familiar sound. It has been a wonderfully convenient scapegoat for truckling politicians, but we women know that it is but another name for greed and profits. Kaiser, Emperor, King and Czar! Yes! they started the war, but we are going to end it. Neutrality—certainly the neutrality of hell—the money changer's pact with death—a bloody bargain with the war lords; peace with damnation, that the profits of these speculators may be protected. How shameful that we must admit that no patriotic passions sway us, no religious frenzy blinds our reason. We are not honest enough to espouse the cause of the nation we think most justified in this murderfest, Germany or England, France or Russia; the blood-stained gold of any nation is acceptable to us. We will furnish the machines of murder to any nation, to kill the people of any nation, if they but bring us "thirty pieces of silver."

AMERICA.   In the name of God, woman, have you no mercy! Why press the white-hot brand of my own soul's condemnation into my heart? Am I not human like yourself, have I not eyes to see and ears to hear and reason that cannot be smothered; have I not a soul that sees and feels and knows the cursed needlessness of the sufferings of mankind? Why add your scorn to my shame, humiliation and self-contempt? The golden chains of international finances and business make me a galley slave. I am helpless!

COLUMBIA.   Forgive the bitter words. My love is far deeper than my scorn. You have at last had one truth seared into your brain—a government, like a home, must have both a father and a mother to be complete. I will call the allies of womanhood and they shall free you from your golden chains of slavery and act as messengers to carry the message of our nation to the world. [*Columbia beckons to Peace, a young woman in white, and Democracy, a young man.*] [*Enter right.*]

PEACE. The world is sick unto death of war and hate, bloodshed and murder, and demands peace. Peace asks of you, the only nation strong enough to make your will law, an official demand for mediation.

AMERICA. How can I give it, when the industrial situation of my nation forbids such action on my part?

DEMOCRACY. The industrial masters of the nation are industrial masters because "THE WILL OF THE PEOPLE" has allowed them mastery. But if our industrial masters insist on deluging the earth with blood in a competitive struggle to fertilize their money crop, the "WILL OF THE PEOPLE" can take from them their power to make wars, or to so order affairs that wars are inevitable. Shorn of this power, the war lords become powerless to wield their despotism and must perforce become peaceful-minded citizens.

The banker, speculator and business man standing near dais listen intently. With the statement of Democracy they burst into a volley of objections, shouting "impracticable," "folly," "socialism," and "utopianism."

The Drummer elbows his way to front of group and addresses America.

DRUMMER. Confound it, Sam! I knew there was trouble ahead when I saw the women getting busy. We can shout "folly", "socialism" and "utopianism" until we are black in the face and it won't touch them. If they want mediation and peace, for God's sake give it to them, or they will be taking our shoe factories next. For, take it from me, they will get what they go after.

DEMOCRACY. Remember, this is a republic. When the people speak it is in the voice of command. The people are demanding that motherhood, as well as fatherhood, shall share the responsibilities of government; that differences between nations shall be settled by mediation, and that war shall be driven off the earth. Declare an embargo on the exportation of war munitions; issue an official demand for mediation and, like dew from Heaven, peace shall bless the earth.

AMERICA. I consent; I shall send a message to the warring nations. In the name of humanity and civilization I shall demand that this war and all future differences between nations shall be settled by Mediation, and the decree of our nation is that peace shall be the price that every king and emperor shall pay for our commodities, and in the future no son of ours shall damn his eternal soul making munitions of war.

COLUMBIA, PEACE, DEMOCRACY AND MESSENGER.   [*Cry in unison*] Glorious! Flash this message to all the world—this manifesto of the American nation.

DRUMMER.   Gee whiz! War sure got a knockout punch that time, but no use to cry over spilled milk—people will still wear shoes, so I must hustle and get to the next move.

American business man, banker and speculator quietly leave the stage. [Exit right.]

The Messenger, escorted by Peace and Democracy, goes back to her place among the European women. During the entire scene the orchestra has maintained the muffled sounds of distant warfare. As Peace and Democracy start on their mission the sound of warfare dies away and the orchestra plays "Lead, Kindly Light."

Peace and Democracy go to the weeping women, lifting the draperies of mourning and dropping them at their feet. The European women, half-blinded by weeping and stupefied by sorrow, try to show their gratitude. Some cross themselves, some fall on their knees, and others cluster about Peace, kissing her hands and garments. The children spring to their feet, shouting in chorus.

IRISH CHILD.   The war is done, Peace has come, daddy is coming back to us, and we will all go home.

The Pilgrim's Chorus is heard afar off, and slowly a pitiful, tattered portion of the men who went to war creep back into view [enter left]. Some are maimed and crippled, some are carried on stretchers. The women and children fall upon their knees beside the stretchers that hold their men, others embrace the cripples, and the women who have received the "Death Letter" gather their children in their arms, crushed by their sorrow. The Belgian mother, who has received a "Death Letter," straightens her shoulders, wipes the tears from her eyes and, leading her son of twelve by the hand, steps forward and speaks.

BELGIAN MOTHER.   Long and black has been our night of sorrow, flame scorched has been the hell we've trod, desolate is the heritage the war gods have left us but our children must live. Someone must smooth down the graves and replant the vines and wheat, someone must rebuild the ruined homes and shell-swept cities, someone must make our blood-soaked continent habitable. The war lords have killed our men, and we women folks must shoulder the burden of rebuilding civilization. An ocean of tears cannot wash away the stains of blood, a lifetime of repining cannot bring back the life of a single man. We must bury our sorrow with the rotting bones of our husbands and make a new earth for the children they have left behind.

Red Cross and Medical Science busily care for the wounded. Charity and Religion offer the gladly welcomed bread, workmen enter slowly with tools of rehabilitation, hammers, spades and trowels. America gazes upon the scene, then turns to Columbia.

AMERICA.   You are right. The blood-stained gold of war is not good business.

CURTAIN.

My Country

I am an American first and a Socialist second." This bombastic statement has been made many times in the last few months by men and women who did not stop to weigh their words or realize the consequences of such an attitude of mind. Nor are the Socialists the only people who mouth such cant—Church members and labor unionists are also guilty.

These human parrots overlook the fact that the very cornerstone of the Socialist movement is the international brotherhood of labor; that the basis of organized labor is the international welfare of the workers; and that the fundamental creed of the church is the brotherhood of all God's children. If God draws no national lines; if Socialism is international and organized labor knows no boundaries, how in the name of reason can a Christian, a Socialist or a labor unionist declare that nationalism is "first" and all other things "second"?

Europe is today a blazing example of "nationalism" first, and all other things secondary. Two groups of the master class, which is also interna-

"My Country" was first published in *Social Revolution* (April, 1917), 5.

tional, foment a war to decide which group shall have the lion's share of
the profits wrung from the toil of the workers. These industrial masters
were far too wise to allow the war to be known as a class war, so they
moved their pawns, the kings, on the chessboard of life and war raged
between the nations. The workers of the nations at war were not consulted as to their wishes in the matter of war; the masters attended to all
details. The workers were simply called from field and workshop to man
the colors of their various nations and do the fighting and the dying while
their wives and children paid the bitter price of war in hunger and misery and untold suffering.

When the master class sounded the trumpet of war, straightway the
Socialists, labor unionists and Christians forgot their ideals, their principles and their vows. The Socialists became nationalists first, and Socialists second; the labor unionists became "patriots" first, and labor
unionists second; and the Christians became soldiers first, and Christians
second. The Socialists repudiated internationalism, the labor unionists
forgot the solidarity of labor and the Christians discarded the "Prince of
Peace" and embraced the war god of Mammon. Because nationalism was
exalted above all else, Europe is one vast charnelhouse, soaked with
blood, reeking with the stench of putrid human bodies, scarred by
trenches and devastated by shot and shell, while famine and pestilence
rages throughout the continent, kindling the fires of misery and hunger-
maddened revolt.

The ten million dead men who rot on the battlefields of Europe were
nationalists "first" and Socialists, labor unionists and Christians "second."
God knows they have paid in blood and death for placing nationalism
above internationalism, the solidarity of labor and the creed of Jesus
Christ.

Can we Americans learn a lesson from the fate of our brothers and
sisters in Europe, or must we, too, wallow in human blood and putrid
human flesh. Must we endure the fires of the hell of war to burn the
dross of sentimental, false "patriotism" out of our souls before we can be
true to our faith?

I can not speak for the Socialist movement of the United States, but
for myself—I am a Socialist, a labor unionist and a follower of the Prince
of Peace, FIRST; and an American, second. I will serve my class, before
I will serve the country that is owned by my industrial masters. If need
be, I will give my life and the life of my mate, to serve my class, BUT

NEVER WITH MY CONSENT WILL THEY BE GIVEN TO ADD TO THE PROF-
ITS AND PROTECT THE STOLEN WEALTH OF THE BANKERS, FOOD SPECU-
LATORS AND AMMUNITION MAKERS.

I am not pro-English; not pro-German; not pro-American, I AM PRO-
WORKING CLASS! Kier Hardie sleeping beneath the heather of Scotland,
Jean Jaurès, dead by an assassin's hand, Karl Liebknecht in a German
prison and Rosa Luxemburg in her dungeon cell are nearer and dearer
to me than Rockefeller, Morgan, Schwab[12] or DuPont.

The world is my country, the workers are my countrymen, peace and
social justice are my creeds, and to these and these alone I owe loyalty
and allegiance.

Good Morning! Mr. American Citizen

Good morning! Mr. American Citizen. I am your Uncle Sam and I have
come to collect $35 for every man, woman and child in your family. I
want it in the 'good coin of the realm' and I want it right now. I will stand
no if's nor and's nor but's about the payment. Wars cost money, and 'you
are the goat.' Have I made myself plain? You understand of course that I
will conscript a few million of your sons and send them to the trenches
in France to fight the battles of the Bank of England, and I will conscript
your daughters and put them into the industries in order that the capitalists may have cheap labor, but these things are merely incidental to
the game. Money is the basis of war, and it's money I want and it's money
you are going to give me, so get busy and hand it over."

Brutally frank isn't it? This crass, raw demand made by the government upon the west while "free and independent" citizens of a nation
that we have always fondly imagined was a republic, YET IT IS THE FIRST
HONEST STRAIGHTFORWARD WORD THAT HAS COME FROM WASHING-
TON. There is no cant, no hypocrisy, no evasion, no juggling of words.
Just the bare, bald statement that before a single shot has been fired,
before a single step has been taken in actual warfare, before the people

---

12. Charles Michael Schwab (1862–1939) was an industrialist who played a key role
in the organization of U.S. Steel Corporation and Bethlehem Steel Corporation. During
the war he was considered a spokesman for the steel industry.

"Good Morning! Mr. American Citizen" was first published in *Social Revolution* (June,
1917), 5.

have had any opportunity to say whether they want to go to war, the profit mongers have demanded their pound of flesh to the extent of $35 for every human being in this nation.

All the maudlin cant about "humanity" and "freedom" and "democracy" with which we were deluged while Congress hesitated to plunge us into the bloody abyss, and while a few brave souls fought to save us from the shame of conscription, has all been dropped. Sentimental cant is not necessary now to force us into war, we are at war; high sounding phrases are not necessary to lure men to enlist, the "selective draft" drags any man out and forces him into the ranks regardless of what his own feelings may be in the matter of man-killing. These two minor details attended to, the very heart and soul of the war stands revealed in all its ghastly hidiousness—IT IS MONEY.

The President who "kept us out of war" and the brave and patriotic Senators and Representatives are fanatically busy now "saving the nation." I don't mean they are doing anything to conserve human life, all activities are in the direction of the destruction of life. They have not made the slightest effort to break the stranglehold of the food speculators upon the food of the nation. They have done nothing constructive towards insuring either intelligent food production or just food distribution. Herbert Hoover[13] declares that with semi-intelligent food control flour could be reduced from $16 a barrel to $8 a barrel and the farmers could be guaranteed $1.50 a bushel for wheat. According to the Associated Press dispatches, Joe Leiter[14] of Chicago has cleaned up $3,000,000 in the last few days gambling in wheat and the English Government about $1,000,000.

The direct tax of $35 a head levied upon the people is merely a little loose change compared to the indirect taxation forced upon us by the extortionate prices of the necessities of life. We are and have been paying an indirect tax to the food speculators of $10 a barrel on flour, $2 a ton on soft coal, $2 a pair on shoes and everything else in proportion.

Bear in mind also that the extortionate indirect taxation by the capitalist owners of the means of life is being levied upon the people with the full and free consent of the government. The Department of Agriculture

13. Herbert C. Hoover (1874–1964) became internationally famous as a humanitarian for his directing of massive war relief in Europe during and after the First World War. He served as Wilson's director of the Food Administration Agency from 1917 to 1919.

14. Joseph Leiter (1868–1932) was a Chicago businessman famous for the number of litigations in which he engaged. In 1898–1899 he attempted to corner the wheat market.

has reported that there is no marked scarcity of food and that the extortionate prices now levied upon the people has no reason but cold-blooded greed. The Commission which investigated the coal situation reported to the President that there was no shadow of justification for the shameful prices of coal, and that the action of the coal operators was plain thievery. There has never been a time when the government could not have stopped the extortion and thievery and protected the lives of the citizens of the nation had President Wilson and Congress cared to do so. THEY DID NOT CARE TO PROTECT OUR LIVES. THEY DID CARE TO FASTEN UPON OUR REPUBLIC THE WORST FEATURE OF PRUSSIAN MILITARISM—CONSCRIPTION—AND THEY DID CARE TO DRAFT A TAX BILL THAT SQUEEZES OUT OF THE VERY BLOOD OF THE PEOPLE $35 A HEAD. THEY DID DESIRE TO PRUSSIANIZE US AND TAX US TO PAY FOR THE PRUSSIANIZING, AND THEY HAVE DONE IT WITH A VENGENCE.

"What are we going to do about it?" Well that is for you to say, Mr. American Citizen. It's your kettle of fish; we Socialists are not responsible. We have been trying for twenty years to make you see that the Democratic and Republican parties were leading you into the shambles; now when you wallow in your own blood, take comfort in the fact that it is your own fault. We have tried by every appeal to your reason to make you understand that as long as the means of life were privately owned, extortion would reign on the one hand and want on the other. When you are as starved as famished wolves and tax ridden to pay for the privilege of being starved, console yourselves by remembering that you were always good Republicans and Democrats and never, never harkened to the ungodly, unpatriotic Socialists. We have tried with all our might to make you see the class character of our government, we have urged that you join with us in electing working class representatives and you have piously declared that "jack-leg lawyers were good enough for our grandads, and they are good enough for us." Now when the government protected cormorants are sucking your very life blood and the government is piling on the taxes, JUST REMEMBER THAT YOU VOTED FOR WILSON BECAUSE HE KEPT US OUT OF WAR.

The jingo press is now shouting that the American Socialists want a separate peace between Germany and Russia, thereby ending the war before the profiteers have squeezed all of the available profits out of the game. NOT FOR A MOMENT, GENTLEMEN! We Socialists did not make this war and we are going to take no steps to end it until you smug Democrats and Republicans get your little tummys so full of capitalist greed and misrule and criminal blundering that you will gag at the very thought of it. WHEN THAT TIME COMES YOU WILL COME TO THE SOCIALISTS BEGING US TO SAVE YOU FROM YOUR OWN SINS. WE WILL BE READY TO ACT AND FURNISH THE LEADERSHIP THAT WILL WIPE OUT THE SHAMBLES OF WAR AND ESTABLISH THE UNITED STATES OF THE WORLD.

Hold the Fort!

Regardless of any position taken by the Socialist party on the war, the subject matter of Socialism itself is so big, the educational work so important, that it is nothing short of criminal to suppress the Socialist press. Giving the administration full allowance for the difficulties involved in the present crisis—the enormous increase of activity that must be reduced to order and executed—one must have a certain amount of patience with its blunders and mistakes. But when all is said and done, the question arises: Can a political party be crushed out, can present officeholders hope to perpetuate their own incumbency, by suppression of all opposition, by the simple expedient of arresting all rival activities and smothering criticism?

The working class is not pleased with the actual administration of things. Their interests are not served. Actual democracy has not been practiced. What I mean is this—that, while the enormous resources of the nation have been called into play, the whole credit of the nation being used by the administration, the form it has taken has been simply an amplification of capitalism. If the war is right, or if it is wrong, the position of the Socialist movement is the same. We demand an administration of things that will place the burdens of the war equally on every shoulder. We demand that if some give, all shall give. We do not consider the taking of a half, or of three-fourths, or of 99/100 of the surplus incomes of the owning class sufficient, if, as is quoted, "wages have ALMOST advanced to meet the advanced cost of living," and the portion of profits remaining to the owning class in spite of increased taxes on incomes continue to mount to dizzy heights.

War or no war, America is not ready for a dictatorship. It is not nec-

"Hold the Fort!" was first published in *Social Revolution* (November, 1917), 5.

essary. It is not tolerable. While one may fight fire with fire, one can not fight Prussia with Prussianism. Look over the long history of the Socialist party. Its sole purpose is to socialize the interests of the people of this nation—to make them identical—so that we shall stand or fall together; not some stand while others fall—not some eat while others look on hungry. And this program is just as vital today as ever before—more so. Let us have food control—but let it reach into the cafes where the wealthy eat, and let it fall upon our honored office-holders at Washington as well as upon the toilers. Capitalism has its own food control. By putting butter to fifty cents per pound, automatically the farm and city workers cease to consume it. But it yet is on the tables of some. Who are the patriotic "some"?

Election time is coming. Not yet has it been "verboten" to nominate candidates and cast ballots. Not yet have the people been informed that expressing their choice at the polls is treason or sedition. In this fact is seen the reason for the hurried suppression of the Socialist press, not particularly for any resolutions or propaganda of the Socialist movement.

As sure as fate, the workers who are still at home will attempt to send some of their own people to Washington to frame laws. As sure as fate, they will attempt to send people of their own class to state government to watch out for the class upon whose shoulders, in peace and in war, all the burden of production in the last analysis rests. Today as never before, the workers see the folly of sending representatives from the owning or retaining class to "guard" their interests.

The second-class mail privilege of many Socialist papers has been arbitrarily taken away.[15] I say arbitrarily, because the law apparently gives the post-office department that despotic right. Now, it behooves every lover of liberty and fair play, by his own action, to assume a larger burden. Every subscriber to SOCIAL REVOLUTION should receive promptly his November number. This will necessitate a one-cent stamp on each copy. There are so many thousands of subscribers to SOCIAL REVOLUTION that many hundreds of dollars over and above the ordinary expenses must be raised to meet this additional cost this month, and next month, and every month this condition prevails. It can be met by the Socialists to whom these words come. Add the extra postage to the normal price of

15. Press censorship during the First World War was, in effect, determined by the post office. Alleged security reasons forced many newspapers and magazines out of business. No specific guidelines were ever provided the press.

SOCIAL REVOLUTION—and the amount in round figures is 40 cents. Let each one secure five subscribers at 40 cents each—$2. This will meet the emergency. Do not fear that you will be violating any law. SOCIAL REVOLUTION is not a law-breaker—not seditious, not treasonable—it is merely revolutionary. Its mission is not to overthrow capitalist-class monopoly of government; not to aid foreign enemies of the government, but to defeat the domestic enemies of democracy.

We can not lie down at this time. We must marshal all our resources to meet this challenge. Until the mails are definitely closed to the voicing of a working-class program, we must sustain the Socialist press. All over the world our comrades are having the same difficulty. They are each carrying their share of the load. We cheerfully assume ours.

And, when the mails are closed to us, we shall in orderly and legal fashion still persist in holding our rapidly growing numbers in compact organization in ways that will develop.

Speech Delivered in Court by Kate Richards O'Hare Before Being Sentenced by Judge Wade

I was taught in High School that law is pure logic. Abstract law may be pure logic, but the application of the law to testimony in this case seems to have gone far afield from logic.

As your Honor knows, I am a professional woman, following the profession of delivering lectures whereby I hope to induce my hearers to study the philosophy of socialism. In the regular course of my profession and work, I delivered during this lecture year lectures all over the United States, or practically all over. I delivered this lecture in North Carolina when the draft riots were at their height; I delivered it in Globe, Arizona, to ten thousand people, two or three days following the deportations from Bisbee,[16] and on the day when the strike vote was taken, when excitement ran high and passions were having their sway; I deliv-

---

"Speech Delivered in Court by Kate Richards O'Hare Before Being Sentenced by Judge Wade" was first published in *Social Revolution* (February, 1918), 6–7.

16. The Bisbee deportations occurred in 1917. Twelve hundred Arizona miners, on strike during the national war effort, were rounded up by local deputies, denounced as foreigners, Wobblies, and German-financed traitors, and were transported out of the state and stranded in the New Mexico desert.

ered it in San Francisco during the Mooney case;[17] and the same thing
was true in Portland, Idaho, and in the northwestern lumber regions
during the great I.W.W. excitement; and at all of those lectures conditions were as tense as conditions could be. The men who were in the
employ of the United States in the Department of Justice were present
at my meetings. These men are trained, highly efficient, and highly paid
detectors of crime and criminals. In all these months when my lecture
was under the scrutiny of this kind of men there was no suggestion at any
time that there was anything in the lecture that was objectionable, that
was treasonable, that was seditious. It was the custom at my meetings to
send complimentary tickets to the district attorney and the marshal and
deputy marshals of the district, in order that they might hear the lecture
and attend the meeting. This plan was followed practically everywhere
that I spoke. And then, in the course of the trip, I landed at Bowman -
a little, sordid, wind-blown, sun-blistered, frost-scarred town on the
plains of western Dakota. There was nothing unusual in my visit to Bowman, except the fact that it was unusual to make a town of this size. The
reason I did was because there was one man whose loyalty and faithful-
ness and unselfish service to the cause to which I had given my life,
wanted me to come, and I felt he had a right to demand my services. I
arrived in the town, delivered my lecture just as I had delivered it many,
many times before. There was nothing in the audience that was unusual,
except the fact that it was a small audience. It was a solid, substantial,
stolid type of farmer crowd. There was not the great enthusiasm that had
prevailed at many of my meetings. There was nothing to stir me, or
arouse me, or cause me to make a more impassioned plea than usual. In
fact, the meeting at Bowman was absolutely commonplace and ordinary,
and there was nothing at all in that little, sordid, wind-blown town, that
commonplace audience, that should have for a moment overbalanced my
reason and judgment and common sense, and have caused me to have
been suddenly smitten with the hydrophobia of sedition. But when I
arrived at Bowman and had delivered my lecture, and spent the next day

17. On July 22, 1916, during a Preparedness Day parade in San Francisco, a bomb
exploded on a sidewalk, killing ten people and wounding forty others. Thomas J. Mooney,
a minor labor leader, and Warren K. Billings, a colleague, were charged with murder.
Although the case against them was weak, they were found guilty and Mooney was sentenced to death and Billings was sentenced to life imprisonment. The case dragged on for
years; various labor and liberal groups fought to win their freedom. In 1939, Governor
Culbert L. Olson pardoned Mooney, and a few months later Billings also was released.

in resting before the continuation of the trip, I found that there were peculiar conditions existing at Bowman. They were not peculiar to Bowman. They are common to the whole state of North Dakota. It is known to Your Honor, and everyone who has had any part in this trial, that in the state of North Dakota, in the last year and a half, the greatest and most revolutionary social phenomena [sic] that has occurred since the foundation of this government, has taken place. The story is one that is so well known I need spend little time on it.

Here to these wind-blown, frost-scarred plains came men hard of face and feature and muscle, who subdued this desert; and men, toiling in their desperate struggle with adverse conditions and with nature, gradually had it forced on their minds that in some way they were not receiving a just return for the labor expended; that after their wheat was raised and garnered, in the processes of marketing, men who toiled not and suffered none of the hardships of production, were robbing them of the product of their labor; and these farmers, smarting under that chaotic condition, came to the town of Bismarck. They felt that the politicians, the men who held the offices in the state, the men they elected to office, were not serving them, but that they were using their offices and power to assist in the robbery and exploitation of the farmers of this state. So they appealed to the legislature, and then there came that marvelous thing that had such a wonderful effect in this state—an insult, a sneer from the lips of the politicians who believed themselves firm and secure in power, and that sneer, that insult, that told the farmers to go home and slop the hogs while the politicians ran the state, had the effect of cementing the farmers in this state into a great revolutionary organization, and that organization went out and swept the whole state, and carried out of power the men who had been in power, and put in power the men chosen by the farmers of this state. This had occurred in Bowman County as it had all over the state of North Dakota. The old order had been deposed. The new order had been enforced, and naturally, as always follows, the appointive offices that are called the spoils of political warfare, were taken from the adherents of the old order and given to the adherents of the new order. I think, so far as I can judge, the fattest, juiciest, most desirable plum in Bowman County was the postoffice. This was taken from the man that had held it and given to the wife of the leader of the new order. This naturally created bitterness, hatred and venom in such marked degree as I have never seen in all my experience. When I ar-

rived in Bowman for my lecture, it chanced that it was the adherents of
the new order that attended, paid for the tickets, appreciated it, approved it, and applauded it, as they stated on the stand. And, among the
adherents of the new order that attended was the postmistress, and she
did the things that the others did. And then the real thing in this case
came out, and that was the contest over the postoffice. There was a certain hungry office seeker in Bowman. He was the principal witness for
the prosecution. He made the statement on the stand that he was a
farmer, but he has never tilled the soil. He has always been a political
hanger-on, a camp-follower of the old political order. Separated from any
political job he became lean and hungry, and looked with a hungry eye
on the postoffice. The deposed boss of the old order was perfectly willing
that the hungry office seeker might have the postoffice if only the present
incumbent could be eliminated; and when the postmistress attended the
lecture, and the next day invited me to her home as her guest, there
grew up in the minds of the deposed boss and the hungry office seeker
the hope that I might be made the lever whereby the postmistress could
be separated from her job, and the hungry office seeker find an opportunity to live without labor. So telegraphic communications were established with Senator McCumber. There was no charge that I should be
arrested for sedition or treason, but the demand was made by the deposed political boss of Bowman County that the postmistress should be
removed for having entertained me. The deposed political boss appeared
before the District Attorney and made the simple demand that the postmistress be removed, and he was told that this was impossible; that the
postmistress had committed no crime; if anyone was the criminal it must
be I; and so, on the testimony of the hungry office seeker, and a few of
the adherents of the old order this indictment was returned—the indictment that does not charge me with a crime, the indictment that in no
place states that I ever committed a crime; the indictment that merely
says that I had an intent to commit a crime. And, Your Honor, it seems
to me one of those strange, grotesque things that can only be the out-
growth of this hysteria that is sweeping over the world today, that a judge
on the bench, and a jury in the box, and a prosecuting attorney, should
attempt to usurp the prerogative of God Almighty, and look down into
the heart of a human being and decide what motives slumber there.
There is no charge that if my intent or my motive was criminal, that that
intent or motive ever flowered, or ever was put into action—only the

charge that in my heart there was an intent, and on that strange charge of an intent so securely buried in a human heart that no result and no effect came from it, I went to trial.

I am not going to spend any of your valuable time rehearsing the trial, except to say that to my mind it is absolutely impossible that under any legal rule or thought a human being can be tried for a thing that he never did, and that there is no charge that he ever did, but only that he might have an intention of doing. But, Your Honor, all through this trial, all through the questions of the District Attorney, all through his appeal to the jury, as the ever-recurring motive in this little drama of life, there ran the charge of a crime, a crime of which I was accused. And this crime is not a new one. It is as old as the human race. It is not peculiar to me. It is universal as life itself. This crime that was charged by inference in the trial was the same crime, was the same charge that was brought against the first slave rebellion, against the first serf revolt. It was the charge that was brought against Moses and Spartacus, Watt Tyler and Cromwell, George Washington and Patrick Henry, William Lloyd Garrison and Wendell Phillips, and it was the same crime that was charged against Jesus of Nazareth when he stood at the judgment bar of Pontius Pilate. The crime is this: "She stirred up the people." And, Your Honor, if by inference I can be charged with that crime, and tried for it, then, Your Honor, at this point I plead guilty of that crime, if it is a crime. For twenty years I have done nothing but stir up the people. As a high school girl, in the first flush of youth, I did my best to stir up the people against the corruption and debasement and debauchery and damnation that came with the liquor traffic of the United States. As a young woman I did all in my power to stir up the people to revolt against the damnation of the vice interests in this country, the interests that debased six hundred thousand women and used them to further political interests of existing political powers. I did all in my power to stir up the people, the working class of the United States to demand more of the wealth of this country. I did my best to stir them up to demand shorter hours and better pay and better conditions; and the one great motive and object of my life has been the ambition to stir up the people of the United States to demand life, and life more abundant. And, Your Honor, if this be the crime for which I was tried in this court, then, Your Honor, I am guilty of that crime. But, having made this statement, and realizing now that the time has come when you are about to pass judgment on me, it seems to me at this time it is meet that we should consider the things that are involved.

There is no doubt that in this hour of travail and sorrow and blood-shed and misery that marks the labor that is ushering in a new order, there is but one thing that should occupy our minds, and that is this: what, at this time, at this hour of our country's peril and travail, will bring the greatest good to the greatest number of people? And this, I believe, Your Honor, is the question that you are to decide. You are to decide whether at this hour it will be better for the people of the United States that I shall be convicted, not of a crime charged in the indictment, but convicted of having an intent in my heart that never found expression, and on conviction of having an intent to which I never gave action, I shall be sentenced to prison. Will this be a matter of the greatest good to the greatest number? If Your Honor believes, as the District Attorney repeated so frequently and so forcefully, that I am a dangerous woman, strong and powerful, with the ability to sway men's minds, and lead them to do my bidding, if you believe that that is true, and you believe the fact that I had a wrongful intent in my heart to which I never gave life or action, and that because of that intent that never matured into a crime, it is better that I should go to prison, then it is your duty to place me there. It is your duty to place me where in this hour of stress and trial and travail I cannot injure my country, or interfere with the conduct of this war. But in the discussion of that point we must consider also this fact; that the big thing, that the vital thing, the all-important thing at this moment is that we should have a nation united. And at this time, taking all of the things that exist into consideration—the fact that passions run high, that hysteria has seized the world, that all of us have more or less abnormal mental processes brought about by this great world tragedy—you must consider well whether my conviction is going to have a ten-dency to unite the people of this country or to disunite them. And in dealing with them, you cannot avoid dealing with the prejudices that have crept into this trial. At this point I want to mention one fact, a fact that has been brought to my mind, to my hearing, and that is this: that from some source of information that I do not know, you have been in-formed that I was connected with a certain publication whose name I never heard, and whose existence I was not aware of, that was published in your home state. This publication was violently anti-religious, and vio-lently rabid, and it was said—

THE COURT: I never heard of that before.

MRS. O'HARE: Very well, I will pass on. We must still consider the question of the prejudices that still exist, and that do exist, and we must take into consideration the effect that the verdict is going to have on the people. And, Your Honor, I want to call this thing to your mind, that the man or the nation whose cause is just is thrice armed; and if the cause of this nation is just in this great war, then is it necessary in order to impress the people of the righteousness and justice of the cause, to convict and sentence a woman on the charge of having an intent but never committing a crime? This you must consider. And you must consider also the danger of arousing hatreds and prejudice and suspicion. Your Honor, there are 100,000 people, and more, in the United States, who know me personally. They have listened to my voice, looked in my face, and they have worked side by side with me in every great reform movement of the last twenty years. My life has been an open book to them. They know what it has been. They know that from my earliest girlhood down to this time I have given all that I am, all that I have—my girlhood, my young womanhood, my wifehood, even my motherhood, for I have carried my unborn children out into this struggle for better conditions for the working class. And, Your Honor, at this time, no judge on earth, and no jury on earth, and no ten thousand judges, or ten thousand juries, can ever convince these hundred thousand people who know me and have worked with me, and these millions who have read my writings, that I am a criminal, or that I have ever given anything to my country except my most unselfish devotion and service. You cannot convince the mass of people who know me that I am dangerous to the United States government. AH! They are willing to admit I am dangerous to some things in the United States, and I thank God that I am. I am dangerous to the invisible government of the United States; I am dangerous to the special privileges of the United States; I am dangerous to the white slaver and to the saloonkeeper, and I thank God that at this hour I am dangerous to the war profiteers of this country who rob the people on the one hand, and rob and debase the government on the other; and then with their pockets and wallets stuffed with the filthy, bloodstained profits of war, wrap the sacred folds of the Stars and Stripes about them and shout their blatant hypocrisy to the world. You can convince the people that I am dangerous to these men; but no jury and no judge can convince them that I am a dangerous woman to the best interests of the United States; and at this hour will my conviction, will my incarceration behind the bars of a prison have the tendency to cement and hold together the great mass of people in this nation, or will it have the tendency to create hatred and bitterness, and arouse suspicion, and make these people who know me, and who cannot be brought to doubt me, feel that this whole case is nothing but an attempt on the part of the war profiteers to eliminate and get out of the way a woman that is dangerous to them? Your Honor, I do not believe that this is true. I do not believe at this point that you are the tool of the war profiteers. I do not believe it is true of the District Attorney. I do not believe at this time that this case is anything but one of those weary, grotesque, fantastic things that has grown out of the war hysteria. But I say that the great mass of the people of the United States are going to have that thing burned into their souls if I go to prison. And you have learned in North Dakota what happens when the working classes have these things burned into their souls.

So now, Your Honor, I am not asking for clemency, I am not asking for mercy. I would scorn to do such a thing. To ask for clemency or for mercy would be an admission of some sense of guilt on my part, and there is absolutely none, and I will not and do not ask for mercy. All I am asking you to consider is the greatest good to the greatest number. What can we do to make this nation united? What are the dangers of arousing hatred and suspicion, and passion and prejudice in these critical times? I am asking you, Your Honor, judging from my appearance in the court room, judging from all that I have said, judging from all that you have read and that I have written - and I have provided you everything that it was within my power to provide - judging from these things, Your Honor, will I be more dangerous outside, following the work I have been doing for the last six months - and my work for the last six months is this: I represent the so-called Minority Wing[18] of the Socialist Party. We are counseling patience, counseling broadmindedness and tolerance. I have gone about at a great sacrifice to myself, and endless weariness, into every corner of the United States, and have said to the Socialists everywhere, "This is not a time for bitterness, this is not a time for passion or prejudice; this is a time for calm, careful, clear thinking. This is a time when we must wait, as the mother waits for the pangs of travail. We cannot stop the coming of this new order that is about to be born any

18. At the time O'Hare was in fact in the majority wing of the party, having promoted, signed, and supported the majority report concerning the party's position on American intervention in the war.

more than the mother can stop the coming of the new life whose time is full. And so we must be patient, and tolerant, and long-suffering, and levelheaded, during this time. We must give this nation the opportunity to prove its statement that this war shall be the last of wars, that this war is being fought in order that wars may end.["] I do not know whether that is true or not, Your Honor. I cannot look down into the motives of men's hearts in Washington, as the Judge and Jury looked down into the motives of my heart and read them. I do not know, I say, whether the motives of these men is that this war shall end war. But I say this: I want this shall be the supreme test of war; I want everything on the face of God's earth to work together to make this the supreme test, to decide this now and for everlasting; that it shall go on at this time, when the bloodshed and suffering is on, until it is decided forever, and not be put aside until some other time. So I want you to decide the question whether, in the months to come, these struggling months that are coming, to demand the service of every intelligent, loyal citizen of the United States, I can serve my country best in prison, or whether I can serve it best doing the work that I have been doing, going about among the people that believe in me, and have faith in me, and asking for their patience, and their tolerance, and their assistance to settle this question once and for all. I ask you to decide this question for yourself, Your Honor, and if you decide that I can serve my country better in prison than anywhere else, I am satisfied. It may be true, Your Honor, that "God works in a mysterious way, his wonders to perform." It may be that down in the dark, noisome, loathsome hells we call prisons, under our modern prison system, there may be a bigger work for me to do than out on the lecture platform. It may be that down there are the things I have sought for all my life. All my life has been devoted to taking light into dark places, to ministering to sick souls, to lifting up degraded humanity; and God knows down there in the prisons, perhaps more than any other place on earth, there is need for that kind of work. So if, as it was necessary that Jesus should come down and live among men in order that he might serve them, it is necessary for me to become a convict among criminals in order that I may serve my country there, then I am perfectly willing to perform my service there. I will do it without a quiver. I will face the prison, I will face the things that go with prison life just as calmly and as serenely as I faced court and judge and jury, and I will do the things that it seems necessary for me to do. And understand this, Your

Honor: if you, this afternoon, decide that I am to serve a prison term, I
want you to know, and I want the District Attorney to know, and I want
these men who sat on the jury to know that I will go out of this court
room to meet whatever you mete out to me with no bitterness in my
heart, with no hate in my soul, but with nothing but the greatest feeling
of comradeship and friendship and appreciation for what you men have
done, because I believe that you have done the thing that you thought
was your duty to do. And so, if it must be that I go to prison, I do not
want a man who sat on the jury, I do not want the District Attorney, I do
not want Your Honor to go out of this room having any feeling that perhaps in some way you have committed a wrong, that you have injured
me, for, Your Honor, you cannot injure me, and the jury cannot injure
me, and the prosecuting attorney cannot injure me. There is only one
human being on earth that can injure me, and that is myself. And as long
as I am right with my God and right with my soul, you cannot, if you
would, injure me. You can send me to prison, but, thank God, you cannot send a great principle to prison. You can shut me behind a cell door,
but, thank God, you cannot put principle in a cell and turn the key on it.
You can degrade my body; you can put it in stripes; you can make me go
down and live with the lowest and most degraded and contaminated on
earth, and still you cannot injure me, for greater men and women have
done this. If the Son of God can come down and partake with publicans
and sinners, and confer with harlots and thieves and murderers, and be
uncontaminated, then, if I have His spirit, I can do the same thing. So I
want you to understand that whatever your decision will be I know you
are making it solely on the basis of the best interests of our country at
this time, and not with any intention to injure me.

And now, there is just one other thing I want to touch, and I am done.
Your Honor, the war is on now. It is a great world tragedy. This thing that
has shaken us all to the very center of our being, that has warped our
judgments and inflamed our passions, and made us different creatures
than we ever were before—possibly for our good—this war must end.
Peace must come. And when the war ends and peace comes, then will
come the trial of the human race. It is no test of humanity to successfully
wage a war. It does not take brains, or courage, or manhood to destroy.
An idiot can destroy in a moment what it took a lifetime to create. Mere
brute force can take a life only God can give. So the test is not going to
be the war. It is going to be the rebuilding of civilization after the war is

over. When the war is done and peace comes, the graves must be smoothed, the grape vines and wheat planted, the cities must be rebuilt, the ways of peace and justice and righteousness must be established. And after peace comes, Your Honor, and after the war is done, then there is just one other thing that you can consider. Will I, in that hour of reconstruction, can I and will I serve my country best in prison? Will that reconstruction go on better, wiser, for my elimination? Or is it possible that when that hour comes, and the maimed, and the broken, and the heartsick, and the soul-oppressed soldier comes home - in that hour when the widow must be comforted, and the sonless mother must be supported, and the orphan must be cared for - is it not possible that in that hour, in that day of stress and trial and heartache and misery that I, who have had twenty years of apprenticeship, twenty years of everlasting study and struggle to fit myself to deal with the downtrodden and the oppressed and the heartbroken, and soulsick, and weary - is it not possible that in that hour I can serve my country better at liberty to write and speak and do my work, than I can serve it incarcerated in a prison cell?

Now, Your Honor, I am only bringing these things to your attention, I am only asking you before you pass sentence to decide on these things, and remember there is but one thing now that I am asking for; and that is the greatest good to the greatest number, a nation united, that we burn into the souls and conscience of this country that this nation is so well armed by her righteousness that she need not persecute any human being - all I am asking you to consider is the danger of arousing hatreds and passions and suspicion. This is all. So now, Your Honor, I am ready to accept judgment, knowing full well that no matter what becomes of me, no matter what becomes of you, or what your action may be, that this great world tragedy is achieving the thing to which I have given my life, and that is it is bringing in the great co-operation instead of competition; a world where greed, and vice, and avarice have been replaced by brotherhood, and justice and humanity. And, Your Honor, since all my life has been given to that ideal of bringing about that new order, and sharing in that time, if this war is to do that thing, then, Your Honor, I can feel at this time that I can retire, perhaps, and rest.

So now, Your Honor, if you decide at this hour that in the service of your country, in the service of the people of this country, I should be sent to prison, then I go, knowing that the onward march of progress will still keep on, and eventually my aim, my goal, and my ideal will be achieved. And knowing this, Your Honor, I can face the court, I can face prison, I can face any sentence that you can give, serene and calm and unafraid.

Your Honor, I await the sentence that you see fit to pass upon me.

Waiting!

I am waiting now, just waiting, and thereby fulfilling the age-old task of women. It has been our portion to wait; to sit with folded hands or labor with straining nerves, but always to wait. We wait with every sense strained and quivering, and with bodies shot through with pain for the call of life that shall send us down into the valley and shadow, to return triumphant with the soft, warm body of a newborn babe to compensate; or that shall send us down the valley in agony while our men go forth to war; we wait in suspense while our loved ones go down into the mines; we wait while they go aloft on the swinging beams of the rising sky-scraper; we wait while they go to sea in ships; we wait while they go forth into the blackness of the night on rumbling trains. Always we wait. It is our portion.

I have waited for the call of life; I have waited while my mate went forth to meet the dangers that lurk in modern industry; I have waited while those I love went forth to war; and now I wait again. This time I wait the call to court. I wait to be arraigned before the august majesty of a judge; I wait to be tried by a jury of my peers; I wait while men decide whether I shall go home to my children, or be sent to prison.

Quite naturally, while I wait, the pictures of courtroom scenes flit through my mind by day, and weave themselves into my dreams at night. I see the smug, self-righteous judge upon the bench, the wrangling law-yers, the motley assortment of humanity in the jury box, the morbid courtroom loafers, the tortured prisoner in the dock; and always I try to imagine myself the central figure in the sordid scene. But my brain will not give me the picture. It is not that I am afraid, for I have never known the sense of fear; it is not that I have any sense of shame, for I have none; it is not that I recoil from being branded as a criminal, for I know that it

"Waiting!" was first published in *Social Revolution* (December, 1917), 4.

is alleged "crimes" that have lifted mankind from the slime of ignorance; and that it has been "criminals," so called by the ruling class, that has given humanity the most noble service. I feel that the reason for my inability to fit myself into the courtroom picture is that for so many years I have fought so ceaselessly and relentlessly for my fellow creatures that I can not fix my mind on the necessity of fighting for myself.

Yet I know that the fight at Bismark, North Dakota, will be a bitter one. Since the day that I was elected Chairman of the War and Militarism Committee[19] of the Emergency Convention in St. Louis last April, there has never been a day or night that I have not been under the eyes of secret service men. My mail has been opened, my baggage and express shipments held up, my grip searched in hotel rooms, and every sort of trap that ingenuity could fashion has been laid for me. The grim walls of the Federal prison are very close. There are hands that itch to clang the cell door upon me; and yet, I have never been more confident, more happy, and more sure of success for the cause to which I have given my life.

Don't imagine for one moment that I am at all anxious to be a martyr. I would far rather be comfortable than heroic. I would much prefer Florida to jail; and I am sure that I can be more useful to my class outside the bars than inside. We are going to make a fight for my freedom, and test the justice of our courts to the limit. We need help to wage this fight, and we are not backward in asking you to do your share. We need money to meet the cost of the legal battle; we need readers to hear and weigh our side of the question; we need the weight of public opinion in our favor; and it is from you soldiers in the ranks of the SOCIAL REVOLUTION that these things must come.

I am ready to do my share. I wait with the patience born of ages of waiting by my maternal ancestors; I will face court, judge and jury without flinching; I will be buried behind prison bars if need be, without cringing, IF—YOU WILL SHOULDER YOUR SHARE OF THE WORK THAT I MUST LAY DOWN.

One soldier more or less counts little in a battle; and, if I go to prison, the battle for human rights will go on and not miss me—IF—YOU PUT YOUR SHOULDER TO THE WHEEL. There is but one thing that counts

19. This committee was assigned the task of developing a party resolution or statement on the American involvement in the world war. The antiwar statement was later affirmed by the membership, in a referendum.

today—SOCIAL REVOLUTION MUST NOT BE THROTTLED. I count for little in a world of human endeavor; but the freedom of the press, the freedom of thought, the freedom of human expression, count for much. If a petty official is allowed to usurp the arbitrary power to crush a great periodical because it adheres to a different political faith than that official embraces, then freedom and democracy are dead in our nation. Usurped power is always arrogant—tyrannical in the face of cringing servility on the part of the people; but it cringes and cowers before the righteous wrath of aroused masses. IT IS YOUR SACRED DUTY, COMRADE, TO DO YOUR SHARE TOWARDS AROUSING THE PEOPLE TO RESIST THE WHOLESALE SLAUGHTER OF RADICAL PUBLICATIONS. . . .

Guilty!

GUILTY! Yes, according to a verdict rendered by a jury of my peers, I am guilty; according to the judgment of the trial judge, I am to serve five years in the prison at Jefferson City, Missouri.

"Guilty? You guilty of a crime meriting five years in prison! I can't grasp that." I can hear you say this, Comrade, as you read the story of my conviction.

It does seem a little difficult to grasp, doesn't it? Guilty of a felony, locked behind prison doors as punishment, an enemy to society. It is very hard to reconcile these facts with what you know of my life, isn't it? It almost makes your world reel and stagger to know that the friend and comrade who has worked by your side through all these long and trying years is a criminal and is sentenced to what in reality means a life sentence. No woman of my age and habits of life could possibly survive five years in that dank and noisesome cell at Jefferson City.

Take heart, comrades. Though the verdict and the sentence are grim realities, I AM NOT A CRIMINAL. This is not a mere statement of a sense of innocence on my part—it is the record of the case as it was tried and decided in the court at Bismarck, North Dakota. I was not indicted for a crime, in no place in the indictment is there any charge that I ever committed a crime. There was no testimony offered to prove that I was guilty of a crime; the district attorney never even suggested that I was guilty of

"Guilty!" was first published in *Social Revolution* (February, 1918), 2.

breaking any law or perpetrating any overt act. There was no charge made in the indictment or during the trial that any bad results followed my words, or that anything occurred that was in the slightest degree detrimental to any individual or to the government of the United States.

The only charge made by the district attorney; the only thing considered by the judge; the only thing the jury was ordered to consider was AN INTENT. An intent that was buried so deeply in my mind and heart that it never became manifest in action or results.

It seems impossible, does it not, that, in the Twentieth Century, when some knowledge of the law and legal processes are common to most men, a government attorney should ask an indictment; that an arrest should be made; that a judge should sit in owl-like wisdom on a bench; that a jury should be drawn; that witnesses should be examined; and that a lawyer who has been honored by a federal appointment, and must know that, according to all rules of law and justice, a court can only convict for a crime, should ask for my conviction on an intent that never developed into a crime? Yet this is exactly what happened in Bismarck, North Dakota.

The whole thing is grotesque and fantastic. It is such a travesty of common sense, law, courts and justice that we can not bring ourselves to feel that it is real. I can not yet feel that I have taken part in anything but some bit of idle buffoonery.

The charge made against me; the whole conduct of the case on the part of the prosecution sweeps us back to the days when witches were tried and burned at the stake in Salem, Massachusetts. The district attorney with impassioned oratory charged me, not with committing a crime, but with being a "dangerous woman," just as Cotton Mather charged "Goodwife" Hibbins with being dangerous to the peace and welfare of the colony of Massachusetts. John Fiske, the historian, says that Goodwife Hibbins was the victim of malice and was hanged only for having more wit than her neighbors. It is interesting to note that at the trial Mr. Hildreth only charged me with being guilty of being a "shrewd, intelligent, powerful woman."

Attorney Hildreth was quite sure that, while I had committed no crime, I had an intent to cast the "evil eye" on the young men of Bowman, and cause them to become slackers. He was not as logical as the clergy and lawyers who were zealous in ridding the colony of witches, however. They always had some tangible crime on which to hang their case. When Goodwife Glover was charged with being a witch, and Cotton Mather prosecuted her as zealously as Mr. Hildreth prosecuted me, there was evidence that the four children of her employer had fits, but never a fit did the young men of Bowman have. Goody Easty was charged with having "sore tormented Mercy Lewis," but, if the saintly Mr. James was "sore tormented," it was not by me or by anything I said or did, but by his own guilty conscience. Mrs. Ann Putman was charged with causing the rooster of Samuel Parris to lay an egg, but so far as is known up to the present time no rooster of Jim Phelan's has laid an egg. I am quite sure, however, that the only reason that Judge Wade did not order me to be bound hand and foot and thrown into the river as a test of my witchcraft was because it was thirty-three degrees below zero and the river was frozen solid.

If I had an intent to cast an evil spell upon the young men of Bowman, it failed to work. There was not a single slacker arrested there. Enlistments were up to the standard of all other counties, and the machinery of the draft went through without a hitch.

Comrades, it has been a long, soul-trying, courage-testing ordeal for me. I had to endure the long wait for trial; then the contest in the courtroom that was only saved from being unbearably tense and dramatic by my sense of humor and the comedy under the tragedy of being gravely tried for a crime that I was never charged with committing. Then came the charge of the judge to the jury which so explicitly and emphatically ordered them to convict me of an INTENT but not of a crime. The grim humor of this saved my sanity and poise for the time being. It also made it impossible for me to feel any bitterness against the judge; one can't be bitter against a person who only succeeds by being ridiculous.

The verdict came as no shock whatever. I knew before the trial had been in progress one hour just what it would be. Neither law nor testimony had the slightest place in the trial. The law most explicitly states, and one Supreme Court decision after another supports the presumption, that both intent and crime must be proven before a verdict of guilty can be returned. No crime was ever charged or proven, yet the judge demanded a verdict of guilty. My testimony was ample and complete. Twelve men and women made the long trip from Bowman on my simple request and without a single summons being served, and swore that the charges in the indictment were absolutely false. It would have been just as easy to have one hundred witnesses who would have testified to the same fact if I could have secured the money for traveling expenses and the judge would have allowed them to testify. This, however, he would not have allowed, for he refused to permit four of the witnesses that I had on hand to go on the stand in my behalf. The jury was out only thirty-five minutes, and they might just as well have returned the verdict without leaving the box, for only one result was possible under the charge of the judge.

After the verdict had been rendered there came the most inhuman and cruel bit of malice on the part of the judge of which a human being could be guilty. The verdict was reached on Friday, and I was kept waiting, waiting, waiting in my hotel room until the next Friday, just one week of eight days that were a century long. Waiting, always, to know what my sentence was to be, and to be allowed to secure bond and go home to spend the Christmas-time with my children. There was no reason on earth why sentence should not have been passed on the very same day or at least the next day after conviction. But the judge knew that no punishment on earth would be so bitter to me as to be kept away from my family and loved ones after such an ordeal as I had endured. It is evident to me that he hoped to break my spirit and bring me before him for sentence, a nervous wreck, willing to plead for mercy at his hands.

Thank God, we Socialists have sources of strength of mind and heart and soul that judges know not of. And I lived through the long, hellish days of waiting, gathering new strength and courage with every hour. No judge on earth can break me, for back of me are my husband and my children and my old grey-haired mother whose faith in me and whose loyalty to the cause of humanity will sustain me through any ordeal, even to the laying down of my life. Back of my family are the hundreds of thousands of comrades with whom I have worked and suffered and sacrificed for many years, and no trial can come to me that they will not share. Behind me in every hour of that trial and that waiting sentence was Phil Wagner and Gene Debs, George Kirkpatrick and Daddy Morgan, Frank Eastwood and Walter Hurt, Walter Milland and Edwin Wagner. Yes, and behind them was every employee of SOCIAL REVOLUTION from the red headed office boy to faithful, loyal Katie, the cashier. I knew that I had their love, and their confidence, and their loyalty; and I knew that they would divide their very blood or their last dime with me, and no petty venom can touch a soul so wonderfully supported as mine.

And I was not without support in Bismarck. During all of the trial and my time of waiting there, I have no memory of hurt or sorrow. No human being gave me even a glance that was not pregnant with sympathy and faith and loyalty. Nothing could have exceeded the kindness and the courtesy of the hotel employees. Clerks, diningroom girls, bell boys and elevator tenders, all gave me such service and attention as no money on earth can buy. Men who had much to lose and nothing to gain but their own self-respect offered me help that I could not accept lest their generosity might be seized upon by enemies to their hurt. A little crippled girl, whose struggle for life must be desperate, came and offered me a five-dollar bill that meant more to me than a gift of a million dollars might. A man, who digs his living in the ditch, came to speak a word of encouragement, and slipped a worn-torn dollar bill under a book on my desk.

I cannot finish the story of my trial without attempting in some way to make you comrades feel how much we owe to my attorney, Mr. V. R. Lovell of Fargo. My sense of debt to this able lawyer and kindly, courteous gentleman is the greater because he is not a Socialist. It is all in the family with us—I can demand all kinds of service, and ask for, and expect to receive, all kinds of help and assistance from comrades who have weathered so many struggles with me. I have every right to expect the Socialists to stand by me and help fight my battles, no matter what the result may be. We are in the same position that Samuel Adams said the Revolutionary forefathers were—"if we don't hang together we may hang separately." I have a right to demand and expect unfaltering loyalty from you Socialists, but Mr. Lovell is not one of us, and the loyalty and splendid courage, the able legal service and unfailing human kindness which he has displayed during the trial, and the weary time of waiting since, has been most marked. It took a lot of courage on his part to take my case; it demanded sheer grit and moral fibre of the highest kind to face the bitter criticisms that have come to him from his friends and associates. It takes manhood of the right sort for a perfectly respectable non-Socialist to deliberately shoulder a large-sized bunch of trouble, by defending me at this time. None but a big man could do it; and, in these trying weeks of stress and strain and ordeal, I have learned that there is at least one big, fearless, loyal, courteous gentleman who has been guilty of voting the Democratic ticket all his life. I know now that there are men who disagree with us (largely because they don't understand) who can still be brave and faithful to a trust, unflinching in the face of criticism, absolutely without mercenary motives and willing to make great sacrifices to serve the ends of justice. Much as your loyalty and unspoken support has been to me in this trying time, it was Mr. Lovell who was on the job from the day the trial started until the hour I was permitted to leave for home; and it was his help, and service, and kindly consideration which enabled me to go through with it all in full command of myself and in a way that you need not blush for. He is a stiff necked, uncompromising Bourbon Democrat, but there is enough of the right sort of stuff in him to make a mighty good Socialist.

It has been a long, hard experience, comrades, but I am not a criminal, and I am not in prison yet. I have no intention of going to prison if I can avoid it. I am going to make the fight of my life for freedom, and you must help me. My greatest need just at this time is money. We must have money and plenty of it to carry the case up to higher courts, and I am going to ask you to help us get it.

This is our battle, comrade; and we must fight it out together. I want you to go down in your pocket and get that sadly crumpled, sweat-stained bill; then gently wave it before the eyes of every Socialist and sympathizer with justice that you know, and tell them that it is going down to St. Louis to make up a defense fund for Kate O'Hare; and suggest that since they are in no danger of going to jail and can earn another that they match it. If every one of my friends in the United States will just sacrifice one day's wages, I may be saved from a five-year prison term. WILL YOU DO IT, COMRADE?

The End of Act One

For almost twenty years I have walked my toilsome path of life surrounded by tragedy; but it has always been the tragedies of other lives, for "only the sorrows of others have cast their shadows over me." Now I am facing the supreme tragedy of life, a prison sentence that virtually means a life sentence. No woman at the turn of life, who has lived an active, inspiring out-door existence, could possibly live through five

"The End of Act One" was first published in *Social Revolution* (March, 1918), 2, 13.

years in the hell-hole at Jefferson City. Strong men have been broken and killed there in as many months, and I would have no hope of surviving the sentence.

I have a husband and four children; and the children are just at the age when they need a mother most. They are a boy just on the verge of young manhood; a girl approaching the critical period of life; and twin boys at the "troublesome age," when only a mother can be patient and understanding. It seems impossible that human beings could fall so low and be swayed by ignorant passion, or bent by economic pressure, to deliberately perjure themselves in order to murder a woman by slow torture, and wreck the lives of her children. Yet that is the grim situation that I face. The jury might have had grounds for reasonable doubt of my innocence. They were not present at my lecture, but every witness for the prosecution knows that the language ascribed to me was a vicious and perjured perversion of the truth.

It has been a source of constant wonder and comment, both by my friends and enemies, that I could face such vicious, glaring injustice, keep my poise and remain unembittered. This was only possible for me because I knew that I was innocent, and more than a million people in the United States share that knowledge. With such mental and moral support I could not weaken. I was protected by the love and loyalty and comradeship of all who knew me; and it was this that made me strong enough to go through the ordeal unscathed. I knew that my old mother, my husband, my children, the SOCIAL REVOLUTION force, and the mass of thinkers of the country, were standing loyally by me, and that knowledge made a barrier that perjury and injustice could not break.

Naturally, I counted on the support and loyalty of those near and dear to me, and of the Socialists of the nation; but the marvelous loyalty and tender courtesy of men and women who are not Socialists, and on whom I had no claim, is one of the most beautiful things in my life.

As a young girl I used to bemoan the fact that the days of knighthood were past, and that no chivalric champion could ever serve me with knightly valor; yet, with youth long behind me, I found that no knight ever served a "lady fair" more valiantly than a young farmer served me. I found it necessary to go to Bowman and secure my witnesses. Those who could serve me best were all ranchers and farmers living from six to twenty miles out in the country. The young man, whose name I may not even mention (lest he be made to suffer for his service to me), owned a car and knew the country and the people I must reach. We left the hotel at Bowman at six in the morning, drove until five-thirty in the evening, covering almost two hundred miles of country roads on a bitterly cold day. When we arrived at the hotel, after a drive that would have taxed the strength and courage of most men to the limit, I found a telegram saying that my case had been put forward on the docket. The only possible way in which I could reach Bismarck in time to protect my bondsmen, was to drive eighty-five miles across the plains to another line of railroad. A blizzard had arisen and the snow was piling up in regular North Dakota fashion. In the face of that roaring storm we drove eighty-five miles through the night, arriving at the railroad station in the early hours of the morning. My driver had duties that he could not neglect, and again he faced the storm and drove the eighty-five miles back through the blizzard. I had never known greater heroism and chivalry than this. And the young man was not a Socialist; he had simply attended my lecture and knew that I was innocent.

All of my twelve witnesses came to Bismarck on my mere request. There was not a single summons issued. They paid their own expenses, amounting to over fifty dollars each, and trusted me to repay them. Nine of the men were farmers—men with farms and stock to care for, yet they left their stock in the midst of a blizzard and came to serve me. Three of my witnesses were women; and they left their homes and children in the care of neighbors, and made the long, weary, bitterly cold journey to Bismarck because I was a woman, and they knew that I was innocent. So far as I know, none of my witnesses was a Socialist, and none had ever seen me until my lecture in Bowman. When the verdict was returned all of the men signed my bond; and, in less than an hour I was at liberty on a five-thousand-dollar bond.

Four of the witnesses who had made such great sacrifices, and whose traveling expenses were so heavy for us to bear, were not allowed to testify. Judge Wade arbitrarily refused us the right to put our witnesses on the stand.

The first act of the tragedy is finished now. We must wait until a higher court acts in the case. That action may mean justice for me; or it may mean a life sentence, a broken home, and four children robbed of their mother. BUT, WHATEVER THE RESULT, I WOULD NOT IF I COULD

UNDO ONE HOUR OF MY LIFE WORK, OR UNSAY ONE WORD THAT HAS PASSED MY LIPS. I HAVE NOTHING TO REGRET, NOTHING TO APOLOGIZE FOR, AND IF I LIVE AND HAVE MY FREEDOM I WILL CONTINUE TO DO IN THE FUTURE JUST WHAT I HAVE DONE IN THE PAST.

Once again I must face the weary months of suspense and WAITING, but while I WAIT, WE MUST ALL BE AT WORK. The human race has never been so ripe for our message as now, and there are a few months left in which I can help to bring that message to the masses. Physically, mentally and spiritually I am stronger than ever before; and, if I must go to prison, I want to make every moment of freedom count. If a DEFENSE MEETING can be arranged in your town, I want to come, if possible. If that can not be done, then help me to speak to your friends and neighbors through the SOCIAL REVOLUTION. Plutocracy, autocracy and injustice are already beginning to tremble and crumble. I WANT TO STRIKE THEM A FEW MORE SMASHING BLOWS BEFORE THE PRISON DOORS CLOSE ON ME.

The district attorney of the Dakota district is, of course, the most prominent of the group; and Mr. Hildreth is a typical prosecuting attorney. Practically all of his adult life has been spent in the practice of law; and, naturally, his profession brought him mostly in contact with the elements in human nature that are hard, sordid, brutal and degenerate. Normal, wholesome people rarely come in conflict with the law; and, as a rule, only the warped and abnormal, the brutal and degenerate, have to do with courts and lawyers. A lawyer, particularly one who has spent years as a public prosecutor, lives and has his being because of the weakness, vice, sin, misery, poverty and degradation of his fellowmen. When a man makes these elements of human nature his means of livelihood, they must and do leave their mark upon him. The only lawyer who escapes the blight of his profession is the man who develops a social conscience and thereby saves his own soul.

Mr. Hildreth has the reputation of being one of the most hard, cold and relentless of his type. I was told by many that his methods in handling witnesses in cross-examination was brutal in the extreme, and all my friends who knew him begged that I would not go on the stand and subject myself to the suffering it would entail. But, when the test came, I found that all their fears were groundless. When I came in contact with Mr. Hildreth, I found a man with the marks of his professional life deep

scarred upon him, but I also found a man suffering keenly from the travail of the birth of a social conscience that is coming into life late in a
hard, abnormal existence. By that wordless language, with which one
soul communicates with another, I knew from the first that Mr. Hildreth
was not my enemy; that he did not hate me or wish me ill; and that he
did not believe me guilty of even the intent with which he charged me.
He simply was not strong enough to withstand the pressure that was
brought to bear by the powers that he had served so long. He was a
reluctant prosecutor, and the newspaper reporters gossiped about the
court-house corridors and the hotel lobbies that "Hildreth was lying
down on the job." He was always kind and courteous to me, and the
cross-examination which we felt would be a frightful ordeal did not bring
me a single moment of pain. I hope that the clouds of war may soon pass,
and that I may have the opportunity to be the friend of Mr. Hildreth, for
he will need friends most bitterly as he walks through the darkness of
the Gethsemane that stretches before him.

The sinister power in the case was the man who never appeared in
the court room, who never testified on the witness stand—James Phelan,
the banker-political boss of Bowman County. Mr. Phelan is, from appearance, what we people who spell our names with an O' call "shanty-
Irish," and that tells the whole story. He is said to have been a railroad
man in early life, but was too shrewd and unscrupulous to remain long
in the working class. Just where, or how, he secured money to go into
the banking business, no one seems to know. Local history simply relates
that he appeared on the scene in Bowman in the early days, started a
small bank, and began to lay his wires for the political and business domination of the county. To anyone who knows the history of the pioneer
community where poor men make the desperate struggle to subdue the
wilds, the rise to power and wealth of the banker-politician is an old
story. It has been enacted a thousand times in the small towns all over
the west and south. An investigation, made by the agents of the United
States a few years ago, laid bare the methods used; and it is a black page
of our national history that I need not enlarge upon. Suffice it to say that
James Phelan, like thousands of others of his type, waxed fat and rich in
money; held mortgages on the business, the activities, the very lives and
souls of the majority of the men in his community—ruled with an iron
hand the politics of the county; and dabbled successfully in the underground politics of the state. None had ever risen strong enough to con-

test his reign until the Non-Partisan League[20] appeared on the scene; and, in a single year, it ousted him bag and baggage from the political control of the county, installing a group of business men in Bowman who were economically independent of him. The man who led the fight that defeated him so completely was Judge E. P. Totten; and Lillian Totten, his wife, was appointed postmistress at Bowman—a job that Phelan wanted for James, his faithful henchman. One thing more that makes Mr. Phelan's hate and animus to me clear—he is a staunch Catholic and a bitter and vindictive enemy of Socialism and all things that tend to human progress and the emancipation of the masses.

Of the witnesses used by the prosecution it is hard to write, for the memory of their faces always brings a pang to me. Mr. James, the leading witness, seemed to be (from what I could observe and what the people of Bowman told me) a poor, weak, inefficient Uriah Heep with a flabby body, bloodless hands, a face the color of bad piedough, and fishy, shifty eyes that never look straight into the eyes of another. The only job that he had worked at for some time, so far as I could learn, was that of passing the collection plate in the stand-pat church—he seems to be the sort of a deacon that Harry Tichnor[21] loves so warmly. He is said to be so inefficient that he cannot stem the tide of life in the stern struggle for existence on the Dakota plains, and is reduced to the position of a political camp-follower, subsisting upon the garbage of political spoils, and desperately in need of the postoffice as a means of livelihood. Mr. James is not the first man, and will not be the last, who will attempt to swear away the life and liberty of an innocent person for a nineteen-hundred-dollar-a-year job and the patronage of a banker-politician.

The second in importance of the prosecution witnesses was Dr. Whit-

20. The Non-Partisan League spearheaded an agrarian uprising in the upper Midwest. The league was organized in 1915 among wheat farmers. Arthur Charles Townley, a bankrupt North Dakota flax farmer and Socialist party organizer, was the founder. The league demanded state-owned storage elevators and mills, package plants, state hail insurance, rural credits, and also taxation reforms. The league elected local candidates to office, and by 1919 its program was enacted into law in North Dakota. Neighboring states, such as South Dakota, Minnesota, and Montana, also witnessed league activities, with the key demand everywhere state-owned marketing facilities, but nowhere was success so marked as in North Dakota. The league's wartime advocacy of conscription of wealth led to charges of its disloyalty.

21. Harry M. Tichenor (1858–1922) was a midwestern journalist who became a socialist around the turn of the century. With Phil Wagner, he founded the *Melting Pot* in St. Louis in 1913 and served as editor until it ceased publication in 1920. He wrote a number of books, most of which satirized orthodox religion.

timore. There is little to be said of him except that he is a typical, young, small-town doctor, who is said to have lost most of his professional business by taking a stand antagonistic to the Non-Partisan League. He is the owner of the stand-pat drug store which is said to be heavily mortgaged to Mr. Phelan. . . .

. . . Upon the unsupported testimony of one hungry job-hunter, the whole prosecution, or persecution, is based. The whole case was such a pitiful demonstration of the blight of capitalism upon the lives of human beings.

Farewell Address of Kate Richards O'Hare

I would not if I could have one day different, one hour unlived, one deed undone, one word unspoken. I have nothing to regret, nothing to retract, nothing for which to apologize. I am willing to leave my life as I have lived it and let the future judge between me and my judges."

So said Kate Richards O'Hare to audiences in Miller's, La Touraine and the East Side Labor Lyceum, Buffalo, N. Y., halls Thursday night. She is to be taken to the Missouri state penitentiary on April 12 to serve five years at hard labor for making a Socialist speech at Bowman, North Dakota, on July 17, 1917. She made the same speech in 72 [*sic*] other places.

"For eighteen months the very atmosphere of the nation has been surcharged with the roaring, shrieking shouts of Americanism, then in a single day a thunderous silence descended upon us and we felt the stunned scene of unreality that fell upon the soldiers in the trenches when the signing of the armistice suddenly stopped the roar and bedlam of war.

"Like the toper suddenly separated from his bottle, or the 'coke' fiend from his 'snuff,' we felt a growing desire for the exhilaration of the intoxicant of rampant Americanism. We resented the gray, colorless, sordid aspects of the life robbed of the rosy glow of patriotism. When the armistice spread the black pall of silence over fervid oratory and burning

"Farewell Address of Kate Richards O'Hare" was published in Oakland *World*, April 25, 1919, a reprint from the *New Age*.

editorials, we felt a deep sense of personal loss; something was missing from our lives.

"And there is another cry—vague, and shrouded in mystery. Sometimes used to express the superlative of disorder and lawlessness—sometimes to indicate in a mild and academic way, a hoped for refuge from the social tornado—the word 'Socialism.'

"And, as the word 'Americanism' goes into eclipse, and the word 'Socialism' no longer evokes terror, comes another word—'Bolshevism.'

"Max Eastman,[22] one of the foremost writers and teachers of the country, went to Fargo, North Dakota, to deliver a lecture on 'Democracy.' A great crowd evidently interested in the thing we were fighting to make the world safe for, gathered in the court to listen to what he had to say. A drunken mob, led by a judge and a 'very respectable' attorney, invaded the 'temple of justice' and would have murdered Max Eastman but for the sublime heroism and unflinching courage of a woman. An attempted murder of Max Eastman was flaunted as an exhibition of the 'spirit of Americanism.'

"During the time when 'Americanism' was so very rampant, I went to Erie, Pennsylvania, to deliver a lecture on 'Christ Before Pilate.' As I sat at the dinner table in the hotel, a dining room girl, shaking with fear and hysterical with excitement, came to me and begged that I would not leave the hotel that evening and would not attempt to do my work. When I pressed her for a reason, she gave me a copy of the Erie Times, and in a box on the front page, in glaring type, was an invitation for all good Americans to be at the court house at eight o'clock that evening with their guns to murder me, as proof of their burning 'Americanism.'

"Then there was written into the history of our country the most shameful story of abject cowardice on the part of elected officials that has ever blackened the pages of human history—the so-called 'espionage act.' In the future our grandchildren will read in their school histories the names of the men responsible for that law with exactly the same

22. Max Eastman (1883–1969), editor of the literary journal the *Masses*, was a Socialist party supporter, and had his periodical barred from the U.S. mails during the war. He immediately commenced publication of the *Liberator*, a similar organ. A decade later he became the publisher of the *New Masses*, and ended his long career as a political and literary commentator in the 1960s as a conservative spokesman writing for *Reader's Digest*.

feeling that we school children felt when we read the name of Judge
Taney, of the Dred Scott decision fame.[23]

"Was this Americanism?

"By the enactment of certain parts of this one act a way was opened
by which we as people lost rights secured by hundreds of years of cease-
less struggle, rights that had been bought and paid for in the blood and
suffering of our fathers, religious liberty, the very ideal that sent the Pu-
ritan forefathers to this savage land, was destroyed overnight. In the land
whose constitution guarantees religious liberty, by the misuse of this act,
scores of men were sent to prison for ten and twenty years for circulating
a book that stated in the mildest, gentlest language that wars were contrary to the teaching of Jesus. Thousands of young men whose religious
convictions made it impossible for them to bear arms or kill their fellow
men were forced by the most brutal methods into uniforms, dragged like
felons to training camps, subjected to tortures that vie with the horrors
of the Inquisition, and that sent many of them to an untimely grave.

Free Speech Crushed

"In all modern history there has never been such a flagrant violation of
the very spirit of free speech. Not even in Russia under the bloody czars
were such brutal laws enacted to curb natural expression of opinions, and
not even by the czar's henchmen were they so ruthlessly and unfairly
enforced. Under the operation of the 'espionage act' it was not necessary
to really commit the crime of having an opinion of the administration; it
was not necessary to do anything at all, or to be responsible for any results. Hundreds of people are now behind prison bars whom the administration never charged with any overt act; they merely were found guilty
for having an 'intent,' and that 'intent' was sufficient to call down upon
their heads punishment far more severe than is dealt out to thieves, bank
wreckers, white slaves and murderers. No white slaver who has made
traffic in human flesh for the profits of vice in this country has ever been
sentenced to five, ten or twenty years in prison, as Rose Pastor Stokes,[24]

23. Roger B. Taney was chief justice at the time of the Supreme Court decision,
March 6, 1857, that denied a slave the right to sue in federal court. Judicial endorsement
of the proslavery point of view, stating that a slave was a citizen of neither state nor
country, further polarized the two sections of the country.

24. Rose Pastor Stokes (1879–1933), a Jewish immigrant from Poland, had worked as
a cigarmaker. She became a labor journalist and a socialist, and married a party comrade,

Eugene V. Debs and others have been sentenced for having an 'intent' that never accomplished any purpose whatever.

Jailed for "Intent"

"And an 'intent' need not be proven, if such a thing could be. All that was necessary to draw a long prison sentence was to have a reputation in the labor movement for loyalty and service to the working class, a couple of nondescript witnesses and a jury hand picked by the 'Council of Defense'[25] and the trick was done. I saw in the tombs in New York City a tiny, half-starved scrap of girlhood that should have been in a grade school, who was sentenced to twenty years at hard labor for saying that President Wilson was a hypocrite, and that girl is now serving this monstrous sentence with Stars and Stripes the emblem of freedom, justice, and democracy, flying over the hell-hole in which she is imprisoned.

Hypocritical Cry of "Disloyalty"

"Then all over this country came a reign of terror, a prostitution of courts and a violation of constitutional rights by elected officials for which our children and our children's children will blush in shame. Soon the country was overrun by spies, seeking not German vandals but Americans who held ideas and beliefs differing from the administration. Soon every vicious element in our society was hot on the trail of every man or woman who had ever stood for social justice and industrial democracy, and found it an easy matter to railroad them to prison. It was only necessary to cry 'disloyal,' 'seditious,' 'pro-German,' 'un-American,' and like the witches of old the leaders of the working class were hounded, imprisoned and murdered.

The New World "Bolshevism"

"What is the strange, new force that is sweeping over the world—this fearsome Bolshevism?

"If we place the slightest dependence on the truthlessness of our newspapers and other censored sources of public information, we well

---

the millionaire J. G. Phelps Stokes, in 1905. She was a party lecturer and agitator, and in 1918 was convicted under the Espionage Act for a letter she wrote in which she criticized war profiteering. The conviction was later overturned.

25. The Council of Defense was one of the many patriotic organizations that sponsored meetings and parades, urged rationing, and promoted the purchase of war bonds.

might shudder before its danger and fear the Bolshevist reign of terror, its orgy of rapine, lust, free-love, robbery, bloodshed, and wholesale murder. But, in spite of all the shouts and groans and cries of the 'press,' we remain quite calm, serene and unafraid. We have learned by long and bitter experience that when the 'kept press' assails a thing, that it must be something very beneficial to the working class; that when the newspapers slander and villify an individual or movement may be serving the masses and endangering the privileged classes.

"Bolshevism is a new word, but the charges brought against it and its supporters have a strangely familiar sound—we seem to remember them of old. Privilege is so sterile of ideas; so barren of imagination, that it has not been able to think of one new lie; to concoct one fresh slander; to turn one new trick or say one new thing about Bolshevism that has not already been worn to tatters in the assaults upon abolition of slavery, trade unionism, woman's suffrage, Socialism, the Non-Partisan League and the I. W. W.

"The scarecrows that it dangles before our eyes have ceased to alarm us; familiarity has bred contempt. Bolshevism may cause the goose-flesh of abject terror to prickle the spine of the 'powers that prey,' but it has no terrors for the working class. We know that robbery, rapine, free-love, and murder have just as much relation to Bolshevism as mob violence, thuggery, and murder have to Americanism.

Socialism Hastened by World War

"Socialism is coming, and it seems poetic justice that it should be thrust upon the world by its most bitter enemies. Industrial and political autocracy run mad plunged the whole world into war, and then the world, in order to save itself from utter destruction, was compelled to turn to Socialism for salvation. The warring nations did not make the long strides towards industrial democracy because they loved the Socialists, or wanted Socialism, but because it is the only thing that can meet the situation and save the world from utter chaos and ruin.

"For twenty years the Socialists have been trying vainly to give you 'great' American sovereign voting kings'—Socialism. We tried so hard to make you understand—we wanted you to take Socialism in peace and intelligence, by the sane, sober use of your ballots, but you would have none of it. You were good Democrats or Republicans and we were a lot of crazy fanatics, and you refused to take Socialism in peace, by lawful, constitutional means.

"Now, you dear old mossbacks, rock-ribbed, hidebound Democrats and Republicans have had a little Socialism thrust into you on the end of a bayonet, and it wasn't a Socialist bayonet, either. Well, if you like it better that way, we must be content. We did our best, there is no blood on our hands and no guilt on our skirts, and if you have been compelled to learn your lesson and take your Socialism in the bloodshed and agony, the hell and horror of war, you and you alone are to blame.

Danger of Insane Revolt

"Friends! I know, and you know, if you have the moral courage to face the facts, that we are on the verge of social revolution. A social revolution that is coming, not because Socialists have preached the gospel of industrial democracy, but because you have turned a deaf ear to it. The streets of this city, and of every other city may run red with the blood spilled in mad revolt; in wild, unrestrained and insane revolution, before the snow falls again unless there is more breadth of vision, more real statesmanship displayed by our elected officials than has yet been displayed.

"And that red revolution will not be stayed by a Supreme Court decision that sends a thousand Socialists to prison by sustaining the 'espionage' act. That decision of the United States Supreme Court handed down on the third day of March, 1919,[26] may be but another Dred Scott decision, that decides nothing but the sublime stupidity of the ruling class. Judge Taney and his associates, by that memorable decision in 1857, sent one poor, humble negro back to slavery, but he also sent one million of the pick and flower of American manhood to death on the battle fields of the Civil War, and he sent three million negroes to final freedom.

"That red revolution that threatens will not be stayed by passing laws making it a crime to display a red flag. Revolution can come under a pink flag, or a green one, or a blue, or under the Stars and Stripes, or under no flag at all. The want of a biscuit, a beefsteak and a job has caused more revolutions than all the flags that ever waved, and when red revolution comes in this country, it will not be because of the bitter want for bread, meat, labor and love.

26. On March 3, 1919, the Supreme Court denied O'Hare's petition for certiorari.

Has No Regrets

"Comrades, I am closing now. This may be the last message that I shall ever give you, for in a few short days I, too, will be one of the political prisoners shut behind steel bars.

"For myself I have no regrets, and only a deep sense of humility and thankfulness if I may be counted worthy to take my place at the very bottom of that illustrious list of those who have died for the love of their fellow-men.

"Looking back over twenty years, I am content. I gave to the service of the working class all that I had and all that I was, and no one can do more. I gave my girlhood, my young womanhood, my wifehood and my motherhood. I have taken babies unborn into the thick of the class war; I have served in the trenches with a nursing baby at my breast; I leave my children now without my care and protection, but I know that I have only done my duty.

"I would not, if I could, have one day different; one hour unlived; one deed undone; one word unspoken. I have nothing to regret, nothing to retract, nothing for which to apologize. I am willing to leave my life as I have lived it; and let the future judge between me and my judges.

"I want you to know that I am calm, serene and unafraid, and face my ordeal without hate in my heart and without fear for the future. Nothing that I may find behind prison walls can injure me. I can and will rise above it all. And I will not be idle there; my work will not end, there is a bigger and more urgent work for me to do in prison than I ever found outside. I have tried to serve the workers because I felt they needed service, but the thousands of helpless victims of our stupid, outworn penal system need me more. If there is any institution in our social organism which needs the light of intelligent study, rational understanding and sane revolution, it is our criminal laws; their administration and systems of punishment.

"When I go to prison, I leave four children outside: a boy of fifteen, a girl of twelve, and twins, boys ten years of age.

"And to my children, I know no one can take a mother's place, but they, too, come of good fighting stock, and they will face the loss of their mother with courage worthy of their ancestry. When they are old enough to understand, they will rather have had a mother inside prison walls true to her ideals and principles, than outside, a craven coward who

dared not protest when our rights were wrested from us and when griev-
ous wrongs were thrust upon us.

"It is not my fate or the fate of my children that I tremble for, it is the
fate of my country. It is not a prison cell that I dread, but blind, insane,
unintelligently directed revolution. It is not the nightmare of gray stone
walls that fills my dreams, but the picture of gutters of our cities running
red with the blood of our people."

PART III
Letters from Prison

April 20, 1919

Dear Sweethearts:

I can only write one letter but Papa will copy it and send it on. First of all, I am quite all right. I feel perfectly well, sleep like a baby and eat like a harvest hand. The quiet after the stress, strain and hard work of these trying times is really restful.

So far I seem to feel no sense of shock whatever. I entered quite as calmly as I have registered at hundreds of hotels and the clang of the cell door did not disturb me more than the slamming of my room door by a careless bell boy. I have either much more poise, courage and strength of character than I dreamed of possessing, or I am psychologically stunned. I suppose that Dr. Zeuch[1] or Dr. Barnes might say the latter.

At any rate I am having a most interesting time. Life is the "Great Adventure" and I am living one of its most interesting and illuminating experiences. I have learned much, so very much, in these strained days; lessons of pride and humility; lessons of laughter and sorrow; lessons of high comedy and bitter tragedy. I have learned that prison cells can teach greater and more useful lessons than college classrooms.

And don't think that I am gloomy and lonely and unloved here, for I

All letters to her family have "Jefferson City, Mo." above the date and are addressed to "F. P. O'Hare, 1011 Holland Bldg., St. Louis, Mo."

1. Professor William E. Zeuch (b. 1892) was a young socialist economist who worked with O'Hare in labor education. He was fired by Clark University for an antiwar comment. He wrote the pamphlet *The Truth About the O'Hare Case*.

certainly am not. Through all the tragedy and heart-ache there come sparkles of wit and flashes of humor, and we really find many things to laugh over.

I have received so many beautiful letters. You must let the comrades know that I will be glad to get letters from all of them, that there is no limit to what I can receive, but I can write only one letter a week, and that, of course, must be to the family.

Have the publishers send me the new books; I can't get too much reading matter. There are 80 girls here, and there is not a book, magazine or particle of reading matter supplied to the women.

I have received my various packages and I am quite comfortable. I got the flowers and candy this morning and the message they brought was very sweet and welcome. I am only short a soft metal knife and fork now and I will be all fixed.

Food is a problem. The kitchen is three blocks from the women's dining hall, and everything is stone cold when served and is uneatable. But we may have everything that does not require cooking sent in from the outside. It will take some thought for me to work out a balanced ration.

Tell the women comrades that I will be very glad to have any sort of home-made jams, jellies and pickles, in fact anything that is put up in small containers. Tell Mrs. Wagner to send me some of her nice cookies, and the Jewish comrades to send me a box of Matzos. I would like some of Mrs. K's tiny pickles and onions also. And, Frank, when you come to Jefferson City, arrange with a grocer to send me such vegetables and fruit as I can manage. And send me a little stand about six inches deep, and two feet wide, the height of a table, with three or four shelves to keep things on.

My cell is about eight feet square, with steel walls, the front is of bars, I have a table and chair, and I have received the rug and table cover, the sheets and pillow cases and bed spread, and it looks quite comfortable. We scrub our cells thoroughly once a week. There is light and ventilation, and happily, no bad smells, for no cooking is permitted in the cells.

Our little world has its comedies, its vanities, its classes and its castes, just like the big world outside. The "federals" are for some reason the "upper class", and the "politicals" are the aristocracy. There are three real "politicals", Emma Goldman,[2] a wonderful little girl of 18, and my-self. There is another "espionage", but she is just a poor, simple old soul, about as dangerous to the government as an old cow.

It is certainly a great thing to have two women like the two "politicals" with me here. Emma is very fine and sweet, and intellectually compan-ionable, while the little girl is a darling. We have really interesting times.

Next in rank are the women who have disposed of undesirable hus-bands, and at this point I want to expound for all of my male friends a bit of wisdom. If you chance to have one of those meek, patient, quiet, long-suffering wives, beware that you do not try them too far, or some morn-ing you may wake up in paradise, or the other place. If you have chanced to get a temperamental lady of shrewish tendencies, you may be uncom-fortable, but you will be safe.

You might tell the Rev. Dr. Bitting that I understand him now. I now know what he feels when he comes into contact with the working class. I feel the same thing here. I want to come close to these women, I want to serve them, but I am conscious of the fact that they feel that I am one apart from them. Quite often I feel that I am reaching a human soul, uncovering a rich vein of underdog philosophy, and then some cynical soul says "Aw cut it—she's a lady." And I am baffled and shut out and realize that "ladies" and "clergymen" are purely ornamental, and can have no relation to real life. But I feel that I am gaining ground and in time I will not be penalized for being a "lady". One thing in my favor is that I can work. I am certainly thankful for my manual dexterity. The work in the factory does not trouble me in the least. I understand that I have broken all records for beginners in making jumpers. I feel a little stiff and sore, but it is nothing serious. I feel sure that I will be able to make the "task" by next week, which is 55 jumpers each day.

I am wondering if you will be able to read this. Writing a long letter by hand is a task for me, and a greater one for those who must read it. I

2. Emma Goldman (1869–1940) was perhaps the most famous (or infamous) woman radical of the era. A Russian immigrant, she became an anarchist by the age of twenty. As the major figure of the minuscule American anarchist movement, she tirelessly toured the country on behalf of her ideology and also spoke on behalf of women's rights and birth control. She was imprisoned for a year during the depression of the 1890s, charged with inciting a crowd to riot for telling the unemployed to demand bread. In 1917 she again went to prison for encouraging men to refuse the draft through the No-Conscription League, which she and her lifelong comrade, Alexander Berkman, had organized. Both were released from prison in 1919 and deported to Russia. The third "political" was an

feel sure that by the time Governor Painter, the warden,[3] has deciphered a letter or two of mine, he will be willing to let me have my little Corona typewriter for his own sake if not for mine. . . .

This is Easter, and I think it means more to me than any other Easter in my whole life. I think that I have come just a little nearer the soul of the universe; that I can touch hands across the ages with all who have walked through Gethsemane and who have found peace for their own souls in service for others.

It seems strange, but it is true, that to-day it is not my own loved ones, not even my comrades, that I long to reach with an Easter message of love and cheer. My own have the memories of long years of love and they can afford to lend me for a time to these poor, despoiled, despairing creatures here. I want you, my children and my husband, to feel that you have only loaned me for a time to those who need me far more bitterly than you do.

I want the Comrades with whom I have worked for years with all my strength, to feel that they must not be bitter if I am taken away for a little while to be with the bitterly wronged victims of our social stupidity.

I am deeply grateful to be where I am to-day and to have found such a place of service. I know that my children are secure. Gene and Victor will be tenderly cared for at Chaminade; Kathleen will be happy with Cousins Mamie and Charles, and Mrs. K. and the St. Louis comrades will take care of my big boys. And there are so many who need me here. The poor little "dope fiend" in the cell next to me needs me more than my own do. You have love and health and the beautiful world; she has only the hellish cry of her nerves for "dope", the black despair born of the neglect of those who should help her, and the gnawing hunger of a long under-nourished body. I can feed her and encourage her and pet her, and I think if Jesus were consulted on the matter, he would prefer that I should be here this Easter Day rather than in some magnificent church.

If I were outside to-day I might be speaking to a great crowd. Perhaps my empty place and silent voice will serve my comrades and my cause better than my presence.

eighteen-year-old Italian immigrant, Gabriella Antolina. For a brief time, there was a fourth "political" who was also a young immigrant, Molly Steimer.

3. William R. Painter (1863–1947), acting warden, was not a trained penologist. He was a Democrat, lieutenant governor of Missouri from 1913 to 1917, and headed the Missouri State Prison Board.

So do not worry about me, and do not be sad. I am all right and I will come back to you a better wife, a more tender mother and a wiser and more efficient comrade.

The floor girl has just come to tell me that it is time to turn in my letter, so I must close now.

You must all be brave and cheerful and go on just as if I had not been taken from you. Tell the Comrades to go on with my work and all will be well.

Love and kisses to my darlings, and greetings to the friends and Comrades.

MAMMA

April 26, 1919

My Darling Sweethearts:

This is Saturday evening, and I will write a part of my letter so it will not take up too much of my time tomorrow.

We do not work Saturday afternoon, and have almost three hours outdoors, so I am feeling fine. I am still doing nicely, eat and sleep well, and do not suffer particularly because of the work. Of course, nine hours per day at a sewing machine is no light task, but I am perfectly well, and quite efficient, so manage very nicely.

I hope that none of you are worried about me, for I am really having a most interesting time. In Emma Goldman, and the dear little Italian girl, I have intellectual comradeship, and in my little "dope" some one to mother; in the management of the institution very interesting study, and in the inmates a wonderful array of interesting fellow-beings.

If it were not for being deprived of my loved ones, I could fully enjoy the new and unusual experience. If I could have my typewriter, and write more often to my darlings, I would be quite content to do my work here for a time. It seems so needlessly stupid that I should be deprived of the opportunity to write, when I have paid the last ounce of flesh demanded by the state at the sewing machine. There is so much that I want to write while the impressions are vivid, but perhaps I will write better for being deprived of the opportunity for a time.

I have received Papa's nice letters each day, also the sweet little letters from Victor and Kathleen, but Gene and Dickie's letters have not come yet. Papa writes me that the twins were lovely, and that he enjoyed their Easter vacation, and that Dick is the dearest and sweetest boy imaginable. I know that you will all be nice and sweet and fine, so that no one can say that Mamma has failed as a mother. . . .

I hope that you will make it plain to all my friends and comrades that the only way in which I can express my appreciation for their letters and presents is to do it collectively in my weekly letter to you.

Please write Theresa Malkiel and tell her to finish the scarf I sent and raffle it for the *New York Call*. It is all that I could do to express my loyalty to all that the *Call* stands for. I got the materials during the last hour of my freedom and fifteen minutes after the cell door had clanged behind me I was busy at work on it. I want this to be my message to all the comrades. Don't waste any time in tears or sorrow over me, but go to work. I want the chances sold for 10¢ each, so every comrade can buy one, and I hope the *Call* will get a dime for every stitch. Children put x's at the end of their letters to indicate kisses. These stitches are my cross marks, and they are words of loyalty to our cause, and faith in ultimate justice, that I cannot speak or write. Ask Theresa to convey my greetings to the comrades who sent me the beautiful letter from the wedding party. Tell Comrade Kate[4] I send my love, and that after almost eighteen years of married life I can testify that it is not so bad, provided!—you start in early to train your husband in the right way. Be firm! be firm! and never let him forget that he is just a mere man! I can't seem to locate the groom in my memory, but send my love and congratulations. I am sure he is all right, or he could never have won a girl like Kate!

Send my letters to Zeuch, and tell him to write to me often. Give Rella my love, and tell her I am glad she is there to help look after my big boys. I hope that you will not be so busy as to neglect the twins. I want them to have their letter every week, and to either come in, or have some one visit them every Sunday. Just ask the YPSLS[5] to see that they are not allowed to get lonely, or feel neglected. Kathleen will be all right, and Dick is with you, and I want my baby boys to be looked after. Have the children write to Mother regularly, and send her copies of my

---

4. Comrade Kate may be Kate Sadler of Washington State. A left-wing socialist activist, she served with O'Hare on the Committee on War and Militarism.

5. The Young People's Socialist League (YPSL) was the socialist association for adolescents. It had its own national secretary and was viewed as a training ground for future party leaders.

letters. Do your best to make her understand that I am all right and not suffering, and that I am merely having a very interesting experience. Her letter was very sweet and beautiful, and I am glad to know that she is a good rebel to the very last.

I receive the *Mirror*, but not *St. Louis Labor*. Ask Comrade Hoehn[6] to send it to me. Give him and Billy and Mrs. L. and all the comrades my love, and tell them not to worry about me, but just go on with the work. I am having a rest and a change of work, and will be in fine shape for the campaign.

I have had really one hard experience, and it was pretty bad. That was the Bertillon.[7] I am not prudish, and not supersensitive, but it took all my poise and self-control to go through it without breaking. The men who put me through the ordeal were kindness and sympathy and courtesy itself, but they could not rob it of its trying effects. When you come down, visit the Bertillon room, and thank the man in charge for his kindness to me. Tell him that while it was pretty hard I have recovered from the shock. Am wondering how Debs will stand it. I am afraid it will be pretty hard on him.

Aside from this there is only one feature that is really revolting, and that is the criminally stupid mixing of the clean women with the frightfully syphilitic. Absolutely no effort to separate them is made. There is an Indian woman here from Alaska, a "federal", who is in the very last stages. Her throat is one mass of open sores, and she bathes in the same tub that I do, and the clean, healthy girls are forced to clean the tub after her baths. There is a white girl in almost as bad condition, who eats at the tables with us, and many of the colored girls are diseased. The dishes are not kept separate and no disinfectants are used.

I have made a formal complaint to the warden, Gov. Painter, in writing but so far have received no answer. I am writing to Judge Krum[8] today asking him for legal advice as to my actions. I have asked him to take the matter up with Mr. Fosdick who has charge of the campaign

6. G. A. Hoehn, a leader of the Socialist party in St. Louis, remained with the party after the schism later that year, and became one of the leaders seeking to formulate a viable postwar program.

7. The Bertillon was a system of body classification named after the French criminologist Alphonse Bertillon (1853–1914). Gross body measurements were taken for purposes of identification. This method, widely used in American prisons, was abandoned a decade later in favor of fingerprinting.

8. Chester Harding Krum (1840–1923), a prominent St. Louis lawyer, had been a judge earlier in his career.

against venereal disease for the "federals". I think Julia Lathrop,[9] chief of the Government Children's Bureau, could do much by personally pressing the matter with the Department of Justice. She is in Washington, and will no doubt be glad to act in the matter. It is a particularly frightful state of affairs, because most of the federal prisoners are young women who are in here for short sentences. I doubt if anything can be done for the state prisoners. Missouri is so backward that I have little hope of anything being done to bring its institutions up to anything humane or modern. "Poor old Missouri."

I would not be telling the truth if I denied that this phase of the situation did not affect me. It does. I can never forget the sickening fact that the country which my ancestors helped to found, and which my father gave his life to protect,[10] has forced me to live in constant danger of contamination from the most loathsome of all diseases.

Aside from this one thing I am quite content. I am making the sort of study of criminology that never has been made before, and which could only be made in this way. I am learning things that will be of inestimable value to the world of science, and, in the future, when I speak of crime and criminals I will have a solid basis of hard-won facts on which to stand. I have such a wealth of material now that I think we will have to revise the questionnaire. I feel now that we are not ready to begin the survey. When I get out you must get in, and study the men as I study the women. It is a hard way to serve science and humanity but it is the only way. I am afraid that you can't get sent up for an "intent", as I have been, so you must discover some crime that can be pinned on you that you do not need to commit.

Send me down that book containing Dr. Barnes' lectures on Nervous and Mental Diseases, I have a wonderful opportunity for such studies here. A most interesting case of dementia praecox in the second cell from me, and an interesting case of homicidal mania that promises some lively developments. Ask Dr. Barnes if there has been anything worth while written on Prison Neurosis. I am certainly gathering a lot of interesting material in that line. If there is anything, ask him to send it to me. Also

---

9. Julia Clifford Lathrop (1858–1932) early in her career was associated with Graham Taylor and Jane Addams, founders of American social settlement work, in Chicago. Her national reputation was established through her work on the Illinois Board of Charities. She was the first head of the United States Children's Bureau.

10. Andrew Richards, a Union soldier, survived the Civil War.

see if he has Hart's *Psychology of Insanity*. If so I would like to have it for a short time.

I am getting some wonderfully interesting stuff on "wish fulfillments" and the peculiar trend that religious emotions take in prison. Here in this grim cell house the battle between the old orthodoxy of the church, and the newer philosophy of Sir Oliver Lodge[11] is being waged, and the new is winning. These poor victims of society feel that God takes no concern for them and they are not strong enough to stand alone, so they find comfort for their sick souls in the belief that their dead comrades in misery come back to care for and protect them. In the weary hours after the lights are out the cell house is peopled by many ghosts, but they are all kindly, comfortable, amiable ghosts, who flit about all night on errands of mercy and love. There is one, more interesting than all the rest, more kindly and humane; some day I will write her story.

All in all, I find this prison life much like the world outside, only things are intensified here. I feel that most of the wrongs committed against these helpless creatures are wrongs and crimes of stupidity and ignorance, and not the crimes of brutality or even callousness. I will write more of this next time, as my paper is almost full.

I have been so well supplied that there is little left to wish for. Some one supplied me with a higher chair, and it has added 100% to my efficiency. I am still waiting for the knife and fork with the soft metal blades. They are in the very back part of the small drawer of the chiffonier. Don't forget the white petticoats, and I want that soft summer corset of mine; I can't remember where it is, but Dickie can find it. Have Dickie get two dozen large kid curlers for me—a paper of pins and two or three sets of little beauty pins. I need the small round point scissors, and some orangewood manicure sticks. You can get all of these at the ten cent store, except the scissors.

The grocery people do splendidly in sending me food. They certainly use intelligence. I am gaining in flesh, and will soon be quite plump. Oh yes—I need some wash cloths also, and some cheap paper napkins. You might send me the spoon also if you locate the silver.

Send me some small gummed labels, to stick things up on the steel walls, and two or three rolls of pretty crepe paper. Let Dickie choose it. When you come down bring me a 75-candle power light bulb. Don't

11. Sir Oliver Lodge (1851–1940), a British physicist and mathematician, was interested in the mental and physical sides of psychic research.

worry about the lace collars. I have some that will do. Be sure to send Emma the pamphlets, and a copy of World Peace.

It is almost time for chapel, and I must close now. Love and kisses to all my darlings. Be brave and sweet and don't worry—I will be all right. Perhaps Dickie will come down soon.

Lovingly,
Mamma

May 10, 1919

Dear Sweethearts:

If Dick can find the package of little calendars that were left from Christmas I would like to have one for each of the women. They are all so eager for calendars that I am sure nothing would please them better. It will require about ninety. This sounds as though I had an acute case of the gimmes, but I have so many to serve, and I know that all the comrades want to share in that service. I know now what Jesus meant when he said: "Inasmuch as ye did it unto the least of these ye did it unto Me." I think so often of Judge Wade and the malignant hatred he expressed in passing sentence, yet all his venom has not injured me, and I am far happier in my prison cell today than he can be in his tawdry glory. I am in prison, but I am surrounded by love that cannot be measured, and I have the greatest opportunity for service that ever came to any woman. I am already repaid a hundredfold for every hour in a prison cell. My time is not wasted here. One month in prison and this is the record that I can write, and the most important must remain unwritten until we are all freed.

The plumbers are busy putting in shower baths. We now get our food nice and hot, and are much better nourished. We now have library privileges and have books with which to pass the tedious hours in the cells. I have volunteered to start a night school to send the inmates out a little less ignorant than when they entered, and therefore better able to stem the tide of life. There is a rumor that the twelve-year-old grime on the cell house walls is to be removed, that the fly specked decorations in the dining room are to be replaced by a coat of fresh paint, and that the tragic histories of uncounted broken lives are to be wiped out with paint brushes. We are hoping that the rumor may become a fact. . . .

I got a wonderful pamphlet of Scott Nearing's, "Violence or Solidarity".[12] Send for a copy. I wish every comrade would read it. I fear that the madness of violence may affect the labor movement and that would be a tragedy indeed. The whole world is so poisoned with the obsession of hate and vengeance that we, of all people, must keep our poise and balance and not be swept into the howling madness of hate and violence. I live in the midst of the mad stupidity that madness can ever make for a better civilization. This is an institution for social vengeance, and it damns every life it touches, and does not help or uplift or reform.

There are only two real criminals here, and they are typical products of prison vengeance. Both are so warped and scarred and hardened by the stupid vengeance of society, that they have ceased to be human, and have become crafty birds of prey, and why not? For nine hours each day we are machines driven to the uttermost to produce wealth of which we are robbed of every penny by organized society. At current wages each woman in the factory earns from twelve to twenty dollars each week. For two hours a day we are imbeciles, moved about like automatons, and absolutely without will or wish or voice. For one hour, we are half human, but under surveillance, and the balance of the time we are wild animals caged like strange creatures in a zoo. This is the vengeance which collective society wreaks upon its victims, and upon those who dare to possess ideas at variance with the economic or political interests of the administration. But no inmate of prison comes back to society better, cleaner, stronger, more intelligent, more able to meet the problems of life.

For a thousand years society has pinned its faith on vengeance, and the world is full of prisons, burdened by courts, hampered and cursed by the blind stupidity of legal procedure, harassed by the ignorance and willfulness and maliciousness of judges, and bedeviled by the odious tribe of parasites called lawyers. And every prison is full and every judge is busy, grinding out social vengeance, and crime is ever on the increase. Now it has become a crime to have an opinion, in the United States, and the judges are working overtime sending us to prison because we have ideas and ideals, and prisons will be just as effective in curing ideas and

12. Scott Nearing (b. 1883), a World War I dissenter, lost his professorship at the University of Pennsylvania and, because of his antiwar writings, was tried for violation of the Espionage Act. Nearing was found innocent. Ironically, his publisher, the Rand School of Social Science, a party to the indictment, was found guilty.

crushing ideals as in curing crime! I know! I have eaten prison bread, slept in a prison cell, slaved at a prison sewing machine, and my ideas are clearer and firmer than ever, and the prison-fanned flame of my ideals burns with a glow that passes through stone walls, travels over land and sea, and kindles the flame of social reconstruction in the hearts of men and women I have never seen.

Just at this point, I might remark that your advice about not overworking is, no doubt, good advice, but like much advice, "it won't work." You must remember that I have ceased to be an individual, that I have no mind, no reason, no judgment, and that I have no more control over the amount of work that I must do than my sewing machine. An illiterate boy of twenty has the absolute power of life and death over me. Fortunately I am strong and well. I am well nourished and sleep well. I am a quick and expert worker and the boy does not seem to have any antagonism toward me, so I manage very well indeed, but the law of the shop is the absolute limit of human endurance, and to that law I must bow. And once again, it is not a law of brutality, but of stupidity. No one connected with the shop has the slightest idea of industrial efficiency. No one knows how to organize the shop, no one teaches the girls the work, no one sees that the machines are cleaned and oiled, and the foreman is as overworked as the girls, and the effect on his temper can be imagined. But, with all that, he is not a bad sort at all, and in my various excursions into industry or as an investigator I have worked under foremen infinitely worse.

But enough of the tragedies of prison life. We will talk of some of its sunshine and of its comedies. One of the most astounding things is the universal kindness of the inmates for each other. I have heard less "cattishness" in my month here than in one West End club meeting. When I compare the honesty and moral integrity of these women with, well, let us say, the Women's Council of St. Louis, the convicts rank infinitely higher. When I compare their loyalty and courteous consideration with the Ethical Society, it makes that perfectly respectable aggregation look very tawdry indeed. I understand now why Jesus showed such good judgment in choosing his associates. There are many bits of comedy, and the supreme comedy is the asinine stupidity of the "powers that be" in sending a trained investigator like myself where there is so much to investigate. I have tried for years to secure permission to make studies of prison life, and prison psychology, and always was denied the opportunity. Then a generous administration chucks me into prison where I have an unparalleled opportunity to make such studies as have never before been made. . . .

I must tell you next time about the fat lady who snores, and the colored girl who jigs so wonderfully. Bring Kathleen and Dick down next Sunday and we can have a nice visit.

Send my greetings to all the comrades, and tell them not to worry. I am getting a necessary and vital experience here, the social revolution is gradually taking shape, and the everlasting march of progress will still sweep on.

It is now mail time, and I must close. Love and kisses to all my darlings, and a message of faith and courage and loyalty to the comrades everywhere.

Lovingly,
KATE

June 8, 1919

Dear Sweethearts:

Sunday. I failed to start my letter yesterday, and so will have to miss my recreation to-day in order to finish it.

We had the first picnic of the season yesterday, and the afternoon in the fresh air made me too sleepy to write. It was really a very enjoyable affair. They loaded all the women in two huge auto trucks, the band in another, and took us out to McClung Park for the afternoon. It is a beautiful park, has one of the most artistic dancing pavilions I have ever seen and wonderfully well equipped. The band played for the dancing and the girls made most of the semi-freedom after the long months of severe repression. The whole thing was a strange and wonderful experience and will make an interesting chapter in the book of my prison memories.

I am still pretty well and getting along splendidly. I have mastered the work until it has become quite mechanical and I can do it without expenditure of any mental energy, but of course the monotony of it has a deadening effect on one's brain. If the amount of work demanded were at all reasonable and the hours not so long, the shop would really be the least objectionable part of the institution. I find that the hours I pass there go very quickly, and if I could only overcome the severe stiffness and soreness of the muscles of my neck and shoulders I shouldn't mind the work particularly. I went to the doctor for something to relieve this condition, and his remarks and treatment would be high comedy if it were not for the bitter tragedy that lies underneath.

The whitewash crew has been with us the past week, and the walls of the cell-house are beautifully clean and white, while the slaughter of the poor defenseless germs was terrific. A little whitewash may seem a trifle to you outside, but it means much to us in here. There is nothing so degrading as dirt, and nothing so reformative as cleanliness. I never realized what a blessing a bath was until I was forced to exist on one a week.

The shower baths are almost finished now, and we are hoping the management will realize that "cleanliness is next to Godliness" and allow us two baths a week at least.

Fortunately the weather has been lovely, and no really hot days, but my heart almost fails me when I think what life will be when our deadly, sultry Missouri Summer is on us in all its sullen fury. The ventilation of the shop is so archaic, the dining-room is a furnace, and our only breath of fresh air must be in a bare court absolutely without shade, and only from five to six o'clock, which is the very hottest part of the day.

I read Lane's[13] article reprinted from the *Survey* in Tuesday's *Post Dispatch*. It made me smile to think that the *Post* should get excited over it, when so much more interesting stories might be found nearer home. How characteristic that the *Survey* should be concerned about the men, yet not have one spark of interest in the women. You know I have never been a particularly rampant feminist; I have always felt that the "woman question" was only a part of the great "social problem" but my two months here have changed my views materially, and I know now, as never before, that "women bear the heaviest burdens and walk the roughest road" and that this is true in all walks of life, and becomes more damnably true as you descend the social scale, until it reaches the very extreme here in prison. I am wondering if Suffrage, which is now prac-

13. Winthrop D. Lane (1887–1962) visited IWW prisoners in federal penitentiaries at Topeka, Kansas City, Wichita, and elsewhere, who had been convicted under the Espionage Act. His series of articles in 1919 in *Survey* magazine exposed the abominable conditions and treatment these political prisoners endured.

tically an accomplished fact, will have any effect. Let us hope it does. However, I am not particularly optimistic concerning the average middle class woman. There is not a place in all the world where there are such opportunities for kindly, humane Christian service as here. Yet not a woman's club, or the women of one church have ever shown one gleam of interest in this institution. The warden, and every member of the prison board, has a wife, yet in the two months I have been here not one of them has ever set foot inside these walls, or made the slightest effort to serve these women who need human understanding so bitterly. Mrs. Gardner, the wife of the Governor, was here, and she really seems to have a genuine interest in the institution. Mrs. Paul Brown, of St. Louis, visited the prison, and did a very sweet, womanly thing, for which I honor her. I have thought a thousand times what a wonderful thing it would be to have a woman like Clara Taylor in charge of an institution like this, but I suppose it will be years before the state realizes that education and scientific training are preferable to "political pull" in the service of state institutions. . . .

By the way, I must tell you that I have moved. The American Revolutionary Soviet is at last together. Emma is on one side of me and Ella on the other, and the executive committee hold nightly conclaves to direct by wireless the affairs of the universe. Just imagine what interesting stories the historian of the future can write of this strange trio and our doings! I miss my little "dope" to whom I had become very much attached, but I have a lighter, more airy cell, and it is convenient for the three of us to be together. . . .

I get plenty of papers and magazines to read, but I enjoy the *Call* most of all, and I am always so disappointed when it fails to arrive. It keeps me in touch with everything that is transpiring now. I get the *Milwaukee Leader* also, and it is very fine too; it has improved lately I think.

Of course I am heartsick over the bomb affairs. Heartsick if it is really the work of radicals whose endurance has given way under the frightful outrages of the "powers that prey", that have been forced upon us during the last two years. Yet murder and violence would be the natural reaction of emotionally unstable minds. For months editors, judges, preachers, writers and artists have lauded murder, sanctioned outrage, glorified mobs and blessed violence. We have heard lawlessness called patriotism, and murder called idealism until what wonder that some should go mad and act upon the teachings of violence that have been forced upon them.

My God! how stupid the ruling class, how blind, how ignorant, how mad. It seems that they can never learn that

> "The robber is robbed by his riches,
> The tyrant is dragged by his chain,
> The schemer is snared by his cunning,
> The slayer lies dead with the slain."

I have never put much faith in prayers, but there is one that I think all of us should ever keep in our hearts—"Oh God, deliver us from hate, that we may love and live."

The only real horror that my ordeal brings to me is the dread that it will teach my children to hate. . . .

Lovingly,
Mama

June 15, 1919

Dear Sweethearts:

Once again the longed for time has come to send a message to my loved ones, and in spite of the frightful heat and discomfort, I shall be happy in my slow task of penning my weekly letter. I suppose it is needless to say that the heat of the last few days has been something frightful. I know how hot it can be in St. Louis, but you at least can stay out of doors until night makes indoors bearable, but we are shut in our cells at six, still heated and sweaty with the long day's labor, and your imagination can supply the further details.

I am still fairly well, but beginning to feel the inevitable sense of weakness from the enervating effect of heat and lack of air. There are sixty women in the shop and seven half-windows, and they are placed at least ten feet above the floor and therefore useless as a means of ventilation. There are three very antiquated fans whose ancient and creaking joints sing an everlasting wailing song of protest, but they are all bunched over the matron's desk and the lower end of the room is absolutely without means of ventilation. The one full-sized window in the shop is right beside my machine and it is the only possible means of securing a direct current of air through the shop, but it is nailed down good and tight and the glass has been painted thickly over, making it utterly useless either for light or air. As a result we are forced to work all the time in the heat and glare of artificial light. Recently, the foreman, who is not a bad sort of kid, chanced to be in a good humor and I asked him why the window had been made useless and suggested that the architect had evidently meant it to provide light and ventilation and asked him to have it opened. He consulted the shop matron and reported that it was impossible. When I insisted on a reason, he said that there was a legend that once upon a time a girl inmate had committed the heinous crime of smiling out of that window at a male inmate of the other side. Naturally, rampant virtue was outraged and from that day down to this, all women have been punished for that crime. The crime was committed years ago and the girl has long since gone, but a long procession of women have had starved lungs and injured eye-sight because of that affront to propriety. It is amazing what an insatiable appetite for vengeance propriety has, for the end seems lost in the dimness of the future. I fear that some of those hot nights there will be nothing left of me but a pool of melted grease under my machine and that the representatives of the "land of the free" will be compelled to gather up the remains with a soup spoon and send it home to you in a milk bottle, but praise the Lord, your giddy young wife will be saved from snares and pitfalls of flirtation. . . .

I get many letters from the comrades everywhere and enjoy them all, and the beautiful thing is that it is the Jewish comrades who are the most faithful, both in writing and sending me good things to eat. I know that in many instances the delicacies they have sent me mean plain, scanty fare for them. And it is from the unknown and obscure, the patient, faithful Jimmie Higginses of the movement that the words of cheer and the hallowed luxuries come. I have not even received the printed matter sent out from the National Office, and except from Gene, not a line from any official or individual prominent in the party. But this does not disturb me for I know that I have the love and loyalty of the rank and file. . . .

So many of the comrades are concerned over how Emma Goldman and I reconcile our differences. Of course, the differences exist. Emma is an anarchist and I a political Socialist, and I presume that the two theories are as far apart as the poles, but somehow theories don't seem very important here. The brutal, naked tragedies of life crush them out. When one lives with wrecked lives, broken hearts and sick souls, abstract theories somehow lose force. So far as Emma and I are concerned,

the shades of Marx and Bakunine[14] can rest in peace. All of our time and
energy is consumed in feeding hungry stomachs and supporting faltering
spirits. Instead of arguing theories, we discuss such vital matters as
which has the greatest amount of nutriment, two pounds of peanut butter or one of the cow variety, at the same price. Instead of hurling anarchist texts at me Emma raps on the wall of the cell and says, "Get busy
Kate, it's time to feed the monkeys, pass the food down the line." I think
it would be a godsend if a lot of theoretical hair-splitters and hobby-riders
went to prison; it might teach them some of the big, vital lessons of life.

It is three o'clock now and I suppose you are out at Chaminade with
the boys. The others have just gone to chapel and I want to finish while
quiet reigns. I am sacrificing my fresh air again to-day, rather than endure the spiritual nausea of the chapel services. You know I vowed that
I would attend chapel regularly so that I need not lose my most valuable
privilege, but I simply cannot do it. It is too much for even my placid
temper. I have too much respect for the message of Jesus to have it made
hateful and disgusting by coarseness and ignorant bigotry. If I could know
in advance when the young priest is to officiate I would take advantage
of the fact. He is not at all objectionable for he has the common sense to
reduce his theology to the minimum and he is well bred, clean faced and
shows some signs of spirituality.

I suppose you read "Joy among the Philistines" in *The New Republic*.
It is a wonderful article and a clean, wholesome confession by Weyl,[15]
who is in that instance the spokesman for millions of Americans. I am
enjoying the divine comedy of being behind prison bars while events
absolutely and completely vindicate me. Surely the so-called Peace
Treaty places us forever in the immortal roster of prophets. In the very
near future a certain document will stand forth as quite as great as the
Declaration of Independence. However, I would rather have less vindication for myself and more justice for war-cursed humanity. My intelligence told me all the time that there was nothing to hope for, but my
heart clung to the hope of a miracle.

14. Mikhail Bakunin (1814–1876) was the nineteenth-century Russian anarchist. His
followers and those of Karl Marx competed for control of the international socialist movement, with the Marxists gradually triumphing by the end of the century.

15. Walter Weyl (1873–1919), of the *New Republic*, had once been associated with
the Intercollegiate Socialist Society and had attended a few party conventions. However,
Weyl was a Progressive and reformer who wrote articles in condemnation of Marxist doctrines.

I must close now and rest for the girls will soon be back and there will be no quiet until the lights go out.

Love and kisses to my darlings.

KATE

July 6, 1919

Dear Sweethearts:

Sunday. I am much disappointed in not having my typewriter this morning, but suppose it has not arrived and I will have to write long-hand. You can imagine what a pleasure it was to me to hear that Gov. Painter said that I might have it. . . .

I know and appreciate the fact that many persons in St. Louis would demand a pardon for me if I would request it, and I know just how annoyed both Judge Krum and Mr. Lovell are that I refuse to ask it. They see the horror of my being in prison, but to them it is only a wrong to an individual. To me it is not an individual but a social matter. I feel no sense of personal outrage over the case, only horror that such outrages could be perpetrated on any American citizen by the United States Government. To me there is no personal horror in being in prison, only the sense of soul-sickness that comes with the knowledge of the prostitution of our courts and the rape on our most cherished American ideals. The horror to me is that my ancestors gave their lives to establish the Constitution and preserve the Nation and that I should live to see the Constitution trampled in the mire of despotism and civil liberties throttled by petty tyrants.

President Wilson will soon be home and we will know what the attitude of the administration is to be on the restoration of civil liberties and the re-establishment of the Constitution. If war-time laws are to be retained, the fight will have to be made and it may be possible that I can serve best where I am. However, Mr. Wilson, up to the time that he went to Paris, always exhibited the qualities of a shrewd politician and I believe he is too shrewd to fan the smoldering fires of revolution by injustice and the abrogation of civil rights. I feel sure that I can live through more imprisonment and I prefer that no move be made until Mr. Wilson has had opportunity to act. In case he should do nothing, the next step would be to present the petition demanding an investigation of the case. I don't want any steps to be taken in the matter of prosecuting the witnesses for perjury until all other means have failed. If the real criminals could be reached I might not be so much averse to it, but I know that only the poor, miserable tools of the real offenders would be caught in the net of the law. One of them is a woman and I could not bring myself to consent to her prosecution. I know what prison means to a woman and I will never have the guilt on my soul of sending one to a living hell. The gathering of names on the petitions should be pushed vigorously, but I feel that aside from the general agitation for amnesty, nothing should be done until President Wilson has had an opportunity to state his position. The world is so cursed by hate and bitterness and rancor that I would not add to it.

And that reminds me; Rev. Dr. A. quite misjudges me and my attitude. I feel toward organized religion of today as I imagine Jesus did towards organized religion of his day, and I am even more polite and tolerant in expressing my opinion than He. In fact, Emma Goldman and Harry Tichenor are the only people that I know who even approximate the vehemence of Jesus. Rev. Stilli of Louisville is quite an artist in that line. Be sure and get his sermon on Debs for Dr. A. to read. Assure Dr. A. that I do not dislike preachers merely because they are preachers; in fact, I have a very warm regard for many of them. Of course, I can not but regret that their education and training so completely eradicates all sense of moral courage and leaves them so supine and spineless as a class; but individually, I like certain ones very much. . . .

I like the young priest here very much, even though he does not seem to feel that my soul is worth bothering about. (I am going to cut your letter short to attend chapel today.) The dislike I feel towards the chaplain here is not because he is a preacher, but because he is unfaithful to his trust. He is hired and paid by the State to look after the moral and spiritual welfare of the women here and they are absolutely neglected, aside from fifteen minutes of cut and dried formalism once a week. Not the slightest personal interest, not a word of help or sympathy or comfort to the soul-sick and the heart-broken. No matter how great the sorrow, how deep the suffering, how terrible the tragedy that comes to these poor women, there is never the slightest personal interest, help or support.

The Protestant Church professes to believe that the Bible is the way of salvation; and there are no Bibles here. Communion is supposed to be an essential of church observance, and in the three months I have been here there has been no communion. Personally, all this does not concern me. I do not need a religious crutch to lean on while I pass through the inferno of social vengeance. Thank God, I am strong enough to stand alone and my strength is sustained by the love of comrades; but there are many here who are weak and organized religion fails them in the hour of their need. What wonder then that they turn to Spiritualism for help and comfort? I want these women to have all of the comforts and the succor that the church can bring; and evidently it has never concerned itself about the matter.

There is one thing certain, and that is I shall come out of prison understanding Jesus better and on terms of closer comradeship with him. Prison may increase my contempt for churchianity, but it will deepen my love and respect for Jesus and the people from whom he chose his friends and disciples. . . .

It is chapel time now, and I must close. Love and kisses to my darlings, and don't worry about me.

Lovingly,
KATE

July 26, 1919

Dear Sweethearts:

Saturday. This is Saturday afternoon. Almost all of the other women have gone to the park but it was so hot and the trip so hard that I decided to stay in my cell and rest and write my letter.

I am quite well but of course have been very unhappy since I knew that my letter of July 19th was held up. It's too bad, it was a very nice letter indeed, I was so happy to have my little Corona that I put especially great interest in writing it.

I had a nice visit with Caroline Lowe[16] who is looking splendid. She is getting younger and more beautiful every time I see her. Certainly she seems to have found the fountain of youth in her magnificent service to

16. Caroline A. Lowe, a former Kansas City schoolteacher, was an organizer and speaker for the party, particularly known for her appearances at the socialist encampments in the Plains states. The woman's general correspondent when the party established a woman's division in 1908, she in effect functioned as the director of daily operations for the Woman's National Committee.

the "underdogs" of society. Dear Carrie—our friendship has been a long and tender one. . . .

I see by the *Post* that Roger Baldwin[17] has been released and like myself is more than ever convinced that prison has no effect on ideals. Dear me! won't we have one talkfest when we meet, and how superior we will feel to you ordinary mortals who have never eaten prison hash and slept in a birdcage. We pay, but God knows we can feel that the love and comradeship that comes to us repays a hundredfold.

Last week I had such an experience as comes to few women indeed. We three politicals received a beautiful box of roses one night, great red roses, and the wonderful thing is that they came all the way from Moscow, straight from the bleeding, quivering heart of Russia. A friend of Emma's sent money to a friend of his in Paris, who in turn sent it to Mrs. Ballantine, and she sent it on to the florist here to bring us that marvelous message of comradeship from half way around the world. Can you imagine anything more thrilling, more inspiring than that? An interruption just occurred; the orderly brought our boxes, and mine contained an exquisite silver loving cup from the Bartlesville, Okla., comrades. It is a beautiful thing, slender, graceful, simple in design and simply inscribed. Yet what a wonderful story it tells. I am sure that my cell is the strangest thing our country ever knew. . . .

I wonder often if Emma and I are not fortunate to be here just at this time of stress and turmoil. Often those too near a great thing or event are too close to get a true perspective, and may see things in a distorted way. We get all the radical papers and magazines as well as the "capitalist" papers and, since we have time for reflection and no opportunity for action, I wonder if our condition does not give us an opportunity for clearer thought and wider vision, and possibly for that reason we will be of more service when we are more greatly needed. The NATION and the NEW REPUBLIC are splendid and the CALL is doing magnificent work. It is certainly a godsend that we have such a publication at this time. I enjoy the LEADER also and admire the wonderful courage and resourcefulness that the Milwaukee comrades show in keeping it alive under such handicaps. I get most of the smaller papers and they are all improving,

17. Roger N. Baldwin (b. 1884), a pacifist, served a prison term of under one year for his failure to respond to an order to report to the military for a physical examination. He was the founder of the wartime National Civil Liberties Bureau (later, the American Civil Liberties Union), which assisted various wartime dissenters and conscientious objectors who ran afoul of the law.

becoming more live and vital; and I am not so much discouraged now over the Right Wing-Left Wing eruption. I know that after the smoke has drifted away and the heated air cooled a bigger and better Socialist movement will come forth. The dross will have been burned out, and only the pure metal remain. . . .

The dear twins have been too busy to write quite so regularly this week, but I know they are quite well and happy. Kathleen is a little tramp, she forgets her Mamma scandalously, but Dick is faithful, if as communicative as a clam. He will never get in trouble for gossiping. I know how hard this week has been for you, doing the most brain-racking and wearing creative work, and always under the suspense of not hearing from me. I am glad you feel that you have the worst of the job done, and I hope we may both have some rest ere long. Kiss all the children for me.

Love and best wishes to all the friends and comrades and many kisses to my darlings.

Lovingly,
KATE

August 2, 1919

Dear Sweethearts:

Saturday. I received such a lovely box from a whole bunch of the New York women, and what pleasant memories it recalled! There was a huge cake in it from Theresa that was so Theresaesque that I should have known she sent it without the card. Dear Theresa, I am sure that she would have been very happy to see pieces of that cake scampering up and down the walks and sailing aloft on the end of a string. One of the colored girls said "Law!, Miss Kate, you sho' is got the mostes' and bestes, friens of any pusson I know", and I certainly agree with her. I did not find any name on the devil's food, but we enjoyed it just as much. Sarah Volicick sent me guava paste and you can imagine how I enjoyed it and how it brought memories of Florida! As I lifted out the boxes and packages one by one I seemed to be back in the Suffrage Headquarters on Lenox Avenue and the impression was so vivid that I seemed to feel the actual living presence of that wonderful group of women with whom I worked that wonderful month. How far away the realization of our ideal

seemed then! What a hopeless task to gain political citizenship for the
women of New York State! Yet it has all come to pass, and I have faith
that the women of that state will use the vote for which we worked so
hard to bring back to this nation something at least of political freedom
and the ideals of democracy which have been wrested from us during the
black and bloody months that have just passed. . . .

Sunday. I had just reached this point in my letter last night when the
orderly arrived with a washtub full of things from the Kate O'Hare Committee of Brooklyn.[18] There were a lot of magazines, many nice books, a
number of little luxuries so rare in prison; and best of all a dozen lovely
knitting bags, each containing some pretty trifle. I don't think I have
ever enjoyed anything more than distributing these beautiful things
among my friends. I tried to choose the women who have the longest
terms and the saddest hearts to receive them and if only the dear comrades who made them could have seen the joy they brought they would
feel repaid for the thoughtfulness and labor. In the dreary greyness of
prison it takes so little to bring happiness to bruised and broken
hearts. . . .

Zeuch and several others seem to feel that I must be heartbroken
over the wild upheaval that is taking place in the Socialist movement. Z.
says it must be a tragedy for me to realize that I have given the best
twenty years of my life to a movement that seems to be disintegrating.
But I do not have that feeling at all. I know that life comes only through
death and that all things decay and pass away when they have served
their period of usefulness. All the work we have done in the past is not
lost. It has been increased a thousandfold. The machine we have used to
do the work may break down; but if so we will get a newer and better.
Why weep over an ox-cart when we may exchange it for a "flivver"?
When all the eruptions and noise are past, the solid, intelligent, creative
men and women will find themselves banded together once more with a
wider vision and a deeper understanding and better tools with which to
accomplish the life work of our generation. So I can face the crisis quite
calmly and know that the outcome will be a bigger and better forward
movement.

18. This was one of the committees of defense established and spearheaded by Frank
P. O'Hare after her conviction; the various committees sent her moral support and cam-
paigned for amnesty for her. The New York committee, founded by leading women radicals including Theresa Malkiel, Elizabeth Gurley Flynn, and Meta Stern Lilienthal, was
the most visible.

I see by the PUBLIC of July 26th that I am a "very moral person". I am really afraid I shall have to protest. I have conceived a great dislike for "moral" persons since coming here, and I really don't think I want to be classed with them. I find the people who are not "moral" so much more intelligent, humane and kindly than the "moral" ones. Of all the women I have come in contact with here who seem to have the real spirit of Christ and comradeship, most of them are prostitutes, and those who have the opposite spirit are dreadfully "moral". In fact, the Satanic trio of our little social inferno are Hell-fire and damnation Religion, Prudish Morality, and Greed-for-Profits. All of the soul-crushing, heart-breaking, life-destroying things are done in the name of one or all three. If ever the Religion of Love, The morality of Normality, and Labor for Service enter the prison doors of this nation, prisons may become really institutions for social healing. But, until they do, prisons will be social ulcers, contaminating the body politic. I think that the reason Mr. P. is so much better and more humane than wardens are supposed to be, is that he probably is not, and does not pretend to be a plaster paris saint. . . .

Remember me to all the friends and comrades and lots and lots of love to my darlings.

Lovingly,
KATE

August 10, 1919

Dear Sweethearts:

Sunday. I had a nice letter from Z. and hope he will spend a part of his vacation with you in St. Louis. Tell him that I do not underestimate the depth and importance of the volcano that has broken forth in the Socialist movement. I think I sense its importance and the vital effect that it will have on all forward movements, but I simply say that it was inevitable and necessary and that out of the disruption will come new alignments, that will be bigger, broader and more serviceable to humanity. I am not one to weep over outworn things, and it is the spirit of human progress and not the letter of an ism that concerns me. You are perfectly right when you say that it will be on a bread and butter basis that the people of this nation and all nations will settle the mighty problems brought to a crisis by the war. The masses of mankind have been

quickened into an all consuming hunger for life and life abundant, and
they will not be hampered by treaties written by old diplomats, creeds
expounded by old theologians, economic theories spun by old econo-
mists, or isms propagated by old propagandists. Mankind vibrant with
the old, old hunger for bread, for love, for life, will pay no more attention
to our isms than to the sophistries of diplomats, the lies of political econo-
mists of the capitalist ilk or the dead creeds of a dead religion. They will
not hunt up the secretary of the Socialist local or peruse Marx to find out
what they should do to be saved. If we have anything to offer that sounds
sensible and workable they will seize upon it, tho they may deface our
label and lay profane hands upon our sacred words.

I have illusions about being a modern Joan of Arc prancing forth to
lead the armies of social revolution to victory, I am just wondering if my
brain is nimble enough and my legs are limber enough to avoid being
stepped on by that "common herd" in the irresistable stampede that is
sweeping over the world.

Z. seemed glad that I was "philosophical". Yes, I am as philosophical
as my physical discomforts will permit me to be, and after the grilling
day in the shop I array myself in a shocking state of undress, sit in my
little rocker and read with vast amusement and many chuckles the capitalist newspapers. It is joy pure and unalloyed to me to peruse the pit-
eous squeaks and despairing wails of the erstwhile arrogant "press". The
antics of the wise men in Washington remind me very much of the sense-
less scuttling about of the army of cockroaches that I uncover when I lift
a book or paper in my cell. How shriekingly funny is all the wild hulla-
baloo about the "profiteers", and poor Rose Pastor Stokes[19] got ten years
for mildly suggesting that there were such animals in a most ladylike
little note.

And how wonderfully our radical papers are rising to the opportunities of the aftermath of war. The CALL is wonderful, the NATION and the
NEW REPUBLIC have gone far beyond anything I hoped for. The DIAL[20] is
painfully highbrow, but sound and deep and truly thoughtful. Both the
LIBERATOR and PEARSON'S are splendid, dear old Billy Reedy[21] is "com-

19. Stokes' letter attacking war profiteering was sent to the Kansas City *Star*. The
conviction was later reversed, and she never went to prison.

20. The *Dial* was an influential small, essentially literary, journal of the era. Its editorial policies tended to be liberal, somewhat like the *New Republic* in attitude.

21. William M. Reedy (1862–1920) published *Reedy's Mirror* in St. Louis, a leading
artistic and literary periodical. He was also active in local Democratic politics.

ing back", and the MIRROR of last week was a masterpiece. The LEADER goes far beyond my expectations also and the boys up there in Milwaukee deserve all credit for the masterly fight they have made and are making. Even the small weeklies that come to me are really wonderful. . . .

Lovingly,
KATE

August 17, 1919

Dear Sweethearts:

Saturday. I shall, of course, give the balance of my life to the fight on our judicial and penal system, but I shall make the fight on the SYSTEM and not on the individuals who are burdened with the details of execution. . . .

I understand by the newspapers that Mr. Palmer[22] and Mr. Wilson are reviewing my case, and well it fits into their high-minded idealism to review it from a well padded swivel chair in front of an electric fan in far off Washington. It is so much more high-minded and idealistic to review it there than to harrow their sensitive souls by watching me do the lock-step in the lineup or make thirty jackets for one cent. But Mr. Palmer and Mr. Wilson really outdo the German militarists who ruled Belgium. Edith Cavell[23] was a barren woman and when the high-minded idealists punished her for being a spy they did not also punish four innocent children. They were far more humane also, for Edith Cavell suffered far less physical pain when the German bullet sped to her heart than I have suffered many, many of these frightful hot nights and work worn days. It would seem far better for one to be an enemy spy at the mercy of German army officers than to be an American mother at the tender mercy of the Wilson administration.

And yet, I would not have things different if I could. I would not have one hour, one day of all these last two years undone if it were in my

22. A. Mitchell Palmer (1872–1936), Woodrow Wilson's attorney general, reacted to postwar unrest, radicalism, and violence, by wholesale violations of civil liberties. Individuals were rounded up and in some instances deported, without due process of law. Palmer's well-publicized raids on dissenters, immigrants, and bystanders were essentially stimulated by his political ambitions.

23. Edith Cavell, a British nurse, was executed by the Germans in October, 1915, for her effort to shelter and tend Allied wounded in Brussels. Her execution was used as part of Allied propaganda efforts to demonstrate German bestiality.

power. I have found, and you and my children will find how true it is
that "he who loses his life shall find it again". We have lost all of our
earthly possessions; we have lost two years of life; we have lost long
months of companionship; we have lost some whom we have considered
friends; I have lost my freedom; and yet we have found a thousandfold
more than we have lost. And we will find as the years go by that these
months, hard and terrible as they have been, are the richest period of
our lives.

So many things occur that mitigate the hardships and heartaches of
the situation. I had a wonderful letter from one of the I.W.W. boys at
Everett, Wash. He had read my letter where I spoke of the annoyance of
not being able to get the books I needed and hastened to assure me that
the "Wobblies" of the Northwest would see that I had all the books I
wanted or needed of any kind. That they wanted me to know that all I
need to do was to ask for them and any book procurable would be mine.
Just think what a wonderful thing, that it is the "Wobblies" who know
and understand the hunger for learning and are willing to spend the
price of their last sack of tobacco for scientific books for me! Has ever the
world produced a more thrilling, a more wonderful incident than this? I
shall write the boys and ask them to get some of the books I want. They
would mean more to me than any other books ever could. . . .

Lovingly,
KATE

August 21, 1919

Dear Sweethearts:

Thursday. We have had two breaks in the monotony this week. On
Tuesday Mr. Joseph F. Fishman, Inspector of Prisons, Department of
Justice, Washington, D.C. spent the afternoon inspecting the prison and
seeking information as to conditions here, particularly as to the federal
prisoners. He seems a perfectly human sort of individual with far more
knowledge of scientific criminology than the usual prison official. He also
seemed to possess a most remarkable amount of intelligence for one connected with the Department of Justice, which was of course a most pleasant surprise to me. Time will tell whether this particular inspection has

any value or not. At any rate, I liked Mr. Fishman's appearance and feel that we may have a common interest in the problems of penology. Will you please send him a set of the booklets?

Mr. Fishman wanted to know, of course, whether I intended asking for a pardon, and when I assured him that I had no such intention, he then asked me if I still wished to be transferred to the Bismarck, N. D., or any other prison. I assured him that so far as being transferred was concerned, I would not trade Mr. Painter for any other prison official that I knew, and that I felt sure that this institution was as good as any other. But that if the policy of the administration was to be that of holding the political prisoners, I would prefer to be transferred to Bismarck, in order to be permitted to do the scientific work I would be allowed to do there. I feel that I have secured about all the data possible here. If Governor Gardner and the Missouri Prison Board will permit me to make the criminological survey, I have no request to make so far as a transfer is concerned.

Mr. Fishman asked me to write to him and discuss my views and opinions on the whole subject of crime, criminals, prisons, prison officials and prison management. If Mr. Painter will permit me to write this without taking away from my letters to home, I shall be very glad to do so, for I really want to discuss my ideas with some one who is in constant touch with the real problems.

I had two talks with Mr. Fishman. It was just as if some visitor from Mars came down and after seating me very politely remarked that it had come to the notice of the managers of the universe that there was considerable dissatisfaction with the capitalist system; would I please state my criticisms and suggest just what should be done to make matters better? Did you ever try to imagine what reply you would make to such a query? Well do so and you can have some conception of how futile the whole thing appeared to me. Where could I begin, what could I suggest, what could be done to make things better, and the more I talked and the more questions he asked, the more trivial and silly the whole thing seemed. In fact what can be done? What could any human being, no matter how wise and humane and sympathetic, do to make the prison system better? We all have our theories, but when you have lived in a prison and faced the deadly realities of prison life they all crumble to dust and leave you hopeless and appalled so far as any real betterment is concerned.

And now that brings me to the second ripple in our stagnant pool of life. At four o'clock the power was suddenly shut down, we were told to line up and, as stupid and dazed as sheep, we trailed up to the chapel. There we found Mr. Painter, looking somewhat uncomfortable and a very beautiful woman dressed in a very rich and beautiful gown. The woman's face was familiar, but to save me I could not remember who she was. Imagine my surprise when Mr. Painter introduced her as Maud Balling-ton Booth.[24] I had seen her several times but always in her uniform and did not recognize her in the beautiful gown. She is a very handsome woman and speaks the most exquisite English, but oh! the tragedy and comedy of her speech. The tragedy of a beautiful, cultured, seemingly intelligent woman standing before a group of women like us and being professionally cheerful, and sanctimoniously uplifting. The tragedy of a woman who had never eaten prison bread, never slept in a prison bunk, never been harried by the prison task, never had every normal emotion and instinct ruthlessly crushed by a prison, standing there with her plas-ter-of-paris smile sprinkling us with her maudlin sentimentality. One mo-ment I writhed in the shame of it all and the next I longed to shriek. Why, oh! why will uplifters persist in adding to our tortures? Why will they insist on making fools of themselves by talking so glibly and so falsely of the things of which they are so absolutely ignorant? How dare any man or woman who has not lived the life here, who does not and cannot know its horrors and its bitterness presume to hand out "advice" that is an insult, and "cheer" that is a sacrilege?

Fortunately I managed to maintain an outward calm at least, but poor Emma Goldman! She went to the chapel because she did not know what was going to happen, and once there the iron discipline made it impos-sible for her to escape—she just swelled up like the toad in the fable until I was absolutely sure she would literally explode. I certainly pity poor Maud Ballington Booth if ever Emma Goldman manages to get her before an audience!

If this letter is ragged and incoherent you will know that it is because I have not quite regained my wonted calm and still feel the sting of the experience. If ever I was guilty of committing such an outrage upon poor,

24. Maud Ballington Booth (1865–1948) came from an evangelistic background in England as the daughter of the founders of the Salvation Army. She emigrated to the United States in the 1880s and, with her husband, founded the Volunteers of America in 1896.

helpless mortals I hope God will forgive me, for I could never forgive myself. . . .

Lovingly,
KATE

August 21, 1919[25]

Dear Sweethearts:

Sunday. The prison system is the most hideous part of the present system of society. It has become the very scapegoat for all of our social crimes. Each and every one of us is individually responsible for its horrors and its barbarities. Our prisons are but a reflection of us, of our ethics, our morals, our ideals, our sense of social justice, and there are none of us who can draw our skirts aside and say that we are guiltless of the crimes of our judicial and penal system. Buried down deep in the subconscious soul of us is the old instinct to hate, to wish to destroy what is unpleasing to us and makes us ashamed and uncomfortable. And our prison population is so very unpleasing, so ugly, they shame us and make us feel so uncomfortable. I sat in the office of the oculist for three hours this morning and watched the male prisoners come and go. A tragic stream of wrecked and ruined lives, marred and scarred, warped and distorted, they were not pleasant to look upon and I could well understand how properly nice, respectable, moral people would be glad to hide them away from the sight of men behind prison walls and forget them as quickly as possible. Oh! there was menace and condemnation, shame and danger in them for smug respectability! What wonder then that respectability would hide them and forget them as quickly as possible?

Our prisons are filled with two groups - the men and women marred in the making by society, the bitter dregs of our social system who shame us by their ugliness, and the men and women who rise superior to the common mass, who by their intelligence and idealism, their love and service shame us for the pettiness of our lives. One group shames us by their sordid, brutal ugliness, the other by the nobility and beauty of their lives, and so we hide them both away in prison. Gene Debs and Red

25. Internal evidence suggests that this date should be August 24, 1919.

McClain - Flora Foreman and Ray McHugh, the man who protested against legalized murder and the man who murdered illegally - the woman who asked the right for all women to own their own bodies and the harlot who sold her body for the profit of a politician. But saviour and slayer, prophetess and prostitute, they are flesh of our flesh, spirit of our spirit, soul of our soul, and for their nobility or their depravity we are all responsible and prison walls can not break the ties that make us one in human brotherhood. . . .

I am so interested in the Actor's strike in New York, how I would love to be there. It must be thrilling. The wonderful spirit of solidarity of the highly paid artists and the lowly chorus girls seems almost beyond comprehension.

I am also keenly interested in the mighty hub-bub this person Plumb[26] has created. He has certainly exploded more like a bomb than a Plumb and I am immensely amused at the consternation in the camp of the reactionaries, and quite as immensely gratified to discover so much real intelligence in the R. R. Brotherhoods. The world do move! I am enjoying also the new game "Hunt the Profiteer," and wondering what would happen if the game should really become dead earnest and the people take the hunt out of the hands of the old ladies in Washington and do a little hunting themselves. La me! these are troubled times for old ladies in trousers. The bold, rude, common people do pester something awful and they are asking such nasty, impertinent questions, too.

It is almost chapel time and as I had no recreation this morning I am going to put on my Sunday-go-to-meetin' dress and go to church for the good of my soul. . . .

Lovingly,
KATE

August 28, 1919

Dear Sweethearts:

Thursday. The hub-bub of the weekly housecleaning is beginning to quiet down and I shall be able to work on my mid-week letter.

I am still feeling quite well and happy over our nice visit. It had been

26. The Plumb plan called for the purchase of the railroads by the federal government, with the establishment of an operating corporation representative of the public,

such a long time since I had seen any of my darlings that I was getting depressed. Now I shall be all right again until Dick and Kathleen can come down. I think it is their turn next, then the twins.

Such a lot of pleasant things have happened the last few days. Your visit, then two of my very best friends have been paroled. Elizabeth, of whom I have written and May, the girl you and Kathleen met when you were visiting me. They are bright, sweet girls and I have become very much attached to them and naturally am very happy that they are to go, tho I shall miss them dreadfully. Next to Emma and Ella they were more congenial than any of the other inmates.

And we have a real diningroom now. I think I wrote you that it had been beautifully decorated in green and white and now we have new tables seating six, nice new chairs and best of all white tablecloths. Tell Paul Wielandy that I said all I need now to make me quite happy is for him to send me a bale of paper napkins (the very cheapest kind will do), and for some one to eliminate the scoundrel who feeds us weinies. There has been an improvement in our food also, no more meatless days and we have had dandy lamb stew on two occasions. Our food is coming over nice and hot now and we get plenty of fresh tomatoes, cantaloupes and watermelons. I think the cows broke in the cabbage patch and ate up all the cabbage for which we are very thankful, I had eaten so much cabbage I felt like a cow myself. Of course I may imagine that our food is better, but I know it tastes better, and the mealtime, which used to be a nightmare to me, is now almost a pleasure and I really enjoy my food, coarse and monotonous as it is. Emma, Ella and I are at the same table and except for the unnatural silence we could almost forget that we are in prison. The effect on the girls is simply marvelous, their attitude and behavior has improved one hundred percent. They are as quiet, well bred and well behaved as any group of women anywhere. When you come down again you must ask Mr. P. to permit you to see us at dinner, it will take away the horror you feel of my position to a great extent.

Another wonderful improvement has been the installation of a sort of community nurse who looks after the girls when they are ill mentally, physically or spiritually. May, the girl who has been paroled held the position, and she was an ideal person for the trying job. I don't know

labor, and management. This postwar plan, following the government's operation of the railroads for the duration of the war, was drafted by Glenn E. Plumb (1866–1922), counsel for the railroad brotherhoods.

who will have the position now, but there is one or two other women
who can fill the place very well, and it is certainly too great an improvement to be discontinued. Of course I am still hoping to see the hospital
properly equipped and when this is done the management shall have
traveled a long way towards humanizing the institution. I shall not be
content either until the splendid facilities of the psychological department of the State University are used here, but I do not hope to see
every thing done at once, I am quite content to be patient while we are
moving forward. Now don't you think all of these are a lot of nice things
to happen all in one week? No wonder I am feeling so much better. . . .

I am very tired tonight and my letter will be short. It has taken a
great deal of self control on my part not to indulge in a long message at
this time to the National Convention.[27] In fact I wrote a letter last night,
then thought better of it. Of course it is natural that I am keenly concerned in what takes place. We have given twenty years of our life to the
Socialist movement, I have attended every National Convention since
1900, carrying my babies with me sometimes and my heart is very heavy
when I realize that at this, the most important meeting the party has
ever held, I can only be present in spirit. I realize that the meeting in
Chicago will decide whether the Socialist movement will go forward and
fulfill the destiny we have had faith it would fulfill, or whether it will
crumble under the strain and leave the big work of reconstruction to
other forces. I feel the whole thing very deeply, but I felt it would be
presumptuous on my part to attempt to influence the comrades in any
way. I have been shut away from the world here for almost five months
now, the most wonderful months the world has ever known. I don't know
whether I am out of touch with the world and its movements, or whether
I see more clearly than those in the thick of the turmoil and struggle. At
any rate I decided that I could not say anything helpful at this time, so
will merely ask you to send a message of love and comradely greeting to
the members of the Convention. Tell them that I have faith in our cause,
faith in my comrades, faith in the honesty and loyalty of all the men and
women with whom we have worked and suffered. . . .

Lovingly,
KATE

27. The convention was the scene of a schism that in effect destroyed the party. Sub-
sequently, a socialist and a communist movement existed on the American Left and displayed mutual hostility.

September 14, 1919

Dear Sweethearts:

Sunday. It is a beautiful day and as we walked round and round in the little courtyard I thought how wonderfully beautiful the roads about Girard must be now. On the ninth of October it will be eighteen years since we met in that upper room with the little group of disciples who had come to be trained for the work of social regeneration. How young we were, how enthusiastic and full of hope for the future! How gaily we had sallied forth to teach the world the ways of peace and human brotherhood, and how little we knew of the ruggedness of the path that lay before us in the performance of our chosen work. I smile now when I think how very human even social crusaders are, and how even a potential Moses may indulge in lovemaking and a would-be Joan innocently tempt disciples to dally at her elbow to the detriment of Marx. We were a little group of "ignorant idealists" then, playing like children at rolling a snowball. Valiantly we gathered our bits of material, tugged and heaved and toiled, but our labors seemed in vain. Then something happened— the tiny snowball slowly rolled down the mountainside, gathering size and momentum as it went, and now, the very foundations of the older order are crashing beneath the mighty onrush of the social avalanche. We are scattered far and wide now. Lucy Hoving and J. A. Wayland have traveled on to the great beyond, yet there is something of their lives that we feel has become a part of our own. Mills, the old crusader who is ever young, has pushed on to the newer pioneer fields of social action and when his work is done he will die with his gaze to the setting sun. I hear from the Backus boys, but have had no word from Benton, I wonder where he is. The Taylors and Fred Johnson, the Cogswells and Will Prahl, they all read the APPEAL and I wish that on the ninth of October I might have a letter from every one of that little group of Girard students. . . .

I had a very remarkable letter from a woman physician in the Columbia Building, St. Louis. I should like to feel that I deserve the things she says of me, but I fear that I do not. I really don't aspire to be either a teacher or a leader, and I doubt if even the germ of an artist lives in me, but I do thank God that I can walk in the darkest most noisome places of life and find work to do, love to light my way and beauty in the midst of ugliness. Please tell her if she has a copy of Kraft-Ebbing I should like it, and perhaps some of Havelock Ellis' later books might be useful; but

literature useful in making a study of prison psychology and prison neurosis is yet to be written, and I doubt if it can be produced except by
those who have lived the life of a convict. How can anyone write intelligently of this life who has not lived it? What can anyone know of the
effects of the constant galling of prison discipline enforced by those absolutely innocent of even the most rudimentary knowledge of human
psychology until one's nerves have been worn to the raw by its stupidities? What can the professor in his college classroom, the physician in his
study, the scientist in his laboratory know of the things that go on behind
prison walls and their effect on human life? When I first came I was
sorely puzzled by the things the girls' conversations revealed. Their
dreams made me shudder in horror; now I understand, but only through
experience. There is a chasm that cannot be bridged, a gulf that cannot
be crossed between the convict and the other men, and only those who
have lived behind stone walls, slept inside steel bars and eaten under
the eye of official espionage can sense what it means. I have studied Mr.
Painter and my heart has ached at the tragedy of his blind groping to
help the women here. I pitied Mrs. Ballington Booth and I have the
deepest sympathy for the prison doctor. All are good at heart, but there
is a wall between them and the convict that they cannot scale. I am
hoping that if I am released before my brain is dulled and my soul too
deeply marred, I may be able to write of prison life in such a way that
the world can understand. I hope too that there will be men in Leavenworth who can tell the story of the man behind bars. But today the literature that would help me in the study of the soul of the convict is, so
far as I know, unwritten. . . .

Lovingly,
KATE

September 28, 1919

Dear Sweethearts:
    Sunday. The most striking thing in all of this experience that I am
undergoing is the amazing variety of people who write me, with their
varied opinions and philosophies, seemingly so far apart and yet so very
close, in the great essentials of life. In the same mail I get beautiful
pictures that show the expenditure of infinite care and patient labor from

an unknown, obscure teaching brother in a Catholic Order, and an offer from an unknown obscure Wobbly to provide me with the scientific books I need in my study of human life. Could anything be farther apart than the I. W. W. lumberjack and the Catholic brother, yet each is truly my brother. I receive on the same day a beautiful letter and a well-chosen selection of literature from a woman who writes on the letter-head of the Unity School of Christianity, and an equally beautiful letter from Upton Sinclair, with a copy of the "Profits of Religion." And strangest of all, the Lady of the Unity School of Christianity and the author of "Profits of Religion" write me almost the same things. In the little pile of letters at my plate I find one from Dr. Zeuch, the cool, polished, cultured college professor, and one from Pat Conway, the rampant I. W. W. agitator, and really, as a letter-writer Pat has rather the best of it. A. will have to acquire several more degrees and devour many more books of psychology before he will ever be able to write so vivid and thrilling a letter as Pat Conway. I have letters from new friends that I never saw, and from old school-mates who drifted out of my life long ago. I have letters and books and literature from Christian Scientists and psycho-analysts, from Wobblies and priests, from Spiritualists and Atheists, from Democrats and anarchists, from Socialists and conservatives, from rich and poor, illiterate and cultured, and yet in the essentials of life each brings the same message and all ask the same question.

It is the message of comradeship and the question of service. Almost without exception, all ask me what they can do, what they can send that will add to my comfort and make my stay in prison bearable. I am a convict, dressed in the coarse, hideous prison garb and locked in a steel-barred cell to-day, yet I am happier than the mistress of the White House, and in my tiny cell I have riches far beyond gifts from Kings and war profiteers. True I am shut away from my husband and children, but there is no guilt on my soul. I sleep on a narrow prison bunk, but there is no blood on my hands and my dreams are not haunted by the boys who died on the blood-stained battlefields of France. I eat prison fare, but it is not made bitter by broken promises. I see the sky only from a prison court-yard but it is not obscured by the clouds of disillusionment, disappointment and resentment. I march in the prison lockstep, but my soul is free; I slave in a prison workshop, but I know the peace that passeth understanding, for I have tried to be true to the teachings of Jesus and the prophets - "Thou shalt not kill - beat your swords into plowshares - love thy neighbor as thyself - do unto others as ye would that they should do unto you."

I don't enjoy prison fare, by any means, but I am learning wonderful lessons, resting my weary body from the strain of constant travel, resting my tired brain from creative work, resting my poor, abused throat from speaking, and from my prison cell I am viewing the mighty turmoil of life far more clearly than you who are in the clangor of it all. I have the feeling that there will be a big and trying work for us to do when the prison doors open and that this period of inaction will give me the strength and poise and courage to do it. I feel sure that you and the children will come through it all without permanent injury and that in the years that are to come we will have no regrets for these days.

It is dinner time now and we must go down. I will finish after we come up. I have so many interruptions that writing is rather a slow job. Now that Emma is gone, I must be mother, confessor and guide for all the women, and it is not a light task or an easy one. . . .

Our dinner was very nice today, and, as I ate heartily, I fear the rest of my letter will be dull. I was rather amused at *The Republic's* story of Fishman's report. Of course the little discrepancy in that I never at any time lodged complaints with the Department of Justice, is a small matter. In six months I have communicated direct with Mr. Painter twice, asking that four different matters might receive his attention, and they were immediately cared for. I may be both "dominating" and "vain", but I want *The Republic* to know that I am fair and wish the management of this institution to have all the credit due them. So please see that the editor gets these facts.

Practically every suggestion that I made to Mr. Fishman had already been put into force. Our meals are served hot; they are of good quality and well cooked. Since the change in the dining room, we have them served as nicely and in as attractive surroundings as one could wish. There are few small town hotels that have diningrooms as attractive as ours now! True, the tableware I mentioned to you is still missing, but those are really minor things. The meatless day has been discontinued; weinies are served so rarely now that we have no objection to them; mutton stew (and it is very good stew, too) now varies the menu. Our bread and coffee-cake is as good as I have ever eaten. The supper is still insufficient as the principal meal for persons engaged at hard, physical labor, as we are, but it has been wonderfully improved by the addition of butter, or, rather oleo, but it is very good oleo, as good as the average working class family eats. I don't agree with Mr. Fishman that we need meat for supper. I think we eat really more meat than is strictly necessary. What we really need is baked potatoes, maccaroni and cheese baked beans and things of that kind. It is perfectly practical to feed us some baked food to vary the monotony of the everlasting stews. Of course there is still the lack of sugar in the diet, but, on the whole I think we are as well fed as the average working class family today. Our milk is skimmed, but it is nice, wholesome milk, and we have about a pint each day. The coffee has improved wonderfully also, and now, while it is rather weak, it is real coffee, and one can drink it quite well.

The bathing facilities were taken care of long ago, and there is no complaint now, except that we only have one bath a week. The hospital has not been equipped, though it has been whitewashed and cleaned, and I imagine proper equipment will be installed in due time. We now have a community nurse, who cares for the sick, and that is a wonderful improvement. The nurse relieves the overworked orderly from the care of the sick, and that means that the orderly is nearly always smiling and good tempered now, which adds immeasurably to our comfort. We have now a third matron, which relieves Miss Smith from many annoying details, and that, too, makes it far better for all concerned.

I don't know whether Mr. Fishman's recommendation that the dark cell should be supplied with sleeping board and three blankets has been complied with or not, but I do know that punishments have been very materially reduced, and that the women are kept on punishment only a short time.

As to the "task"; I feel that no one could really know just how possible or impossible it was to make the task until she has been at the work for at least six months. I am sure that it will take that long for anyone to reach her highest point of production. Of course, I have had very decided opinions concerning the wisdom and efficiency of driven labor as a corrective, and I have also very decided opinions as to the wisdom of allowing a contractor's profits to determine the means and methods of handling subnormal and defective women. However, I am sure that the reporter was drawing on his imagination, and that no member of the Prison Board would make himself ridiculous by stating that "the women completed their tasks in the morning and had practically nothing to do in the afternoon." No visitor ever entered the shop in the afternoon and found the women idle or the machines unoccupied. Every person who has visited the shop knows that it is during the afternoon hours that the maddest rush is on and the women show the most marked physical and mental strain. In due time I shall have an opinion of the task, but when I discuss it, it shall certainly be with Mr. Painter himself. Of course the really big, vital problem of the shop is not touched upon in *The Republic* story, and naturally I cannot discuss it.

I don't know the other members of the board, Mr. Andrae and Mr. Poole or Mr. Gilvin, the warden. So far as I know, none of them have ever been inside the female wing in the six months I have been here. I do know Mr. Painter, the President of the Board, and I have said over and over again that I consider him one of the kindliest, most humane prison officials in the country. I fully believe that he is doing all in his power to keep pace with modern methods of prison management. I am sure that as long as he is in authority here he will do all that he can to improve the institution. I fully agree with Mr. Fishman that this is as good as any prison in the country, and that the wrongs and horrors that I find here are not peculiar to this prison, but common to the whole prison system. . . .

Lovingly,
KATE

October 5, 1919

Dear Sweethearts:

Sunday. For two years elected officials, editors, educators and clergymen have glorified slaughter, idealized killing, sanctioned mob-madness and physical outrage upon every human being who dared to disagree with the administration. For two long bitter years they sowed the winds, now they are reaping the whirlwinds. When savage blood-lust is unleashed it is not always careful to choose socialists and labor leaders for its victims; sometimes it chances to be mayors and governors and senators. There is serious danger that the mob spirit may sooner or later turn upon some who have fanned the flames of disorder and seared men's souls with the gospel of hate and unlawful vengeance. At this hour a monument is being unveiled over the grave of Prager,[28] one of the first victims of mob madness, and I wonder if there will be any one with the courage to say what I am saying now—that Prager was not murdered in the high road of Illinois by a mob of drunken miners; Prager was murdered in the editorial rooms of respectable newspapers by sober sane editors.

I can't help but be depressed by all of the horrors that are taking place out in the world, the strikes, the outbursts of mob-madness, the willful and wanton murder of working men and women, yet I know that all of these things are but the birth pangs of the coming of the new order. They are but the natural reaction of a betrayed, disillusioned, embittered humanity that is rapidly awakening to the wrongs that have been heaped upon it in the name of democracy, the outrages that have been forced upon it in the name of patriotism. How long this night of horror will be, how rough the road and how bloodstained the way, none of us can say. But there is one consolation we Socialists can take to our hearts: We know our hands are free from bloodstains, and our garments are clean. For years and years we have tried to lead the feet of mankind to the paths of internationalism, cooperation, peace and justice, but the workers were too stupid to hear and the rulers too blind and ignorant to heed and now the deluge is upon us. Who can say what the end will be or when the night of horrors will break!

Lovingly,
KATE

November 2, 1919

Dear Sweethearts:

Sunday. I received a fine letter from the boys in Sheridan County, Mont., and a copy of the dandy paper they are publishing. I don't seem to be able to place the editor but it is certainly a first class county paper, - no wonder the "old gang" loves it so much. If you drop a line to THE

28. Robert Paul Prager, a German immigrant, was a registered enemy alien in a small town near St. Louis. He had not been involved in any antiwar activities and, in fact, had sought to enlist. In April, 1918, a drunken mob attacked the young man. Although he was placed in jail for his own safety, the mob broke into the jail and hanged him. Those who were indicted were found not guilty, in an atmosphere of patriotic enthusiasm and hysteria.

PRODUCERS NEWS, Plentywood, Mont., they will be glad to put you on the list and you can keep in touch with what is doing in the Northwest. Tell the boys I send them all my love and that they are not to worry about me. I still have health and strength to be loyal to our ideals even behind prison bars, and that they can do more for me by organizing American farmers into a successful, militant, political, and co-operative movement than in any other way. I am in hearty sympathy with the work they are doing and think they are using the best of commonsense tactics. What difference does it make what name we call the movement of the producing class, just so it moves, and moves in the direction of the emancipation of the workers, both of the farms and of the industries! For twenty years, I have looked and longed, worked and prayed for the day when the farmers and the industrial workers would join hands and vote together for the good of the people, and now that day is dawning in glorious splendor. Perhaps because I am a farmer born, and bred, the wonderful movement of the farmers of the Northwest is the most inspiring thing in all the world to me today. How I enjoy the shrewdness with which these "hayseeds" outwit vicious politicians and corrupt lawyers! So far, they have won at every trick, and I feel sure they will continue to do so. I see that the bonding companies have refused to underwrite the state bonds of North Dakota. I am waiting with eagerness to see how the farmers will meet this vicious move, but I am serenely sure they will meet it and win. Tell the boys I am looking forward to the day when we can load up Charley Westphal's old "Case" and risk our necks by his wild driving and rattle over about Sheridan County, meeting the farmers of those wonderful plains. Sometimes, the horror of confinement, the staring blank walls of the cell-house, the windows so crusted with the accumulated dirt and grime of many years that no ray of sunshine can penetrate; the steel bars and the cramped muscles that come from hours at the machine, and more hours in a cell become almost maddening, and then I always think of those wonderful moonlight drives over the Montana prairies, of my long rides as a child over the Kansas hills and of our long walks thru the mountains of Kentucky. I have always been a child of the great out-of-doors and loved freedom and distances, so confinement is more terrible for me than housed souls whose outlook is cramped to the space between four walls. . . .

Lovingly,
KATE

November 23, 1919

Dear Sweethearts:

Sunday. . . . We had a nice letter from Emma telling of the dinner of the K.R.O. Committee in New York, and of course read the account in the CALL. I am glad that all my friends could gather and that Emma could bring them a cheerful message from the prison. Knowing how generous she is, I want to warn my friends that they must take all of the nice things she says of me with a grain of salt. I was sorry to hear that A.B.[29] had been ill. Hope he is better by this time, and that Emma's jaw is in good working condition.

Had a nice letter from Theresa. No thought that she or any of my friends had deserted me has ever entered my head. I know them too well, and have had too many evidences to the contrary. Yes, I received her box, and I am sure I mentioned dividing most of the cake among the colored girls, because I knew how deeply she felt on the race question. I certainly realize that everything is in a mighty muddle, and that the whole world is suffering from dire effects of the "morning after." When the whole world goes on one grand spree, the resulting headache is terrific.

This reminds me that I wonder if all of you read the news of the grand and glorious fizzle of the Peace Treaty[30] with the same mixed emotions I did. I felt much like the man my father used to tell of, who was strong on praying, but weak on work. Food was getting pretty low, and he decided to call God's attention to the matter after the manner of many good Christians who are prone to give Him much free advice about running the universe. He prayed: "O, Lord! Thou knowest how poor and needy we are, and we know it is not Thy will that Thy children should suffer for material comforts. Send us, O Lord, a barrel of pork and a barrel of meal, a barrel of salt and a barrel of sugar, a barrel of pepper—Aw hell Lord! that's too much pepper." For four years now, we Socialists have been hoping and praying that time would vindicate our stand on war, but when that Peace Treaty just naturally fizzled out in one disgusting sputter, I said "Aw! hell God! that's too much vindication." Four years of

29. Alexander Berkman (1870–1936), who spent fourteen years in prison for his attack on Henry Clay Frick following the Homestead strike of 1892, had been tried and convicted in 1917, as had Goldman, for campaigning against conscription.

30. On November 19, 1919, the United States Senate voted several times on the Versailles treaty with various reservations attached. The treaty was rejected, but would again come to a vote in the months ahead.

war—ten million slaughtered men, twenty million heartbroken women, a world of fatherless children, a millstone of war debts about each nation's neck, six months to write a Peace Treaty, six months yowling over it, and the achievement just a fizzle. I don't mind in the least that capitalism should commit suicide, but I object to its messing up the whole world doing it.

I see by the papers that Attorney General Palmer is on the verge of a nervous breakdown. No wonder, poor chap! I should think he would want to find a nice dark hole, crawl in to it, and pull the hole in after him. Just imagine how pleasant it must be to occupy his position with all the horrible, filthy, disgusting mess that he is supposed to clean up. Wow! Don't you wish you were in his shoes? . . .

Lovingly,
KATE

December 7, 1919

Dear Sweethearts:

Sunday. Irene Benton, of Granada, Minn., writes a fine, brave, cheering letter that has the ring of the right spirit in it. I agree with her absolutely as to the foolish comrades who insist on wasting their energies in fighting among themselves. I wish they could all go to prison for a few months, and they would learn if they have any brains, how stupid it is to squabble over nonessentials, when the big, all important job is crying for their attention and energies. I too, want C**** K**** to know that I received her letter, and that they are always welcome, but I disagree with her decision. No one knows the shortcomings of the Socialist Party and its officials better than I do, and I doubt if any other person in the United States has suffered for them and from them more than I have, yet I still insist on retaining my membership in the party and feel that any move to disorganize and disrupt it is criminal at this time. I have no desire at this time to become more narrow and exclusive. On the other hand, I am hoping that all radicals, pink, cerise, and RED may find a common ground of absolutely essential things and unite on it for the common good. The Socialist who takes the "holier than thou" attitude and refuses to work with the N.P.L. after the marvelously sane and splendid work that has been done in N.D. is a narrow egotist and not likely to add much to the sum total of human progress. I am more than glad that the Labor Party has been formed, and I am hoping with the deepest intensity that the Committee of 48[31] will work out some intelligent plan whereby ALL of the radical and progressive forces of the country can combine to sweep the forces of reaction from the places of political power all over the country. I don't think anyone can question my loyalty to the Socialist movement, yet I am ready to join hands with all forces that are willing to help remove the political barnacles from the ship of state.

Please tell Comrade K**** not to be so heartbroken over the fact that the great Amnesty meeting in Milwaukee practically overlooked amnesty altogether in the enthusiasm of political fervor, and that none of the male speakers, and there were all male, remembered that I existed. I don't mind, really. They did not overlook Flora Foreman[32] or me because they were bad, or unfriendly, but simply because that is the psychology of the male. And it is a fact that the return of Berger[33] by a heavy vote will do more for amnesty than all the oratory in the world. Political and economic power used by the workingclass is the only thing on earth that the ruling class fears. We politicals will stay in prison only as long as the workingclass is willing that we should. The United Mine Workers or the Railway Brotherhoods could open every prison door for every political prisoner in twenty-four hours if they wished to do it. The workers opened the prison doors in France, and they can do the same in the United States whenever they are ready for action. And there is simply nothing for us to do but wait as patiently as we may until the workers act.

31. The Labor party was an embryonic group which she eagerly hoped would lead to some sort of radical-Progressive coalition. Eventually the Farmer-Labor party, it was centered in the upper Midwest, especially Minnesota, and emerged in different manifestations in several states in 1919 and 1920. Those who joined tended to be former socialists, usually reformist, Non-Partisan League members, and labor representatives. The Committee of Forty-Eight, originally composed of Teddy Roosevelt Republicans who left the party in 1912 and never returned to the fold, was one of a number of heterogeneous groups which would meet in Chicago in February, 1922, at the invitation of the railroad brotherhoods to discuss a labor-Left coalition. With Socialist party participation, it formed the Conference for Progressive Political Action and nominated Senator Robert M. La Follette as its presidential candidate in 1924.

32. Flora Foreman, a schoolteacher, was convicted in northern Texas for advising soldiers to shoot their officers.

33. Victor Berger (1860–1929), the Milwaukee socialist leader elected to Congress in November, 1918, had been excluded by a vote of the House of Representatives for having "given comfort to the enemy," as evidenced by his conviction for conspiracy under the Espionage Act. In a hastily called election to fill his seat, Berger easily won again in December, 1919. The House once more excluded him.

God knows how long it will be, but I know they will act sooner or later. Of course, I also realize that many of us may pay with our lives for their inertia and slowness. I know perfectly well that every month I spend here means a year from my life, and that if I should stay many more months, I will come out a physical wreck, but hundreds of thousands have died in this last mad struggle of capitalism, and my life is no more valuable than the thousands that lie sleeping on the blood soaked fields of France. Death that seems so fearsome to normal people under normal conditions, has no terrors for those behind the bars.

Lovingly,
KATE

December 14, 1919

Dear Sweethearts:

Sunday. It is eight months today since I donned the garb of a criminal and took up the life of the damned. They have been long months, hard months, sad months, but they have made me one with all the sick and sad, the downtrodden and oppressed, the outraged and the outcast of earth. In many ways the experience is much like that of motherhood, and these months have been akin to the months I spent waiting for my babies to come. Soon now, I shall have spent as long here as the months that one spends in discomfort and misery to bring a new life into the world; let us hope that out of this travail will come something as well worthwhile as our children have been.

I am feeling more serene and content the last few days than for some time past, so many big and vital things are occurring outside in the world and some of the more nerve-racking and soul-torturing things here are gradually improving. . . .

As to what I can judge of the real work of the Conference, it seems to have been sane, constructive and progressive. The postcard platform is a masterpiece, and seems to cover most of the really vital things, and will, I think, appeal to a mighty mass of men and women as sane and eminently practical. The thing I am interested in now is the task of working out a plan of coalition between the Trades Unions, who have declared for a Labor Party, the Nonpartisan League and the Socialists. If such a coalition can be made, and the political power of all of these groups can be fused, it may mean that we can yet make the transition from crumbling capitalism to industrial democracy, without the hell of revolution and bloodshed that is sweeping over Europe. Only in such action can I see any hope for accomplishing necessary changes in our political and industrial structures by political action. If such an alignment is not made between these groups, I can see nothing but the onward march of blind, stupid, panic-crazed reaction, until its tyranny and horrors will force blind, bloody revolution.

I realize that it is going to take tact and patience and much forbearing wisdom to work out a plan of coalition that the three groups will accept. Of course, the most dangerous shoals will be narrowness, prejudice, and petty personal ambitions. I don't know whether or not we have yet been hounded and pounded enough to give us wisdom and tolerance, but fortunately the hounding and the pounding will go right on, and we will be forced to learn our lesson, - if not this year, then later. Be sure and send me all you can of the reports of committees and anything else that will help me to visualize the men and women and form some judgment of the value of the work. I presume I shall receive whatever is sent out from Headquarters. I don't remember whether this was suggested or not, if not, then I want to suggest it. When the postcard platforms are printed, they should have a return card with a declaration of either support or interest, or both, in the movement, with space for the signer's name and address, and his or her choice for President and Vice-President. The cards would furnish a mailing list of supporters and sympathizers and would give an opportunity for what would really amount to a referendum of candidates. . . .

Such a beautiful letter came to me from Rev. Robert Whitaker, Los Gatos, Calif.[34] In so many things, it was much like the letter from Father C*****. I wish I could send them both on to you, but the rules forbid. He served three months in jail in Los Angeles for acting as chairman of the Christian Socialist Pacifist Conference there, and he feels as I do about the whole matter of going to prison for principle. I agree with him that it is a splendid thing for a few "respectable" people to go to prison, and I have never felt bitter because fate chanced to choose me as one of

34. Robert Whitaker (1863–1944), a California-based Baptist minister, was active in a variety of labor, pacifist, and civil libertarian causes. He ran for Congress as a socialist in 1912 and he participated in the formation of the California Communist Labor party in 1919.

them. In fact, sometimes I feel that all my long, hard years of training both as a writer and a speaker has merely been to fit me for the work of arousing ALL respectable people to the stupid horrors of our whole prison system. For, after all, it is stupidity, and not brutality that permits it to exist. How many people in the state of Missouri know anything about our prisons, jails, and reformatories, (God save the mark), or give the slightest attention to what is hidden behind stone walls and locked behind steel doors? It is not so much that these women are here that makes me soul sick, as that seemingly sane, intelligent, decent, citizens should amble thru the shop and never inquire as to the right or wrongs of the task system, or as to who profits by this slave labor. It is not that we are caged like wild animals in a zoo, but that visiting women should walk by these cells with never a question as to the mental, moral, and physical conditions that are forced on other women.

Strange to say, it is the physical that makes me revolt most. I sit here night after night hearing language of such lewdness and vulgarity that I do not even understand the meaning of much of it, yet I never feel the sense of mental pollution. But I live in constant horror of loathsome disease germs, and I feel that months of scrubbing and bathing will be necessary to make me fit to live in decent society. The whole place reeks with every known veneral disease, and so far as any prophylatic measures are concerned, we might be living in the Middle Ages. There is an insane woman just below me in an advanced stage of syphillitic dementia, and she walks all night. Above me is a girl well advanced with both sy. and t.b. Just around the corner is another t.b. who coughs all night, and she works in the diningroom, and handles our food and dishes. Alice creeps about, a constant menace to all of us, and now we have the added horror of an old woman who is a dope fiend, and slowly dying with cancer of the womb. And who is to blame? The management. Not at all. The Prison Board keeps us in the buildings provided by the state legislature, and work us under contracts made by the state, and they dump in here together what the various courts dump on them. The old woman with the cancer was in a poorhouse in a certain county, the county authorities got tired of caring for her, and did not have the nerve or decency to painlessly put her out of the way, so when she dropped a match on a strawbed, and set it afire, they tried her for arson, and sentenced her to prison for two years. And aside from this case, and one other, all of the worst are Federal prisoners.

I think that the only real humiliation I have felt since being here has been a deep, burning shame for my country. I came here with much of love of country and idealism concerning it that I had inherited from my pioneer ancestors. Take the three of us here, side by side, Ella, Rose and me. Ella was only a child when she came, clean in body and mind, Rose is the daughter of a businessman in a northwestern city, and the wife of another businessman. She is refined, fairly well educated in a conventional way, and as ignorant and innocent as a kitten, and has a beautiful little girl of ten. All of us came here clean and free of disease, yet it will be one chance in ten thousand if we escape without infection. Is there any record of any German atrocities, even when German atrocities were all the style, that could be more cursed than to force three clean women to live where loathsome infection is almost a certainty? Yet it is our federal and state legislatures that are to blame and not the prison officials who do their bidding.

And we are only three. In the prisons of our country, there are thousands. The administration is busy now wrecking army training camps. Millions of dollars worth of building will be sold for a pittance, and thousands of men and women will be infected for want of decent care. Why should not the government take one of these southern army cantonments, and transform it at a very slight cost to a federal hospital where all syphilitics, consumptives, and drug addicts could be cared for in a humane way, and according to modern methods?

Lovingly,
KATE

December 21, 1919

Dear Sweethearts:

I will write my Christmas letter today so you will be sure to have it by Christmas. For the last few days I have been thinking back over all the Christmas days of the past. They have been many and varied and most of them very happy, so I feel quite sure that I needed this one here in The Sorrowful City to make me comprehend what Christmas meant to the sick and sinful, the sad and sorry outcasts that guilty society hides away from sight behind prison walls.

As I sit here in a steel walled, steel barred cell, and let my mind retrace the long and winding path of life, I know that I have lived more fully, more deeply and more broadly than is the lot of the average woman. The first Christmas I can dimly remember was spent in a sod-walled, dirt-roofed pioneer shanty on the plains of Kansas. Toys for the child of the pioneer were few and rare in those days, but that Christmas was far from barren indeed. Mother made me the most beautiful Red Riding Hood cloak and hood of wonderful scarlet cloth, and no queen was ever prouder of her ermine than I of my scarlet cloak.

There was a beautiful, gay, girl-wife—Liza—who lived on an adjoining claim. When she and her young husband, who is but a blurred memory, came to spend Christmas day with us, she brought me, as far as I can remember, my first doll. The little girls of today would turn up their noses in scorn at "Rose" but to me she was all that any embryo mother's first doll is. She was only made of china, her hair was painted on, and her eyes were staring blue smudges, but she was my very first baby and of all the gifts I have ever received, I doubt if there has been one that I loved and cherished so much. A strange coincidence has reached down into my subconscious mind and brought out my memories of Liza, for hers was a tragic story that is painfully vivid to me now. She was so gay and beautiful, so full of life and love that she was a favorite all the way from the Solomon to Springcreek and from the Saline to Delphos way. Soon she began to fade and fell ill. I remember that Mother and the other women shook their heads sadly, but whispered that she would be better after the baby came. But when the baby came, it was dead and Liza soon followed. The memory of that tiny, waxen baby face in the tiny coffin is my first memory of death. Then just a little later, I saw Liza shut in her narrow bed, and my heart was almost broken for I loved her well, and she is still one of the sweet memories of my childhood. When I was old enough to understand, Mother told me her story; and it is the old, old bitter story of so many blasted lives. It was just the simple story of a cowboy who went to the city with a load of stock, went out to see "life", and who later brought to his gay and laughing bride the taint syphilis. . . .

I am sending you a little kodak picture of Glendale schoolhouse recently sent to me. This is where the foundations of my education were laid. It will look tiny and shabby and funny to you, but we were mighty proud of it, and it was the best building for twenty miles in any direction. The first Christmas after it was built, we celebrated with a perfectly gorgeous dance. Every woman in the neighborhood cooked up a washtub full of "eats," the men sent all the way to Kansas City for a tub of oysters, the gay young blades like Cousin Jim Richards, Jay King and Dave Roy, imported Jim Kallon from way out east of Minneapolis, Kansas, to assist Riley Austin, our local fiddler. Od Colby was the champion "caller off". He practiced on the cattle until Father threatened to shoot him for cruelty to animals. The few unmarried girls kept their hair in the lead frizzers for a week and the gay young matrons like Lucy Richards, Teenie Tibbits, and Mrs. Hubbard let out a few inches on their "holdback" Polanaises, just to show the girls that they could shake a toe even if they were married. It was bitter cold when Christmas night came, but we snuggled down in the armloads of sweet smelling hay Father put in the bottom of the wagon, and Mother wrapped us up like papooses in buffalo robes, and we were snug and cozy as the wagon wheels sang thru the frozen snow. Uncle Clarence suffered in dignified silence the agonies of his first "biled" collar and Uncle John slipped in the kitchen at the last moment and oiled his hair with Grandmother's goose grease to make it lie down. I have looked upon many of earth's beauty spots, but none hold for me a tenderer memory than that winding road across the snow covered hills, the dancing lights of swinging lanterns, the song of the wheels in the snow, the winking lights from the schoolhouse windows, and the cheery shouts of "Christmas Giff" as Father drove old "Bill" and "Miller" up to the schoolhouse porch. Inside all was laughter, music, good things to eat and dancing. The memory of that Christmas sort of trails into a hazy blur; for Uncle John and I, stuffed like Christmas turkeys, and satiated with enjoyment crept into a pile of robes behind the stove to rest, and the last thing I remember was Riley Austin's billygoat whiskers waggling in the most amazing way as he sawed away on the "Irish Washerwoman."

Then there was the Christmas when I had the awe inspiring experience of my first beau. He was only a neighbor boy that I had played with and quarreled with all my life, but it was a wonderful moment when he rode defiantly up to the kitchen door, and still mounted, so he could beat a hasty retreat in case it seemed wise, asked me if he might "have my company to the Christmas tree." Does any woman ever forget I wonder, the blissful agony of her first public appearance with a real, live beau? I am sure that I have not. Long years have passed since then. Our paths have wandered far apart, yet I am sure that in the heart of each of us, there will be a little thrill as we think of that long gone Christmas.

Then, there is a long succession of Christmases of happy young womanhood; then that Christmas in Girard, Kansas, in 1901. It was a part of the wonderful experiences of the Mills' School, of the prelude to love, marriage and life. Papa and Professor Mills were in a state of expansive happiness so they invited seventy-five guests to take dinner with us, and generously handed over to me the job of preparing that dinner, with a smoky stove and an assistant whose culinary skill was exhausted in boiling water. But Mother Tubbs and some of the other good Girard matrons came to my rescue, and Daddy Tubbs fed the balky stove with pine kindling wood and at the appointed hour that mammoth Christmas dinner was ready to serve. Fortunately, the guests were all good comrades, and they did not mind that the oyster soup had been slightly scorched and the mashed potatoes were somewhat lumpy. There is a tie particularly warm, strong and tender between the Mills' School students and that group of Girard residents, and I am sure that no matter where any of them may be this Christmas time, their love will come to me and each will remember that Christmas dinner.

Then, there was that wonderful Christmas in our beautiful home in Rosedale. Once again the Mills' School students were our guests and Dick, who was just one month old, was the center of attraction. It is when I think of that Christmas that I realize to what a marvelous extent both Father and Mother exercised that exquisite hospitality that gave them so many lovers. I am sure that every one of the young men and women who shared that Christmas with us will think of it tenderly. . . .

One Christmas time that stands out in my memory was that spent in London in 1913, the first I had ever spent away from my husband and children. How strange a contrast it was to this. At that time it seemed I had all the honors that can be given to any woman by the best and greatest thinkers, writers, and artists of our time; but here in my prison cell, dressed in the garb of a convict, I know that I am serving better than at that time, and that if I ever walk out from these steel gates, I will be capable of doing bigger and better work than I have ever done. So on this Christmas day I want you, my husband, and my children, my old mother, my brothers and sisters, my friends and comrades to be as serene and calm as I am. It will be lonely for you, this Christmas day, but remember that you have only loaned me to those whose needs are greater far. . . .

So while our home has no mother on this Christmas day; while our table will have its empty chair; while our hearts will ache and our tears will fall, you will fill the mother's place with greater love for each other; fill my empty chair with some one whose heart is heavier than ours; you will make your tears bring forth the flowers of loving service for others, and your heartaches bring help and comfort to the sad and sorrowing that come your way. Be as happy as you can on Christmas day; enjoy whatever comes to you, and go out among our friends who will do everything in their power to make up for my absence. Don't worry about me. My hands will be full, and I shall be too busy to find time to be unhappy. There are ninety souls here who need me, and you are only five. Already loving messages and beautiful gifts are coming and I shall make this the best and richest Christmas day of my life. You must all do the same.

The world will remember this as its darkest Christmas, darker far than the bloodiest Christmas of the war; but it will precede the greatest and most sublime New Year that the world has ever known.

And may hope, faith, peace and love be with us all.

Lovingly,
KATE

January 10, 1920

Dear Sweethearts:

Saturday. I am rather annoyed at failing to receive my papers last night. Things go with such a rush these days that if you are out of touch with the world for two days, it is almost hopeless to try to overtake the mad race. The things that "constituted authority" is doing to "constitutional rights" these days make ones head whirl. Raids, deportations, mobs, outrages and murders follow so fast, one upon the other, that one feels like being pricked with pins to see if one is really sane and wide awake or indulging in a frightful nightmare. The birth of a new social order is no twilight sleep affair, but humanity must pay to the last pain and the extreme of agony for the coming life. The Democratic administration seems to be rushing the labor in a heroic, if somewhat mistaken zeal. Old Doc Palmer seems to be administering unheard of doses of—is it thyroidin, or thyroprotein that busy doctors use when old mother Na-

ture is a little slow? How strange it is that we Socialists are the only sane,
restraining force in the United States today while the whole weight and
power of the Democratic administration is being hurled into the effort to
plunge the nation into the throes of a bloody revolution. Not one thing
that could possibly be done to enrage and inflame the masses is being
overlooked by elected officials. Law is put at naught, justice is trampled
underfoot, courts and injunctions used in the most gallingly unlawful
manner, men elected fairly and by great majorities are being denied their
rightful places in the legislative branches of government and a horde of
petty spies are turned loose with no law but their own mad passions to
invade the homes and meeting places of every human being, alien and
citizen, who is even suspected of having an opinion differing in the slightest degree from that of the administration.

Such methods can have but one result, first surprise, then resentment, and then revolt. I had hoped that the Committee of Forty-Eight
would be able to amalgamate the sane vote, (one can call it the radical),
for the radicals are now the conservatives who cling to constitutional political action, while the reactionary forces are now the radicals who would
overthrow constitutional political action by force and violence and replace it by mob autocracy. But I fear now that bloody revolt will be forced
upon the masses by the mob autocracy of petty officials long before the
time comes for the expression of the popular will at the ballot box.

It is fortunate for me, no doubt, that I am behind prison walls. It is a
safer place than outside. I can easily imagine the hounding and the ha-
rassment that I would be compelled to endure if I were at "liberty".

Don't think that I am merely depressed and unhappy. I simply know
that we as a people must go thru our period of travail; but I naturally
hope it may be as short as possible and pass with as little bloodshed as
the natural processes of evolution permit. I hope, of course, that the
workers will be able to maintain their poise, reason and common sense,
and bring order out of the chaos that exists; but they will be tried to the
limit, and I fear for the immediate outcome of the reign of terror which
the administration seems determined to force upon us.

Of course, the quiet, orderly, sane, unimpassioned workers' move-
ment of the great Northwest is hopeful and the recent actions of the
Railway Brotherhoods in the co-operative field is a splendid indication.
If only we can go thru the next few weeks without violence, a peaceful

reaction against official violence may be possible. At any rate, we can only hope for the best and take what comes with as much courage and poise as possible.

I have just returned from the picture show on the other side, and must cut my letter short as the orderly will soon be here to take up the mail.

I am writing a little play for the women and want you to ask V. L. to get me a copy of words and music of "Rock Me To Sleep Mother" which I wish to use.

Must close now. Will write again Tuesday. Love and kisses to my darlings.

Lovingly,
KATE

January 17, 1920

Dear Sweethearts:

Saturday. Von H. and his panacea for "the woman question" is really very amusing. I should have enjoyed the discussion, I am sure. I think I mentioned once before that when Mr. Painter was Chairman of the Senate Commission investigating women's wages, etc., it was his cureall also. Every time something particularly appalling was brought out in regard to working conditions for women and girls he would deliver a sermon on the beauties and safety of domestic work for girls. He felt quite sure that if all working girls would become housemaids, the social problem would be solved. After coming here I decided to take a census of his guests and I found that about eighty per cent of them had been housemaids before they turned prostitute and thief. There are only two women here who have reached High School, or had any training whatever, myself and the judge's daughter. All of the others are barely literate and have had no trades, professions or training whatever. There is not a bold, bad stenographer or a naughty manicurist in the lot, but there are something like fifty housemaids. Every woman here for eliminating an undesirable husband is a regular old plug workhorse of a housewife and there is not a Socialist, Bolshevik or Anarchist among them; mostly they are perfectly good Democrats. And the very funny thing is that they are all

dreadfully respectable. One of them is still terribly agitated over the
Christmas presents I received from MEN.

What you say is true. Events move with mighty velocity now and we
will emerge from this black night of terrorism much more rapidly than
our parents did from the same madness of the slave autocracy. I have
been reading REBELS AND REFORMERS, by Ponsonby. I suggest that Dick
or Kathleen get it from the Library. The story of William Lloyd Garrison
will help the children to meet their experience philosophically and understandingly. The early Abolitionists faced exactly the same conditions
seventy-five years ago that we face and suffered exactly the same outrages. Then it was the panic stricken fear of the slave autocracy that
resorted to mobs and prostituted courts; now it is the mad panic of the
industrial autocracy that resorts to the same methods. But the reaction is
coming more quickly than I hoped. Berger's reelection and the storm of
protest loosed by the unseating of the five Socialist Assemblymen[35]
shows that the day of reckoning is much nearer than we had thought. If
Palmer will only stage a few more "bomb explosions" and indulge in a
few more "raids" the storm will break in all its fury.

You can imagine with what intense interest I am reading of the expo-
sures of the stupendous robbery of the government by the big lumber
and shipping interests of the Northwest. And mark my prophecy, the
tiny whiff that we are getting now is only an atom of the stench that will
be uncovered soon. In due time, and I sincerely believe it will not be
long - the whole vicious, brutal, murderous story will be uncovered and
the world will know why I am in prison and why such reversions to savagery as the Centralia affair[36] take place. We will find the link that con-
nects James E. Phelan to the Milwaukee Railway, the Milwaukee to the
lumber thieves, the lumber thieves to the shipbuilding thieves and all of
them to the political administration in power. The whole story of why I
should have been chosen the victim of their wrath is plain to me now,
and we can afford to be patient while the scroll of infamy unrolls. The

35. This occurred in New York State. These socialist assemblymen, like Berger in
Congress, had been legally elected. They were excluded on the general grounds of lack of
patriotism.

36. The Centralia Massacre occurred on Armistice Day, 1919. The local IWW hall
was attacked by American Legionnaires after a parade. Wobblies in the hall fired at their
attackers and killed at least four men. In retaliation, one Wobbly was castrated and murdered by the mob.

I. W. W. was the first thing that ever challenged the despotic and murderous reign of the lumber kings, and while I never aligned myself with them, I did understand them and I had the power to make others understand. Then came the N. P. L. and I was almost the very first person who ever undertook to carry to the Eastern and Southern workers the wonderful story of this mighty uprising of the farmers of the great Northwest. Then in the spring of 1917 came the thing that struck terror to the hearts of the thieves and plunderers of the Pacific coast. The I. W. W. was organizing the underdogs of the industrial world out there and the N. P. L. was organizing the plundered farmers: as the harvest time neared that summer, the N. P. L. farmers made terms with the "Wobblies" and this alignment struck at the very foundation of the power of the Northwestern plunderbund including the lumber interests, the mining interests, the grain speculators and the railways. They were wise enough to know that if the plundered farmers and the plundered wage workers ever joined forces their days of unrestricted plundering were done. The war was the golden opportunity of the plunderers.

Human jackals have always preyed both upon the people and the government under the clouds of war. When logic and reason and civilization are swallowed up in the mad vortex of war, thieves and plunderers and murderers are freed from the restrictions that sane civilized society imposes upon them, and under the guise of patriotism they are permitted to commit any crime as long as they cover it with shouts of patriotism and drape it with flaunting flags. Out there in the great, rich Northwest were the lumber interests who controlled the spruce needed by the government for aeroplanes, the copper interests who controlled the copper necessary for munitions, the ship building interests who controlled the shipping needful to wage the war and the grain speculators who hoped to, and did to a certain extent control the bread supply of the world. Interlocked with these were the railroad interests who must transport these necessities not only of life but of death also. They knew their servile lackeys were safely placed in where they could serve them best in the political administration of the government and the only thing that threatened their wild orgy of unrestricted thievish profits was the awakening sense of solidarity between the industrial workers and the farmers and the astounding efforts of the farmers to boycott the old parties and build a political party of their own.

When I look back over that fateful lecture trip of 1917 in the light of these recent disclosures the whole tragedy unrolls, a mighty epic of human progress in which fate throws me to the crest of the wave. When I left St. Louis I traveled east and south and everywhere record breaking crowds heard me gladly. I delivered my *lecture in Washington* under the very nose of the administration and every department of the government was represented and none discovered that there was anything treasonable in my address. Then I turned westward and it was Democratic farmers who had voted for Wilson because "he kept us out of war" who flocked to my meetings. When I reached Phoenix, Ariz., ten thousand miners stood packed in one solid mass of humanity for four hours and listened and cheered and insisted that I go on and on long after my regular lecture was finished. All the way to the Pacific it was the same; up the Coast I talked to farmers, wobblies, miners and lumber workers. The newspapers were full of I. W. W. outrages, they were said to be burning lumber mills, destroying crops and burning the wheatfields. All the way from the Oklahoma oil fields to the California beet fields, from there to the Washington forests and later to the Montana and North Dakota wheatfields I followed that will-o'-the-wisp of "wobbly outrages" but I never overtook it. It always happened - not in the place where I chanced to be - but just over the state or county line, but when I too went over the line the outrages were always somewhere beyond!

On the way into Spokane I shared the observation of the deluxe train with one of the Weyerhausers and his young son about Dick's age. We became quite friendly and when I told him I was a magazine writer from the east he unfolded a wonderful tale of "wobbly outrages" and the "I. W. W. menace". But when I insisted that my magazine would not be satisfied with the word of even a lumber king, but wanted actual details and real photos of a burned mill and insisted on being led to the spot where one of these outrages had taken place he retired to the seclusion of his stateroom and he cut me dead when I bowed to him in the dining room of the hotel in Spokane. On the way from Seattle to Tacoma it was the Federal District Attorney who shared the observation with me, and when I again insisted on being led to the very spot where a "wobbly outrage" had been committed he said it would be as much as my life was worth to venture out among these desperate villains and he as a gentleman could not permit me to take such chances. When I told him that I had been hobnobbing with these same desperate villains for a number of years without harm, he grew very angry and said I was not a magazine writer at all but a "damned dirty agitator" who should be put in jail for the good of the country. At Lewiston, Ida., I was billed as the Fourth of July speaker for the A. F. of L. central labor body, but when the Federal Attorney announced that I would not be permitted to speak it was the farmers and the wobblies that put the meeting over. Then I entered the wheat regions and the stronghold of the N. P. L. and it was the farmer members of this organization who paid for and attended my meetings.

I can understand now just what a fly I was in the ointment of the interests who had everything fixed to clean up their billions on the profits of war. But I was modest about my work and there were always too great crowds at my meetings and I was too wise to talk to individuals, so no opportunity came to "frame me" until I reached Bowman. Here Phelan, who owned a string of elevators on the Milwaukee and had a mortgage on the very lives of certain of the villagers, was able to "put it over". But behind James, the cringing, crawling perjurer, was Phelan the Milwaukee retainer, and behind Phelan the lumber interests and the copper interests and the grain thieves and the railway plunderers. Before another year has passed the whole slimy tale will be public property. I can afford to wait and be patient here in my prison cell. I can stitch jackets all day long and sleep peacefully at night, for out there in the world of free men mighty forces are fighting my battles for me. And every stitch I sew is a stitch in the shroud of the Plunderbund. The jackets I have made since coming here will prove to be the most expensive garments ever made in the slave pens of Capitalism; they will be the grave clothes of the vicious spirit of the despoilers of human life; they will be the swaddling clothes of the newborn spirit of social justice that is now being brought into the world.

Lovingly,
KATE

January 20, 1920

Dear Sweethearts:

. . . I don't know that I am particularly unflinching, or "willing to stand absolutely alone in the world rather than to make any allowances for the prejudices of others", but I do insist on my right to make a distinction between human beings and their particular theories and beliefs. Good Heavens! Emma Goldman is not the only person I have defended in my lifetime. I have brought down a storm of wrath on my head from my most devoted friends because the same evening that the jury returned a verdict finding me guilty I issued a statement defending the jurymen, not for a criminally unjust verdict, but from the purely human standpoint. Surely if there is any person on earth that I would naturally be presumed to hate, it would be the prosecutor who used what I believe to be perjured testimony and resorted to every legal trick made possible by the abnormal psychology of the time. Yet over and over again I have defended Mr. Hildreth, in print and on the platform, much to the disgust of my friends and supporters. I do not defend Hildreth the prosecutor, but Hildreth the human being.

I am not in the least inclined to the theory of anarchy - even the denatured variety known as philosophical anarchy. I may not be sufficiently intellectual enough to fully grasp the theory, but what of it I do grasp seems to be the impractical phantasies of psychopathic minds. I think I stated once before that I felt that the emotional reaction known as anarchy was but the soul scar of social injustice and that so-called anarchists should be handled, not by ignorant judges and jailers, but by intelligent psychologists. In fact when brought down to the last analysis I feel that the whole theory is as impractical, but not as stupid, as erratic, but not as vicious as the tenets of the Democratic party.

Emma Goldman has been preaching anarchy for thirty years in this country and anarchy is presumed to be productive of lawlessness and disorder, of crime and danger to stableized [sic] government. Yet more crimes have been committed in the last three months by alleged members of the American Legion[37] than by alleged anarchists in thirty years. Emma and all the followers she could rally about her have not endangered stable government, assaulted the constitution and disregarded law one thousandth's part as much as the Department of Justice in the last three weeks. When it comes to actually doing all the things that anarchists are presumed to teach, the Democratic party is there with the goods.

37. American Legion crimes is a reference to a series of government raids, without warrants, aided by vigilantes, all along the West Coast. American Legion *ad hoc* involvement seemed clear in this effort to rid the region of its radical element.

But that does not prevent me from having the friendliest feelings for individual democrats.

Lovingly,
KATE

January 21, 1920

Dear Sweethearts:

I am going to do a part of my letter tonight for Thursday is always bedlam. It is housecleaning night and grocery ordering night and by the time one goes thro the grinding grill of the "task" in the shop and cleans and makes out the grocery order, there is little strength or energy left for writing. Until the last two weeks I have been able to hire my cleaning done which helped me greatly, but recently that privilege and also the privilege of keeping my perishable food in the ice box has been revoked which naturally makes things much harder for me. I have not the slightest idea as to the whyfores of it all, it is simply a part of the arbitrary domination which we may not even inquire into. But I have always been able to adjust myself to anything and make the best of it and I hope to be able to continue to do so.

Received Pop's little note this evening and a nice long letter from Ella. She gives me the welcome news that her bond has been reduced to $5,000, and that she hopes to be at liberty soon. I sincerely hope there has been no hitch, and that she has been able to get a free breath by this time. Mercy! What a sight it must have been to see her "crying two hundred tears" when she read my letter. I really did not know they had such an effect on persons. But it explained something that had been puzzling us here. The water was very muddy one day last week and someone said that the River had risen very suddenly and no one knew what caused it. But please tell the poor kiddie not to worry about me, I am feeling fine again, and while I am terribly lonely I just keep busy all the time and manage to exist. We still have fairly good work and I have been able to make the "task" so far and have some jackets on the book. Rose is nice and sweet to me and Lady S. keeps me busy most of the time. Yes, I have talked to Ida, she seems very nice and is getting acclimated quite well. She told me a great deal about the jail life there in St. Louis. What interesting stories Gabriella Antolina and I will write some day of the Dark Ages in America and the prisons that yawned for any one daring enough to express a real, live thought.

And that reminds me that I can sew on jackets all day now quite contentedly because I know that when the slave has done her "task" I can go to my cell, clang the steel door behind me and behind the steel bars I can read my newspapers and laugh at the tragic-comedy of life. Root[38] has at last discovered that the only way to destroy the power of Lenine and Trotsky is to lift the embargo and permit the Russian people to trade with the allied nations. Of course the Allies have not changed their attitude towards the Soviet government; certainly not; it will not be recognized, but the trading will be done with the co-operatives which have escaped the power of the Soviets. Sure! the co-operatives have escaped; it would be just like greedy, blood-thirsty villains like L. and T. to permit them to flourish unmolested. Kolchak[39] is now in cold storage, the American troops are being brought home from Siberia and the United States is too busy quashing the wild and wooley "REDS" at home to assist the Japs in wiping out the Soviets over there. "The Tiger" had his claws clipped in the recent French election, the English Laborites are winning in every contest and last but not least, Sammy, dear respectable old Sammy, is raising his voice in a squeak against the "sedition" laws pending in Congress.[40]

If such amazing things keep on happening Mr. Palmer may unearth from some long-buried archives a certain old and venerable document known as the CONSTITUTION OF THE UNITED STATES. And if its faded ink is still decipherable he may discover that it contains the quaint provisions that "free speech", "free press" and "free assemblage shall not be abridged." Actually it may happen; stranger things have occurred.

Thursday. Well I have cleaned house, ordered groceries, cooked sup-

38. Elihu Root (1845–1937), considered an elder statesman of the Republican party, following his service as secretary of state and secretary of war in Republican administrations, led an American mission to Russia in the summer of 1917. This mission, like those from the Allied countries, sought to persuade the provisional government led by Kerensky to continue the war effort. The delegations sent by European nations were socialist in ideology; the American delegation was supposed to represent a variety of political viewpoints. Root reported optimistically on the Kerensky government's chances for survival.

39. Admiral A. V. Kolchak (1874–1920) led the White forces in Siberia during the civil war following the Bolshevik assumption of power.

40. Georges Clemenceau, known as the Tiger, former premier of France, was defeated in 1920 and retired. Samuel Gompers failed to oppose pending sedition laws.

per, washed the dishes and now I will finish my letter. Received yours of last night only to find another disappointment about the bond. But fortunately I have reached the point where nothing seems to be of particular importance. I presume that this feeling of weary indifference must possess the souls of every one at this time. I imagine that it is the psychological state that makes it possible for a nation to go on with a war until utter destruction forces it to cease. However I have an amazing power of recuperation, and when I have had a night's rest I will be ready to take up the fight for life once more.

Dear me! this thing of acting as attorney, counselor, and guide for such a bunch of helpless women has a sad effect on one's literary efforts, but I will be ready to enter the legal profession by the time I have finished my schooling here. I no more than get my paper in the machine when someone comes for me to write something for them, so if my letter is ragged you will understand.

I have been more intensely interested in the pending sedition legislation in Washington than anything that has happened since coming here. It seems to me to be the test of whether we are to come thru the after-the-war chaos without bloody revolution or in a welter of terrorism, mobbery and bloodshed that appalls the mind to contemplate. If the five Socialist assemblymen are actually denied their seats in Albany and the Graham bill[41] is enacted I can see little or no hope of escaping more sickening horrors than any nation in Europe is now enduring. If the Graham bill really becomes a law it will let loose such a flood of official despotism and petty official terrorism that it makes me soul sick to even think of it. Yet it may be that this nation must pay in blood as all of the nations of Europe have paid. There is one truth that we cannot but face, and that is that if peaceful political action is taken from the people and sedition laws rob them of the last vestige of the protection of constitutional guarantees there is nothing left.

The action of Congress is so problematical that it is very difficult to forecast what will happen. It is true that the revolt against such legislation is mounting rapidly. Even the most reactionary of the capitalist

---

41. The proposed Graham bill, bearing the name of Representative George S. Graham of Pennsylvania, combined several proposals for peacetime anti–civil liberties legislation. The bill invoked twenty years' imprisonment, a ten-thousand-dollar fine, or both, for seeking the overthrow or destruction of the American government or for seeking to harm or terrorize any federal official. This measure, and others to restrict freedom of opinion in peacetime, did not pass.

newspapers admit it, but so much blind, assinine stupidity has been displayed in Washington that one wonders if the administration is not so totally out of touch with the people that nothing less than a political earthquake could jar it loose from its stupid complacency.

The fact that a hearing will be held on the bill sometime in the near future is hopeful, but not assuring. I should like, in some way, to get the story of my case before that hearing. It is quite a striking and dramatic example of the real workings of a sedition law.

I am really too tired to write more tonight, so must close now. Hope to feel more cheerful tomorrow. Love and kisses to my darlings.

Lovingly,
KATE

January 31, 1920

Dear Sweethearts:

Saturday. Emma Goldman too had that rare gift; in her it was the all-embracing, intensified sacrificing maternity. Thwarted in physical motherhood she poured out her whole soul in vicarious motherhood of all the sad and sorrowful, the wronged and oppressed, the bitter and rebellious children of men. Warden Gilvin was right when he said the women here worshipped her with an idolatrous worship. They did. And largely it was because the women here are mostly the weak and inefficient, the arrested and infantile who have never achieved adulthood and still sorely need the sheltering mother love. The girls love me too, but never as they loved Emma Goldman. To them I am the dispenser of chewing gum and peppermint drops, a perambulating spelling book, dictionary and compendium of all known wisdom, I am lawyer, priest and physician, I am an authority on everything from crochet stitches to the meaning of dreams; but I do not and never can fill Emma's place in their hearts. I read many of Emma's letters - letters that expressed the deepest and most sincere love but practically all displaying marked evidence that the writer suffered from the "Oedipus complex". It was Emma's passionate maternal spirit that appealed to them and not her anarchistic philosophy.

Love and kisses to all my darlings,
KATE

Jefferson City, Mo.
February 8, 1920

Mr. Otto Branstetter[42]
National Office, Socialist Party
803 W. Madison St.
Chicago, Ill.
Dear Otto:

I feel that the time has arrived to take the next step in my case. I have asked Mr. V. R. Lovell, Fargo, N. D., my attorney to go to Bowman and secure the legal evidence of the use of perjured testimony in my trial. He informs me that he is at present occupied with cases coming up during the term of court now in session but will be ready to go to Bowman in a short time. I presume about the first of March.

I have considered the whole matter very carefully and it seems vital that the S. P. should not leave this work entirely to a hired attorney. If there was ever a time when every true Socialist should wish to avoid anything that could possibly cause friction and inharmony in the party it is now. There is a deep and very bitter feeling among the rank and file of the party members that I have been most shamefully treated by the National Office. How much basis there is for this feeling is aside from the point at issue, but all reasonable means should be used to eradicate it.

There is also some feeling in North Dakota that because Mr. Lovell is a staunch Democrat and very conservative there is doubt as to his sincerity in handling my case. Personally I do not feel that there is the slightest question, I feel that Mr. L. was far more loyal and faithful to me than the N. E. C. or the N. O. ever was and that he did all that any attorney could do, and did it under the most trying circumstances, and with wonderful courage in the face of the terrorism that raged in North Dakota. However there are two things that must be done - the bitterness caused by the actions of the N. O. in the past must be removed as far as possible and all question as to my having the best legal service possible must be settled. So when Mr. Lovell goes to Bowman it is very essential that the N. O. should have an attorney on the grounds to assist in the work, and a press representative to cover the story. Engdahl[43] is of

42. Otto Branstetter, longtime party functionary from the Plains states, was the national secretary of the Socialist party in the postwar years.
43. Louis J. Engdahl (1884–1932) was a socialist journalist who, before the war, had

course the press man to send, and Stedman[44] should go as the N.O. attorney. But S. is not friendly to me, and he is no doubt extremely busy with the New York case. If he is not available, and I doubt very much if he will be, Comrade Wm. Remphfler of South Dakota (I can not remember his address, but you will have it in the files) is quite near and it would be less expensive and quite as well for the N.O. to send him to Bowman.

I suggest that you write Mr. Lovell telling him that the N.O. wants to send an attorney to assist in the work, and I am sure he will be more than pleased, and will give you as soon as possible the exact date of his intended visit to Bowman. Write Remphfler and find out if he can assist in the work. I know he will be glad to do so if conditions permit. Louis is in Chicago I presume and would be willing to undertake the trip at any time.

Otto, I think you know me well enough to understand that I am not asking any personal favors from the N.O. but only trying my very best to do what seems to me to be the loyal and comradely thing to do under the circumstances. For myself I ask nothing, but I am as deeply concerned for the harmony and solidarity of the movement as any human being could possibly be. Naturally I have been deeply hurt by things that have happened and are happening now, but I would not have my hurts used to cause friction in the movement. So let us use good tactics and sound common sense and smooth over a bad situation as well as possible.

Fraternally yours,
KATE R. O'HARE

[Branstetter replied] . . . I deny most emphatically that you have been shamefully or unjustly treated by the National Office. I do not know of any wide-spread resentment amongst the rank and file over this alleged shameful treatment and I think you and Frank are personally responsible for such unjustified resentment as does exist.

---

served as editor of the party newspaper, *American Socialist*. One of the five defendants in the Berger trial, he would soon change allegiance and join the Communist party.

44. Seymour Stedman (1872–1948) was a socialist attorney in Chicago and handled many of the socialists' wartime trials. From 1912 to 1916 he served in the Illinois legislature and in 1920 he was Debs's running mate as the Socialist party's vice-presidential candidate.

I also desire to say that your method of presenting this matter is not very felicitous. You ask for the co-operation and support of the National Office in the further pushing of your case. You do this very diplomatically and in a comradely spirit by instructing me without previous notice or communication, to send a lawyer and a press agent to North Dakota in your behalf under penalty of further dissension and trouble in the organization. I think your request for this support and co-operation could as well have been made without the attack upon the past conduct of the National Office and without the threat of future attacks.

This, however, is beside the point and is made necessary only by the tone of your communication. The essential thing, of course, is the measure of assistance which the National Office will be able to give you in the future prosecution of your case. As frankly as I have stated my opinion above, I want to assure you that it will not in any way prejudice or interfere with my giving you all the assistance that is in my power. The situation in the National Office at the present time is this: we are bankrupt. During the internal trouble last summer and fall with the expense it involved and the reduction of income due both to the loss of members and cessation of all real activity, we became heavily involved in debt. Since I have taken charge of the office, the financial condition has grown even worse than it was, due to the fact that on account of the reduced membership our dues receipts are not sufficient to meet the ordinary requirements of the office and to the fact that new cases constantly arising have required more than the defense funds secured. . . .

Your letter was received yesterday and yesterday our finances were so low that I allowed a note of $500 to go to protest because I did not have the money to meet it, so that your communication comes at a most embarrassing and inopportune time for the National Office.

I am presenting the whole situation to the National Executive Committee for their consideration and I am sure they will do whatever is just, and at the same time possible, under the circumstances. In the meantime, I am writing to Comrade Rempfer asking his assistance and co-operation in the matter. . . .[45]

45. Otto Branstetter to O'Hare, February 14, 1920, in Socialist Party of America Papers, Duke University Library, Durham, N.C.

February 24, 1920

Dear Otto:

Yours of recent date received, and my dear man what a case of nerves you must have developed. If this letter is a fair sample of what has been going out of the National Office for the last year no wonder the Party had a brainstorm last summer and proceeded to do the Kilkinney cats act. Be calm for Heaven's sake and get down to normal.

I am sure after reading your letter that what you need very badly is a little dose of Freud. Get MAN'S UNCONSCIOUS CONFLICTS by Lay and FREUD'S THEORIES OF NEUROSES by Hitchmann and read them carefully. You will not only find these books mighty interesting but very helpful to you in your present position of emotional stress and nerve strain.

Now to the business at hand, why need we argue the matter of what has happened in the past, it is what is going to happen in the future that interests us. But just the same the many letters I receive from the Comrades all over the country are more emphatic than I that the N.O. has commited many sins both of ommission and commission against me during the last few years. One thing I want to remind you of and ask that you remedy it, not only for my peace of mind, but for the effect it must have on my relations with the Party in the future.

I have been here now almost one year and yours was the first communication I have received from the N.O. except the most perfunctory messages sent when it was absolutely necessary to do so. I have never had a single report of party activities, financial conditions, nominations and elections and other things that you must know are of the most vital interest to me. I am as ignorant of what has been transpiring within the party as if I were the most rank outsider. Not even the Chicago Socialist papers have been sent me. And no blame can be attached to the management of this institution for Mr. Painter permits me to have everything that is sent me. The I.W.W., the Communist Party, the N.P.L., the Labor Party, the Christian Scientists, the Society of Unity and the Catholic church keep me in touch with their movements but nothing doing so far as the S.P. is concerned. Sure I cussed you out and I have a perfect right to do so, that is always a woman's privilege.

Now please get this very clearly - I am not asking the N.E.C. for help or even co-operation, tho it should not be necessary for me to ask for either. I am merely trying to induce it to have a little foresight as well as hindsight. We have spent blood and tears and untold money during the last two years in the farce of legal defense and always we have been on the defendant's side of the table. Now the tide has turned, mass psychology is coming to us, and it is time we got on the other side of the table and became prosecutors. Mine is the only case, so far as I know where we have a splendid chance to convict the prosecution witnesses of perjury. My case is such a simple one of the matter of two sentences being used in a certain lecture, nothing else enters into the case to confuse the issue. Even at the time the case was tried only two people who attended the lecture could be induced to testify against me. Now practically every person present at the lecture is ready and willing to testify to the perjury being committed. The "paytriots" have insisted on dragging me into the fight on the N.P.L. and the N.P.L. is willing to make a political issue of the case. Governor Frazier[46] has already taken his stand in the most fearless and public manner. The N.P.L. and Mr. Lovell are quite willing to see the thing thru, but the S.P. can not afford to have this done, for first, last and all the time I am a Socialist, a vetren member of the party and to save its own self respect the party must stand by me.

And the issue is much bigger than me personally. I have stood the year in prison pretty well, could no doubt stick it out until the coming election will force the issue of the political prisoners, but why should we lose the political value of the fight to convict the perjurers? And tho the tide has turned we are not out of danger yet. Two more struggles loom big in the immediate future. The Graham bill has gone to its last long rest, the Davey bill[47] is very wobbly, but that does not mean that no more attempts will be made to enact sedition legislation. When the Graham bill which was of the most vital importance to us came up for consideration at a public hearing the S.P. had no carefully prepared testimony to offer against it, the reactionary A. F. of L. had to do the job. I feel that the question of amnesty will come before Congress soon. Wilson seems to be utterly batty, and Palmer determined to run amuck, but there are some canny Congressmen who will not care to go into the campaign with

---

46. Lynn J. Frazier (1874–1947) was elected governor of North Dakota in 1917 on the Non-Partisan ticket. He served as senator from 1923 to 1941 and, himself a farmer, was a persuasive spokesman for agrarian interests.

47. The Davey bill, introduced by Martin Luther Davey (1884–1946), Democratic representative from Ohio, on November 19, 1919, attempted to define further the law of sedition.

the U.S. the only country holding its political prisoners, so I look for some move in Congress to force the issue. When that time comes we will want every bit of available amunition ready for immediate use. A carefully prepared review of my case and if possible an indictment of the prosecution witnesses for perjury would be mighty good amunition. Not because I am important, but because my case is one of the most flagrant and has so many dramatic features.

Lovell is an able lawyer and has been both kind and loyal to me but he is deaf, dumb and blind to the class struggle, particularly in courts. That is the reason I wanted Remphfler on the job. I had no idea of Louis (Engdahl) doing a press agent stunt, God knows F.P. is quite sufficient on that line. I wanted Louis on the job to get the local color and to help the lawyers work up the case with the proper news interest and dramatic sequence. And I want the whole thing ready to spring when it is needed. Of course I am not in love with my present abode and do not overlook the effect that this work properly done might have on hastening my release. In fact I wrote Mr. Lovell today that as soon as absolute proof of my innocence was secured I would permit him to apply for a pardon, not as a matter of mercy, but purely on the grounds of a grave miscarriage of justice and I have a hunch that even such an application would be welcomed in Washington.

Sure that N.O. is in debt, it always is so far as I have known anything about it. I know perfectly well that the cost of the defense of the officials has been frightful, but that is just the point. When some old Comrade down in the sticks reads the figures and notices that mighty discrepency between what the party has spent in my defense and what it has expended in the defense of the five, they scratch their heads in puzzlement for a bit then sit down and write me a letter that is both amusing and heartbreaking. One sent me a heading clipped from a certain appeal that was sent out for funds for my defense and attached to it was a financial statement telling how those funds were spent and the letter that accompanied it was so hot it scorched the envelope. And by the way this Comrade was one that went "Left", and with him as with thousands of others it was a mere matter of emotional reaction, not reason at all.

Some day I will be released, naturally I will be back on the job, and we will have some job of harmonizing the squabbling factions and getting back into working trim. When that time comes I want to be able to go to the comrades and work for harmony without being forced to spend two thirds of my energy thinking up convincing lies to tell to explain how it all happened. Now when it comes to thinking of lies to protect my new friends I am some artist, I have had such an awful lot of practice. But I don't want to be like the old lady who found herself in an impossible position. The story runs that once upon a time a man brought an unexpected guest home for dinner and found an embarrassingly scanty meal on the table. When the guest had gone, he after the manner of all men reproached his wife and wanted to know why she did not have a better meal. She replied that it was all she had to prepare. He then said: "Well you could have made excuses". And she replied, "I couldn't either, I didn't have anything to make excuses out of". Now when the time comes for me to get back into the harness I don't want to be in the position of having nothing to make excuses out of.

Please make it perfectly plain that I am not asking for any favors for myself when you discuss the matter with the N.E.C. I have never asked a favor and never will no matter how much I may suffer. I am now as I have at different times in the past merely prodding the N.O. into what seems to me to be absolutely necessary action, necessary not to me, but to the harmony and well being of the party.

Give my love to Winnie[48] and the girls and tell Gertrude that I have her fastened up on the wall with a dab of chewing gum. But I would also like Tressa.

Better take my advice Otto and relieve the racking nerve strain of your work by imbibing a little Freud since you can no longer imbibe Schlitz. Really my study of psychoanalysis has kept me sane during my imprisonment.

Greetings to all the comrades and love to the family, I am

Fraternally yours,
KATE

Kate Richards O'Hare
Reg. No. 21669

---

48. Winnie E. Branstetter, Otto's wife, was a longtime party functionary. She had once served as a key figure in the woman's sector of the party, and the two women had worked together then and also at the encampments in the Southwest.

March 7, 1920

Dear Sweethearts:

Sunday. During the months I have been here I have felt very strongly that I have finished one phase of my work. Everything seems to point to the utter destruction of all old political alignments and the formation of new ones. I would not be at all surprised if a new capitalist party were formed from the reactionary elements of both the Democratic and Republican parties and a labor party combining all the elements of the trades union, the farmers' and the Socialist movements. It may not come this election, but it may before two years have passed. Should this occur I should feel that I am no longer needed to fight the battles of an unpopular political and economic movement. I can then give all my strength and energies to the destruction of our prison system and the building of a sane system of dealing with subnormal and delinquent human beings. I almost feel tempted to apply to the Soviet Republic of Russia for employment in its Department of Prisons and Reformatories! I know that Russia is the only country on earth today that dare face boldly and attempt to solve scientifically the tangled problems of crime and criminals. Since Mr. Palmer considers me so very "dangerous" he should be delighted to get rid of me by shipping me to Russia; I feel sure that Russia would be willing to have me and give me the job I most want.

I am anxious to get Mott Osborne's book;[49] I want to see if he has really touched the heart of the prison problem; nothing I have ever read on the subject has more than scratched the surface. In fact I was here months before I really began to grasp the problem in its entirety. I know now that I have not been here one day too long. Any shorter period would have left me with a partial and hence distorted view of the conditions. I have been here long enough now to see with my own eyes and study with minute care the disintegration of body, mind and soul under prison regime. I have learned a new language, whose very words were unintelligible to me, because they hark back to the dark night of our savage past. I should never have been able to discover the symbolism of

49. Thomas Mott Osborne (1859–1926) was a New York State manufacturer who dabbled in Democratic politics. In 1913 he was appointed to a state commission on prison reform, and henceforth penology became his major interest. As warden of Sing Sing (1914–15), he fought political patronage and won public attention by serving one week in Auburn prison, posing as a prisoner under the name of Tom Brown. He was a spokesman for the New Penology and wrote *Within Prison Walls* (1914), *Society and Prisons* (1916), and *Prisons and Common Sense* (1924).

this language of the underworld except for that book of Abraham's we read on "Myths and Legends". Mrs. E.C.R. of St. Louis sent me a most remarkable book called "A Mind That Found Itself", by Beers. It deals with the problem of insanity in exactly the way in which I want to write of crime when my opportunity comes. Mrs. R. will pardon me, I am sure, for not thanking her for the book before this, but it arrived just as I was coming down with the flu and so many things have been neglected since then.

> Lovingly,
> KATE

March 21, 1920

Dear Sweethearts:

Sunday. I have just read George Cram Cook's "Chasm"[50] again and it is positively uncanny in the light of present conditions in the United States. How little I dreamed when I read it some years ago that here in this republic we should see re-enacted the black terrorism of the Russia of ten years ago! Had anyone made the prophecy that in less than ten years there would be prisoners in American prisons for the crime of expressing opinions I would have ridiculed it as a mad phantasy of a disordered brain; yet it has come to pass. And how perfectly logical. The workers of Russia revolted against the feudal landlords and the despotism of a czaristic government and the landlords and the parasitic government officials put down that revolt, using every method possible from keyhole spying to wholesale slaughter by trained soldiers. Here in the United States the workers show signs of revolting against the industrial overlords, and here in the United States, as in Russia ten years ago, the industrial overlords will use every method possible to put down that revolt. Our very social system of cruel inequalities breeds men and women with abnormal brains and scarred, twisted souls who can be hired to become keyhole spys and agent provocateurs. Public offices come to be filled by men who know that their official tenures are based upon their service to industrial overlordism and they will see that the prisons are gorged with men and women who dare to threaten their masters' inter-

50. The book made an impact when it was published in 1911. Through the protagonist, Cook dramatized a conflict between Nietzschean and Marxist philosophy.

ests. The tank, the machine gun and the trained soldiers may be used for wholesale slaughter here as in Russia. History re-enacts her tragic role again and again, and I am convinced now that we too may walk the same blood-stained, corpse-strewn path that Russia walked and that the other nations of Europe are now traversing. Many of us may fall by the way-side, many die before our dead bodies fill the chasm that yawns between industrial despotism and industrial democracy, and builds the bridge over which mankind may walk to sanity and safety. . . .

Someone sent me this clipping from the NATION; don't know the date for I have not been receiving it for some time now. It is a splendid, a wonderful thing, but how tragically funny that "A Clergyman" should display by not signing his name to the article, exactly the same moral reticence for which he chides the church as a whole so severely. But what strikes me most forcibly is that, according to this article, I took exactly the stand on war sanctioned by the authorities of the Catholic Church. "A Clergyman" weakens his case by not giving the names, chapters and pages of the official theological textbooks of the Church. I wish you would write to the NATION and ask them either to forward a letter to "A Cler-gyman", or to give you his name. I want the names of those theological textbooks and then I will make things very interesting for a few Catholic gentlemen of my acquaintance. Wouldn't it be screamingly funny to quote those Catholic textbooks in one column, my Bowman speech in the second, and Catholic Judge Wade's speech when he sentenced me in the third? What a joke that Kate O'Hare the Socialist should be sent to prison for five years by a Catholic judge for stating the position of the Catholic Church on war! Deary me! but funny things do happen when the world goes on a jag, and churches and judges do the funniest stunts of all.

Several of my friends have written asking me what they can do for the colored girls here. It is a tragically hard question to answer. Some-how whenever I think of them, and I think of them much, a bit of verse flits thru my mind: "Alas! since women bear the heavier burden and walk the rougher road." These colored prison companions of mine are women, with all that that implies; they are working women, and they are women of a downtrodden and outraged race; so their hardships and their wrongs are threefold. Some of them are innocent; we here know who is innocent and who is guilty; for it is the innocent who feel shamed, and the guilty feel a certain sense of pride in the fact that they "got theirs" before the heavy hand of the law "got" them. In almost every case their trials were travesties on fairness and justice. Only a cheap "shyster" lawyer will defend them; judge and jury take it for granted that if they are "niggers" they are guilty and if they are not guilty they should be sent to prison for general cussedness. Unless they are valuable prostitutes for whom the cadets are willing to pull political wires there is no hope of parole for them; their sentences are outrageously long, the "task" is murderous; so they just drag on until they threaten to die and put the state to the expense of burying them and then they are released to carry the scourge of syphilis and consumption back to some alley shack where others become contaminated. I have watched them come and I have watched them go. They come with great possibilities of a life of service under a decent social system and they go with tragic possibilities of death and destruction, the fruits of our brutal prison system. But the problem is a social problem and must be solved for all. It cannot be solved for one or two or fifty. There are many here to whom I have become much attached; there is little Rachel Epps, who is a "federal" and has already served eight years, and Rachel never harmed a human being in all her life. She is the sweetest, gentlest, most loyal and faithful soul I have ever known, black or white. Then Willie Wilkinson, the most tragic soul I have ever known. Willie is one of those accursed by being neither white nor black and hated by both. Her mother must have been a quadroon and beautiful, her father no doubt an aristocratic Southern Democrat who "hates Socialism, be Gad" because it would mean "nigger equality and free love". Oh! Willie's white blood is of the best; she has the features of a Greek goddess and the most beautiful form and hands and feet I have ever seen; and she is proud and a rebel to the marrow of her bones. Your imagination can supply the details of what life must be to her here. But fortunately there is hope that she won't be here long. I understand that she is somewhat advanced with t.b. and I am hoping it will take her quickly. Whenever I look at Willie I long so keenly for the power to put her face on canvas. Oh! if I could only paint as the artist painted who created my Beautiful Girl, I would paint Willie in the ugly prison dress with all her tragic beauty and call it "The Sins of The Fathers". There is Penelope Hill who has almost woven her shroud of flying stitches; and Annie Pollard, my laundress, who would give me her last drop of blood and do it with a smile; there are Evalina Roberts and Mattie Purvis and Icey Arnold, all long-timers and all friendless and hopeless. Letters to them are a Godsend. Dear Jessie Bronson has written some beautiful letters to some of the girls whose names I mentioned and they have been passed about until worn out. They need little luxuries and above all sweets, but they and all the rest need most of all social justice, decent living conditions outside and sane, scientific handling here. And these things cannot be achieved for a few; they must be achieved for all women, black and white, "good" and "bad".

A friend from New York sent a hundred beautiful collars and I distributed them yesterday afternoon. Now every girl will have her bit of Easter finery and to these love- and beauty-starved hearts that bit of lace and lawn will hold more of the Christ spirit than all the incense and flowers and pealing music and glib sermons that will mock the proletarian Christ in the fashionable churches of the land on Easter Day.

Lovingly,

KATE

March 24, 1920

Dear Sweethearts:

Wednesday. I came directly to my cell from the dining room and read alot of my accumulated papers while the others were having recreation. What an amusing and yet shameful and tragic mess the administration is in over the Peace Treaty. The war has been over now for sixteen months and yet we have no peace. We are at war and we are not at war, and only God or the Devil, I don't know which, knows where we are. When I first read that the poor, illbegotten child, sadly battered and abused, has been returned to the White House rejected and forsaken, I said "too much pepper". But on second thought, perhaps it is the wisdom of fools that has brought the strange condition about. I doubt if anyone could accuse the Senate of vision, foresight or real statesmanship, and yet I am beginning to feel that out of their stupid, selfish, partisanship may come real leadership of the world for a genuine World Federation. Even the blindest of fools have been forced to see that the vicious, grasping, brutal treaty of Versailles[51] must be rewritten. The United States is the one

51. The Treaty of Versailles was rejected finally by the Senate on March 19, 1920. While a majority of senators favored the treaty, the vote fell seven short of the necessary two thirds. The failure of the United States to accept the treaty and to join the League of

great nation that has not signed that treaty and this very fact may be of the most vital importance. A presidential election is at hand, President and Congressmen will be elected and stranger things have happened than that at this election a real man, a genuine statesman, a builder with world vision might be elected president. It is conceivable that the people, sick unto death with narrow, ignorant, selfish politicians, might revolt at the ballot box and elect intelligent, forward looking, constructive minded men to sit in the seats that have been occupied by political pygmies in the House of Representatives and the Senate. Should this occur, and it is not impossible, we would be unfettered and unbound and might really dictate and dominate in the sane reconstruction of the terms of peace. It is quite possible that the rejection of the Treaty will put the whole matter of amnesty for political prisoners far into the future, but no matter. If it hastens the coming of a real peace we can afford to stay behind bars for a little longer time.

One can't tell just how much truth there is in the newspaper reports of what is transpiring in Germany, but it seems quite possible that the impossible peace terms have hastened by some months if not years the coming of a Soviet government there. And poor old England is quaking in terror and the murder of the Lord Mayor of Cork will not have a reassuring effect. God! what a mess the old world is in, and Socialism did not make the mess. I wonder how certain gentlemen explain that fact. . . .

Lovingly,
KATE

April 3, 1920

Dear Sweethearts:

This is Easter eve and at last the long, weary, heart-hungry days have dragged their lonely hours thru, and one year of our Gethsemene is passed. One year—how swiftly it passes when love and joy and useful labor gilds the hours with life's gold, but how slowly it creeps away when prison bars shut out life and love and joyful labor and shackles each

---

Nations was the result of political maneuverings and was further complicated by the incapacitation of President Wilson, the architect of the original document.

weary moment with loneliness and longing, with degradation and the leaden ball and chain of chattel slavery.

One year—from behind the grim grey walls and the brutal bars of steel I have watched the seasons come and go. The tender beauty of awakening springtime, the full, rich noonday of the summer, the brown and gold of autumn when nature is aweary and the hoary frost of wintertime when nature sleeps. And here as the long, long days have dragged their weary hours by and the longer nights have passed with leaden feet I have watched the slow and devilishly cruel crucifixion of the humble sisters of the Nazarene. In ten thousand churches tomorrow will the old story of Passion week, of the sufferings of Jesus, the dark and lonely night in the Garden of Gethsemene and the climax of the crucifixion on Calvary be told. From ten thousand pulpits will the story be told of death, the darkness of the grave and the Resurrection of Easter morn. About the legend that told our prehistoric ancestors the age-long tale of ever-reconstructed life that burst into being from seemingly dead and inert things, has been woven the story of Jesus. And tomorrow in every church, from the tiny, shabby mission to the magnificent cathedral will clergy and choir sing and chant and preach this story and as the organ notes die into silence, as the smoke of the incense drifts into nothingness and the benediction rests upon the heads of the worshippers, clergy and congregation will hurry forth to the struggles and the pleasures of life, deaf and dumb and blind to the fact that here—today—at our very doors is being re-enacted again, increased a thousandfold, the passion, the sufferings, the Gethsemene and the Calvary.

Caesar still sits in power absolute upon the throne of international commerce. His far-flung armies encompass all the earth, the thunder of his cannons have not been stilled by the peace that is no peace. His minions sit not only in the halls of Albany and Washington, but in all the seats of legislation in all the countries of earth, save one. His Pilates sit on uncounted benches and do the bidding of his will. In a thousand jails and prisons and dungeons thousands of the modern prototypes of Jesus of Nazareth are entombed and ten thousand Barrabases flaunt their war-won wealth before our eyes. And the symbolism of the Passion and suffering and death of Jesus—aye, yes and His Resurrection too, are today being made more perfect, more rounded and complete. For the church has given us only the symbol of the man Jesus, it has ignored the fact that no man liveth except by woman and that a man God without the complement of a woman God is hideous and incomplete. But Caesar of the kingdom of International Commercialism is wiser and more scientific than the church. For when his soldiers go down to the garden of Gethsemene to seize the criminals who breathe sedition against his reign, he brings to the court of Caesar's justice, women as well as men, maiden, wife and mother,—all are equally dangerous in his eyes. And when the dark hours of our social Gethsemene are passed, when the long march up Calvary is finished, when we have borne our cross to the very end, when in the prison cell we have gone down to the grave with Him, when the Easter morn of the Social Resurrection shall come, man and woman, harmonious, complete and whole, we will emerge into the perfect love that casteth out all fear.

Oh! the hours are long in prison and our thoughts are longer still. The work of our hands becomes mechanical long before we "make the task" and the whine and snarl of the machinery merges into a sort of harmony that aids deep, careful thinking. And in the hushed stillness of the long, long hours of the night we are face to face with our naked souls and face to face with God. I remember that a certain man was sharing my last hour of freedom. He said: "There in prison you will have many hours for retrospection and introspection, and I fear that when the grim realities, the damnable horrors of prison life, press heavily upon you, you will suffer from bitter regrets. You will know then that you have loved too much, given too much and stood too unflinchingly for the things that are after all the ideals and not the realities of life." I have lived thru a year of prison life now; I have had many long, lonely hours of retrospection and introspection and the only regret that I have known is that in the long years of life and freedom I failed to give so much that I might have given. I valued too lightly and was too self-conscious to give freely and wholesomely of the things that I have been taught by bitter deprivation to estimate more correctly now.

No, the leaden hours of this year have not been given to regrets for having given too much. Thru most of them I have tried to find some rational, logical explanation for the actions and reactions of mankind. Of course the eternal questions that have been always with me are WHY do semi-sane people submit to war and permit prisons to exist?

Psychologists tell us that there are three primary urges—nutrition, reproduction and self-preservation. They tell us that the urge of nutrition means not only the satisfaction of our stomachs, but of every physical, mental, artistic, ethical and spiritual hunger. The urge of reproduction, they say, includes all that embraces sex life, and the urge of self-preservation is the instinct to protect our egos from everything that endangers our continuity of life. War negates and violates and outrages every one of these primal urges. WHY DO MEN TOLERATE WAR? And prisons? These shackle liberty, which is the very essence of life, for without it every urge is nullified. Prisons starve us physically for food, action and fresh air; they pervert every normal urge of sex and ruthlessly and brutally violate and outrage every instinct of the ego. They do not successfully segregate the anti-social and subnormal persons; they merely toss them like photographic prints into baths of vice and degeneracy where every vicious, perverted, dangerous abnormality is developed and fixed for life. Then they are turned loose to be a thousandfold more of a social menace than before courts and prisons did their vicious work. Prisons never have and never will reform, reconstruct or heal a perverted, diseased body, brain or soul; neither do they protect society from its own vicious products. There is nothing of social value gained by our prison system, and it breeds a thousand social curses. Then WHY DO MEN PERMIT IT TO EXIST?

Thru all the hideous months of prison life I have been groping for an answer to these questions. Dimly I have formulated something that seems to give some glimmer of explanation to me, but I am not sure that it will be any explanation to others. I knew that so great a crime as the world war could not curse the human race without some human beings being guilty, but who are they? It was not that puny, stupid handful of kings, emperors and presidents who played at ruling the destinies of nations; they are disgustingly and pitifully weak and impotent. Can you fasten the crime upon the international bankers, munition makers and food profiteers? Are they numerous enough and have they influence enough upon the actions and reactions of men? I cannot lay it on the souls of the working class,—not even to their stupidity. For tho the workers are the masses, and tho I know, Oh! how bitterly I know, that they are stupid, they are not criminal in that stupidity. How could they be anything else but stupid? They have borne the burden of the world upon their shoulders, they have bended their necks to the yoke of productive labor and like the oxen they have treaded out the corn while muzzled. So heavy, so exhausting, so stupefying has been the burden of feeding, clothing, and sheltering the human race that the intellects and souls of the workers have been deadened and paralyzed. So if they went like dumb driven cattle into the shambles of war the crime was not really theirs. The workers wanted no war; they had everything to lose and nothing to gain by one. Then why was the world swept into a war that violated every normal urge?

What of its intellectuals? Its clergy first of all who like Peter denied Christ and forgot God and His command, "THOU SHALT NOT KILL" and prostituted every pulpit to preaching hate and slaughter instead of love and brotherhood? Its lawyers who spun legal theories making wholesale murder glorious while holding retail murder felonious? Its teachers who forgot the lessons of history and proclaimed brute force a more righteous and efficient weapon for solving human problems than intelligently applied scientific facts? Its physicians who glorified war by using their skill to mend the broken and maimed bodies of men mutilated in battle, that they might fight more? Its artists who permitted their art to be prostituted, its ethical teachers who overnight exchanged their "ethics" for blatant jingoism? And last, but most powerful of all, the newspaper men, mild, unassuming men whose very names not one reader in a thousand knows, are the ones whose hands are dyed the deepest crimson in the blood of young men.

The known, trusted, loved "intellectuals" had more power than all the capitalists and all the workers. They proclaimed their hatred of war and their love of peace. The crucial hour came. If these had stood firm, could they not have carried their whole cities with them, and the cities the nations, and the nations the world? Who can blame the profit-mongers who are rich and powerful because they have killed out every other instinct but that of profit-taking, for waging a profit-making war? Not I. Who can blame the mass of workers, conscious of their lack of education, culture and intellectual grasp, if they became bewildered when their leaders forsook them and betrayed them, and stumbled blindly into the shambles of war? Not I.

Easter Day. The long dark night has gone and now I must finish my message. As I read what I wrote last night it seems a gloomy message to send forth on Easter Day, but this is NOT OUR Easter, it is the Easter of the clergy who denied Christ, the Easter of the teachers who denied history, the Easter of the "intellectuals" who made their intellectual leadership slave to the great, unreasoning, superstitious FEAR. Oh God!

What comedy under all the tragedy. The men and women who could
have saved the world from the shambles were afraid - AFRAID as Peter
was afraid; they feared as moral cowards down all the ages have feared;
and yet in the fire of the Crucifixion the dross of fear and respectability
was burned out of Peter, and in the fire of a world war it may be that fear
and respectability may be burned out of the intellectual leaders of the
race.

And because I believe so ardently that it must be love and intelligence that will save the world, I look back on this year of prison life as a
marvelous privilege. It has taught me to glimpse "the perfect love that
casteth out all fear" and I know that out of the blood bought intelligence
of the spirit of international brotherhood will come the message "I AM
THE RESURRECTION AND THE LIFE".

There is so much more I long to say, but my allotted space is full and
it must wait for another day. With tenderest love to my darlings and the
message of faith and hope and steadfastness to the comrades I wait the
coming of OUR EASTER DAY OF LIBERTY AND LIFE AND LOVE.

KATE

April 11, 1920

Dear Sweethearts:

Sunday. This is a glorious day and I understand that we are to attend
the first ball game of the season this afternoon, so I fear your letter will
be somewhat brief; for of course I can't possibly miss that ball game.

No letter from home yesterday, so naturally decide that you are all
very busy; but will look for a nice one Monday. But Easter letters continued to arrive all week, so I did not feel neglected. I had a nice letter from
Pauline Newman.[52] Tell her that it is not indifference on the part of organized labor that makes it seem so careless of the lives of the political
prisoners, and so willing that civil liberties should be abridged—it is
simply bewilderment. In the crash and chaos of the rapidly crumbling
capitalist system their old moorings are being swept away and they have
not as yet found the new. She wanted to know what book she should send

52. Pauline Newman (b. 1891), an immigrant garment worker and socialist, was the
first woman organizer for the International Ladies Garment Workers Union.

me, and just now I would like "The Freudian Wish in Ethics" by Holt. I am having the most interesting experiment in making dents in Katherine's adamantine, New England conception of "good" and "bad", "right" and "wrong", "morality" and "immorality", "ethical" and "unethical". I would also like "The Psychology of Intoxication" by Partridge, for she and I have great arguments as to the whys and wherefores of intemperance, and as she is intelligent enough to read understandingly and reason with effect I think these two books will help win the battle. I would like also something really good on phallic worship, but just now I cannot think of any book that is just what I want. She is of course obsessed by the idea that everything connected with sex is "bad" and that really "nice", "respectable" people never admit that such a thing exists. I horrified her beyond measure by pointing out that symbolism of the architecture of the prison buildings, (and the architect certainly outdid himself in that line). I think she is quite sure that I am either a monumental prevaricator or insane, but she has child-like faith that anything and everything that is printed in a book is gospel truth, so I want some books to substantiate my arguments.

I received the little book you sent, "The Golden Key" by Graves. You are quite right, I think; the author has found the realities of this life very, very hard to bear so he has attempted to transfer himself to the spiritual world. Such a book would naturally come from California, which is the land of narcotic religions. I am sure that there is no place on earth where so many different varieties of anaesthetic cults exist as there, unless it be India. We poor, harassed, bewildered human beings who find grim reality unbearably hard, so often try to run away from ourselves. Some get drunk, some use cocaine, some indulge in sex debauch, some become rampantly "RED" radicals and many go to California and invent a lovely narcotic cult. But ever and ever the Holy Grail of our endless seeking is to find the forgetfulness of self and the too hard realities of life. But there is no land, no matter how beautiful, where we may escape ourselves; neither drink, drugs, sex excesses, neurasthenia, radicalism or transcendentalism can lay the ghosts of our own souls, or blot out the hard realities of life. If I believed in the sort of a God that most religionists do, if I thought that all that was necessary was simply to call his attention to unpleasant facts, I would pray, "Oh! God, give us strength and courage, wisdom and reason to face life as it is; to know the worst; to understand

and conquer it; to realize that SELF is the only vehicle of life and that we must live with ourselves as long as life lasts and that it behooves us to make SELF so beautiful that we shall need no narcotic to drug us into forgetfulness."

Please tell Jessie Bronson that the candy for the long time colored girls arrived and that really candy is the very best thing to send these girls. I think it is generally understood now that sugar is an absolute essential of human diet; yet here are ninety women, doing fearfully hard, heavy, trying work under the worst possible conditions and month after month and year after year they have a diet in which there is not one grain of sugar. In the year I have been here not an ounce of sugar has ever come into our dining room, except that paid for by the women themselves. Some of us have friends on the outside who furnish money to pay for sugar, but most of the women have not and they are simply ravenous for sweets. It is better and cheaper to have the candy sent in from a local grocery than to mail it from a long distance. Asel Bros. Grocery Co. of Jefferson City are not only very reliable, but exceedingly kind and helpful. If she will send whatever money she wishes to them, they will send the candy to me and I will see that it goes to the girls.

And to the lady who wanted to know if I could use certain school books. No; I feel that it is useless to send them. When I first came I was quite indignant that there were no school facilities for the women and volunteered my services to teach. My offer was rejected and now I understand why. The task is so heavy that vampire-like it sucks the last drop of life and energy from the women and when the day's work is done there is not enough vitality left to attempt any educational work. There is not one woman in a thousand as strong and energetic as I, and I have everything that money will buy in the way of food; yet when I have "made the task" I am usually too utterly weary to read my newspapers. No one will ever realize with what stern measures I drive myself to write my letters, and you cannot even guess the dogged courage they represent. Z. has asked many times if I was not doing any writing. No, my letters are all I can manage and they are terribly unsatisfactory. I can't keep notes, for I would not be permitted to take them out; but he need not fear that I will forget; the memories of prison life are burned too deeply into our consciousness to ever be erased.

MAMMA

April 17, 1920

Dear Sweethearts:

Saturday. And the kiddies want to know something about Quakers and the Single Taxers, do they? Mercy! Neither of them are safe subjects just now when opinions are being so rampantly sterilized by the eagle-eyed Palmer. I wonder what started the youngsters off after information concerning such dangerous and disloyal creatures? Surely nothing is being taught in the St. Louis schools that is so disreputable as the theory of Single Tax or the pacifist creed of the Quaker religion!

I really never tried to explain Single Tax to eleven year old boys, but it is not so very complicated. You know that all city, state and government expenses are paid by taxes on property. From the cookstove and piano to the great factory and railway system, all property is taxed, and for each dollar's worth a citizen owns he must pay the city, state and federal government a certain number of mills in taxes. The Single Taxers say that land is the basis of all property, the original source of all wealth, and that all taxes should be based on land values instead of other kinds of property. For illustration you remember that for several miles the road from Ruskin to Tampa ran thru land owned by Mrs. P***** P***** of Chicago. This woman owned thousands and thousands of acres of land in Florida. She made no use of it, would permit no one else to use it, and neither would she sell it to people who wanted to use it. It was not for sale. Because it is unimproved land she pays practically nothing in taxes on the land and simply holds it out of use. You remember Mr. S****, the truck gardener who lived just across the inlet, who raised such marvelous vegetables on his few acres of intensively tilled land. Well, Mr. S**** paid more taxes on his five acres of truck garden than Mrs. P***** P***** paid on five thousand acres of her unused land. The Single Taxers would just turn the thing about and make the improvements on the land pay no taxes, and the unused, unimproved land pay taxes. This would free the hard working truck gardener from heavy taxation and force Mrs. P***** P***** to either pay very heavy taxes or sell her land to people who could and would use it. Mrs. P***** P***** has gone on to a different climate than Florida, but the unused thousands of acres of land are still there and still untaxed, while every house and fence and fruit tree and saw mill and turpentine still put on the land in Ruskin is taxed to pay the expenses of protecting Mrs. P. in the ownership of her land. Now who do you kiddies think should pay the taxes, Mrs. P., who has gone to a place where no land is needed, or the settlers in Ruskin, who are making that wilderness into a place of wealth and beauty?

Quakers are a religious sect who really take their religious beliefs seriously. They believe that the simple life is the beautiful life; that simple dress is beautiful dress and that simple language is beautiful language, so their lives are marked by sweet and dignified simplicity. The old Quakers believed implicitly in the brotherhood of man and they felt that the golden rule was law sufficient to rule the lives of men. They settled their differences without laws or lawyers or courts or jails or prisons, and justice was the simple, ordinary everyday thing of their lives. They believe with all their hearts that God meant just what he said when he gave the command "Thou shalt not kill", and Quakers never went to war. They believe that Jesus was in dead earnest when he said: "Do unto others as ye would that they should do unto you", and "Love thy neighbor as thyself", so they could find no glory, or grace, or righteousness in slaughtering people weaker than themselves.

We gave Gene and Victor a year in Catholic boarding school so they would not have their lives warped by the stupid, vicious prejudice against their fellow men who chanced to be of that religion. I sincerely hope that we will be able to give all of you children a year or two in some good Quaker boarding school. Kathleen and Victor particularly need the quiet, calm courteous discipline of Quaker environment to help them overcome certain tendencies of temperament. If it should be that I am not restored to my family soon, I want if humanly possible, for Kathleen to be placed in some good Quaker school.

But when I think of either Quakers or Single Taxers it is not of their theories or beliefs; these words bring to me some of the happiest and biggest memories of my life. When I was just Kathleen's age, and just the same sort of a precocious, eager-minded girl that she is, Father belonged to what I think was the first Single Tax Club ever organized in Kansas City, and they used to meet at our home. There were not more than ten or fifteen men in the group, but they were men of marvelous culture and breadth of mind. There was A. P. Warrington, a school principal, Henry Julian, a lawyer, Dr. Knoche, a physician, a Mr. Reeves, whose profession I have forgotten, and a young man whose name I cannot recall, but whose personality is a vivid memory to me. John Crosby came to Kansas City on the invitation of this group to do propaganda work and to know him was to a girl like me a rare privilege and joy unbounded. Perhaps I was an interesting youngster, or more likely they were men of rare kindness and patience, but at any rate I was permitted to attend the meetings, keep the records and stagger under the stupendous responsibility of caring for at least $3.21 that at one time accumulated in the treasury. I presume I was an eager-eyed, pigtailed joke to those men, but their companionship was one of the big and determining factors in my life. They gave me books like "Progress and Poverty", "Looking Backward", and "Caesar's Column" to read and each one of them inspired in me the ambition to really know something of their special profession. One young man whose name I cannot remember was a geologist and he took me for walks out over the hills where now Scarritt Park is located and he made the story of this old earth's creation the most vivid and thrilling romance and to this day every hill and mountain, every rock and crag, has its wonderful story to tell me because of the things that young man taught me so many years ago.

When I was about twenty-two business chanced to take me to Richmond, Indiana, and there I was for several weeks a guest in the home of one of the most charming Quaker families of that town. Stephen Wiggins and his lovely wife were the most cultured and charming of the old Quaker type, now I think almost extinct. They wore the simple dress of the Friends and used the soft, sweet "thee" and "thou" and everything about their staid, old-fashioned home was simple, sweet and beautiful. Their friends, too, were of the old Quaker stock and as Stephen Wiggins was blind I used to take him about to visit his old time friends; and their kindly welcome and beautiful courtesy to a rather brash snip of a girl will always be one of the wonderful memories of my life. There was a queer old-fashioned "meeting house" among the trees in Richmond where the old "Hicksite Quakers"[53] met for worship and its dim quiet and sweet peacefulness was like cooling waters to my hot, passionate, questioning girlish heart. Stephen Wiggins and his dear old wife, Mrs. Starr, and all of my old Quaker friends have passed to the Great Beyond, but the mark they left upon my life is ineffacable. And if it be true that those we love

53. Hicksite Quakers were followers of Elias Hicks (1748–1830), whose teachings led to a split in the Society of Friends in 1837. In the twentieth century the Friends have tended to draw together.

come back to ease the burdens of our aching hearts—who knows but it may be Stephen Wiggins whose love and faith and courage helped to give me strength to stand for peace in the madness of war! . . .

Drop a line to Otto for me, will you, and tell him I received his letter and feel sure that everything is being done that is possible. Explain to him also that I received a letter from Max Shonberg asking for some sort of a statement from me for the Convention Journal, but I knew Gene would not be permitted to write anything and I decided to refrain also.

Presume you read Clarence Darrow's[54] article in the MIRROR; it is really very fine. What he says of the overthrow of constitutional safeguards during war is just what I said in my speech at Bowman. His attitude on the inevitability of the war is directly in line with the St. Louis Manifesto of the Party and his exposition of mass psychology is quite scientific.

Lovingly,
KATE

Kate Richards O'Hare
Reg. No. 21669

April 26, 1920

Dear Sweethearts:

Sunday. The National Convention of the Socialist Party will soon convene and when it does, it will be the group of quiet, sane, modest comrades who for years have been called "yellow" and "middleclass", who will be there to do the work, while those whose principal occupation was calling names will be noticable by their absence. Naturally I am intensely interested in the Convention, for I feel that it will be a momentous one. I wish of course that I might attend, but if that is denied me, I can still feel that I am doing my share of the work here. Three years have passed, three years of fire and blood and hell—three years that have tried men and principles as never men and principles have been tried before, and

---

54. Clarence Darrow (1857–1938), leading defense attorney of the era, was often associated with American socialists, although he was never a socialist. During the war he was one of the prominent attorneys sent by the National Civil Liberties Bureau to seek a clarification from the attorney general on freedom of the press.

out of the blazing hell of war madness the Socialist Party of the United States is the only organization which has emerged unscathed. Oh! we bear our body wounds, but the soul of us has come thru the fiery furnace unmarred. Some have crept home torn and maimed, many of us are in prison, we have endured fratricidal strife, but by the very hell of war our enemies have proven to the world that we are right.

We have come thru these years of social hell with the soul of the Socialist Party unharmed; we stand before the world vindicated; we have nothing to regret, nothing to retract, nothing to apologize for. This coming campaign is our supreme OPPORTUNITY, the very forces of Heaven and Hell seem to be working for us and nothing can prevail against us but a lack of solidarity and harmony between ourselves.

Uncounted forces are doing our propaganda work for us now; we need spend little energy on that phase, but the re-organization and the re-building on a better and more solid foundation of our party machinery is the matter of vital import. Numberless comrades have written me asking: "What can I do for you?" The one thing I would ask of all of my comrades is that if they are out of the organization they immediately get back in and shoulder up the share of the work I would be doing were I not behind the bars.

Lovingly,
KATE

May 13, 1920

Dear Sweethearts:

Thursday. Genevieve sent me an exquisite copy of "Our Saviour" by Da Vinci. It is a striking face, and of course a masterpiece of art, but it does not express the man Jesus as I have always pictured him. The great ideal we express by the name of Jesus is the love that embraces all and gives all in the service of mankind. And because to love and serve is to know the heights and depths of happiness, I have always been repelled by the conception of Jesus as "the Man of Sorrows". I don't think he was a "man of sorrows"; I think he was a man of love and joy and laughter, a man who smiled more often than he wept, and who loved far more than he hated. I have never known a man or woman who lived and loved and

gave their all to service who went about bewailing their sad lot or who
bore upon their faces the outward marks of sorrow. They who love and
serve are always cheerful and the gloom-dispensers are the selfish ones
who love no one but themselves and never serve but for a price. Who
has given more and suffered more for mankind than Gene? And yet the
things that will live long, long after Gene's old tired body shall have
returned to dust are his love and his smile. And Mother Bloor![55] who has
loved and given more than she? I have a hundred memories of her; on
the platform and in the picket line; in the strike meeting and facing the
street hoodlums; in the scorching heat of the summer day and the bitter
cold of the winter night, and all of my memories are of love and smiles
and laughter, but not one tear or complaint or expression of personal
sorrow. When she bade me good-bye on my way to prison she smiled
and said, "Well, so long, Kate. You've got some dirty work to do behind
the bars, but you've got the grit and backbone to do it, and we'll hold
down your job out here until you get back—see you later." And away she
trotted with a smile to live and love and serve. Few are ever called upon
to give more than you, my darlings; few have a more just cause for expressing sorrow; yet the thing that always thrills my heart with pride is
that when any of you, from Papa down to little Gene and Vic, come to
visit me the memory that I carry back to the roaring shop and the
cramped cell is always of smiles and never of tears. In the year I have
spent here not one word of rebuke, complaint or regret has ever come to
me from my loved ones. I have no memories of gloom or sadness or
repining; my darlings come with a smile and kiss me good-bye with as
brave a heart as if I were only leaving for a day's work at the office. So if
I could wield a brush and paint a portrait of our elder brother Jesus, I
would paint him with Papa's steadfastness, Dick's courage, Vic's tender-
ness, Gene's smiling brown eyes and Kathleen's passionate love.

MAMMA

55. Ella Reeve "Mother" Bloor (1862–1951) spent her long life organizing workers.
She joined the Knights of Labor in 1884 after several years with the Woman's Christian
Temperance Union. In the 1890s she fell under the influence of Eugene Debs and joined
the Social Democracy of America. Briefly a member of Daniel De Leon's Socialist Labor
party, she was an organizer and speaker for the Socialist party from 1902 until 1919, when
she became a founding member of the Communist Labor party and, after 1922, a member
of the Communist party.

May 18, 1920

Dear Sweethearts:

Tuesday. I have been working on very small boys' jackets the last few days and was able to come in at noon and have a good rest and a most refreshing nap this afternoon, so I feel more like writing than I usually do on week nights.

Naturally the Convention and its work has occupied a large part of my thoughts this last week. The paper containing the platform has at last arrived, and I have been digesting it as well as I am capable of doing. It is a splendid document, but I fear we Socialists will never get away from the habit of writing a book when we start to write a political platform. The platform put out by the Committee of Forty-Eight was ideal, I thought, in its lucidity, compactness and completeness. Then they added a sort of exposition of the platform which was excellent. I see that the *Call* summarized the Socialist platform in just the same lucid, exact and compact manner. Now if the N. E. C. will just make the CALL's summary the platform, and make the platform written, or rather adopted, by the Convention an exposition of our position, we may be able to really make the average working man and woman really understand us; but I fear that few will have the patience to wade thru the beautiful piece of literature which we call our platform.

Of course there was not an hour of the time that the Convention was in session that I was not there in heart and spirit. I have attended every meeting of the Socialist Party of any importance whatever since I went to the Convention in Chicago in 1904 with Dick, a seven-months-old baby, in my arms, and our lives have become so woven into the Socialist movement that they are one. I received the following telegram from the convention, and will you please ask Otto to transmit to the comrades my appreciation and greetings?

Convention Hall,
New York City.

Kate Richards O'Hare,
Federal Prison,
Jefferson City, Mo.
The National Convention Socialist Party in nominating Eugene V. Debs and Seymour Stedman as its standard bearers, is not unmindful of the great service you have rendered our party and our cause. Initiating a campaign of

enlightenment throughout the United States we hope for it to result in the opening of the iron gates and restore to our councils yourself and hundreds of others in prison for devotion to working class ideals. We know that you are with us in spirit, and we send you a unanimous message of love and good cheer.

> Walter M. Cook,
> Secretary.

I feel the deepest and most sincere gratitude to the loving, loyal, faithful comrades whose love and comradeship no walls or prison bars could shut out, and whose sustaining influence has given me the strength to walk serene and unafraid the road to Gethsemene. And if that love and loyalty opens the prison doors for me, as it seems possible it may, I ask no greater privilege than to serve the comrades wherever my service will count for most. Please send 'Gene and Steady my greetings—tell them that the Socialist Party has chosen two of its staunchest, ablest and most loyal men as standard bearers, and that we are blessed indeed to have such men to take the brunt of the fight in these trying times. I am with them heart and soul and whether I remain behind bars or I am freed I ask nothing better than to do all and give all that I possess to the coming struggle.

I received a letter from Dr. Madge Stevens[56] who attended the Convention. She seems to feel very optimistic that things will be moving in my case within the next ten days—let us hope that it may be true, but we have, as you say, learned patience and fortitude in these long, hard months and our hearts are staunch for whatever comes or does not come, for we know that in due time things must be made right.

I also had a nice, long letter from W.T.M. tonight and he tells me many interesting things that are happening out in the great Northwest. Tell him I said I really thought it required a very vivid imagination to see any "literature" in my letters, but I am humbly thankful that they seem to have the faculty of bringing hope and cheer and solace to many sad, weary hearts. There is one sentence that occurs in almost every letter I receive from rich and poor, educated and uneducated, priest and "wobbly", business man and housewife: there may be a slight difference in wording, but the thought is always the same, and a very strange thing it seems. They say: "We wait for your letters so eagerly, for they bring us

56. Dr. Madge Stevens was a socialist in Terre Haute, Indiana, who worked locally with Gene Debs, the town's most famous socialist.

new hope and inspiration, new faith and strength to meet the bitter struggles of life." Can you imagine anything so paradoxical as that men and women who walk their various ways of life in freedom and unmarked by the stigma of "crime" should wait for the hurriedly written words of a weary woman who has given her last ounce of physical strength to a brutal "task" in a prison sweatshop, and who bears society's mark of a "criminal" and wears the ugly garb of a convict? Could anything surpass it in absurdity? And can life give to any human being a richer reward, a deeper happiness, a greater joy than to know that even in a prison cell, branded as a criminal, garbed as a convict, she can still send words of hope and faith, strength and inspiration to sad hearts and sick souls.

Lovingly,
KATE

May 23, 1920

Dear Sweethearts:

Sunday. Please tell Clarissa Kneeland that I received her letters and the scrapbooks which are in great demand among the younger girls here. Poor creatures! Hope springs eternal in their souls and they are pathetically sentimental. The hunger for love is the last beautiful thing to die in their hearts. Then every other normal impulse has been killed by poverty and degradation, punishment and brutality, that one spark of the divine still cowers beneath the sodden ashes of a ruined life. Communication between the inmates of the men's and women's departments is more frightfully and fiendishly punished here than any other thing, yet in spite of the brutal worst that can be done, both men and women will run risks that make my blood run cold, to send their tragically pathetic little love notes over the walls. I can influence the girls in most things, can reason and coax them into at least outward submission to the rules, but when I try to induce them not to run such frightful risks with their love notes, I am up against a stone wall. Sometimes with tears and sometimes in blazing rage they say: "Yes, it's all right for you to preach; the man you love writes you every day and comes to see you every month; but if he were over there and you couldn't see him or hear from him for months and months, you would break rules and run risks to get your letters thru." And I know that it is true. I can live thru the hell of prison life, I can rise above the petty persecutions of ignorance and venom because I have love—love that no bolts or bars or locks can shut out—love that is as bountiful as the gifts of God—love that can lift me out of the sordid, brutal ugliness of a convict's lot and give in my prison cell a joy in life that no millionaire's gold can buy and no fame or glory can attain.

And that reminds me that we have the two extremes of life here now, Mollie, the tiny four-foot, eighty-pound maiden and an old, white-haired woman tottering down the path to the grave. Mollie is the incarnate spirit of youth—youth that loves and hopes, gives and suffers for its ideals, and Mary Deming is the pitiful tragedy of poverty stricken old age. It is hard, oh! terribly hard not to be bitter when one looks at Mollie and Mother Deming. Mollie whose crime was that she never protested. Mrs. Deming's story is so heart-breakingly tragic. She is the typical well bred, modest, refined, conventionally religious old lady of the upstate New York village. Her husband was the village postmaster and received the starvation wage paid by the "richest government on earth" to its postal employees. They pinched along, as only old fashioned upstate New Yorkers can pinch, but as the cost of living soared and their pitiful wages shrunk somehow there grew a shortage of twelve hundred dollars in their accounts. They were both indicted and the old man, almost seventy, was sent to Atlanta and the old wife, past sixty-five, sent here. Only one who knows the narrow, rigid, harsh conceptions of life that is the psychology of the old fashioned New England villagers can sense the crushing tragedy that has damned the closing days of Mary Deming and her husband. The poor old creature creeps about like a distraught ghost and all but breaks our hearts with her dumb misery. Please see Miss Bates and ask her to see that some of the church women of St. Louis write her. Ask all of my friends there to just forget me for a while and send messages to Mrs. Deming. If my men friends at the City Club want to do something for me, just ask them to drop a note to the poor old lady and send her a dollar bill. Not more than that, for more would make her feel embarrassed and under unbearably heavy obligations, but she does need a little money to buy extra food. I wish she had arrived before Mike Kinney[57] came, I would have taken all his loose change for her. And Frank, ask

57. Mike Kinney was an old-style machine politician. His visit to O'Hare that spring seemed to touch her.

Miss Bates to mobilize all the influence she possibly can and appeal to Mr. Palmer to make a special ruling in her case that will permit her to send and receive letters from her husband in Atlanta. There is a rule, I don't know who is responsible for it, that no one here can send letters to an inmate at Atlanta, and it will be unbearably hard if these old people are prevented from even hearing from each other for a whole year. The poor old soul worries constantly lest her husband is ill or suffering more than she from their imprisonment.

I have written several times of Rachel Epps, a federal girl who has served almost eight years. She is one of the quietest, nicest colored girls here and we have been very good friends. Yesterday her parole blanks came and since she has already served so long and has a perfect record I feel sure there will be little difficulty in securing her parole. She has no friends and I want you to sign her papers as sponsor and we will get her employment as a maid. She will be awkward and untrained in housework now after all these years, but she is kind and faithful and loyal and will serve to the best of her ability. I am sending you the paper to fill out. If you need any advice Mr. S. will give it. I will fill out the other paper here. Send it back as soon as it is properly executed and it will be forwarded to Washington from here.

Lovingly,
KATE

Kate Richards O'Hare
Reg. No. 21669

Girard, Kansas
February 15, 1921

Dear Friends:

Since the day I was released from prison I have been looking forward to the happiness of writing a real, honest-to-goodness letter to our friends of the *Bulletin*. My prison letters were all written under the eye of hostile censorship and I wanted to write just once in absolute freedom. But with the very first day of freedom came imperative duties that could not be put aside, and not until today has it been possible for me to find time to fulfill this long cherished wish.

Naturally my first few days of freedom were given to the family; to being quizzed by newspaper reporters, and to reading the wealth of letters and telegrams that came from every corner of the earth, and from all manner of people. And with the very first mail came the insistent demand that we make a trip covering the larger cities east of the Rocky Mountains to speak in behalf of amnesty for political prisoners. It seemed a crime against the children for me to leave home even for this purpose. But Eugene settled the matter by saying: "Mamma, of course we want you; but we must remember that if all our friends hadn't worked so hard for you, you wouldn't be here. You will have to go say 'Hello!' to them and ask them to work for the other political prisoners."

Mr. O'Hare made the first trip with me, and it was one of those experiences that can come but once in a lifetime—a joyous pageant of love and fellowship and thanksgiving everywhere. We met old comrades with whom we had worked for years in the labor movement and new friends who had come to us through the *Bulletin*. Later trips I made alone, but from June 13th to November 2nd, I traveled thousands of miles and spoke to record breaking crowds in appeal for amnesty for political prisoners and for a complete reconstruction of our entire prison system. The response was far beyond our wildest hopes and every day emphasized the keen interest in these great problems.

Nothing in my prison experience was so unutterably horrible as the constant and revolting contact with venereal disease, and the brutal indifference of the prison officials in forcing clean human beings to risk contamination. I came out of prison convinced that nothing could be of greater importance than to wage a warfare upon this foul plague. So far as I was concerned "the spirit was willing, but the flesh was weak". I was ready to start the fight instanter, but I had sense enough to know that I lacked training. And here was an instance where I believed in "preparedness."

You remember that I used to tell Emma Goldman that "the Lord will provide", and He must still be on the job. In November I received a letter from the Mayor of Milwaukee[58] telling me that I had been appointed delegate to represent that city in the Institute on Venereal Disease Control and Social Hygiene, and the All-American Conference on Venereal Disease Control held in Washington, D.C., from November 22

58. Daniel Webster Hoan (1881–1961), mayor of Milwaukee from 1916 to 1940, headed a socialist administration.

to December 10, 1920, under the direction of the United States Public Health Service. Needless to say I accepted the commission and hied myself to Washington where I once more became the guest of Uncle Sam. This time a voluntary one.

I thus had almost a month of intensive training under a faculty of world famous physicians, surgeons, biologists, psychologists and sociologists. Here I had an opportunity to study under masters all of the things that I needed so much to know. And of greater value perhaps than the lessons were the contacts with five hundred men and women who are already veterans in the warfare on venereal disease. The comedy that spiced the whole experience was the fact that but for the chastening hand of a pious lady uplifter from Noo Yo'k who was scandalized at finding herself in such close proximity to a "convict", I might have become puffed up with pride by the flattering attentions I received because of being the only person present who KNEW prison conditions from the inside. I came home from Washington fully convinced that somehow, somewhere, we must create a magazine that could handle the problem of social hygiene with scientific accuracy and yet expressed in the language of the common people. I was loaded with valuable information—but—I was also threatened with lockjaw from trying to say the words that the famous specialists use to express very simple facts.

The blissful ignorance of the prison officials concerning the most elemental facts of human psychology, the brutal treatment of feeble-minded and patently insane prisoners by keepers, forced me to realize that nothing could be of greater importance than the sane and scientific study of human behavior; the whys and wherefores of human action and reaction and their effects on delinquency. I had been sort of nibbling at Freud before my imprisonment, and in those long and tragic months the psycho-analytic theory of human behavior ceased to be an amusing speculation and became my anchor to sanity, my hold on faith in humanity and my hope for a better social adjustment. I know that Freud is both insidious and exhilarating, and I may be indulging in a sort of Freudian jag just now, but I know he saved my sanity behind the prison walls. In Washington I had a regular psychological spree. And once again I feel the necessity for a periodical in which I can translate the hope-inspiring wonders of modern psychology into the plain and simple language of the common people.

The long months since last we wrote to you have been filled with

fruitful and inspiring work, but always we have been faced with the
necessity of choosing what should be our permanent life work. Naturally
we could not turn our backs upon the prisons and helpless human beings
hidden there. A part of us will always be within prison walls and never
again can we walk in freedom as long as our brothers and sisters are shut
away from life. When I came out, we felt that we owed a debt to our
friends that could only be in a measure paid by serving, to the limit of
our ability, those who needed service most. Thousands behind prison
walls are voiceless; the scourge of venereal disease menaces our civilization; mental hygiene has much to offer in making the lives of the people
sane and wholesome; the co-operative movement on the industrial field
and sanity on the political field must be developed before we can have a
just economic system and a sane social order. We feel that a magazine is
abundantly necessary that will bring to the common people an understanding of these dynamic facts.

So it seemed to us that we could best serve by establishing a magazine
that would be the voice of the voiceless, the hope of the hopeless, and
the help of the helpless. We have revived the *National Rip-Saw*, a magazine that for many years served the most needy people of the United
States. It bears a rather crude and homely name, but a wholesome one.
Without the sweat and toil of the lowly lumberjack and the cheery song
of the "rip-saw" neither homes nor human progress would be possible.
We want to help build better homes and better people and a better world
for them to live in; so we are proud of our sweat-stained symbol—the
Rip-Saw. It may be "of the earth earthy", but about ninety-nine per cent
of the human race lives mighty close to the earth, and if we hope to lift
their eyes to higher things we must go down and become like them, as
Jesus did.

We have made the price of the magazine low, so that every one can
become subscribers. We must use inexpensive paper and economical
methods of printing and our salary looks like a ten dollar bill after paying
for a ton of coal; but nothing cheap or tawdry shall ever go into its columns. We use the simple language of the common people, and homely
illustrations drawn from every day working-class life, but we try to bring
the best that science and literature have to offer to our readers. It is
not the sort of a magazine we would publish if we were trying to serve
only the people who received the *Bulletin*, but we believe that it is the
sort of a magazine that our friends will be glad to support. . . .

Girard is a nice little one-hoss town in Kansas, with a courthouse in the middle of the square, a lot of dinky stores fringing it, and flivvers hopping about like restless grasshoppers. The wide old streets are lined with catalpa trees and your neighbors' chickens scratch up your garden. We walk back and forth to work through tree-lined streets made warm and homelike by grinning urchins and kindly neighbors going about the business of life. The O'Hare children take to village life like ducks to mud puddles and it is all very sweet and restful after the stress and strain and horror of the last three years. The great printing plant of the *Appeal to Reason* gives us access to ample facilities here in the quiet and homey atmosphere of a small town, and we expect to pass the happiest days of our life here editing and publishing the *Rip-Saw* and serving our fellow-men "as God gives us light."

This letter marks the end of *Frank O'Hare's Bulletin*—one of the most unique publications ever issued in the United States. It was born of a great need, written in the heart's blood of our family, and went forth to the uttermost ends of the earth to find love and loyalty and light in the hour of darkness. The only acceptable expression of our appreciation of your fellowship in the time of need, is to try to so live and serve that you may be glad to have been a Bulletineer.

You have lived in spirit with us through long, tragic months. You have visualized my prison walls and my husband and our children suffering far more than I. Your hearts have accorded with ours and you have shared your love and your money with us. Now the brighter, happier days have come, and when you think of us let it be this picture. A modest cottage on a tree-lined street, a shabby office on a sleepy square where we find useful joyous work to do; roaring presses and deft-handed girls sending out the *Rip-Saw* to carry its message wherever that message is needed. Think of Dick as a high-school lad just nibbling at romance and Kathleen as a high-school girl hurrying fast toward young womanhood. And Gene and Vic—well, they are just healthy, normal boys, always noisy, often dirty, always hungry, and oftimes naughty—but just boys. And now may love, peace and fellowship rest and abide with you.

Fraternally yours,
KATE O'HARE

PART IV
In Prison

In Prison

The Function of the Prison

As a rule we have very hazy ideas indeed as to the proper function and the requisite efficiency of the prison as a social institution. So general is the impression that prisons are a necessary part of our social machinery that for the time being we will accept that impression as true, and consider only the questions of function and efficiency. In a general way we agree that prisons should serve a threefold purpose: they should be places of social vengeance where we punish persons who break the law; they should be safe places to segregate unpleasant and dangerous persons; and they should be places where some indefinite thing called "reformation" is achieved by some unknown and mysterious process.

No one denies, I think, that our whole prison system as it exists today is based on the idea of social vengeance. So far as I have been able to determine, the problem seems to resolve into certain questions for which we must find intelligent answers.

Is social vengeance the proper purpose of our penal institutions?

Who shall determine the nature of this social vengeance?

Is the loss of liberty sufficient punishment for misdeeds, or shall there be added the deliberate violation of every normal human impulse?

Should social vengeance include undernourishment, bad housing, degrading raiment, enforced unpaid labour, contamination from loath-

From *In Prison*, 49–55, 73, 74–82, 93–95, 100–102, 181–83.

some diseases, mental stagnation, moral degeneracy, and spiritual disintegration?

Must social vengeance include physical violence and excessive brutality, and if it must, should we have a body of public servants trained for
that purpose?

If we must have public servants trained for prison brutality, where,
and how, shall they be secured?

Shall we breed and train administrators of brutality and torture, or
shall we leave to chance the problem of securing prison keepers sufficiently brutal to carry out the requirements of social vengeance?

What standards shall be used to measure their ability to administer
punishments?

Who shall determine the natural fitness and degree of training in
prison brutality which is proper to these public servants?

Is it possible for one human being to inflict mental and physical torture on another human being without himself being injured?

If the infliction of torture on prisoners injures the public servants who
act as prison keepers, how shall society compensate the servants so injured?

Have we any reliable information as to whether or not the methods
of prison cruelty as now applied have a tendency to graduate from our
prisons ex-convicts less disturbing to the public peace, and safer persons
with whom to live, than the criminals whom we sent to prison?

If it is true that social vengeance is just and efficient, and that society
has the right to punish by prison brutalities any member who violates its
laws, must we not determine the share of responsibility which society
bears, in order that the delinquent may be punished with an approximately exact justice?

If we admit that punishment, in order to be effective, must be just,
and if we admit that in many instances individuals are punished for the
sins of society as a whole, is not crime added to crime, and no good end
served?

When we have found rational, scientific, common-sense answers to
these questions we shall have reached the heart of the prison problem.
As yet we are much befogged on all of them.

To the unthinking the grim grey walls with their shrouding cloak of
mystery, and the steel-barred windows, sinister in their silence, give a
comforting sense of social security against the depredations of criminals.

We feel, somehow, that walls and bars make us safe, and that massive locks and armed guards give us protection. "The wish is father to the thought," so we have come to consider our prisons safe places for the segregation of the criminals that prey upon society. We know that in the field of physical hygiene the segregation of the infected from the uninfected is recognized as necessary to the control and cure of physical diseases, and somehow we feel that prisons protect us from moral contamination.

This myth is no doubt comforting to the unthinking—but it is a myth. If criminality is an infectious moral disease, jails and prisons have not provided, and under present methods of management never will provide, the security of real segregation.

I have often watched the police patrol wagon go clanging down the street carrying some malefactor to jail, and in some unexplained way it seemed to bring a soothing sense of security. I felt that the sleepless eye of the law was ever alert for my protection, and that criminals who might endanger my property or life would be quickly and safely shut behind prison bars. I am wiser now. I have seen the inside workings of prisons, and I know that all the clanging patrol wagons, all the stolid policemen, all the mysteries of the courtroom, all the evil-smelling jails and frowning prison walls can not make me safe from the depredations of the criminally bent.

I have seen the federal court and the prison in operation, and after my release I sat in other courts and watched the workings of the law there. The first man brought in was a noted automobile bandit who drove the arresting officer to the station in a car noted for its speed and high price. Any cub reporter in the city could tell thrilling stories of the skill and daring and amazing depredations committed by this ultra-modern thief. The policeman who arrested him, the judge before whom he was arraigned, and all the courtroom loungers knew his record. But he was represented by a high-priced attorney, a notorious political ward heeler, and a multi-millionaire professional bondsman provided bond for his appearance in court, and he drove away to indulge in his profession of banditry, gaily undisturbed by his experience with the law.

Then there was a shambling moron, vacant-eyed, listless, and degenerate. He had been arrested for making lewd remarks to a group of school girls. His mother worked as cook for a well-known saloon keeper who provided the fine, and the pervert went on his way.

Then came a street walker arrested for soliciting, but her cadet was on hand, a whispered conversation took place between the panderer and the judge, money was deposited, and the girl went back to her profession.

The next was a "hop head" arrested for peddling "dope." But the charge was changed to vagrancy, and he got thirty days in the work-house.

Then came a wild-eyed woman sobbing and muttering that someone had insulted her. She was charged with assault, but a worried looking husband and a fat, sleek lawyer conferred with the judge, a Liberty bond was deposited for bail, and the woman muttered her way to freedom. And so the monotonous grind went on and on, and at the end of the day a score of really dangerous persons had been freed, and five merely annoying ones were in jail.

The judges had administered the letter of the law; they had done all that can be expected of the type of men we elect to the duties of police judge; but they had not segregated the dangerous criminals, nor had they safeguarded the lives and property of the people of the city.

Had these courts had, instead of merely ignorant politicians, the services of a trained physician and psychologist, fitted to detect dangerous traits of human character and abnormalities, the story would have been different. The scientifically trained man would have known that the bandit would immediately return to his criminal activities, and that to release him on bail would merely make the law-enforcing machinery of the city a partner in his crime.

In the degenerate moron the psychologist would have recognized the potential rapist and possible murderer, and he would have been committed to an institution for the feeble-minded.

The physician would have known that the street walker was almost sure to be infected with venereal diseases which she would transmit to her customers, and she would have been placed in a segregation hospital for treatment.

Trained men would have known that thirty days in the work-house for the drug addict would merely mean a period of hellish torture while in prison and continued degeneracy when released, and he too would have been committed to a hospital for treatment.

The psychologist would have recognized in the woman arrested for assault, not a criminal, but a dangerous dement, who must be sent to a psychopathic hospital.

I know, of course, that laws permitting persons charged with crime to give bond for appearance in court are necessary to protect the innocent from unjust punishment while waiting trial, but surely no person should be released on bond until he has been carefully observed and painstakingly examined by a competent physician and psychologist, who alone can determine whether or not a delinquent is really dangerous to society.

We reassure ourselves that, while it may be true that dangerous criminals are sometimes released on bonds, we are actually quite safe once they are in the penitentiary. We feel that after a criminal has had his day in court, after he has been found guilty and shut behind prison walls, we are safeguarded. This too is a comforting myth, but a myth only.

Prisons do not segregate, and they do not permanently and adequately protect us from the criminal by shutting him behind prison walls. And neither does the prison segregate the various grades and types of convicts who go to prison. We know that not all persons who go to prison are equally criminalistic and dangerous. We know that some are young and new to the ways of crime, and some are old and hardened. We know that some are shrewd and highly trained in criminal practices, and many are merely the stupid victims of circumstances. We know that some are habitual criminals, some are accidental, and some are being punished for the crimes of others. We know that some are approximately normal and many are abnormal, some free from physical disease, and many contaminated. Yet within the prison where I served, for whose conditions the federal government, by sending prisoners, accepts responsibility, there was no attempt at intelligent segregation, no recognition of mental or physical abnormalities, no attempt to prevent the spread of diseases, physical, mental, or moral.

And there was not the slightest effort to segregate the young offenders from the old and more hardened and vicious criminals. . . .

The Prison

I was not permitted by the prison officials to keep the data gathered in a survey of the prisoners, but I think that seventy-five per cent were mentally and psychically abnormal, and an appalling number were obviously insane. No effort was made to segregate the mentally diseased; no intelligent consideration was given their mental condition in the amount of work demanded or the discipline exacted, and no helpful treatment was ever given. It is a tragic and soul-sickening thing that the most revolting instances of brutality and downright fiendish cruelty were directed toward the women utterly unable to make the "task" or conform to required discipline—women who should never have been sent to prison, but should rather have been committed to institutions for the feeble-minded or insane.

The methods and facilities for dealing with the psychopaths were, if possible, more benighted still, for the prison management seemed blissfully unconscious of everything related to modern psychology. They dealt with the psychically ill with the same degree of intelligence that the old witch doctors used in dealing with the physically ill. The witch doctors beat sick men with clubs to drive the devils out of them, and in our prison the officials punished the psychically sick to obtain the same results—and their methods were just as efficient in curing criminality as the witch doctors' in curing jungle fever. . . .

The Prisoners

I lived for fourteen months the life of a Federal prisoner in the State Penitentiary at Jefferson City, Missouri. I had, perhaps, a better opportunity to study female prisoners and the conditions existing in this, an average prison, than any other person has had who is really interested in female delinquency. I had the advantage of having some previous training and an intellectual background not common among women convicts. I had what the criminologist does not have—the actual experience of being a convict—and I also had sufficient time in prison to check theories and impressions with well tested facts.

I managed to escape bitterness and rancour and to devote my time to studying, as honestly and fairly as I could, the prison system as I endured it; attempting to evaluate, as nearly as my training permitted, its efficiency as a place of social vengeance and of segregation, and the results of its methods of reforming socially undesirable persons committed to its care.

The women themselves were, of course, the vividly interesting feature of my prison life. My first studies in criminology had been in the older schools of which Lombroso[1] is the best known exponent. The theories of this school I had acquired at the most impressionable period of my life, and, in spite of later studies in the directions taken by the Freudian school, the earlier impressions were dominant. I held the convictions, quite common, I think, that there is such a thing as a "criminal type," a distinct "criminal class," and that certain symptoms called "criminal stigmata" might be found in all delinquents.

My first view of my prison mates was disconcerting. They did not measure up to my preconceived idea of what a group of the "criminal class" should be. On that never-to-be-forgotten first day that looms so large in every prisoner's memory, after the ordeal of being "dressed in," I waited for my first meal with the women who have come to mean more to me than any other associates I have ever known. With the women who cleaned the halls and worked in the prison laundry, and with those too ill to work, I lined up in the narrow hall and watched these modern chattel slaves march from the workshop to the dining room to eat their coarse and scanty prison fare.

It was a tragic tale which that line of weary, toil-stained women told as they shuffled by—a challenge to our civilization, an indictment of our social system. There were women there scarred by the marks of toil, marred by the curse of poverty, and broken by the sordid struggle for existence. There were young girls there marked by the stamp of vice before the childish roundness of cheek and chin had settled into the hard lines of degraded womanhood. There were old women, some burned out by vice, and some bent with honest labour and child-bearing. There were cripples and degenerates, consumptives and epileptics, dements and sex perverts, morons and high-grade imbeciles, and a very few who under ordinary conditions would be classed as normal. The few normal women in that tragic group, practically all political prisoners, were for the most part women and girls so fine and clean, so intelligent and womanly, that the horror of plunging them into that human cesspool gripped my heart and seemed to wring it dry.

When my place in that long line of human tragedy came, some com-

---

1. Cesare Lombroso (1836–1909), an influential criminologist, taught that "the criminal population" exhibited a high ratio of physical and mental abnormalities, and that criminals could be identified by certain physical characteristics.

panion gave me a gentle push, and I fell into the prison lockstep with a few of the noblest women God ever made and many of the saddest wrecks life ever marred. Except for the hideously ugly prison dress they did not differ startlingly from the sort of women one might find crowding about a bargain table in a department store basement or dragging a cotton sack on a tenant farm.

Naturally I studied these women with keen interest. But I was never able to discover the expected physical marks of the "criminal type," and none displayed, so far as I could determine, the stigmata of criminalism of which Lombroso writes, and of which I had been wont to speak so glibly. The only stigmata that I could discover were those of poverty, excessive child-bearing, undernourishment, and overwork. In every phase of most of the women's outside lives these things were commonplace, and I think I am justified in feeling that they were the great determining factors in their delinquency.

In my very first attempt to study the women prisoners I came in contact with the most common and vicious results of women's economic dependency. The warden and the chaplain both assured me that it was useless to attempt to make any study of causative factors, or to arrive at worthwhile conclusions, because "they all lied like troopers." And the women did lie. Certainly they did—and why not? From my own experiences and what they told me, I am quite sure that their experiences in life would have no tendency to induce them to be strictly truthful. Certainly their experiences with the law and its application would not. They had learned by bitter experience that truth is an outcast from the courts, and that their prison life was a maze of lies.

The very first thing I was compelled to do when I went to prison was to stitch a lying label on the overalls I made. This label stated that this prison-made garment was manufactured by a respectable firm hundreds of miles away in another state; and it bore no indication that it was one of the most hated things in modern commerce—prison-made goods. The warden lied to the women prisoners, the chaplain lied to them, and so did the matron and the guards and the "stool pigeons." Society lied to them also when the pretense was made that the purpose of their imprisonment was to "reform" them, whereas every woman knew that the real object was social vengeance and exploitation for the profit of the political party in power and the prison contractors.

And I am not sure that women convicts are the only women who lie. I rather think all women do. We are forced to do it in order to live. I am afraid I shall have to confess that I am somewhat of an expert myself. I have evaded the truth for all the men I know—my father, brothers, schoolmates, sweethearts, husband, sons, employer, and employees; for my doctor, lawyer, minister, and co-workers in the labour movement. And I presume I shall keep right on prevaricating for men to the end of my days. All women do. It is the price we pay for even approximate peace. The effect on our social relations, should all women proceed to tell the truth, the whole truth, and nothing but the truth about all the men they come in contact with, would be appalling to contemplate.

Judy O'Grady and the captain's lady are much akin. So the women convicts did lie to me, not always consciously; as a rule, I think, unconsciously. The first stories they told me of their tragedies and their crimes were never true. In fact, they almost never knew the real causes for their delinquencies, and they did not tell them if they did. Why should they? I found that getting the real story of a woman convict's life was not so easy as turning on a phonograph. It required cartons of chewing gum, pounds of candy, unlimited patience, and endless work to get the true stories of only a few of the women with whom I served in prison.

I could only get the facts piecemeal, bit by bit, from time to time; and always I must get them when the tellers were off guard, when they did not realize that they were laying bare the inmost secrets of their sin-scarred souls. I found that my dearly beloved notebook was worse than useless. I had to cultivate a memory that would retain the fragment of a life history and fit those fragments into a mosaic of human frailty. To gather the facts it was necessary to hold their respect, command their faith, gain their love, and touch into life the mute, deadened strings of their hearts. It was not an easy task, but the rewards were great; for I found that in every woman convict's life there appeared to be economic, psychological, and sociological causes for her crime, and in almost every case, it seemed to me, social responsibility for her criminality was far greater than individual responsibility.

The prison population of the Missouri State Penitentiary is usually about 2600, 100 women and 2500 men. Basing conclusions on these figures one might think that men are something more than twenty-five times as bad as women. Flattering as this conclusion may be to my sex,

I do not think it is true. In spite of the fact that there were twenty-five times as many men as women in this prison—and the ratio is approximately the same in all states—so far as I can judge, men and women are "good" and "bad" to about the same degree, and sex has little to do with criminality. That is, women are not less criminal, nor men more criminal. Human nature is about the same, male or female.

A very large percentage of both men and women, about eighty or ninety, so far as I could determine, were in prison for offenses against property—most of them petty offenses committed in the pursuit of the necessities of life. The next largest group of the men had committed offenses against sex. While women have even greater insecurity in the struggle for existence and must meet aggravated problems in selling their labour power, they have one advantage: in addition to their labour, women have another saleable commodity—their sex. So when women are faced by the alternatives of prostitution or crime, they usually choose the former. Women are the passive and receptive in sex transgressions, men are the aggressive and active; so that women rarely come in conflict with the laws governing sex relations except for pandering or procuring women for the profession of prostitution, and these crimes are very infrequently punished by penitentiary sentences. It is also, no doubt, true that women are not punished so severely by the courts as men, and that a woman will receive a jail sentence for the same offense that will send a man to the penitentiary.

I found that many of my fellow convicts were from the old and well established profession of prostitution; but I also found that women of this profession very rarely go to the penitentiary until they are old and worn out and no longer profitable to the men who control the business of vice. The younger prostitutes were almost without exception "rebels," women who had rebelled against the political machines that controlled the vice interests of the cities in which they lived and plied their trade. They were girls who tried to "go it alone," who refused to "line up with the gang," who rebelled against taking a politician cadet for a "protector," and who refused to "split" their earnings with cadet, police, and ward politicians.

These young courtesans who flouted the power of the men who make a business of politics and vice were frequently "sent up,"—usually, on a charge of "rolling" a customer, or shop lifting—to be "broken." And broken they were! Of all the ghastly memories I brought back from prison, none are so terrible as the breaking of these women.

Evelyn was one of these young rebels, and the memory of her breaking is still a nightmare to me. She was young and strong and obstinate, and the brutalities and horrors necessary to break her were beyond the possibilities of the human language to express or the normal mind to comprehend. But, strong and stubborn as she was, prison life broke her, and when she had been reduced to a half insane, cringing travesty on womanhood, a powerful politician of St. Louis secured her parole. I met her on the street after my release and she told me that she was plying her trade, but that she was "regular" and "split" without protest.

Evelyn's fate is a common one, I found. The young white women usually remained in prison but a short time if they were prostitutes or potential ones; they were too valuable to their cadets and the politicians to permit the prison contractor to have the cream of their lives. A certain state senator of St. Louis and a state representative of Kansas City seemed to have the power to secure pardons or paroles for these women at will.

Most of the young coloured women in the "stir" had been convicted of "rolling." Technically this means highway robbery, but actually something else. Many white men consort with negro prostitutes and refuse to pay them. There is nothing a girl can do but wait her opportunity, and the next time the man comes to her she gives him knockout drops and takes his roll, which means all the money and valuables he may have on his person.

Of the state prisoners one was charged with forgery, two with bigamy, and one with embezzlement—enough to show that women are not given to committing crimes of skill and daring.

Perhaps the most interesting group of the women were those sent up for "eliminating undesirable husbands," as they expressed it. They were not only the most intelligent of the state prisoners, but they were the exact opposite of what one would naturally think a husband-murderer would be. They were practically all middle-aged, some quite old, and they were quiet, diffident, toilworn women; the type that bears children uncomplainingly and endures poverty and hardship, neglect and brutality. Then, some day, there is laid upon their burden the last straw. The repressed emotions, the outraged love, the mother ferocity that makes a woman fight for her young, flame into rebellion; taut nerves snap, a man is killed, a home broken up, children scattered and branded; and a woman enters the living tomb of a prison—to be forgotten. And usually she stays there until death ends her misery. She is too old and toilworn to be of value to the vice interests, too poor and obscure to command political influence. The prison doors close behind her—and the world forgets.

The most tragic group of all were the women convicted of killing their newborn babies—illegitimate babies, of course. They were of two types: young mentally deficient girls, and faded, worn, love-starved spinsters. These fagged-out, love-starved women were either domestic servants from small country towns or country school teachers. They all worshipped at the shrine of respectability; they were prudish to a degree that would have been amusing had it not been so tragic; and they were all very religious. . . .

Prison Food, Clothing, Education, and Recreation

There were no provisions in our prison for educational or vocational training. The women, at the expiration of their sentences, go out not only worn to physical depletion, but as illiterate and untrained as they entered. I found that about twenty per cent could neither read nor write, and with few exceptions the others had not finished the grade schools. Only three of the women, aside from the politicals, had entered high school, and only one had finished.

At the time I entered, no library facilities were provided for the women. They were entirely without reading matter except what they could purchase, and where the food problem was so pressing it was natural that what little money they could secure should go to feed their stomachs and not their minds. I made a row about the lack of reading matter and finally secured permission for the women to have one book a week from the library on the men's side. This library is old and almost worthless for educational purposes. The non-fiction includes little of value except a few fairly good but very old histories of the United States. The fiction was of the lightest and least educational sort, but in spite of its limitations the library privileges were a great comfort to the women and relieved the monotony of the long hours spent locked in the cells.

A few weeks after I entered I sent a formal request to Mr. W. R.

Painter, chairman of the prison board, asking permission to open a night school. One of the girls who had finished the grade school offered to teach the beginners, and I tendered my services to teach the more advanced. The women were pathetically eager for the opportunity to attend school, but the prison board ignored the request, and the prison still has no school for the women prisoners. The work which the women do has no educational value and will not in the least help them to adjust themselves and their lives to accepted social standards.

One of the things which make adjustment almost impossible for the convict released after serving a prison sentence of any length is the complete suppression of initiative on the part of the prisoner. He is not permitted to think, or plan, or act for himself in even the most trivial matters. We employed in our home as a housemaid a woman who had served five years in the Missouri State Penitentiary. We found that, while she was eager and willing to work, her initiative had been so completely destroyed that the simplest tasks were beyond her unless some one followed her about continually to give endless directions. For five years this woman had moved like an automaton, always under rasping orders and never permitted to have the slightest control over her actions. Naturally, when she faced the world she was unable to think or act on her own initiative—incapable of doing the common, ordinary work of life.

The women were as ruthlessly dominated in their mental and spiritual lives as in their physical. Many of them had lost relatives in the World War, and when Memorial Day came it was a day of deep meaning to them. Several weeks before Memorial Day, 1919, a letter signed by all the inmates of the female wing was sent to the prison board asking permission to arrange their programme and hold the service after work hours, but they wanted to conduct it themselves. This perfectly courteous and modest request was ignored, not even a reply being made.

At Christmas time the women again requested, this time of the matron, permission to arrange an entertainment. This request was also denied, with a vivid eruption of profanity. Later I asked the matron for permission to coach the women in the production of a little play which I had written. This was also denied. The matron gave as her reason for refusing these requests that the women were too tired after work hours to rehearse. There was logic in that position, for when the task had taken its share of human energy, there was little left for life and mental growth.

I thought a series of simple lectures on psychology would be interesting and possibly helpful to the prisoners. On Christmas Day, 1919, Governor Gardner and all the prison officials visited us, and I personally requested permission to do this work. This request was denied also. In the minds of all the prison officials with whom I came in contact, there was a marked antipathy to any sort of educational work among the prisoners, and seemingly a firm and deep-rooted conviction that ignorance in the prisoners is to be desired and maintained. . . .

Task and Punishment

I found that, under the guise of punishment for crime and in the name of reformation of criminals, a tremendously profitable form of chattel slavery has grown up in this country. When I reached prison I found that for all practical purposes, I had been converted by the United States Department of Justice into a chattel slave. The process whereby the Department of Justice supplies chattel slaves is very simple. Our government maintains prisons to care for none of its female prisoners and for only a fraction of its male prisoners. At stated times the Superintendent of Federal Prisons sends out letters to the wardens and prison boards of state penitentiaries asking for bids for the care of male and female prisoners. A prison, like the Women's Reformatory of Massachusetts, which cares for its prisoners in something approaching a civilized manner, and which does not indulge in the convict leasing system or the task system, bids twenty-five dollars a month. The Missouri State Penitentiary bids eighteen dollars a month.

Federal law absolutely forbids the working of federal prisoners under contract or under the task system. This means nothing to the State of Missouri—and I was sold to its prison board.

The Missouri Prison Board in turn sold me for nine hours each day to the Oberman Manufacturing Company, who manufacture overalls. The state of Missouri is forbidden by law to sell its convicts to contractors of convict labour, and I do not know the details of the evasion or violation of this law. I know only that it is evaded or violated, or both. I also know that the Oberman Manufacturing Company made garments that bore the label of reputable firms located in states which have laws forbidding the sale of convict-made goods.

The government pays for the maintenance of the prisoners, so the profit on the labour of the federal convict is what thieves call "velvet."

Possibly this "velvet" softens the shock of prison brutalities for politicians and muffles the cries of prisoners for decency and justice.

The profits from these chattel slaves are enormous. The state provides the building, heat, light, power, and convict labour, and the contractor pays the state a pittance for the right to exploit the prisoners and the taxpayers. Every day I worked in the prison shop I earned, at nonunion wages paid in the worst sweat shops in the country, from $4.80 to $5.20 a day. I was paid fifty cents a month the first three months, seventy-five cents a month the next three months, and one dollar a month thereafter. I earned about $1800 at ordinary wages, making unionalls. I was paid $10.50 for this work, and all the difference between the wealth I created and the pittance paid me went, not into the treasury of the nation I was presumed to have injured, not into the treasury of the state of Missouri, but into the pockets of the prison contractor as profits. If the profit on the labour of each convict is only $1000 a year, the profits on many thousands of convicts explain why politicians are so universally in favour of our present prison system. There is a law on the statute books of Missouri that all convicts employed at gainful labour shall be paid in cash five per cent of the value of their labour. But this law, too, is evaded, and the prison management unlawfully robbed me of even the five per cent of my earnings which the law says shall be paid the convict. . . .

Appendix: Statement by the Author

When I found that I might be compelled to spend many months in prison I felt that I should like to make my incarceration of social value, if possible, by making a detailed study of my fellow convicts.

With the co-operation of the heads of departments of universities, heads of social service organizations, scientific societies, employers of labour, labour leaders and other interested individuals I prepared [an] outline . . . for a case book on criminology.

When the outline was completed I visited (1918) Governor Frederick D. Gardner of Missouri, submitted a copy of the schedule, and asked his co-operation in securing permission to make the survey in case I should be compelled to serve as a federal prisoner in the state penitentiary at Jefferson City. Governor Gardner seemed to feel quite sure that such a survey would be of great social value. He called in his private secretary, discussed the matter with him at length, and then gave his unqualified promise that he would arrange that the prison officials should not only give me permission to make the survey, but that I should have every co-operation needful.

I then visited the University of Missouri at Columbia, and found that the department of psychology and the medical school would be willing to make the psychological and medical examinations, and were keenly anxious that a case study in criminology should be made.

I also visited Governor Lynn J. Frazier of North Dakota, the state in which my presumed offense was said to have been committed, the University of North Dakota at Grand Forks, and the warden and physician of the state penitentiary at Bismarck.

The North Dakota officials were eager to arrange with the Department of Justice for my incarceration in the penitentiary at Bismarck. They were deeply interested in the data the survey might make available and offered every opportunity for the work to be done, as well as the services of certain convicts capable of doing clerical work.

Before entering the prison at Jefferson City I had prepared myself for the work on the case book. The schedules had been printed and I expected to undertake the work which Governor Gardner had promised that I should be permitted to do. But the prison officials were of another mind. I was strong and in good health and capable of doing more than the ordinary amount of work in the prison workshop, so I was told that I was there to work and not to make a prison survey. However, my husband was permitted to bring me a bundle of the schedule blanks and I made the survey "under cover" during recreation hours. I managed to get the case histories of about two hundred women. I not only had no difficulty in getting the information I desired, but the prisoners felt slighted if I failed to ask them for the data. When Mr. Fishman, the U. S. Inspector of federal prisons, visited me in Jefferson City I gave him the above facts, and made a formal request to be transferred to the penitentiary at Bismarck, North Dakota. I thought that this work might be of greater social value than making overalls in the prison workshop, but the Department of Justice refused to make the transfer.

When I was released I was permitted to take out my library of several hundred books which had been sent me by friends, as well as paintings, gifts and other personal belongings, except my bundle of case histories. This had been taken to the matron's office by a trusty with my other property, but when I looked for it to pack with my books I found that it was missing, and I was told that it had been destroyed. I feel that this action on the part of the prison officials at Jefferson City was anti-social. Such data as I had secured would certainly have been of some value in the study of delinquent psychology. Because of the months I had given to the work, and the eager co-operation of the prisoners, the work constituted an exhaustive survey. Because I was a convict I secured information inaccessible to the ordinary research worker. In destroying the case studies the prison officials robbed themselves of what might have been of value to them, and deprived scientists of the opportunity of considering the fruits of my original researches. . . .

Recommendations

I recognize the fact that crime and prison systems have their causes deeply laid in the economic conditions of modern society and that prisons are merely the cesspools of our mal-adjusted social system. I believe that crime will not be considerably lessened until the economic struggle for existence is mitigated and the living conditions of the masses cease to breed human abnormalities. I believe that the ultimate goal must be, not the reformation of prisons, but the reconstruction of our whole system of dealing with unfit members of society; I realize that the prison as we know it today must go with all of its stupidities, crudities and cruelties, and that the reformative institutions of the future must be hospitals where trained physicians and psychologists, sympathetic and kindly nurses, cultured and understanding teachers shall deal with subnormals, not as criminals to be punished, but as unfortunate children upon whose helpless heads have fallen the "sins of the fathers." I understand quite well that "prison reform" is but a palliative, a sort of narcotic to ease the pain of unbearable social ills, but I also understand that there are conditions under which palliatives and narcotics must be made use of until time and progress have had an opportunity to work a cure.

There are certain things that can be done during this transition period of social progress that will make prison life less degenerating and pave the way for really sane and rational handling of the vexing problem of social delinquents. To narrow the question down to the Missouri State Penitentiary and the care of female federal prisoners there are certain recommendations I make in the light of my fourteen months actual prison experience.

"Recommendations" comes from "In Prison," O'Hare's report, which was first published as a booklet in St. Louis by Frank P. O'Hare, in 1920, pp. 62–63.

Build Model Female Reformatory

The federal government should immediately build and equip an institution of its own for the care of its female prisoners to be a model for the many state institutions. To peddle the women out to any prison authorities willing to accept them for the niggardly sum of eighteen dollars per month is a disgraceful proceeding. None of the better and more humane penal institutions will receive female federal prisoners and the institutions that do receive them seem to be the least desirable. The Superintendent of Prisons of the Department of Justice cannot control the conditions surrounding the female prisoners when peddled out to the lowest bidder among the state penitentiaries, and while he is morally and legally responsible, cannot protect them from the most terrible abuses.

There are never more than a few hundred of these federal women, two hundred perhaps being the limit. For the most part they are women convicted under the "Harrison Drug Act," and are not really criminals, but drug addicts, and should be cared for in a hospital under trained physicians and employed so far as possible in healthful, outdoor work. This federal hospital for delinquent women should be separate from the prisons for men, or at least far enough distant to avoid the constant friction caused by the perfectly normal desire of the men and women to communicate. It should be a large farm where complete segregation of the diseased from the normal can be secured. It might be placed near some great universities where specialized work in abnormal psychology is being carried on, and the prison could furnish clinical cases for intensive study by those who are giving their lives to the investigation of these problems. If this federal hospital for female delinquents is placed near enough to a high-class university for the civilizing influences of knowledge and culture to reach it; if only the doors are opened to scientific study and research, I feel sure that prison abuses will tend to disappear, and that the whole problem of the care of delinquents will receive much needed attention and be nearer solution.

Useful labor under healthful conditions should be provided for the inmates suitable to their capacities and the women should be paid for this work at current wages less a deduction for their subsistance.

PART V

Postprison Writings

Smoldering Fires of Unrest

Since June 1st I have followed the long trail that has led to the Pacific Coast and back twice. I have crossed the western half of the United States four times—once near the northern border, once near the southern border and twice through the central section. I have talked to farmers and stock ranchers, fruit raisers and cotton producers, lumberjacks and miners, city wage workers and college students, business men and professional men in every state west of the Mississippi River. Everywhere I have found the same disillusionment, bitterness and despair. Never have I seen the soul of mankind so harried and distressed, never have the smoldering fires of social unrest been so apparent.

Through the wheat producing regions of the Northwest restricted credits and low-priced wheat have brought even the most substantial farmers to the verge of bankruptcy, and the same restricted credits and low prices have ruined the stock and wool raisers. The Federal Reserve Bank drained every possible dollar of money out of the West and locked it in the vaults of Wall Street bankers who glutted themselves with the bloody profits of war, are now gorging on the profits that can be made by buying up the depreciated Liberty Bonds and other non-taxable securities and wrecking the whole system of agriculture by cutting off the necessary credits that are the very life-blood of the capitalist system of farm production.

"Smoldering Fires of Unrest" was first published in *National Rip-Saw* (September, 1921), 1–2.

The great lumber interests which profiteered so successfully and so criminally during the war that they can now shut down practically all operations and starve the lumberjacks at their pleasure. The same thing is true of the mining interests and unemployment in these industries is appalling. The thievish freight rates that the railroads have been permitted to levy on industry have made it impossible for the fruit and truck farmers of the Pacific Coast to ship their products, and I have never seen such wicked and wanton waste of food as is now rotting on the ground in the most fertile and highly developed country in the United States. And while freight rates and passenger rates soared skyward, the wages of the railroad workers have been cut to the bone.

In all the twenty years I have been upon the platform I have never seen such universally successful meetings; never have the crowds been so large, never the types of people so varied and never the interest so intense. Every meeting has been a surprise to the people handling it. The crowds have been far beyond the wildest hopes of the groups handling the meetings, and in spite of the hard times and unemployment, every committee has been astounded to find that the income had more than paid the expenses. The intense misery and unrest which is so universal makes people hungry for some message of hope, some glimmer of light on the dangerous path they are traveling.

All of these conditions made my western trips intensely interesting, and heart breakingly tragic, lighted now and then with the gleams of hope and flashes of humor. My daughter, Kathleen, followed the long trail with me and no doubt learned more of real life than any college or university will teach. North Dakota is as hard hit industrially, as bankrupt as any state we visited, but it is the one bright spot on the trail, the one place where hope still lived. And this is because in North Dakota the people are not sitting down and waiting in their disillusionment and despair, but they are standing up like men and making the most inspiring fight for their lives. At Bowman, North Dakota, Kathleen met for the first time the real West, the fast disappearing remnant of the West that I knew as a girl; and I found how many friends I had in the very town where, in 1917, it was charged that I had "insulted" the mothers of this country by using vile and vulgar language. If I ever said anything to insult the mothers of Bowman they must have liked it, for they were out in full force to greet me and to listen to the message that I had to give. And if I had "insulted" the ex-service men of Bowman they must have enjoyed being "insulted" for they were there by hundreds to be "insulted" again and they expressed their resentment to me by making me dance until my feet were blistered and feeding me ice cream and soda pop until I felt like a walking soda fountain.

At Cole Harbor, North Dakota, which is not even a speck on the map, the meeting was held in a farmer's barnyard, and when a sudden shower came the women climbed up in a great haymow, and men stood outside in the rain and I perched in the hay door and talked both ways at once. At Williston, North Dakota, the American Legion had decided that I should "not be permitted to pollute the public mind," and forbade the meeting. But J. I. Todd owned a farm three miles from town and did not mind being "polluted," so we held the meeting in his grove and about two thousand farmers and their wives, who were not afraid of "pollution" attended. After I had finished my lecture they decided that it would be a shame for the town of Williston to miss it. At five o'clock they decided to go to town for a meeting that night. The Legionaires said that it would not be permitted, but the sheriff of the county, who is a Non-Partisan Leaguer, picked out about a hundred of the biggest, huskiest farmers he could find and announced that he was going to deputize them to enforce the law—and well; the Legionaires changed their minds about the danger of "pollution" and five thousand people jammed Main Street and fairly wallowed in "pollution" for almost three hours. At Kenmare, North Dakota, we again held our meeting in a farmer's barnyard and somehow as I watched the thousands of tillers of the soil who had been driven from the churches of the town to meet on that Lord's Day evening in a barnyard, I thought of Jesus who preached to the camel drivers in the stable yards of Judea.

At Plentywood, Montana, Charley Westphal was on the job. The dust-covered "Lizzies" began to rattle in from the far outlying reaches the night before the meeting and the baseball park was the only place big enough to hold the crowd of five thousand people when the time came to open the meeting. At Wolf Point, Montana, the meeting was handled by the railroad men, and at Burke, Idaho, by the Miners' Union. At Seattle the meeting was handled by old-time Socialists and I spoke to a great crowd from a ring where prize fights are staged. At Portland my meeting was handled by the I. W. W. Defense Committee and it was one of the best organized and most systematically handled meetings I have ever addressed. At Salem, Oregon, I spoke in the State Armory and my

meeting was handled by professional men who were interested in criminology from a purely scientific standpoint. At Vale, Oregon, the audience
was of farmers. The meeting was handled by a civil engineer and a doctor. . . .

Then came Twin Falls, Idaho, and the kidnapping; and of this there
is one little story that has not been told. When the ranchers and farmers
and cowboys drove in to Twin Falls for the meeting the night of July 1
and found that I had been kidnapped and that the county and city officials, seemingly as guilty as the thugs, had flatly refused to do anything
that their oath of office made it their duty to do; when they realized that
everything indicated that I had been handed over to the tender mercies
of a mob of thugs by the connivance of elected officials, who had refused
to make any effort to protect my life and person, the ugly spirit of the
mob was bred. As night came the streets of Twin Falls were filled with
angry groups of men needing only a leader to break into violence. They
said that if mobs were to rule the city, and if violence was to be the order
of the day, that they would take a hand in the mobbing and give the
guilty officials a taste of violence. Then Kathleen, who knew nothing of
my fate, whether I was still alive or had been murdered, went out on the
streets and appealed to every group of angry men to keep the peace and
not add crime to crime or violence to violence. She begged the people
to be calm and patient, and urged that the laws of the country were
sufficient to deal with the criminals. She pointed out that even if some
officials were corrupt, we still had faith that justice would be done. And
because the girl was wise and poised beyond her fourteen years, the only
crime committed in Twin Falls was by the catspaws of Big Business. Our
next date was Pocatello, Idaho. The train left Twin Falls at 5 o'clock in
the morning. At this time no word had come back from me, and no one
knew whether I was alive or dead. But Kathleen took this train, traveled
to Pocatello and wired the committee in charge to go on with the meeting, that she had the manuscript of my lecture and would read it to the
audience.

The rough handling I received from the mob, the shock and exposure
of the wild night ride over mountain and desert trails, the excitement of
my escape and all that goes with soul scars that comes from having vicious men lay profane hands upon your person were too much for even
my iron constitution and we were forced to cancel remaining meetings
on the trip and come in home for the rest from Pocatello.

To the Coast Again

One month later I was sufficiently recovered to take the trail again. I spoke at Elk City, Oklahoma, to a sweltering mass of farmers packed like cattle in an old barn because the business men who lived on these same farmers would not permit them to use the city park. At Enid the parasites were not powerful enough to keep the thousands of farmers and wage workers out of the Court House Park and we held a wonderful meeting in the shadow of the "temple of justice." At Seymour, Texas, two or three old warhorses of the Socialist movement handled the meeting. Train schedules made it necessary for me to speak at ten o'clock Sunday morning, but the farmers were there in full force and thronged the Court House Square. After the meeting a young man who said he was a Democrat, an ex-service man and a member of the American Legion handed me five dollars and said he wanted it used in the prosecution fund to put the Twin Falls kidnappers behind the bars. He said he could ill-afford this donation, but that unless the American Legion disciplined its lawless members, the Legion as a whole was as guilty as they. . . .

At Tucson, Arizona, my meeting was managed by the World War Veterans,[1] ably assisted by a University student and the editor of an A. F. of L. newspaper. At Phoenix, Arizona, the World War Veterans were again in charge and the people packed the huge auditorium of the High School. My chairman was a Baptist preacher and a group of young girls were such efficient collectors that the committee almost dropped dead when they found that the collection had covered all expenses and left a comfortable surplus. The soldier boys had feared that they could not raise the expenses of the meeting and only decided to make a try for it two days before the meeting was held, yet on two days notice and a hat collection they met all expenses and had some surplus.

At Anaheim, California, one lone buck private in the *Rip-Saw* Army decided that he wanted a meeting there. And he had it. He packed the High School Auditorium, inveigled a Christian preacher into acting as chairman and extracted a collection that more than paid the expenses of the meeting. Some buck private!

At Los Angeles the meeting was held under the management of the Socialist local. The largest available hall was packed long before meeting

1. The World War Veterans was an organization founded in 1919 to aid veterans in securing adequate employment.

time at fifty cents per person. A collection of $194 was secured to help defray the debt of the National Socialist office, and in addition to this local, Los Angeles made about $300 to apply on its local activities.

At Fresno, California, two young girls who pack raisins in a local fruit warehouse were in charge. The meeting was held in the city park and five thousand people attended. Surely that was some stunt for two modest little raisin packers of the female persuasion to pull off. . . .

At Oakland, California, the Chief of Police decided at the last moment that I was "not a fit person to address an audience in Oakland," and the meeting was postponed until the Chief of Police can be shown the error of his way. At San Francisco a splendid meeting was held which not only paid for itself but helped to defray the debt on the Oakland *World*. . . .

The next stop was Wells, Nevada, to confer with the local attorneys who are handling the prosecution of the kidnappers. These dashes------- are the things I say, but can't write, when I think of all the things that I am aching to tell you of that conference. But the attorneys have emphatically forbidden any discussion of our plans for the prosecution until those plans are all perfected. I have a lump on my jaw that looks like the mumps from gritting my teeth every time I remember that I have been forbidden to talk about the case.

Montello, Nevada, is a real bit of the old West inhabited by the genuine type of he-man that I knew as a young girl. There are the railroad men with the hard-boiled shell that covers the warmest hearts and the most loyal friendships that ever made friendship a holy thing. And there are the bowlegged cowboys squatting on the stools in the restaurant, and the restaurant keeper and the lanky sheriff who seems to have stepped from the pages of one of Brete Harte's novels. I stopped off in Montello to round up witnesses and try to pay back the money the boys gave me when I reached Montello at 2 a.m., July 2, after making my escape from the kidnappers, bruised and sore, cold and hungry. And in all the golden memories of life that has been blessed by comradeship and loyal friendship there are none more beautiful than my reception on my return to the little town of Montello. I was the guest of the restaurant man's lovely young wife. I perched on the wobbly stool at the lunch counter with the bowlegged cowboys and the hard-boiled railroad men and consumed the sort of steak you often dream of but seldom meet. In the evening I spoke in the town hall which is slightly larger than a city hall bedroom and the entire population turned out. It was not much of a crowd for quantity, but I want to state most emphatically that it was QUALITY all right. And when one of the hard-boiled gentlemen with a stern and glittering eye put his big sombrero under a man's nose he gravely dug up a silver dollar and tossed it in. I held my breath in awe wondering what would happen if any man failed to dig up the dollar, but none did and I had no opportunity to see the glittering-eyed gentlemen in action. I am sorry for all of you who don't know the real West and the wonderful men and women it breeds.

About a year ago the people of Grand Island, Nebraska, got sick, tired and disgusted with dirty, petty politicians so they elected a big switchman who had climbed to the job of yard master to be mayor. Mayor Elsberry has tamed the Commercial Club and impressed the Legion with the fact that he is mayor and we had a wonderful meeting in the High School Auditorium. At Sioux Falls, South Dakota, an old veteran in the *Rip-Saw* Army handled the meeting, and everyone was astonished at its success. At Fort Dodge, Iowa, the railroad men managed the meeting which was held in the city park. Some threats had been made that I would be roughly handled, but about twenty big, husky switchmen parked right near the stand and nothing happened.

My last meeting was at Des Moines, Iowa, the scene of many outrages against constitutional rights and human decency recently, but a great crowd gathered in Library Park and I talked to them for three solid hours and everything was serene and peaceful as a summer day.

The whole *Rip-Saw* family, including the pup, has just arrived in St. Louis. I must hunt a house and get the family settled. Frank is frantically hunting office quarters and trying to get the machinery of the *Rip-Saw* buzzing once more. If your September magazine is just a little late, just remember the sign that hung above the piano in a western mining camp, "Don't shoot player, he's doin' the best he kin."

The Children's Crusade

Inasmuch as ye have done it unto the least of these my children, ye have done it unto me."

"The Children's Crusade" was first published in *National Rip-Saw* (April–May, 1922), 3–4.

Like the refrain from some great masterpiece these words of the Nazarene have been the marching song of the Children's Crusade. Sometimes they were soft and sweet as a cradle song as when some great
mother heart gathered a weary, travel-worn child in her arms and
soothed the weariness and kissed away the tears. Sometimes they rang
like a mighty battle song when great men, strong men, powerful men
thundered their denunciation of the conditions that had made the Crusade necessary. Sometimes they were weighted with prophecy when politicians turned deaf ears to the pleas of the children—when the door of
the White House was closed to them. But these words have been burned
into the hearts and souls of the American people. They are today the acid
test of real manhood, womanhood, citizenship and statesmanship.

Three months ago the cry of the children for justice for their fathers,
for life for their mothers and for succor for themselves, went out to the
highways and byways of the United States. And the cry of the children
reached answering hearts in many places, the big, loving, sympathetic
hearts that are always attuned to the sorrows and the wrongs of humanity.
Nickels and dimes and dollars came flowing into the Crusade Fund until
there was enough to gather up the wives and children of many of the
political prisoners at St. Louis and start the Children's Crusade towards
Washington.

Unfortunately all the wives and all the children of the political prisoners could not come. Some were too ill to travel, some too heartsick
and discouraged to make the effort and some so far away on the Pacific
Coast that the cost seemed too great.

But on April 17, 1922, the Children's Crusade for Amnesty left St.
Louis for the long, long trip to Washington to seek the holy grail of justice
at the hands of President Harding. The very heavens wept at the spec-
tacle and the children plodded wearily through rain, too inured to hardships and too intent on their mission to be disturbed by physical discomfort. At the Union Station the children found that first response to the
words of the Nazarene, and strange to say that response came from the
least expected source—the Big Four Railroad. At the station they found
that a great, powerful corporation had heard and responded to their cry
for justice and had placed at their service every resource of its great
railway system. A railway official was on hand to bid them Godspeed and
to see that every facility for comfortable travel was at hand. No mother
could have cared for her child more carefully and more faithfully than

the great railway system cared for the Crusade, and this care and priceless service continued over the New York Central Lines and the Pennsylvania System until Washington was reached.

Like the disciples of old, the Crusaders started out without money in their purse or script in their wallet, and like them, they were welcomed and fed and lodged and provided with means to travel.

Terre Haute

The first stop of the crusade was at Terre Haute for the blessing of Gene Debs. All knew how worn and ill Gene Debs is, and only hoped to march past his home and receive his blessing. But when the train pulled into the station Gene was there waiting with his great arms outstretched to gather every child to his heart and his great heart ready to embrace them all. In its own way the meeting of Gene Debs and the Children's Crusade was as sublime and wonderful an occasion as Debs' homecoming. Doctor Madge Stevens and a loyal committee had provided cars to carry the children to the Central Trades and Labor Hall where a bounteous dinner was waiting. As the Crusaders sat at the long tables, spread with such loving care, served with such tender love, and listened to the words of love and benediction from Gene Debs, I felt that we were back in that upper chamber breaking bread with the Carpenter of Nazareth. That evening the friends and comrades gathered to meet the Crusaders and Gene Debs spoke the first address he has attempted to deliver since his release. No one dreamed that Debs could come, no one thought his strength would be sufficient, and so no stenographer was present to give the world that speech. Perhaps it was too sweet and intimate and holy to reproduce in cold type, but whether this is true or not, the greatest speech Gene Debs ever made was to this little band of Crusaders.

Indianapolis

From Terre Haute the Crusade went to Indianapolis and there the blight of the American Legion upon the soul of the city was set forth with ghastly vividness. No Socialist, radical, or liberal came forward to greet the children. The city officials would not permit the children to walk through the streets with their banners, unless they carried them upside down. No street meeting could be held, and the city officials forbade the children to even distribute handbills telling of their mission. There was not quite sufficient money in the treasury to pay the hotel expenses so

Dorothy Clark and Mrs. Reeder went out and found a trade union in session and the members gave all they had, which was enough to pay the balance of the hotel bill.

Chicago

In Chicago Jane Addams and Mr. Mathes of the Church Federation and Professor Lovett[2] of the University of Chicago, and many other friends of like character, had arranged a beautiful meeting in a Methodist Church as a send-off for the Chicago contingent of the Crusade. The President of the Church Federation presided. University professors and clergymen and famous women took part in the program and money enough to meet Chicago's quota of the expenses was contributed.

Dayton

In Dayton, Ohio, all the old Socialists and many new friends had joined to give the Crusaders a welcome that would wipe away the shame and bitterness of the experience at Indianapolis. The Crusaders were fed and sheltered and made welcome and sent on their way with money enough to carry them to Cincinnati. To the little Crusaders and their mothers, Dayton, Ohio, will always be a sweet memory of love and welcome and sacred comradeship.

Cincinnati

At Cincinnati Mrs. Mary D. Brite had secured the co-operation of fifteen different organizations to arrange the welcome to the Crusade, and these organizations ranged from conservative women's clubs to Communists and I. W. W.'s. They were taken from the station to the People's Church, of which Herbert Bigelow is pastor, and had another of those banquets spread by the loving hands of friends and comrades. Homes and hearts were opened everywhere and the little band of Crusaders was scattered among some of the most aristocratic as well as the humble homes of the working class. The mass meeting in the evening was one of the most successful of the trip, and once again ample funds were contributed to carry the Crusade on its way. The Crusade decided that Mrs. Brite had done such magnificent work in arranging the Cincinnati meeting that she

2. Robert M. Lovett was renowned as a civil libertarian.

was conscripted and sent on ahead to act as advance agent, and she is still with the Crusade in Washington.

Toledo

At Toledo, Ohio, Millard Price and his wife and a splendid group of comrades were waiting to welcome the Crusaders. A big red bus waited at the station, and they were carried to the Machinists' Union Hall where a hot supper was served. Again the homes of rich and poor were opened and the weary Crusaders rested from their journey.

Detroit

At Detroit, Agnes Inglis[3] was in charge of the reception for the Crusade, and it was beautifully done, as is everything Agnes Inglis does. They were taken to the Auto Workers' Hall where the Finnish women comrades gave them a hot dinner and a group of Roumanian children came to sing for them. A mass meeting in the Auto Workers' Hall again furnished money to carry the Crusade to the next town. For supper they were taken to the House of the Masses and the Finnish women comrades spread a bounteous feast and provided a lunch for the next day.

Cleveland

Cleveland was the next stop and Reverend David R. Williams was in charge of arrangements. As the little Crusaders toiled wearily out of the grimey old station the whole thing seemed like a fantastic dream. For awaiting them were the luxurious limousines of the richest business men, the most famous editors and the most illustrious writers and clergymen of that city. So many of Cleveland's most famous citizens were clamoring for the privilege of having a Crusader for a guest that it seemed they might have to be disappointed, so they were taken to the Hollenden, one of the best hotels in Cleveland, where every luxury that modern hotels can supply was at their disposal. The mass meeting was held in the largest church in Cleveland, Trinity Congregational, where the pastor had given up his regular Sunday evening services for the Crusaders. Two thousand people were jammed into the great church and almost as many were outside who were never able to squeeze in. Fifteen promi-

---

3. Agnes Inglis was one of Emma Goldman's most steadfast loyalists, and she later preserved some of the Goldman papers in archives at the University of Michigan.

nent clergymen, writers, editors and business men made three minute speeches each demanding the release of political prisoners. . . .

New York

Mary Heaton Vorse has written of the New York reception so beautifully that I need say little more. Elizabeth Gurley Flynn was in charge of arrangements and they were perfect in every way. One interesting incident of the New York visit was the reception given by Mrs. Willard Straight[4] in her beautiful Fifth Avenue mansion to the women and children of the cotton fields and factory towns. As is always the case, the contributions in New York were very generous.

Philadelphia

In Philadelphia Mary Winsor was in charge of arrangements. The Crusade was met at the station by a committee of women from some of the oldest and most famous families of the City of Brotherly Love, and a city of brotherly love it proved to be to the Crusaders. They were taken to the San Souci Hotel for lunch, then autos were provided and the Crusaders spent the afternoon sightseeing. They visited the famous buildings and saw the Liberty Bell. Little Elbertine Reeder gazed at it a long time and finally said, "The Liberty Bell is cracked. I wonder if that is why our fathers are in prison? Do you think liberty got cracked when the bell busted?" There was a splendid mass meeting in the Labor Temple and one of the best collections on the trip.

Baltimore

Baltimore was the last stop and here the reception was managed by Elizabeth Gilman, the daughter of Dr. Daniel Coit Gilman, the great founder of Johns Hopkins University. Automobiles carried the Crusaders to the Y.W.C.A. for lunch, then on a wonderful sightseeing trip which ended at the grave of Edgar Allen Poe, where little Ivan Chaplin, the son of Ralph Chaplin,[5] placed red roses on the grave of the great poet in the name of the Children's Crusade. Instead of the usual mass meeting, there was a wonderful dinner. About two hundred people of the finest,

4. Dorothy Whitney Straight used her wealth to help her husband found the *New Republic*.

5. Ralph Chaplin, editor of the official IWW newspaper *Solidarity*, was among the IWW leaders convicted in a wartime espionage trial, which effectively destroyed the organization.

the oldest, and the most genuinely American families of that famous old city broke bread with the children. It was a love feast that will hallow the days of every person who shared it. A fund was started here to provide the families of the political prisoners means with which to reunite their families and rehabilitate their homes when they are released. The Crusaders spent the night with loving friends and started the next morning for the last lap of the long and wearisome journey, yet a journey so blessed and hallowed by love and comradeship.

Washington

Washington at last! The weary Crusaders stumbled out of the train, marched through the great beautiful union station and out to the plaza. Before them Washington in all its beauty of springtime was spread; the great white dome of the Capitol reared its head and beauty and grandeur was everywhere. Kind friends were waiting and the children, too intent upon their mission to heed the beauty or be inspired by the grandeur, resented for the first time the army of photographers and movie men who blocked their way with clicking cameras. For months they had dreamed of but one thing; they had but one inspiration to sustain them in the long weary trip; they were going to the President to ask for the release of their fathers and they resented anything that stopped them for even a moment. They had been told that he was a kindly man who loved children and wanted to do justice to all men; they felt that they had only to see the President, tell him the truth of their fathers' lives and acts and he would make things right for them.

Many men and women felt as the children did; they believed that Warren G. Harding was a kind man, a just man, and a man with the courage to do justice, so they hurried the children away to the White House. But when the children reached the Mecca of their dreams, the goal of their tragic pilgrimage, policemen barred their way; the President was too busy receiving Lady Astor and a circus freak to see them. The great man of whom they had dreamed would not receive them. The just man in whom they had placed their faith, the kindly man of whom they had heard, the man whom they had been told loved children, turned them away from the White House door with the message that they were free to play on the White House lawn.

But after the first soul-sickening disappointment the Crusaders wiped away their tears, closed their lips in heroic silence—and took up their banners and marched away. Kindly friends, shocked and disillusioned men, grimly determined women, rallied to the Crusaders with the holy spirit of love and common brotherhood. A home was provided at 938 New York Avenue, and individuals and organizations promised to assist with funds. The Children's Crusade has settled down to stay in Washington until the White House doors open to them and the prison doors open for their fathers.

THE CHILDREN'S CRUSADE WILL NOT DISBAND UNTIL THE CONSTITUTION OF THE UNITED STATES IS RESTORED TO THE PEOPLE—UNTIL THE POLITICAL PRISONERS ARE RESTORED TO THEIR WIVES AND CHILDREN.

The Cleveland Conference

So many and conflicting have been the reports given by delegates attending the Conference called by the Committee for Progressive Political Action which was held in Cleveland December 11–12–13, 1922,[6] that most persons who did not attend feel both confused and pessimistic.

There is really no grounds for either confusion or disappointment. The Conference was well worth while and marked an important milestone in the march of the American labor movement towards its ultimate goal. I attended the Conference and watched each move from the vantage point of the press table, and I came home neither confused nor pessimistic.

The outstanding fact of the Conference is that for the first time in the history of the labor movement a real cross section of America sat down together in a political labor conference and found that they were all "just folks." Every conceivable group of our population was represented from the wealthy and cultured liberal to the dirt farmer and the coal miner with the marks of the picks on his hands. Conservative unions, radical

"The Cleveland Conference" was first published in *American Vanguard* (January, 1923), 2.

6. This conference of labor and the Left represents the type of wide coalition that her prison writings anticipated after the Socialist party schism. Republican Senator Robert M. La Follette of Wisconsin had been the probable candidate of the Progressive party in 1912, but lost the nomination to Theodore Roosevelt. In 1924, La Follette would wear that mantle, as the Progressive party candidate. A party in name only, it was the offshoot of several conferences such as this Cleveland gathering.

unions, foreign-born workers and genuine hillbillies, breezy folk from the great Northwest and "crackers" from the Southeast, Socialists, pink and red, Farmer-Laborites and Non-partisan Leaguers, wobblies and Legionnaires, "highbrow" and "Lowbrow," they were all there.

Overshadowing all the lines that have divided the producers in the past was the realization that Wall Street had the whole nation by the throat and that the only way to break that strangle-hold was for the producers of the farms and the producers in the industries to get together and make common cause against the common foe. The delegates from the West and Middle West strutted pridefully because of their political victories and the Easterners were amazingly chastened and respectful. There was neither suspicion nor jealousy between the farmers and the industrial workers; they had found that they could work together during the last campaign and in the election, and they expected to go right on doing it. The "conservatives" were much impressed by the fact that the "radicals" were for the most part perfectly well fed intelligent people, and the "radicals" found the "conservatives" fair-minded and anxious to promote harmony. The value of such conferences in promoting understanding which must lead to solidarity is inestimable. When North meets South, and East meets West; when farmer meets industrial worker, and conservative meets radical; when from the far corners of our nation we meet and deliberate, plan and hope, then co-operate to make our dreams come true, we have accomplished much.

But the Cleveland Conference was not without its contest, not without the struggle that makes for real progress. All life is an eternal struggle between the old that is passing away and the young that is coming into power, and the Conference was a phase of that struggle. There were two distinct groups there, each fighting for power, and the end is not yet. The line of cleavage was not between farmer and industrial worker, liberal and radical, conservative and progressive unions, high brow and low brow, man and woman, Socialist and non-Socialist, Leaguer and Legionnaire. It was always between the rank and file of every organization and the "leaders" and "officials."

From the first moment of the Conference to the last, a veiled, and perhaps subconscious, but nevertheless relentless contest waged between the farmers who farm and the workers who work, and the paunchy, sleek, high salaried "labor leaders" and lame duck politicians who have fastened themselves upon the farmer-labor movement. On every point at issue the rank and file lined up on one side and the "officials" on the other. The rank and file wanted progress, real progress towards a very definite objective, and the "officials" wanted to move forward, but always in the same old vicious circle of Gomperism. The rank and file wanted action, and the leaders wanted action also—but not too much of it—not action that would endanger the sacred cow which is their political party.

In the Cleveland Conference was made quite clear the real object of the Committee for Progressive Political Action. It was not at all a dishonorable object, and no one has been willfully deceived or led astray by its founders. Back of the whole move is Robert La Follette, who has long nursed an ambition to be president of the United States, this is certainly a laudable ambition and La Follette would certainly be a great improvement on any president who has occupied the White House since Lincoln. There is no denial, so far as I could discover, that the railroad brotherhoods and other conservative unions launched the Committee for Progressive Political Action for the sole purpose of electing La Follette, on the Republican ticket, if possible, to the presidency in 1924. But of course to achieve this end the support of the whole working class is necessary, hence the hope inspiring appeal for "progressive political action." As a matter of fact I think a great mass of the working class, both farmers and wage workers, are perfectly willing to support La Follette, but the big question is whether they are willing to swallow the whole sickening mess called the Republican party, or whether they shall demand that he "come clean" by running on a straight labor party ticket. So since the day that the railroad brotherhoods brought the Committee for Progressive Political Action into being they have been compelled to wage a strenuous and losing fight to keep the child of their loins in hand. Progressive political action sounded so good, held so much of hope and inspiration for the masses that they have flocked to its standards regardless of the fact that the rank and file really had not been invited to the party.

Both the Chicago Conference held last February and the Cleveland Conference were very carefully hand-picked affairs. Everything possible was done to make them meetings composed of "leaders" committed to "safe and sane" policies, which of course meant nothing so radical as "progressive political action" sounded. Rather elaborate rules were laid down in the call for the Conference which should have excluded almost entirely the rank and file of the workers and made them perfectly respectable gatherings of "leaders," who would then transmit the sacred fire to the masses.

But the sentiment for real progressive political action; real genuine co-operation between the farmers and industrial workers is so strong that it swept over the barriers set up to harness it to the leaders' political ambitions. The rank and file ignored the fact that they had not been invited to the Conference, swept aside the rules formulated to deny them seats, and keen, clear-sighted and determined they almost kid-napped the child from its parents.

Naturally the real contest between the rank and file and the "leaders" was on the question of "independent political action," which is of course a less fearsome name for a labor party. On the direct vote on this question the conference stood 52 for and 64 against the immediate formation of a labor party. And this despite the fact that the delegates had been so care-fully hand-picked from officialdom and the seating of the rank and file made so difficult.

It is also quite possible that the vote for "independent political action" would have been larger, had it not been that many felt there was nothing to be gained by forcing the issue at that time.

The constitution adopted by the Conference makes it mandatory upon the executive committee to call state conferences in each state in the immediate future, and each state Conference is left perfectly free to adhere to Gomperism or organize an independent labor party. Many of the delegates who favored "independent political action" felt that these state Conferences provided means of taking the whole matter out of the hands of officialdom and putting it in the hands of the rank and file.

The real test of whether the producers are ready to break with the two old parties and build a political party of their own, was not settled at Cleveland, but will be determined at the state Conferences that will be held during the next six months. If the workers are really ripe for a labor party they will dominate these Conferences, and if they are not, no suc-cessful labor party could be launched.

Those of us who believe that a labor party must be formed have no quarrel with the men who brought the Committee for Progressive Politi-cal Action into being. They performed a valuable service in centering the minds of great sections of the working class on "progressive political ac-tion," and bringing together, whether they intended to do it or not, rep-resentatives of all sections of the producing classes who have found that

they can work in harmony. Ours is now the task of educating the sentiment for "progressive political action" into a real labor party and translat-
ing harmony of interest into definite action.

Our first advice to the farmers and workers is to get together immediately in each town and county and form local farm-labor blocs in order
to control their state conferences.

What Commonwealth College Means to the Workers

Commonwealth is a new adventure in working-class education, and before we can determine what it means to the workers we must have some
conception of the true meaning and purpose of education. . . .

The history of education in the United States has been very largely
the story of the efforts of the ruling classes to impose their ideals of culture upon the growing generation. Historians now admit that our free
school system, and our state-supported institutions of higher learning are
monuments to the tenacity, genius, and struggles of unknown and un-
honored trade unionists who waged the battle for free schools for more
than half a century. Free schools were won by the organized workers in
open warfare with the rich and cultured, as well as with the church and
the press. But the free schools are too powerful a force in shaping the
ideals of the coming generation to be overlooked by the ruling class, and
in the last quarter of a century our public school system has been seized
upon by the owning class and made a most effective machine to shape
the development of the coming generation in accordance with its ideals
of life. Tho the workers create all the wealth and provide the majority of
the pupils and teachers for the public schools, it is rare indeed that labor
has any representation on the school boards, or that labor's viewpoint is
fairly presented in the teaching. Under the domination of the ruling class
our public school system has developed into an efficient method of mold-
ing and shaping the growing generation to the ideals most useful to the
exploiters of labor.

Our privately-endowed institutions of higher learning are, for the
most part, things apart from the every-day life of the masses; they are
reserved for the use of the privileged classes. Unlike the public school

"What Commonwealth College Means to the Workers" was first published in *American
Vanguard* (October, 1923), 6–7.

system the history of privately-supported higher education in the United States does not touch the life of the common people; it has to do only with the landlord class and the church, the machine lord class and the gospel of profits. Harvard college, established in the early days of the colony of Massachusetts, was the first institution of higher learning, and it, like the other colleges later established in other colonies, was established, controlled, and utilized by the church to train men for the clergy. The founders of these early institutions of higher learning had no idea of bringing culture to the masses; their sole idea was to train men for the ministry of the church that it might dominate the social life of the people and teach them how to endure the misery of this life in such a way as to escape everlasting punishment in the next.

When this attitude of mind prevailed in the educational world, and when the institutions of higher learning were in the hands of the ecclesiastical caste, arts and sciences were "radical, revolutionary, and irreligious." Scientific educators were suspected of being "tainted" and were as undesirable as the "radical" in the modern college.

But as the hunger of the human race for knowledge cannot be suppressed by bans, nor satisfied with religious dogma, two warring factions were created to battle for supremacy in the world of education. The battle between Ecclesiasticism and secularism raged for more than a century. Other learned professions clamored for social standing and educational opportunities equal to those of the clergy. There was a wide-spread revolt against the narrowness of the field of higher education, and the educational radicals and revolutionists of that day demanded that the physical sciences be placed in our institutions of higher learning. Thousands of young men, largely from the rising middle class, who had neither the birth nor the breeding to make them welcome in the aristocratic colleges, rebelled at higher education being so completely monopolized by the very few, and the budding business magnates sympathized with them. They had great need for educated men to assist in developing and managing their rapidly expanding industries. Secularism finally triumphed.

In the battle that raged between the rising middle class and the decaying aristocracy, between secularism and ecclesiasticism, a new type of institution of higher learning was born. These new institutions were organized, endowed, and managed by groups of business men who sought schools where managerial forces might be trained, where their sons might be educated without being subjected to scorn because of their

lowly origin and vulgar occupations. The very name "college" had come
to stand for social snobbery and intellectual suppression, so the new
middle-class schools were called "academies" or "universities."

Many of the academies and universities founded by the middle class
as a protest against the exclusiveness and narrow culture of the old colleges grew like mushrooms. The United States was a new and wonderfully rich country where marvelous natural resources, a complaisant government, marvelous machinery, and unlimited emigrant labor to exploit
brought fabulous wealth to the new industrial capitalists. The laborer of
yesterday became the millionaire of to-day. Smarting under the scorn of
the aristocrat and the learned, and eager to buy culture for their children
as they bought other commodities in the market, with all their millions
the new-rich middle class could no more buy or conquer the old college
than a man can buy the soul of a woman who scorns him. There was
something in the very air and atmosphere of the college, something of
soul and spirit that the children of the new rich could not attain; with all
their wealth they were aliens and outsiders. So, in self-defense, to maintain their self-respect and to salve their wounded pride, the new-rich
middle class established schools of its own, based on the criterion of
wealth instead of the criterion of birth.

Capitalism grew like Jonah's gourd vine, and industrialism became
the mighty giant of our civilization. And it came to pass that neither the
old college nor the new hybred university sufficed to meet the needs of
on-rushing industry. The railroads that stretched over mountain and
plain, the mining shafts that burrowed into the bowels of the earth, the
steel mills that spat out rails and bars and beams, the chemical laboratories that solved nature's riddles, and the electrical shops that chained the
lightning—all had need of specialists, but not of truly cultured men. To
fill this need for trained specialists, who in the estimation of the industrial magnates, had no need for culture, the privately endowed technical
schools, state universities, and state colleges of agriculture and mechanical arts came into being. For more than half a century they have been
training young men and women to become efficient subservient instru-
ments of "big business," but they have not, and never can produce well-
rounded and truly cultured human beings with social consciousness.
There is but a shallow pretense which deceives no one, that they are
cultural institutions. They are a kind of educational department store

where courses in the management of economic resources and labor power may be purchased for the purposes of profit.

These great schools were founded by the industrial magnates that the physical sciences might have free and unhampered development, for business had need of physical science. As these middle-class schools grew in power and influence, science gradually became more respectable and, slowly, ethics, culture, social custom, law, and quite recently, religion, made it welcome. But science has a most annoying tendency to ignore proper bounds. The ungrateful scientists, whom the industrial magnates had fostered and made welcome in their scheme of education, refused to confine their studies to plants, animals, minerals, and natural forces, and insisted on making studies of human beings in their relations to each other. While the new-rich industrial overlords were busy building colleges and universities, the scientists were just as busy developing the new science of human relations. One morning the scandalized captains of industry awoke to find the disreputable urchin, social science, sitting on the front door step of the institution of higher learning, clamoring for admission. Uninvited urchins are never welcome in high society, and social science was repulsed with scorn. But social science is just as pushing and aggressive as physical science was a century ago, and a merry war is once more being waged in the world of education. A hundred years ago it was secularism against ecclesiasticism, and now it is socialism against secularism; but it is the same old war under a different name.

The development of social science holds out to the workers the same hope for the mastery of the means of life that the development of physical science held out to the capitalist class a century ago. Physical science promised, and kept that promise, to turn dirt into gold for the industrial masters, and social science promises to turn poverty, unrighteousness and war into social justice for the workers.

With faith in that promise the workers are demanding that higher education shall be placed within their reach. The workers are becoming restless under the knowledge that in all the history of education in the United States, they, the majority of all the people, have had so little part. They know that the old colleges were the property and the servants of the landed ruling class that has always dominated the church. The newer colleges and universities they know were created by the industrial magnates for the education of their children and intellectual servitors, and the endowed trade schools, state universities, and colleges of agriculture and mechanical arts to provide suitable managerial material for their industries and technicians and specialists to handle the problems of modern production, distribution, and financing. And the workers are beginning to awake to the shame of the fact that no institutions of higher learning have as yet been created by the workers to fit their children to secure more of the products of their labor and to enable them to have a broader life.

It is true that isolated members of the working class, both farmers and industrial workers, have managed to force their way into the educational preserves of the ruling classes. Even in the old colleges, with their ironbound castes, there have always been a few working men—men in whose souls burned so steadfastly the love of learning that they were willing to endure menial labor, social ostracism, and pitying scorn, that they might gather the crumbs of learning that fell from the tables of the rich. In most of the newer institutions some provisions have been made for young men and women to "work their way" through the college. It means, as a rule, that they must do menial labor, be shut out from the social activities of college life, and snatch their study hours as best they can. Many have been willing to endure the hardships and discomforts and pay this heavy price for education.

For several decades the children of the working class, in ever greater numbers, have trod that weary, heartbreaking, disaster-inviting path to higher education, that the new-rich industrial class trod a century ago, forcing their way into institutions foreign to them in the effort to secure culture. They find the icy walls of exclusion shut them out of the social life of the college, that no amount of intellect, character, or spiritual worth can break down the barriers, any more than money could break them down for the new-rich in the old colleges, and that the things they want are not there for them. The things they are offered are foreign to their lives and the culture they so ardently seek is not in harmony with their place in the social structure. The son of a locomotive engineer or a farmer goes to a college and is educated in the ideals of the capitalist class. When he graduates he has been educated away from his economic group and lacks the capital to enter the group that formed the educational ideals of his alma mater—he is intellectually and economically neither "flesh nor fowl," and the only place he is fitter to fill is that of "labor herder," or under-paid instructor in an institution of so-called higher learning.

But from the time the children of the working class began to invade the institutions of higher learning in any numbers, the social sciences began to take form. Naturally this brings about endless warfare between the ideals and culture of the ruling classes and the ideals of the workers struggling for expression. The educational institutions were the creations of the industrial masters, but some of the students and many of the instructors came from the producing classes. And these men and women have a psychology of their own. They inherit from their ancestors a deep reverence for learning, and their working class background gives them a sense of fellowship with all who serve—the desire to be of social value, and conviction that none should receive income without performing labor, and that to the useful workers rightfully belong the fruits of labor. Quite naturally, when instructors who spring from the soil begin teaching working class ethics and the working class students demand more of the same sort of teaching, the war of the classes rages in the educational institutions. On one side are vested interests and special privilege fighting to impose their ideals of culture on the growing generations, and on the other side the rapidly awakening working class fighting to shape the development of coming generations in accordance with its ideals of life.

And out of this struggle has been born Commonwealth College. Almost universally, and more or less clearly, the mass of the workers are beginning to realize that higher education makes possible the application of those laws of life which make for man's improvement a generally higher type of life. Since the university and the college, with the equipment which modern science provides, are able to produce a greater strength of body, mind, and character, thereby improving the common life and adding to its naturalness, efficiency and joy, the workers are now demanding that they shall not be shut out from them.

And profiting by the example of the new-rich middle class whose children never did, nor could, invade and capture the old college and who therefore built a new type of institution, Commonwealth College is established by the workers, for the workers, with a cultural ideal harmonious with productive life, as a new type of educational institution.

We, who have gathered here this autumn day to open this new type of institution of higher learning, are the sons and daughters of toil; the children of the farm and the industry; the common people who must feed, clothe, and shelter the race; the masses upon whose shoulders must ever rest the weight of civilization. Since the foundation of our country our working-class ancestors have been, very largely, shut out from the learning that might have lightened their burdens and the culture that adds beauty to life, breadth to mind, and power to live life more bountifully. To be a worker has, far too often, meant to be condemned to the life of a beast of burden, with a stunted mind, an uncouth personality and a dwarfed soul.

But we of Llano Colony[7] and Commonwealth College revolt against this state of affairs, and we have started to build our own cultural institution, one suited to the needs of the common people. We must tend the earth and make it give forth the things needful to mankind, but we refuse to longer permit useful labor to shut us out from the things that make life more efficient and more beautiful.

As our pioneer fathers and mothers went out into the wilderness to build a new civilization, we go forth, pioneers of a new culture. With the crudest of material equipment we must build slowly, build in the sweat of our own brows and in the labor of our own hands. We must blaze new trails of learning where no trails have led before; we shall choose the good in the old cultures and develop new elements to meet our needs.

We cannot use, and do not want, the selfish, white-handed culture of the old college that sought to divide mankind into two castes—decorated parasites and boorish, ignorant workers—the culture that has declared that the gentleman must never bear the marks of labor. We do not want the harsh, materialistic culture of the industrial magnates whose ideal is to produce highly-skilled technical servants and maintain a slavish, ignorant working class. We have no ambition to share the grotesque architecture, the garish display of wealth, the crude social snobbery, the department-store learning, and the jazztime activities of the middle-class college and university.

Commonwealth comes into being to build a culture in overalls and workmarked hands; a culture whose ideal is a working class fit to inherit and hold the earth and the fulness thereof. But because it is to be a working-class culture is no reason that it should be coarse and uncouth.

7. The Llano Colony was founded by Job Harriman, a socialist attorney, in California in 1914. Three years later it moved to Louisiana. In 1922 the O'Hares joined the cooperative venture, then in Arkansas, and for a while headquartered their periodical there and joined the faculty of Commonwealth College, an experiment in labor education.

Boorishness is not strength, and true refinement and gentleness are not weakness.

Harsh and materialistic as are the colleges and the universities of the industrial masters, they have performed a mighty service to mankind in the development of physical science, and all that they have brought forth we shall claim as our heritage. We shall take from the old college all that is fine and useful and beautiful and make it our own. We shall claim all the best of literature, music, art, and the thoughtful consideration for others that are the foundations and ornaments of manhood and womanhood.

On the firm foundation of physical science we shall erect our laboratories for the development of social sciences, the while making our lives rich in every-day association with all things that make life more abundant and more satisfying.

Commonwealth College means to the workers the opening of the long-locked doors of learning, the transforming of physical science from a greed-sodden master into a joyous fellow worker, a laboratory for working out the technique of co-operative life, and a crucible for refining the ore of common humanity into pure and precious metal.

Are We Headed Straight for Perdition?

One of the sad, sad tasks of ye editor is reading the plaints of the tearful who insist on weeping in our ear, to the extent of at least six pages written on both sides. And gloom beshrouded and direful are the tales they tell: "Then World War destroyed civilization, the Socialist Party is shot all to pieces, the A. F. of L. is a doddering senile old wreck, the Nonpartisan League has gone flooey, co-operation won't work, our colleges are 'goose-stepped,' and the churches are as empty of life as last year's bird-nest."

Yea, verily. O! weeper, it's all true too true—but so far as I can see weeping isn't going to help in the least. And before we find a hole and creep into it and then pull the hole in after us, let's sort of take stock of ourselves and the world and see just how much of the old wreck can be used in rebuilding our worldly habitation. For just as sure as fate the youth of the land is too blindly swayed by the age-old instinct to live and

"Are We Headed Straight for Perdition?" was first published in *American Vanguard* (November, 1923), 1.

reproduce to crawl into the hole with us. They won't take our word for it that life is not worth the struggle; they will insist on trying it out; they will go right on loving and marrying and bringing children into this world no matter how weepy we tired radicals may be. And since we tired middle-aged ones are responsible for all the young people being here, it is a mighty "sorry" attitude on our part to crawl into our holes and leave them to clean up all the mess we have made of life.

The World War did wreck civilization. There is not question about it. The world that was is gone, never to return. Old systems and old institutions are broken beyond repair by the weight the war placed on them, but what is left of the human race must go right on living notwithstanding.

And, after all, the civilization that was wrecked by the war was not so much to boast of; if it's the best the human race can do, we might be excused for looking for a hole to crawl into. It was a civilization based on force and exploitation; a civilization based on the rule by might by the few and the ruthless subjection and robbery of the masses; a civilization based on the glorification of war and ill-gotten wealth and the degradation and insecurity of human life. Its glories, its wealth, and its culture were distilled from the blood, the poverty, and the ignorance of the masses, and its best was scarred by man's inhumanity to man. The World War smashed this unrighteous civilization. It may be for the best. Now it behooves mankind to get busy and build another. And I have never known a weeper that was worth a hoot as a builder.

The Socialist Party, in the United States at least, is shot to pieces. The splendid thing it once was is no more, but sprinkling the ashes with tears is not going to rekindle it. And it is not the first great political movement that has gone the way of all flesh, when its work was done. The Abolition Party and the Greenback Party lived, and then died when their proper work was done. In my lifetime (and I am not so terribly old) I have seen two great working-class political movements rise, do their work, and crumble. I lived through the stirring days of the old Populist movement, in which my father and most of my male kin took part, and which possibly fixed my childish mind on social problems. I saw Populism rise to a nation-shaking power, saw it hated and feared by the predatory class and hailed as a star of hope by the producers. I saw it burn itself out into grey ashes. But in the burning it branded itself so deeply into our national psychology that the planks of its one-time radical platform have become commonplaces in our political thinking, and its soul lives in practically all of our progressive legislation.

I helped, a little, to build the Socialist Party. I saw it spring from the ashes of the Populist movement and gather strength and power until it swept over the land, a glorious flame of mental and spiritual illumination. I saw it shape the hunger of the human heart for a greater measure of social justice into concrete demands and burn them so deeply into our national psychology that its fundamental principles ceased to be the exclusive property of the Socialist Party and became the very basic things in our thought, the seed of a new culture. I saw the Socialist Party grow into a mighty movement, and the Socialist press become the most dynamic power in the country—and I have seen both fall into decay.

We should like to blame Burns,[8] Palmer, Burleson, Wilson, and war hysteria for the crumbling of the Socialist Party, but if we have the courage to face facts we know that it is the ghost of its former glory because it has served its proper purpose and, like all things mortal, must pass away. The Socialist Party was primarily an educational machine whose function was to fix certain principles in the minds of the American people, and in this it gloriously succeeded. The Socialist political machinery was built on the theory of the all-sufficiency of political action and political governments, and the World War proved that the real governing forces of the world are not political but industrial. The Socialist Party could not adjust itself to the changed conditions, and hence could not survive in an outgrown form.

Many who gave the best years of their lives in building the Socialist Party and press see nothing for their labor but a heap of grey ashes, hope faded, hearts grow weary—hence the weepers. But they are mistaken. If we read history intelligently, we know that the soul of a great movement never dies. From the embers of every human revolt have been kindled greater movements all down the road of human progress. Not one hour of labor nor one ounce of human energy that we gave to the Socialist movement has been lost. All the things to which we gave our faith and our labor are taking form again in numberless new movements which give them wider scope.

8. William John Burns (1861–1932) was the founder of the Burns Detective Agency, well known for its support for management during labor disputes. Burns was appointed director of the Bureau of Investigation (now the Federal Bureau of Investigation) in 1921 and served for three years.

The A. F. of L. may be a doddering, senile old wreck; Gomperism may be tottering into the grave; but the labor movement is not dead, nor dying. The new spirit of amalgamation and industrial unionism is traveling forward in seven-league boots, and the newer vision in organized labor, which for want of a better name, we call Fosterism,[9] is laying the foundations for a bigger and far more powerful labor movement.

The Nonpartisan League may have gone flooey, though I doubt it; and fake co-operatives may have failed, and fleeced the unwary; but the principles of industrial organization for the farmers, making possible the co-operative control of the markets by the producers is taking form in the Farm-Labor Union[10] in the South and the great producers' co-operatives in the Northwest. The Socialist Party may have passed off the stage as a great political factor, but the trend towards a Farmer-Labor political party gives promise of accomplishing all that can be done by political action.

Our colleges may be "goosestepped," but there is nothing to hinder us building some of our own. The churches may be barren and empty but the quickening spirit of the fellowship of all who serve still lives and manifests in many institutions more powerful and closer to the common soul than the churches decked out in the gawds of the master class.

I know just how sore are your hearts, O beloved weepers! My own is so bruised and torn that I must smile that I may not weep; but I also know that good honest-to-God work is the best cure I know for the bruised heart, and that mere idle repining is the most useless of indulgences. Why not try eliminating the weeps for a while and join the sturdy army of brave, strong, clear-visioned souls who are the embers from which the next great labor movement must be kindled? You may not think there are any left, but there are, and they are at work and their numbers are growing.

In the old pioneer days it was the duty of the housemother to tend the "seedfire" from which the household fires must be kindled. The army

9. William Z. Foster (1881–1961), an American communist, was known in the 1920s as a proponent of aggressive industrial unionism.

10. The Farm-Labor Union emerged in Texas in 1921 as a grass-roots farmers' organization with tenuous links to organized labor. Concerned essentially with cooperative marketing, it saw itself as a competitor to the more established Farm Bureau Federation. The Farm-Labor Union spread to Oklahoma, Arkansas, Louisiana, Alabama, and Mississippi, but after five years, declined.

that has faith in itself and in humanity is the mother of future progress and the workers and not the weepers will be the "seedfire" of the newly-forming labor movement. Then let's stop weeping and go to work. Sighs are mighty poor kindling wood. There are thousands of worth-while things waiting to be done. There are war wounds to heal, broken hearts to be strengthened, anchorless souls to be re-anchored, new standards of life to be formulated, new labor movements to be organized, and a new civilization to be built. Weeping will never do the jobs waiting to be done—work will; then let's stop weeping and go to work; let's stop wailing over the past and begin building for the future.

We Protest Stop or "Congressman's Nightmare"

It is not heat, humidity, Supreme Court cat and dog fight nor the pressing need for political fence fixing at home, that most harasses members of Congress at the moment. It's telegrams! The most unwelcome person on Capitol Hill is the Western Union boy. These modern birds of ill omen flit about hot corridors delivering their pesky yellow envelopes that are as welcome as a bouquet of poison ivy.

Sometimes they are addressed to the Congressmen, but most often they are copies of messages that have been sent to the President. Some are short, with words carefully counted to keep inside the minimum rate, and others are long, bitter and vituperative. They come from individuals, organizations and groups ranging all the way from powerful international labor unions to groups of women relief workers on a disbanded WPA sewing project. But long or short, hysterical or dignified, courteous or vituperative, this is the gist of them:

"Strongly protest dismissal of WPA workers stop these people have the right to live stop industry will not or cannot give them jobs stop we recognize their social value to education health recreation culture and welfare groups stop these dismissals lower living standards security and morale the whole American people stop we urge the immediate reinstatement of all WPA workers stop."

"We Protest Stop or 'Congressman's Nightmare'" was first published in *American Guardian*, July 23, 1937.

Bitter Cry of the People

What is the President or Congressman to do when harassed by telegrams like that? Poets, prophets and demagogues have long used the phrase, "the bitter cry of the people." Now Washington is the sounding board of that cry. The President's well-guarded sanctum and the Congressman's office are as near to every citizen as the nearest telegraph office, and the doors are open to anyone who can scrape together a few pieces of silver to pay the telegraph toll. Never before has the "bitter cry of the people" beat so relentlessly on the unprotected heads of democratic government, and never has a government been put to it to find an answer to that cry.

When the scarcity system, careening like a behemoth diesel truck out of control, crashed seven years ago, all the powers of government were turned to salvaging the wreck and attempting to get it started under its own power. The Federal Government, through the RFC, poured billions into wrecked corporations, bankrupt railroads and wobbly banks. Congress worked frantically at "priming the pump" of private industry by hectic financing, subsidies and purchases of vast quantities of commodities, often at fantastic prices. The government hoped that if it poured enough money into the pump that had lost its priming, private industry might right itself and reabsorb the millions of unemployed. This did not happen, then the government started the most colossal job of charity dispensing ever conceived by the mind of man; the SERA, the FERA, CWA, WPA, PWA, RA, AAA, and all urgently PDQ.

It was a spending debauch such as the world has never seen, but all directed towards turning civilization back to a system of scarcity which modern mass production methods had destroyed. For seven years Washington has drawn its inspirations from graveyards, worn its eyes in the back of its collective head, and progressed like a crab, traveling backwards.

The Tinkers Have Failed

Now the crab has bumped his tail against the rock of the inability of the government to borrow itself out of the depression and into prosperity, and Congress has the economy jitters.

The tinkers who have failed to mend the old wreck and make it go, are now yelling about the cost of the repair job. They who face their own failures have wept all over the halls of Congress until they are soppy with tears and gloom. Milling about like lost sheep they bleat, "Balance the budget, cut the cost of government, go back to the good old days, stop the charity racket, swat the Communists, no one must starve, but don't spend any money on relief." Sure! That all sounded noble and patriotic when the relief bill was up for action. So "swish swosh, hack! Do a good job while you are about it!" "Guess that will take care of the lousy bums who want the government to feed them." Relief appropriations were slashed to a billion and a half dollars, with millions still unemployed, and the primed pump still wheezing only hot air. Members of Congress sat back in air-conditioned legislative halls and licked their whiskers like cats who had raided the cream jar.

Congress on the Hot Spot

None of us are so naive as not to know that Federal relief reeks with inefficiency, pork and graft. There are many indications that it has made worthless, whining dole takers out of what were once self-respecting citizens, it may be the hang-out for all sorts of subversive influences, but it has been the last ditch for the scarcity system. When artificial scarcity denies men the opportunity to work and produce their own keep, there is nothing that can be done but for the government to step in and feed them.

When Congress slashed the relief appropriations, Harry Hopkins[11] went grimly to work slashing the rolls to fit the cash they had to spend. There was nothing else he could do. Now Congress is sitting on the hot spot. Telegraph boys are pests, yellow sheets of paper are danger signals, the "bitter cry of the people" has an ominous sound, and Congress sweats, more from fear than the famed Washington climate.

It requires no Roman augur with a rooster's gizzard to discern that in that relief appropriation cut, blind Samson may have pulled down the pillars, and the priests and vestal virgins may be buried under the wreckage. I am a kindly soul with a noble Christian spirit, I admit it, but if that is that, I don't see what we can do about it, except thank God we were not squashed. We might also move out of the wreckage and shadows of the past and forward into an economy of abundance that will permit each human being to "eat his bread in the sweat of his brow," and toss doles and relief clean out of our civilization.

11. Harry Hopkins (1890–1946) headed several New Deal agencies, including the Federal Emergency Relief Administration, the Civil Works Administration, and the Works Progress Administration. His earlier career had been in social work administration.

Index

Addams, Jane, 9, 103, 103n, 212n, 336
American Federation of Labor (AFL), 5, 72n, 263, 273, 331, 351, 354
American Legion, 264, 264n, 329, 331, 333, 335, 341
American Socialist, 19, 170n
American Vanguard, 29
Ameringer, Oscar, 13, 93, 93n
Amnesty, 22, 29, 224, 249, 273, 281, 300, 333–40
Anti-Saloon League, 84, 84n
Anti-Vice Crusade, 84, 84n
Antolina, Gabriella (Ella), 25, 208n, 219, 237, 253, 265, 266
Appeal to Reason, 1, 16, 19, 39, 39n, 51, 239, 303

Bakunin, Mikhail, 222, 222n
Baldwin, Roger, 226, 226n
Bebel, August, 11, 117
Bellamy, Edward, 39, 39n
Berger, Victor, 4, 5, 12, 13, 14, 15, 17, 21, 249n, 260, 270n
Berkman, Alexander, 247, 247n
Bertillon, 211, 211n
Billings, Warren K., 171n
Bisbee, 170, 170n
Blacks, 6, 12, 44–49, 50, 99, 247, 278–79, 288, 299, 317
Bloor, Ella Reeve, "Mother," 294, 294n
Bolshevism, 195, 197–98
Booth, Maud Billington, 234, 234n, 240
Bowman, North Dakota, 19, 20, 21, 125, 128, 171–73, 184, 189, 190, 192, 193, 194, 263, 269, 278, 292, 328
Branstetter, Otto, 269, 269n, 270, 292
Branstetter, Winnie E., 275, 275n
Brewer, Grace D., 10
Brotherhood of Timber Workers, 51, 51n
Bureau of Investigation, 353
Burleson, Albert S., 129, 129n, 353
Burns, John Williams, 353, 353n

Cable, George W., 29
Caesar's Column, 38, 291
Calumet, 70–78, 103, 104, 139
Cavell, Edith, 231, 231n
Censorship, 18–19, 129n, 182–183, 292n
Centralia affair, 260, 260n
Chaplin, Ralph, 338, 338n
Child labor, 7, 31, 52–56
Chasm, 277, 277n
Civil Works Administration, 356, 357n
Clark, John G., 30
Collins, Peter, 96, 96n, 125, 125n
Committee of Forty-Eight, 28, 249, 249n, 258, 295
Committee on Public Information, 18
Commonwealth College, 30, 344–51
Communist Labor party, 28
Communist Manifesto, 39
Communist party, 5, 22, 28, 270n, 272
Conference for Progressive Political Action, 249n, 340–44
Connolly, James, 89–90, 89n, 138
Contract labor, 23, 24–25, 207, 215–17, 220–21, 243–44, 252, 263, 265, 266, 283, 288, 295, 297, 314, 320–21. *See also* Prison system
Convict leasing, 60–62
Cook, George Cram, 277, 277n
Cook, Walter M., 296

Council of Defense, 197, 197n
Cunningham, Charles C., 30
Cunningham, Kate Richards O'Hare. *See*
  O'Hare, Kate Richards

Darrow, Clarence, 19, 292, 292n
Davy Bill. *See* Sedition legislation
Debs, Eugene V., 4, 13–14, 15, 16, 186,
  221, 292, 294, 294n, 296, 335; and
  prison, 14, 21, 26, 29, 197, 211, 235; as
  candidate, 94n, 270n, 295; mentioned,
  1, 94, 97, 224, 296n
Debs, Kate, 29
De Leon, Daniel, 11, 294n
Dial, 230, 230n
Donaghey, George W., 59, 59n, 60
Donnelly, Ignatius, 3, 38n
Duffy, Clinton T., 31

Eastman, Max, 195
Ellis, Havelock, 239
Encampments, 13, 14, 93, 145, 225n, 275
Engdahl, Louis, 269, 269n, 270, 274
Engels, Friedrich, 10–11
Espionage Act, 19, 20, 195, 196, 197n,
  199, 249n

Farm-Labor Union, 354, 354n
Farmer-Labor party, 28, 249n, 341
Farmer's Union, 51
Federal Emergency Relief Administration,
  356, 357n
Feminist, 9, 218
Fenian, 86, 87, 88
Fishman, Joseph F., 232–33, 242–43, 322
Flynn, Elizabeth Gurley, 1, 228n, 338
Foreman, Flora, 236, 249, 249n
Fosterism, 354
Foster, William Z., 354n
Franklin, H. Bruce, 26
Frank O'Hare's Bulletin, 299, 300, 302,
  303
Frazier, Lynn J., 273, 273n, 322
Freud, Sigmund, 27, 275, 301, 313

Gardner, Frederick D., 233, 320, 321, 322
Gardner, Mrs. Frederick D., 219
George, Henry, 3, 37n
Germer, Adolph, 15
Gilman, Charlotte Perkins, 11
Glennon, John J., 7, 112, 113
Goldman, Emma, 26–27, 207n, 219, 224,
  226, 234, 242, 268; related to O'Hare,
  25–26, 209, 221–22; mentioned, 1, 207,
  214, 237, 247, 264, 300, 337n

Goldstein, Davy, 125, 125n
Gomperism, 342, 343, 354
Gompers, Samuel, 5, 266, 266n
Graham Bill. *See* Sedition legislation

Hardie, Keir, 92, 92n, 93, 165
Harding, Warren G., 334, 339
Harriman, Job, 17, 30
Haywood, William D. (Big Bill), 21
Hicksite Quakers. *See* Quakers
Hildreth, Milton A., 184–85, 191–92, 264
Hillquit, Morris, 4, 12, 14, 17
Hoan, Daniel Webster, 300, 300n
Hoehn, G. A., 211, 211n
Hoover, Herbert, 167, 167n
Hopkins, Harry, 357, 357n
Huerta, Victoriano, 149, 149n
Huysmans, Camille, 92, 92n

Industrial Workers of the World (IWW), 1,
  5, 19, 171, 198, 218n, 232, 241, 260n,
  261, 262, 263, 272, 329, 336, 341
Inglis, Agnes, 337, 337n
Intercollegiate Socialist Society, 222
International Association of Machinists, 3,
  42
International Conference of Socialist
  Women, 10
International Socialist Bureau, 6, 16, 91–
  93, 93n, 144–45
International Socialist Congress, 16, 144
International Socialist Review, 19
International Union of Mine, Mill, and
  Smelter Workers, 72n
Irish Transport and General Workers'
  Union, 85n

James, anti-O'Hare witness, 184, 193, 263
Jaurès, Jean, 16, 91, 91n, 92n, 93, 128,
  143–46, 165
Jefferson City Prison. *See* Missouri State
  Penitentiary
Jesus, 7, 127, 129, 174, 196, 214, 216, 222,
  224, 225, 229, 282–83, 293–94, 329,
  334, 335
Jones, Mary Harris "Mother," 3, 13, 38,
  38n, 103

Kate O'Hare's Prison Letters, 27
Kate Richards O'Hare Committee of
  Brooklyn, 228, 228n, 247
Kautsky, Karl, 93, 93n
Kinney, Mike, 298, 298n
Kirby, John J., 61, 61n
Kirby Lumber Co., 51n

Kirchwey, G. W., 23
Kirkpatrick, George R., 14, 186
Kolchak, A. V., 266, 266n
Krafft-Ebing, Richard, 239
Krum, Chester Harding, 211, 211n, 223

Labor party, 249, 250, 272
La Follette, Robert M., 249n, 340n, 342
Lane, Winthrop D., 218, 218n
Larkin, James, 86–90, 86n
Larkin, Margaret, 86
Lathrop, Julia, 212, 212n
Lawrence, Mass., 104, 104n
League of Nations, 122, 280n
Lewis, Lena Morrow, 14
Liberator, 230
Liebknecht, Karl, 18, 128, 128n, 165
Lilienthal, Meta Stern, 94, 94n, 228n
Liquor question, 3, 36–37, 78–85, 174
Llano Co-operative Colony, 29–30, 350
Lloyd, Henry Demarest, 3, 38n
Lloyd, William Bross, 21
Lodge, Sir Oliver, 213
Lombroso, Cesare, 313, 313n, 314
London, Meyer, 94, 94n, 95
Long, R. A., 61, 61n, 149
Longuet, Jean, 92, 92n
Longuet, Paul, 145
Looking Backward, 39, 291
Lovell, V. R., 21, 187, 223, 269, 270, 273, 274
Lovett, Robert M., 336
Lowe, Caroline, 225, 225n
Ludlow, 104, 104n, 139, 149, 150
Lusitania, 138, 138n, 148, 149
Luxemburg, Rosa, 18, 93n, 128, 165

McCumber, Porter James, 121, 121n, 173
Malkiel, Theresa S., 8, 10, 94, 94n, 95, 210, 227, 228n, 247
Marx, Karl, 59, 222, 222n, 230, 239
Marxism, 10, 12, 18
Masses, 19
Milholland, Inez, 104, 104n
Mills, Walter Thomas, 4, 40, 40n, 117, 239, 256
Milwaukee Leader, 19, 219, 226, 231
Minimum Wage Commission, Missouri, 63, 64, 66
Minor, Robert, 112, 112n
Mirror, 211
Missouri Prison Board, 233
Missouri State Penitentiary, 10, 16, 21, 28, 183, 189, 194, 312, 315, 319, 320, 323

Molkenbuhr, Hermann, 91, 91n, 93
Mooney Case, 171
Mooney, Thomas J., 171n
Morgan, J. P., 149, 165
Morgan, Lewis Henry, 114, 114n, 116

Nation, 226, 230, 278
National Civil Liberties Bureau, 19, 226n, 292n
National Rip-Saw, 1, 7, 16, 51, 51n, 62, 70, 111, 113, 302, 303, 331, 333
Nearing, Scott, 215, 215n
New Deal, 30
Newman, Pauline, 286, 286n
New Penologists, 2, 23, 27
New Republic, 222, 222n, 226, 230, 230n
New York Call, 19, 210, 226, 230, 247, 295
Non-Partisan League, 19, 193, 249n, 273, 351, 354; achievements of, 28, 193n, 261; O'Hare hopes in, 248, 250, 341; mentioned, 20, 194, 198, 263, 272, 329

O'Hare children, 4n, 14–15, 16, 20, 189, 190, 200, 208, 220, 241, 289
O'Hare, Dick, 209, 210, 213, 214, 227, 236, 256, 260, 294, 295, 303
O'Hare, Eugene, 208–209, 227, 236, 290, 294, 303
O'Hare, Frank P., 4, 4n, 16, 21, 25, 26, 27, 29, 40, 51n, 189, 228n, 241, 265, 270, 294, 300, 303, 333
O'Hare, Kate Richards: early life of, 2–4, 35–44; and religion, 2, 7; and temperance work, 3, 36–37; and socialist conversion, 3–4; marriage of, 4; on lecture circuit, 4, 13–14, 18, 19, 29, 40, 93–97, 262–63, 300, 327–33; as International Secretary, 5, 15–16, 91–93, 144–45; as candidate, 14; and World War One, 2, 16–20, 109–110, 121, 126–43, 146–68, 198–99, trial of, 13, 20–21, 121–22, 170–80, 181–82, 183–94, 269, 273; and imprisonment, 1, 2, 13, 23–28, 178, 179, 205–299; and commutation, 28; and prison reform, 29, 30–31, 231, 233, 235–36, 301–302, 307–24; death of, 31
O'Hare, Kathleen, 29, 208, 209, 210, 227, 236, 260, 290, 294, 303, 328, 330
O'Hare, Victor, 208, 209, 227, 236, 290, 294, 303
Olson, Culbert L., 30, 171n
Osborne, Thomas Mott, 23, 25, 276, 276n
Oviereau, Louise, 26

.

Painter, William R., 208, 208n, 211, 223, 229, 233, 234, 237, 240, 244, 259, 272, 318–19
Palmer, A. Mitchell, 231, 231n, 248, 257, 260, 266, 273, 276, 289, 299, 353
Palmer Raids, 257
Peace Treaty (Versailles), 247–48, 247n, 280–81, 280n
Pearson's, 149n, 230
Phelan, James E., 121, 185, 192, 194, 260, 263
Plumb, Glenn E., 236, 237n
Plumb Plan, 236n
Political prisoners, 1, 25, 28–29, 206–207, 226, 233, 273–74, 277, 281, 286, 300, 318, 334, 338
Populist party, 57, 57n, 352, 353
Prager, Robert Paul, 245, 245n
Prison system, 23, 58–59, 60, 231, 233, 235–36, 240, 253, 276, 279, 283–84, 300. See also Contract labor
Progress and Poverty, 3, 37, 291
Progressives, 5, 9, 12, 30, 340n
Prostitution, 8, 36, 43, 63, 67, 68–69, 75, 81, 82, 109, 174, 229, 279, 316, 317
Public, 229

Quakers, 289, 290, 291–92, 291n

Railroad Brotherhoods, 236, 237n, 249n, 258, 342
Rebel, 51, 51n
Reedy's Mirror, 230n, 231
Reedy, William M., 230, 230n
Religion, 2, 36, 78–79, 81, 108–10, 124–26, 127–28, 152, 224–25
Remphfler, William, 270, 271, 274
Republic, 242, 244
Richards, Andrew, 3, 37, 41, 212n, 252, 256, 290
Robins, Margaret Dreier, 67, 67n
Rockefeller, John D., 115, 149, 150, 165
Roosevelt, Theodore, 42, 249n, 340n
Root, Elihu, 266, 266n
Ruler, Bessie, 99–103, 99n
Ruskin, 30
Russian Revolution, 21, 22

Sadler, Kate, 17, 210n
St. Louis Labor, 211
St. Louis Post-Dispatch, 218
Sanger, Margaret, 110–14
Schneiderman, Rose, 103, 103n
Schwab, Charles Michael, 165, 165n

Second International, 1, 6, 8, 15–16, 91n, 92n
Sedition legislation, 266, 267–68; Davy Bill, 273, 273n; Graham Bill, 267–68, 267n, 273
Shiplicoff, Abraham, 96
Simons, A. M., 17
Simons, May Wood, 10, 17
Sinclair, Upton, 30, 241
Single-Tax, 289, 290
Socialism, 8, 40, 44–49, 51–52, 55–58, 79, 83, 84–85, 91; and religion, 124–26, 127–28; state socialism, 139, 139n; and World War One, 121–43, 163–65, 167–68, 198–99, 247–48
Socialist Labor party, 11, 294n
Socialist party, 1, 4, 5, 8, 9, 11–13, 19, 28, 38, 59, 123, 177, 249n, 250, 269–75, 276, 293, 296, 351, 352, 353, 354; Suffrage Campaign Committee of, 9, 94–95, 227; Woman's National Committee of, 8, 9–10, 15, 225n; Emergency Convention of, 15, 17–18; National Executive Committee of, 15, 22, 269, 271, 272, 275, 295; schism of, 4, 16, 22, 28, 227, 228, 229–30, 238n, 245–46, 248, 340n; National Committee of, 144; and censorship, 168–70; Young People's Socialist League of, 210, 210n; National Office of, 221, 269, 270, 271, 272, 274, 275, 332; 1919 convention of, 238; 1920 convention of, 292, 295
Social Revolution, 17n, 18, 169–70, 183, 186
Solomon, U., 95, 95n
South, 2, 6, 44–49, 49–52
Stedman, Seymour, 270, 270n, 295, 296
Steimer, Molly, 25, 208n
Stern, Meta. See Lilienthal, Meta Stern
Stevens, Madge, 296, 296n, 335
Stokes, J. G. Phelps, 17, 197n
Stokes, Rose Pastor, 196, 196n, 230, 230n
Straight, Dorothy Whitney, 338, 338n
Sunday, William Ashley, 92, 92n

"Task." See Contract labor
Totten, E. P., 193
Totten, Lillian, 20, 193

United Mine Workers, 74n, 249

Vandervelde, Émile, 92, 92n, 93

Wade, Martin J., 20–21, 120, 185, 190, 214, 278

Wagner, Phil, 16, 186, 193n
Walling, William English, 17
Walsh, Frank P., 19
Warren, Earl, 31
Warren, Fred D., 62, 62n
Wayland, J. A., 4, 39, 39n, 40, 62, 239
Wealth Against Commonwealth, 3, 37
Western Federation of Miners, 70n, 72, 72n, 77
Weyl, Walter, 222, 222n
Whitaker, Robert, 251, 251n
Whittimore, A. A., 192–93
Wilson, Woodrow, 28, 138–39, 149, 150, 167; and League of Nations, 122, 281n; reelection of, 134, 262; and World War One, 148, 353; and civil liberties, 197, 223; and O'Hare case, 224, 231, 273;

mentioned, 16
Woman Question, 9–11, 31, 114–18, 218, 259
Women's suffrage, 8–9, 65, 94–95, 97–106, 137, 159, 218–19
Women's Trade Union League, 67n, 69–70, 70n, 103n
Women workers, 7–8, 63–70, 106–108
Works Project Administration, 356, 356n
World War One, 16–17, 109–10, 146–63, 165–68; and socialism, 121–43, 163–65, 167–68, 198–99, 247–48; mentioned, 291, 351
World War Veterans, 331, 331n

Zeuch, William E., 30, 205, 210, 228, 229, 230, 241, 288